Christian Tradition
in Global Perspective

CHRISTIAN TRADITION IN GLOBAL PERSPECTIVE

Roger P. Schroeder, SVD

ORBIS BOOKS
Maryknoll, New York 10545

Founded in 1970, Orbis Books endeavors to publish works that enlighten the mind, nourish the spirit, and challenge the conscience. The publishing arm of the Maryknoll Fathers and Brothers, Orbis seeks to explore the global dimensions of the Christian faith and mission, to invite dialogue with diverse cultures and religious traditions, and to serve the cause of reconciliation and peace. The books published reflect the views of their authors and do not represent the official position of the Maryknoll Society. To learn more about Orbis Books, please visit our website at www.orbisbooks.com.

Copyright © 2021 by Roger P. Schroeder.

Published by Orbis Books, Box 302, Maryknoll, NY 10545-0302.

All rights reserved.

No part of this publication may be reproduced or transmitted in any form or by any means, electronic or mechanical, including photocopying, recording, or any information storage or retrieval system, without prior permission in writing from the publisher.

Queries regarding rights and permissions should be addressed to: Orbis Books, P.O. Box 302, Maryknoll, NY 10545-0302.

Manufactured in the United States of America

Manuscript editing and typesetting by Joan Weber Laflamme

Library of Congress Cataloging-in-Publication Data

Names: Schroeder, Roger P., author.
Title: Christian tradition in global perspective / Roger P. Schroeder, SVD.
Description: Maryknoll, NY : Orbis Books, [2021] | Summary: "A one-volume history of Christianity for undergraduate students, written from a Catholic perspective"— Provided by publisher.
Identifiers: LCCN 2021005447 (print) | LCCN 2021005448 (ebook) | ISBN 9781626984349 (trade paperback) | ISBN 9781608338979 (epub)
Subjects: LCSH: Church history. | Tradition (Theology)—History of doctrines. | Theology, Doctrinal—History.
Classification: LCC BR145.3 .S37 2021 (print) | LCC BR145.3 (ebook) | DDC 230—dc23
LC record available at https://lccn.loc.gov/2021005447
LC ebook record available at https://lccn.loc.gov/2021005448

Contents

Maps   vii

Acknowledgments   ix

Introduction   xi

1. **The Early Church**   1
   Beginnings to ca. 300
   Historical Context   2
   Moving in All Directions   8
   Threads of Christian Tradition   15
   Conclusion   31

2. **The Age of the "Imperial Church"**   33
   ca. 300 to ca. 600
   Historical Context   33
   Threads of Christian Tradition   45
   Conclusion   63

3. **New Challenges and New Beginnings**   67
   ca. 600 to ca. 1000
   Historical Context   67
   Threads of Christian Tradition   83
   Conclusion   98

4. **New Political Horizons**   101
   ca. 1000 to ca. 1453
   Historical Context   102
   Threads of Christian Tradition   114
   Conclusion   134

vi   Contents

5. **Conquest, Reformation, and Indigenous Growth**   135
   ca. 1454 to ca. 1600
   Historical Context   137
   Threads of Christian Tradition   149
   Conclusion   168

6. **Global Religious and Secular Encounters**   171
   ca. 1600 to ca. 1800
   Historical Context   172
   Threads of Christian Tradition   188
   Conclusion   210

7. **Colonialism, Progress, and Mission**   211
   ca. 1800 to ca. 1900
   Historical Context   212
   Threads of Christian Tradition   228
   Conclusion   249

8. **Post-Christendom West and Non-Western Christians**   251
   ca. 1900 to ca. 2000
   Historical Context   252
   Threads of Christian Tradition   268
   Conclusion   292

Conclusion   293

Works Cited   295

Index   303

Maps

Map 1.	The Chief Cities of the World near the Beginning of Christianity	4–5
Map 2.	Boundaries and Jurisdictions of the Roman Empire in the Year 300	34
Map 3.	Arabic-Islamic Empire and the Christian World, about the Year 900	70
Map 4.	East Asia and T'ang Dynasty China, about the Year 800	76–77
Map 5.	The Mongol Empire in 1227 and 1280	108
Map 6.	Approximate Boundaries of Eurasian Religions, about the Year 1450	136
Map 7.	Asia and Adjacent Islands, 1500–1815	173
Map 8.	North and South America in the Late Eighteenth Century	185
Map 9.	The Colonial Partition of Africa in the Early Twentieth Century	218
Map 10.	Oceania at the End of the Twentieth Century	267

Acknowledgments

The proposal for this book project was accepted in 2008. Here I am, twelve years later, with a final manuscript in hand. I used to say "one chapter a summer," but it has taken even a bit longer than that. I guess it is not surprising when one strives to cover two thousand years of Christian tradition from a global (polycentric, multivocal, ecumenical) perspective.

This research and writing ran parallel with experiences, teaching, and many conversations about how individuals and groups describe and live their understanding of Christian history and tradition, of the past and present. I have learned so much from many diverse people.

- *Experience*: Observing that the Lakota had nailed the word *massacre* over the word *battle* on a roadside signboard to describe what happened at Wounded Knee in December 1890 on the Pine Ridge reservation and standing within a few miles from that place at the grave of Nicholas Black Elk, a Lakota spiritual leader and catechist, who is in the process of possibly being identified as a saint by the universal church.
- *Teaching*: Sharing with today's first generation of lay Mongolian Christians the story of their national Christian ancestors of the thirteenth-century Mongol Empire (with existing correspondence between popes and khans) and seeing the excitement of a priest in China identifying the topic of my teaching—an eighth-century Christian stele (monument) and monastery outside the first Chinese capital of Xi'an—with the identity and faith of his local Christian community near that very site.
- *Conversations*: Learning, through a conversation with scholars from varying perspectives regarding the relationship of slavery and Christianity, that using the term *enslaved persons* rather than *slaves* avoids unintentionally affirming that human beings could rightfully be considered chattel or "things"; and learning from others how anti-Semitism and Islamophobia can continue to surface, intentionally or not, within our current understanding of Christian history and tradition.

As for additional acknowledgments, I begin with Lawrence (Larry) Nemer, SVD, who introduced me to the vast field of history of Christian mission as my teacher and mentor. Scott Sunquist, Dale Irvin, and the wonderful group of international and ecumenical consultants on the History of the World Christian Movement project at Orbis Books opened me up to a new way of understanding the history of Christianity. I have also gained so much from my colleagues in the American Society of Missiology, the International Association of Mission Studies, and the local Committee on Global Mission of three theological schools in Hyde Park, Chicago. And then, of course, my community of learners includes my colleagues, staff, and students at Catholic Theological Union in Chicago. In particular, I want to thank Steve Bevans—my frequent coauthor, companion in prophetic dialogue, and SVD friend of many years—and Amanda Quantz—my co-teacher (Tradition course), ongoing conversation partner, and lasting friend.

As for this book, I want to thank professors and friends James Okoye, CSSp, Laurie Brink, OP, and Paul Bernier, SSS, for offering me feedback on the sections related to the threads of scripture and ministry/organization, and to my student Cathy Solano, RSM, who volunteered to proofread the entire manuscript. Last but certainly not least, I want to thank William Burrows, the former managing editor of Orbis Books and fellow PNG missionary for enthusiastically supporting the initial book proposal; publisher Robert Ellsberg for his long-term shepherding of this project to completion with patience and wisdom; and the many members of the competent editorial team at Orbis Books.

I also would like to remember the following deceased colleagues and friends who taught me so much, particularly in the areas of Christian history and tradition and, more important, about faith and life: Janet Carroll, Cyprian Davis, Charles Forman, Ogbu Kalu, Gary McGee, Samuel Moffett, Frederick Norris, and Lamin Sanneh.

I hope that this book contributes in some ways to allowing the voices and perspectives of more and more women and men—past, present, and future—to be added to the recorded global history of Christian tradition.

Introduction

> For as the rain and the snow come down from heaven,
>   and do not return there until they have watered the earth,
> making it bring forth and sprout, . . .
> so shall my word . . . not return to me empty,
> but it shall accomplish that which I purpose,
>   and succeed in the thing for which I sent it.
>
> (Isa 55:10–11)

This beautiful passage from the prophet Isaiah reflects the power of God's word itself to bear fruit and bring forth life. All grace comes generously and lovingly from God, and all humanity and creation are being drawn back to God. This is God's mission (*missio Dei*) of love, salvation, and justice. The natural phenomena of rain and snow can also open up a powerful image or parable. As moisture falls, it forms an intricate network of waterways—trickles, streams, rivers, lakes, and oceans—and in the process people, earth, and creation are "watered." And at the same time, the moisture evaporates, being drawn back to the heavens.

A significant part of the waterway system represents the church's participation in God's mission, as the church serves as a visible sign and community of the reign of God. However, the waterways cut and flow through a variety of terrains, both shaping and being shaped by the physical environment around the world—water trickling over gentle hills into Asian rice fields, the swift Colorado River cutting into the floor of the Grand Canyon over centuries, fresh spring streams in the Alps, the seasonal streamlet through a desert area, the complex network of Iguazu waterfalls of Argentina and Brazil, a still pond in an African savanna, and the powerful waves of an ocean.

This book strives to describe two dimensions of this phenomenon. My first goal is to describe the various waterways of Christianity over time and space. We call this the history of the world Christian movement or Christianity from a *global perspective*. We recognize through faith that the water of God's word nourishes all peoples and lands and that other religions also somehow serve as waterways of God's grace. Of course, there are also underground streams representing the movement of God's Spirit in ways unknown to us until they find their way to the surface or we make an effort to tap them. While acknowledging this more expansive movement of God, here we shall focus on the "Christian waterways." The second goal of this book is to describe the common components of the Christian waterways found in many different contexts throughout history. I refer to these as the "threads" of Christian Tradition. They are constant and changing, common and diverse. These two formidable goals intersect in order to understand Christian Tradition in global perspective. We begin by introducing the global perspective contribution.

In the year 635 CE, Alopen and his small group of East Syrian Christian monks came to the end of their long journey across Asia and over the Silk Route. They arrived in Chang'an (present-day Xi'an), the first capital of the ancient Chinese Empire and the largest city in the world at that time. The Chinese emperor welcomed them as religious and peaceful persons and invited them to translate their sacred writings into Chinese. Later, after hearing about Jesus Christ in his own language, the emperor gave the monks permission to share the Christian message in China. He even funded the building of the first church in the capital. The number of churches, monasteries, monks, and Christians grew. This amazing story marks the beginning of the first era of Christianity in China, which lasted over two hundred years.

Most Christians and students of church history are not familiar with this movement, which occurred before Boniface, the Apostle of Germany, was even born. Or that there were thriving Christian communities in present-day Iraq, Iran, and India for several hundred years before Patrick stepped foot in Ireland. The history of Christianity has normally been told and retold—whether in Vietnam, Germany, Chile, or the United States—from a Eurocentric perspective. In fact, the "good news" in the early centuries of the church spread more quickly north, south, and east of Jerusalem rather than westward into Europe. Only much later, in 1500, does Christianity for the first time in its history find itself in "a rather lopsided situation" whereby the "majority of the world's Christians resided in the European West" (Irvin and Sunquist 2001, 504). That perception unfortunately continues to a great extent even though the majority of Christians since the end of the twentieth century live—or were born—in Africa, Latin America, Asia, or the Pacific. It is estimated that by 2025, two-thirds of Christians will be of the Global South (Jenkins 2002, 3).

I personally became aware of this problem of perception in the early 1990s, when two of my Filipino students critiqued the brief description of the beginning of Christianity in the Philippines from Anglican Bishop

Stephen Neill's *A History of Christian Missions* (1964/1986), stating, "That's not the way we understand our history." On the one hand, Bishop Neill, who worked in India, taught in Nairobi, and contributed significantly to the ecumenical movement, and Kenneth Scott Latourette of Yale Divinity School, author of the seven-volume work *A History of the Expansion of Christianity* (1937–45), were more aware of the geographical expanse of Christianity than their contemporary church historians. The latter were writing what was called *church* history, in contradistinction to the *mission* history of Neill and Latourette. On the other hand, both Neill and Latourette proceeded "to tell the story of Christianity as essentially a phase of Europe's worldwide ascendancy" (Sanneh, 98). People like Nosipho Majeke, K. M. Panikkar, and J. F. Ade Ajayi, and E. A. Ayandele represent the earliest voices signaling the need for a new perspective for understanding Christian history. The comments of my Filipino students reflected this growing wave of postcolonial critique.

A number of historians began developing the theory and methodology for such an approach (Irvin 1998, González 2002, Sanneh 2002, Shenk 2002, Walls 2002) and the second generation includes the work of Tan and Tran (2016) and Cabrita, Maxwell, and Wild-Wood (2017). Gambian-born Yale professor Lamin Sanneh, who succeeded Latourette, made the connection between the shifting Christian demographics and a new way of understanding and writing the history of Christianity, and he called for "fresh navigational aids" (2002, 113). Using the metaphor of geography, Cuban-American Justo González described "the changing shape of church history" in terms of the need for a new cartography, topography, and evaluation of continental shifts (2002) to reflect the changes of perspective from "one center" to "polycentric," from a limited "mountaintop" view of the powerful and important to include a "down-to-earth" view of the ordinary and often marginalized Christians, and from an evaluation of the major shifts in history and developments based on a single perspective to one based on several perspectives.

Attempts to offer such a "'new' church history" (Bevans and Schroeder 2003) have been written or edited by scholars such as Adrian Hastings (1999), David Chidester (2000), Martin Marty (2007), Robert Bruce Mullin (2008), Dana Robert (2009), Robert Louis Wilken (2012), and Lalsangkima Pachuau (2018). The eighth and ninth volumes of *The Cambridge History of Christianity* (2005–9) should also be mentioned. Two prime examples are *Christianity: A Short Global History* (2002) by Frederick Norris and the three-volume *History of the World Christian Movement* (2001, 2012, unpublished) by Dale Irvin and Scott Sunquist. The latter drew from over a hundred scholars representing the full spectrum of ecclesiastical and national backgrounds and expertise in developing a single historical account from multiple perspectives. For this book I want to acknowledge my incalculable debt in particular to the monumental, multi-volume *History of the World Christian Movement*, which is the fruit of so many live and virtual conversations among those representing the multi-vocal histories of Christianity. I was fortunate to be included as one of those conversation partners along the way.

Alongside these attempts to write a broad global history, the post-colonial shift has also lifted up the urgent need for non-Western local, regional, and/or denominational histories. They benefit the particular peoples and serve as a necessary contribution to the overall history. Of the literally thousands of such recent studies, some representative examples (included in the bibliography at the end of this volume) are by such authors as Cyprian Davis, Enrique Dussel, Mark Noll, Samuel Moffett, Angelyn Dries, Lamin Sanneh, Peter Phan, Paul Kollman, Ogbu Kalu, and Alan Anderson. Multi-volume works have also been sponsored by such ecumenical groups as the Church History Association of India (CHAI), Comisión de Estudios de Historia de la Iglesia en América Latina (CEHILA), and Third World Theologians (EATWOT). Furthermore, the lacunae of written histories of women in the church and in mission is thankfully being filled by such authors as Mary Malone, Dana Robert, Susan Smith, and Frances Adeney.

Christian Tradition in Global Perspective is situated within this field of the "'new' church history." Therefore, this book attempts to recount the history of Christianity from a polycentric perspective and to be inclusive of the roles and movements of non-Western people, women, laity, and others who often have been excluded from the written histories of Christianity. This history strives to include, as much as possible, the lived reality of Christian communities along with the official councils of the church, and it places the history of Christianity within its various social and political contexts. While written from the author's Catholic perspective, the book is inclusive of other Christian denominations, churches, and movements, that is, the various streams within Christianity. From this perspective the church is not just an institution but also the emergence of a movement.

Writing such a global history also raises the issue of distinguishing chronological periods and shifts. How will the parameters of a particular historical period be determined? The choice of beginning and end dates, such as the Edict of Milan (313) or the French Revolution (1789), is influenced by certain geographical, ecclesiastical, and/or other perspectives. However, Susan Smith (2007, xv) warns that thematic periodization tends to be drawn from an androcentric reading of history. I chose particular dates around global themes in *Constants in Context: A Theology of Mission for Today* (2004), coauthored with Stephen Bevans, for the models of mission. However, in this current volume the periods consist of blocks of centuries, while allowing some occasional overlap and flexibility between them for the sake of understanding particular developments and movements. As one exception, the year 1453 was chosen as the midpoint from a global perspective in line with the international body of consultants working with Irvin and Sunquist. It marks the end of Byzantine Christianity and the beginning of a new distinct phase of Christian history with the Portuguese in sub-Saharan Africa, and of course with Spain and Portugal in the Americas and Asia soon after that. How the world changed in those fifty years!

As mentioned earlier, this history of world Christianity from the Acts of the Apostles until the end of the twentieth century serves as the context or backdrop for understanding the nature, breadth, and pluriformity of the church's Tradition. A clarification of the term *Tradition,* as used in this volume, is necessary. It is both a noun and a verb. As a noun, *Tradition* encompasses the "stuff" of Christian faith, action, and thought—scripture, theology, liturgy, doctrine, ethics, and the lives of holy women and men—with its pluriformity and the ambiguity of grace and malpractice. "Tradition, in other words, is the way that the faith we believe today is the same faith that Christians *have always* and *will always* believe" (Bevans 2009, 92). However, what is handed down is not just content, but a *sense* and a *love* of the faith. As a verb *Tradition* represents the "process" of passing on, internalizing, and shaping the Christian faith in new contexts. It is "the faith of the church in action." The "stuff" of Tradition provides the source, parameters, and agenda for "traditioning," which needs to be both faithful and accountable to the past and responsive and creative in the present. My colleague Stephen Bevans uses the image of the baton in a relay race. Tradition is both what is passed and the process of the passing. Furthermore, references are made to specific traditions, such as the Franciscan or pacifist traditions. Without denying the legitimacy of such terminology, these smaller traditions (spelled with a lowercase "t") will be treated as specific elements or manifestations of the more long-term threads of Tradition (spelled with a capital "T"), such as the "Franciscan tradition" as a religious movement of Christian Tradition.

I approach the deep and varied Christian Tradition by focusing on six primary threads throughout its global history. In reference to our initial image, the threads of Tradition could be considered common components within the Christian waterways. They also express the rich variety of diversity both synchronically and diachronically. The primary threads to be treated explicitly are (1) scripture; (2) liturgy, sacraments, and art; (3) ministry and organization; (4) spiritual, religious, and social movements; (5) theological developments; and 6) mission, cultures, and religions.

The choice of key threads developed to a great degree from the course "Tradition: Sources through History," a formerly required foundational core course in the curriculum for graduate-level theology and ministry students at Catholic Theological Union in Chicago. I acknowledge my debt to Dr. Amanda Quantz, with whom I developed and often taught this course. I learned much from Dr. Quantz, an academic church historian in the interdisciplinary area of historical theology and visual art, with an additional interest in Franciscan religious history, Eastern Christianity, and papal history from a global perspective. I also team taught this course and learned a great deal from Dr. Stephen Bevans, a systematic theologian whose particular areas of study are contextual theology, mission theology, ecclesiology, and ministry. Quantz and Bevans were also consultants for the History of the World Christian Movement project referenced earlier.

As for other literature, my particular choice of components was drawn from the nine threads of Christopher Bellitto's *Ten Ways the Church Has Changed* (2006)—with its Roman Catholic and more Eurocentric-leaning perspectives—and the three thematic chapter subsections of Norris's *Christianity: A Short Global History* (2002), which have broader ecumenical Protestant and strong global perspectives. While such a title as *Christian Tradition in Global Perspective* could easily require a multi-volume work, this work is intended to present an overview or panorama with a minimum of detail necessary for that purpose. After reading this book, the reader should hopefully be able to (1) identify from a global perspective the nature, breadth, and pluriformity of the church's Tradition; (2) interpret key eras, centers, figures, movements, and some particular threads of Tradition in a basic global historical framework of Christianity; and (3) make helpful and insightful connections among historical and contemporary events, issues, and developments.

Methodologically, each chapter, arranged chronologically from the beginning of Christianity until the end of the second millennium, begins with a description of the historical context from the global perspective and then focuses on outlining the six threads of Christian Tradition for that particular period of time. One can then focus not only on a single thread but also see the interrelationships among the threads. Recommended further readings are given at the end of each chapter.

Writing a book with such an ambitious scope is quite daunting and humbling. I am very aware of my own limitations and social location. I am a Roman Catholic priest of the missionary congregation of the Society of the Divine Word, and I am a male of the Baby Boomer Generation from the United States. All of these elements influence my fundamental approach to understanding and writing the history of Christianity. At the same time, I continue the process of situating and expanding my faith and my theological, historical, cultural, political, and human understanding in relation to a Christian spectrum that is ecumenically and contextually ever expanding for me. I have found myself enriched and challenged culturally, ecumenically, professionally, and personally in such settings as the following: living and working for six years in Papua New Guinea; communicating for thirty years with colleagues in the ecumenical American Society of Missiology; participating in two summers of linguistic studies with evangelicals of the Wycliffe Bible Translators; lecturing at Asbury Theological Seminary (Kentucky), Andrews University (Michigan) of the Seventh Day Adventists, Unisa–University of Pretoria in South Africa; and providing an interview for Moody Bible Institute (Chicago). I have also been enriched through a thirty-year relationship with Lakota on two South Dakota reservations; engaging encounters with Christians in places like China, Vietnam, Indonesia, India, Ethiopia, and Mongolia; and interactions with Christians and followers of other religions from around the world, who are or were my students at Catholic Theological Union. Finally, I am constantly stretched and informed by the perspectives and history of many others through my reading and study.

I want to offer several final points. First, the use of the term *global* in the title is not linked to the complex phenomenon of globalization but rather is meant to represent a polycentric and inclusive approach to Christian history and Tradition as explained above. Second, a number of eminent scholars argue for the use of *world Christianity* over *global Christianity*. However, like Lalsangkima Pachuau, I consider the terms "synonyms and use them interchangeably" (2018, 2). Third, I have not included extensive quotations from primary texts. And, finally, the style of in-line references (rather than footnotes or endnotes) is intended to facilitate a more fluid narrative style in the text and reduce the overall length of the book.

Christian Tradition in Global Perspective is not just a collection of "their" stories and traditions but a collage of *our* rich, shared Christian Tradition—the waterway system of the church's participation in God's mission over two thousand years.

1

The Early Church

Beginnings to ca. 300

Jesus embodied the mission of God, and that mission of Jesus was centered on the reign of God. "The time is fulfilled, and the kingdom of God has come near; repent, and believe in the good news" (Mk 1:14). His healings and exorcisms marked the breaking in of that reign, and Jesus used parables to describe it. His life witnessed to the fact that the reign of God is not confined to human categories, as Jesus reached out to those considered marginalized and "impure"—sinners, tax-collectors, and women—through his attitudes and actions, particularly through table fellowship. While the actual public period of Jesus's life in mission was very limited in terms of time and space, its meaning had universal significance across both. The early disciples of Christ witnessed to Jesus and carried his mission, with and without words, to the ends of the earth.

In this first chapter we begin with this post-Pentecost Jesus movement that led to the birth of the church, which with time and discernment distinguished itself from Judaism and welcomed Gentiles as fellow believers into its community. The disciples of Christ became the seed of Christian communities as they moved in all four directions from Jerusalem—east across Syria, into the Persian Empire, and by another route, to India; north into Greece, Asia Minor, and Armenia; south into Egypt and across the northern part of the continent of Africa; and west to the area north of the Mediterranean. During this period of over two-and-a-half centuries, the early church with its tremendous diversity formed the beginnings of the "threads" of its tradition. The church started to form its scriptural canon, liturgy, ministry, leadership, and overall structure. Its spiritual life shaped and was shaped by house churches, martyrdom, asceticism, and social environments. These early Christians made theological attempts in art, worship, and written texts to express an understanding of God, Jesus Christ, the Holy Spirit, and the relationship of faith and philosophy. They shared their faith in mission, with and without words, as they encountered other cultures and religions. By approximately the year 300 the church had taken the very important first steps of laying a foundation for an identity marked with diversity in unity.

Historical Context

The World at the Time of Jesus

Narrating the history of Christianity from a global perspective implies the need to situate it within the panorama of the world at the time of Jesus. As a starting point, four major empires or urban civilizations stretched from the Atlantic to the Pacific. Beginning with Jesus's social location, the Roman Empire that circled the Mediterranean is often referred to as the Greco-Roman world, although in fact it included ancient Egyptian, Syrian, Greek, Jewish, Mesopotamian, and Latin cultures. This empire was unified through its use of Greek (in addition to its primary language, Latin) and an extensive network of roads from its capital of Rome. The diverse religious world included an emperor cult and belief in Greco-Roman divinities, a mixture of strong traditional religions in rural areas, an influx of new mystery religions from the east, and a population that was 7–10 percent Jewish.

East of the Roman Empire was its enemy, the equally multicultural Persian Empire (approximately present-day Iran), stretched from the Euphrates River to the Himalayan Mountains. While Judaism and other religions were present, Zoroastrianism was more prominent. Like the Roman Empire, Persia consisted of a network of urban areas and a strong system of trade and military power. At the time of Jesus, the Parthian Dynasty was in power, and the capital was Seleucia-Ctesiphon on the Tigris River (see Map 1).

Moving east and south of Persia was the third urban civilization of India. Some 260 years before Christ, the competent leader Ashoka had united most of the subcontinent with the region of Magadha (present-day Bihar) as the political center. Later, he became Buddhist and united the people under a religion that became a missionary movement beyond India. India also had the ancient sacred writings of the Vedas, the most ancient Hindu scriptures. The fourth empire was that of China. Building upon an existing common written language and collection of sacred texts, China was politically united about two hundred years before Christ under the Han Dynasty with the capital in Chang'an (present-day Xi'an). Confucianism became prominent particularly among the ruling classes at that time.

The movement of peoples across these empires and urban civilizations was associated with war and trade. The famous Silk Road traversed all four empires, and other land and navigational routes filled in an elaborate network of travel and connections. Furthermore, soldiers, prisoners of war, refugees, settlers, and merchants were not only agents of intercultural exchange, but also agents of interreligious exchange. For example, soldiers had brought elements of mystery religions into the Roman Empire, and Jewish captives and merchants carried their faith into the Persian and Indian empires, respectively, before the time of Christ. The new religion of Christianity would follow these same trade routes.

North of these four urban civilizations were many nomadic tribes—Germanic, Celtic, Slavic, Turkish, and Mongol, to name a few—that belonged to broader groupings. South of Egypt was the ancient kingdom of Meroë (present-day Sudan) and the Aksumite Empire (present-day Ethiopia and Eritrea). The descendants of all these people would somehow become part of the Christian history within the first thousand years of Christianity. The indigenous people, with their traditional religions, living south of the great Saharan desert and in Australia and parts of the Pacific, would not be touched by the Christian message until much later. The same is the case for the inhabitants of the Americas, which included the Olmec and Mayan civilizations with some urban centers in Central America and Mexico before the time of Christ.

In shifting our focus to Jesus's local context, the Jewish people were of course under the authority of the Roman Empire, but they had earlier been under the Greeks, Persians, Babylonians, and Egyptians. The Sadducees, Pharisees, and Essenes were three major Jewish parties during the time of Jesus. Religiously, some suggest using the term *Judaisms* in the sense that "competing schools of interpretation and the various influences of other cultures from outside of Israel combined to make for a diversity of religious practices" (Irvin and Sunquist 2001, 11). However, some Jewish scholars don't like this term and prefer to speak simply in terms of various ways of expressing one's Jewish faith. Such diversity is characteristic of all world religions. Occasional movements of social unrest and resistance in response to the economic and political circumstances are also significant aspects for understanding the context of Jesus's life.

Jesus Movement after Pentecost

The final chapter of the gospel of Luke contains powerful accounts of encounters with the resurrected Jesus: women at the tomb (24:1–12), the two disciples on the road to Emmaus (24:13–35), and the appearance to the eleven (24:36–49). The Acts of the Apostles, as the second volume of Luke, continues with a description of the first years of the Jesus movement. While Luke is generally reliable as a historian of his time, a critical reading is also

Map 1. The Chief Cities of the World near the Beginning of Christianity

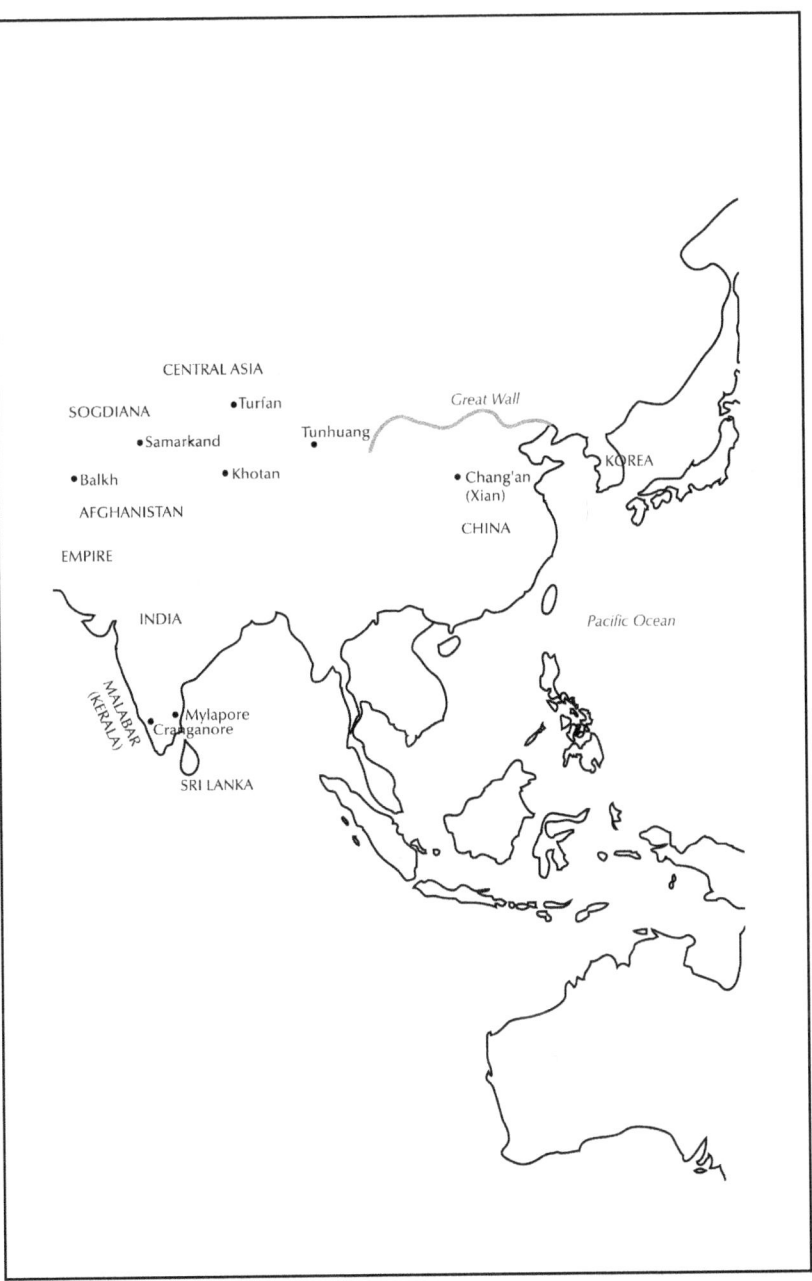

necessary, and it is important to note that the order and choice of events is determined by his primary role as a theologian. In that way Luke wrote an excellent theological history of the beginning of Christianity. In the gospel of Luke, everything moves toward Jerusalem with the death and resurrection of Jesus, and in Acts everything moves from Jerusalem to Judea, Samaria, and the "ends of the earth" (Acts 1:8). One can identify distinct stages in this theological narrative (Bevans and Schroeder 2004, 13–31).

After Jesus's death and resurrection and before Pentecost (Acts 1), one can imagine that the women and men who followed him were probably expecting the imminent inauguration of God's rule on earth. There was most likely a sense of anxiety and emptiness as they prayerfully waited in Jerusalem for that eschatological event. An eschatological event does happen at Pentecost (Acts 2:1–4), but it was not what was expected. Rather than the second coming of Christ, it was the coming of the Spirit. Rather than the end time, Israel was given a second chance, and the Jesus community was the promised remnant. The crowds who heard Peter's preaching came from many parts of the known world, but they were all Jews (Acts 2:11). While Pentecost is often considered the "birthday" of the church, Jesus's disciples saw themselves more as a Jewish sect that continued to pray in the Temple, and outreach to the Gentiles was very far from their thoughts.

In a very idealistic image of that early community, the first signs of serious discord appear with the stage associated with Stephen (Acts 6—7) over the unequal allotment of food between two groups of widows. Favor is given to the Hebrew-speaking Jewish Christians (Hebrews), or those who live in Israel, over the Greek-speaking Jewish Christians (Hellenists), who live outside Israel in the diaspora and who were more influenced by the Hellenistic Greek world of the Roman Empire. Seven men, including Stephen, called deacons, were selected from among the Hellenists to oversee a just distribution. Not only was there linguistic and social diversity between the Hebrew-speaking and Greek-speaking Jewish Christians, but there was also a theological difference. The Hellenists tended more quickly to identify and distinguish the soteriological significance of Jesus Christ, which led to the hostility toward Stephen (see Acts 6:14). According to Luke's description, Stephen died a Christlike death, and his cloaks are piled at the feet of Saul.

With the stoning of Stephen, the Hellenists flee from Jerusalem. However, the events surrounding Samaria and the Ethiopian eunuch (Acts 8) indicate that this didn't stop them from preaching about Jesus. When Philip, another of the seven deacons, performed healings and exorcisms, the Samaritans, whom some Jews considered "half Jews," responded positively and were baptized. The apostles Peter and John were sent from Jerusalem to see what was happening, and they approved and completed Philip's work by extending their hands over the newly baptized to receive the Spirit. Philip then encountered the Ethiopian eunuch who was reading the words of Isaiah upon his return home from a pilgrimage in Jerusalem. While it is not clear if the eunuch was a Jew or a Gentile, the baptisms of the eunuch and the Samaritans earlier represent a widening of the circle of the Jesus movement.

The story of Cornelius and his household (Acts 10:1—11:18) represents a further stage of development. The Roman centurion Cornelius was definitely a Gentile, a good and holy one. Through prayer and a vision Cornelius sends for Peter, who is in Joppa. At the same time, also through prayer and a vision, Peter is challenged to reexamine his traditional understanding of what and who is pure and impure. "What God has made clean, you must not call profane" (Acts 10:15). Peter receives the Gentile messengers of Cornelius as guests in his own home. Later Peter goes to Cornelius's house, where he preaches to all those assembled. Upon seeing their openness, Peter realizes that "God shows no partiality" (Acts 10:34), and the Spirit comes upon the household. The companions of Peter exclaim, "Can anyone withhold the water for baptizing these people who have received the Holy Spirit just as we have?" (Acts 10:47). This was not only the conversion of Cornelius and his household, but also the transformation of Peter as he realizes that the mission of Jesus went beyond the categories of his Jewish religion and culture. It is noteworthy that later, at the Council of Jerusalem, Peter and others will be confronted more for breaking the rules of table fellowship and food taboos than for baptizing the Gentiles.

What happens next in Antioch (Acts 11:19–26) is described in just eight verses, but it is probably the high point in Luke's theological narrative for several reasons. First of all, we find Jewish Christians preaching not only to a single household but to Gentiles in a general way, and "a great number became believers and turned to the Lord" (11:21). Second, the gospel was presented in terms of "Lord Jesus" (11:20), whereby in addition to the ordinary indication for the significance of Jesus with the Jewish title Messiah (*Christos*), in Antioch the significance of Jesus is also attested to by the title Lord (*Kyrios*), which had been attributed to Hellenistic cult divinities and to the emperor. This radical step indicates that salvation through Christ and the meaning of the gospel extend beyond the understanding and people of Judaism. Third, when the community in Jerusalem heard about the happenings in Antioch, they sent the Hellenist Jewish-Christian Barnabas to investigate. He encouraged the new believers, and he didn't have to complete the process of making disciples that had been done earlier by Peter and John in Samaria (Acts 8:15–17). Later Barnabas would take a very important step when he persuaded Saul to join him in Antioch. Fourth, "It was in Antioch that the disciples were first called 'Christians'" (11:26). While the term *Christian* likely had a negative connotation with the Roman authorities, it indicates that outsiders recognized a new movement coming from Judaism. This parallels a shift in self-understanding on the part of the followers of Jesus, as they realize that they are a part of something new. The universal significance of the gospel and the Spirit has led them to embrace the Gentiles. Later tradition will see this moment in Antioch as the birthday of the church—the birth of a new and distinctive identity and an expanded consciousness of mission and church. Following the mission of Jesus (and God) led to the formation of the church. Later, the Second Vatican Council will reaffirm that the church is "missionary by its nature" (*Ad Gentes* 2).

The final stage in this theological history is the ongoing Mission to the Gentiles (Acts 12—28). However, there continues to be an initial outreach to the Jewish community. Acts 12 records the execution of James (son of Zebedee) and the arrest of Peter; Paul then becomes the primary agent throughout the rest of Acts. A watershed moment occurred around the year 49 CE with the Council of Jerusalem (Acts 15:1–29). In response to the controversy regarding the necessity of circumcision for Gentile Christians, the community of Antioch sent Barnabas, Paul, and a few others to Jerusalem to clarify the matter. After listening to both sides of the question and the experience of the Antiochene community, James, as the leader of the Jerusalem community, spoke with approval of how God was taking from among the Gentiles "a people for his name" (Acts 15:14) and stated that "we should not trouble those Gentiles who are turning to God" (Acts 15:19). Therefore, the council decided that Gentile Christians were not required to be circumcised or to follow the Jewish Law, except for a couple of conditions to avoid scandal (Acts 15:28–29). In the rest of Acts, Paul continues the mission in Asia and Europe. The pattern is preaching to the Jews, leading to rejection by most, and preaching to the Gentiles, leading to acceptance by many. The concluding chapters of Acts present Paul's trial and arrest in Jerusalem, his captivity in Caesarea, and his journey to and stay in Rome. The last line in Acts provides the final image of Paul in Rome "proclaiming the kingdom of God and teaching about the Lord Jesus Christ with all boldness and without hindrance" (28:31).

Having described the earliest developments of the Jesus movement, we now trace how Christianity moved geographically and culturally in every direction from Jerusalem by the year 300 CE (see Irvin and Sunquist 2001, 47–153).

Moving in All Directions

Syria, Mesopotamia, Persia, and India

The importance of Antioch for early Christianity was already highlighted in the Acts of the Apostles. Antioch was the third-largest urban area in the

Mediterranean area and the capital of the Roman province of Syria. The gospel of Matthew was probably written in Syria, and the following post-apostolic writings are even more certainly products of Syria: the *Odes of Solomon* and the *Didache* (Teaching of the Lord to the Gentiles through the twelve apostles) date from the end of the first or the beginning of the second century, and the gospel of Thomas from the second century. A widely known church leader at the beginning of the second century was Ignatius (d. ca. 107), bishop of Antioch, whose letters provide important information about the early church. We will return to some of these writings later.

Moving eastward from Antioch outside the Roman Empire into eastern Syria and Mesopotamia across the Euphrates River was the city of Edessa (in present-day southeastern Turkey), which was the capital of Oshroene, a small buffer state between the Roman and Persian empires at the time of Jesus. Edessa was strategically situated at the intersection of two major trade routes, making it a crossroads not only of trade, but also of culture, philosophy, and religion. The large Jewish population in the city provided the initial foundation for the Christian community. According to their tradition, which cannot simply be dismissed as legend, the people of Edessa first received the gospel from a Galilean Jewish Christian, possibly an original disciple of Jesus, by the name of Addai (Thaddeus in Greek), who is still considered today the founder of the Syrian church. Later, around the year 200, there is a report that King Agbar VIII of Oshroene had "come to the faith," and one also finds evidence in Edessa of the first public church building. Both factors suggest that Christianity found a more favorable welcome here than in the Roman Empire, where Christians experienced occasional persecution and hardships at this time. The independent Kingdom of Oshroene became a Roman colony in 214 but was taken over temporarily by Persia around 250. Throughout these years the predominantly Jewish-Christian community maintained relationships with fellow Christians in both the Roman and Persian empires.

Around this same time there was a Christian community four hundred miles east of Edessa across the Tigris River in Arbela, the capital of the Kingdom of Adiabene in the empire of Persia (present-day Iran). Although its Christian origins are unknown, there is evidence that around the middle of the second century Tatian the Assyrian, a theologian and ex-pupil of the apologist Justin Martyr, brought the gospel to the community in Syriac, a dialect of Jesus's language of Aramaic. Representing this important ancient branch of Christianity, "Syriac became the language of choice among Christians in eastern Syria, Mesopotamia, Persia, and eventually India, Mongolia, and China" (Irvin and Sunquist 2001, 57). Also, many people went to the Syrian wilderness seeking a more ascetic life, and from this spiritual movement a form of monasticism would develop and quickly spread across Asia.

The early Syrian theology associated with Antioch and Edessa was found more in their hymns and liturgy than in philosophical texts. In terms of Christology, the Syrian theologians emphasized the humanity of Jesus and the connection between Jesus and the Spirit. Syriac literature contains positive feminine images in liturgy and theology, with images of the Spirit as a woman and references to God as both Father and Mother during an early Eucharistic prayer. The Odes of Solomon, a collection of hymns, uses feminine imagery for the three persons of the Trinity. Edessa became the main theological school outside of the Roman Empire, and Bardaisan (ca. 154–222) was its most prominent theologian during this time period.

Another independent beginning of Christianity in Asia occurred in India. The coming of the gospel to southwest and northwest areas of India is associated with the apostles Thomas, Bartholomew, and/or the Christian teacher Pantaenus. The apocryphal *Acts of Thomas* is a product of legend and oral traditions, but there is some supportive historical data as well. Travel by Roman ships from Egypt across the Red and Arabian seas to India and the presence of Jewish communities in India before the time of Jesus certainly make these journeys possible. One or more of these men quite possibly were in India, but the historical evidence for the first foundation of a Christian community is not decisive. However, one can say that a community was probably established as early as the end of the second century (Moffett 1998, 39). The community of Saint Thomas Christians from southwestern India (present-day state of Kerala) grew, became linked ecclesiastically in time with the East Syrian Church, and exists today as a Christian community founded on the apostolic tradition of Thomas. One can still visit his tomb in Mylapore outside Chennai (formerly Madras) in the state of Tamil Nadu.

Greece, Asia Minor, and Armenia

Possibly the greatest area for Christian growth during this time period was in Asia Minor (comprising most of present-day Turkey) and Greece, both in the eastern part of the Roman Empire. Paul, Timothy, and Titus were primary evangelizers and church founders in that region. Paul's letters and the Acts of the Apostles offer a rich description of these early Christian communities. For example, in Greece we know of early developments and challenges in the communities of Corinth and Thessalonica, and Paul delivered his famous speech in the Areopagus in Athens regarding the altar to "an unknown god" (Acts 17:22–31). The gospel and other writings associated with the apostle John were probably written in Asia Minor. Most of the letters written later by Ignatius of Antioch on his way to martyrdom in Rome are addressed to communities in Asia Minor.

Unlike the Christians outside the Roman Empire, those within the empire suffered hardships and sporadic local persecutions before 250 CE. After that year there were three major systematic attempts to wipe out Christianity by Decius (250), Valerian (257), and Diocletian (after 303). The oldest written account of martyrdom, outside of the New Testament (NT), is by the renowned historian Eusebius on the martyrdom of Polycarp (d. ca. 156), the eighty-six-year-old bishop of Smyrna in Asia Minor. "Actual martyrdoms were relatively few, but those who did go to their death inspired others to face hostility" (Irvin and Sunquist 2001, 73). Within this context, apocalyptic and prophetic impulses continued in Asia Minor to foster hope in the coming reign of God in the face of persecution, following the tradition of John's book of Revelation and the four prophesying daughters of Philip (Acts 21:9).

Irenaeus (ca. 115–ca. 202) was the key theologian of this stream of Christianity. He was born in Smyrna and learned about the faith from Polycarp. He became a bishop in Lyons in Gaul (roughly present-day France), where he migrated with others from Asia Minor, but is representative of the theology of Asia Minor. His theology was also not based on philosophy but on the lived situation of Christians. Writing in Greek, Irenaeus emphasized the humanity of Jesus, and he described Jesus and the Holy Spirit as the two hands of God. This thought is an expression of the same theological school of Antioch, noted above, which would be further developed in eastern Syria and across Asia.

Northeast of Asia Minor was Armenia, a semi-independent kingdom between the Roman and Persian empires. It seems that Christian merchants were the first to bring the gospel message to Armenia, probably as early as the first part of the second century and probably from Edessa and other centers for trade. Eusebius recorded a letter being sent around the middle of the third century from the bishop of Alexandria to the Armenians, where a certain Meruzanes was bishop (Moffett 1998, 113). However, the founder of Christianity in this land is traditionally considered to be Gregory the Illuminator. Born of Parthian-Persian parents who settled in Armenia, he left Armenia, became Christian in Cappadocia (present-day Turkey), and then returned home around the year 300. Gregory baptized King Tiridates III, and the king declared Armenia a Christian nation. Traditionally 301 is the date of this event, although it more likely occurred around 314 (Cowe, 48). The scriptures would eventually be translated into Armenian, and a very strong link was established between the Christian faith and Armenian culture. It is interesting to note how the history of Gregory and Christianity in Armenia followed the paths of trade and migration with Persia, Mesopotamia, and Asia Minor. However, while Armenia was influenced by other Christian centers, it also developed its own particular expression of Christian faith.

The Western Mediterranean

As noted above, Irenaeus had migrated from Asia Minor to Gaul in the western part of the Roman Empire. Rome was the capital of the entire empire and the most influential city politically and economically in the West. Although the details about its origin are unknown, a Christian community existed already in Rome as early as the year 50 CE, with Paul writing his letter to them in the mid-50s. There is evidence of Christianity in other parts of Italy and in Gaul and Spain by the end of the second century. The first major persecution in Rome occurred in 64, when the emperor Nero falsely accused the Christians of starting a major fire in the city. Peter and Paul were among the hundreds executed at that time.

Most Christians in Rome were foreigners, which isn't surprising given that the majority of the city's population was born in other places. This included many slaves and captives in war and their descendants, who could become Roman citizens if and when they were freed. Although Latin was the language of the ruling classes, the early Christian community used *koine* (common) Greek, which in Rome at that time "identified someone as a member of a lower class or a foreigner" (Irvin and Sunquist 2001, 76). They began using Latin in the second half of the second century and were bilingual into the third century. By the middle of the third century the bishop of Rome gathered about sixty bishops from around Italy for a local council.

The Christian life was centered on people's homes. Some were designated as house churches, where Christians would meet regularly for prayer, Bible study, meetings, and breaking bread together. Some homes underwent major adaptation to accommodate the growing numbers, and the use of large houses indicated that a number of high-class people were also becoming Christians. Christians had the custom of burying, not cremating, their dead. At first, they used the private property of Christians, and on occasion the remains or relics of martyrs were also kept and honored in homes. With time, the dead were buried in large underground catacombs outside the city. Contrary to popular belief, Christians did not live or hide in the catacombs, and having more regular worship services there would only start in the fourth century. However, the catacombs were very important for Christian faith and identity.

Shifting south of the Mediterranean to the other section of the western part of the Roman Empire was Roman North Africa. The first historical evidence of Christianity is an account of martyrdom in 180 outside the city of Carthage (near present-day Tunis in Tunisia), which was a multicultural Roman city. Rather than inhibiting the Christian movement, a rapid growth followed this persecution. In 230, around seventy bishops from that region attended a local council. To a lesser extent than in Asia Minor, but still to some degree, one also finds the prophetic and charismatic aspects among some of the women martyrs, notably Perpetua and Felicitas.

It is not surprising that this environment of occasional persecution fostered a strict moral code. A serious controversy both in North Africa and in Rome developed over the terms for readmitting those who committed apostasy during the period of persecution. Cornelius, selected as the bishop of Rome in 251, promoted the moderate position, while the presbyter Novatian denied any readmission and was elected as an alternative bishop of Rome. Those of this latter approach, known as Novatianism, established congregations during the third century in the Mediterranean area, particularly around Carthage, where a controversy with a similar perspective called Donatism would arise after 300.

The theologian of this period who set the tone for the theology that developed in the western part of the Roman Empire was Tertullian of Carthage. Whether he was a lawyer or not, his writings reflected a legal mindset and were based on the prevalent philosophy of Stoicism, which held that the universe had a fundamental order. Christians were to align themselves completely to the divine order and law, and Tertullian was opposed to any perceived compromise. He accepted the human and divine natures of Jesus, which became the orthodox understanding, although he considered the divinity of Jesus as the starting point. Later, Tertullian was associated in North Africa to some extent with a group called the New Prophecy or Montanists, with its strict discipline and charismatic characteristic. This movement would eventually be considered heretical, but there is no clear evidence that Tertullian ever left the church.

Alexandria and Egypt

Continuing in the broad counter-clockwise movement, one arrives full circle back in the eastern part of the Roman Empire and west of Jerusalem in the Egyptian city Alexandria, the intellectual center of the Mediterranean near the mouth of the Nile River. While the exact origins of Christianity in Alexandria are unknown, Apollos in the Acts of the Apostles (18:24–25) is described as an Alexandrian-Jewish follower of Christ. The apostle Mark is traditionally considered the founder of Christianity in Alexandria. While there is no historical evidence for this claim, it is possible that a longer version of his gospel may have been composed there by Mark. Jews may have composed as much as 25 percent of the city's population, and they provided the initial springboard for Christianity. With time, Gentile Christians would become the majority, following the general pattern.

With one of the best libraries ever known, Alexandria was the intellectual and religious crossroads for people like Mesopotamian astrologers, Persian Zoroastrians, Greek philosophers, and worshippers of Egyptian gods. The Jewish scholar Philo lived in the city around the time of Jesus, and later the Christian teacher Clement of Alexandria was one of the first in the West to understand who the Buddha was and to associate him with India. Such a hotbed of ideas welcomed the new mystery religions and also became the source of some syncretistic Christian thought. One major development of this latter kind was Gnosticism, which emphasized salvation through knowledge of secret teachings about God and Jesus by a select limited number of members. While the earliest Gnostic teachers probably came from Palestine and Syria, Alexandria had the most famous ones, like Basilides and Valentinus. Irenaeus and others condemned the Gnostics for restricting the public invitation of salvation to all people.

Bishop Demetrius opened what would become a famous catechetical school in the late part of the second century to provide a healthier context for integrating Hellenistic thought and Christian faith. The name of Pantaenus, the first teacher of the school, is associated with bringing the gospel to India, as noted above. His successor, Clement, was born in Athens and became a Christian in Alexandria. This wonderfully gifted philosopher and theologian strove to reconcile Greek philosophy with scripture. His greatest student was Origen, considered the first Christian systematic theologian and the key developer of Alexandrine theology.

Origen was raised in a Christian home and educated in Hellenistic philosophy in Alexandria. Theologically, he valued both reason and revelation as the means for humanity to recover its holiness. Origen saw a line of perfect compatibility and continuity between philosophy and faith, both of which sought truth, at least partially. Human experience and philosophical reason helped in understanding the meaning of scripture and Christianity. Origen emphasized the divine nature of Christ, who gave Christians an example to follow to receive the truth of God's love. Origen would eventually leave Alexandria because of a dispute with the bishop Demetrius. He spent his last twenty years in Caesarea in Palestine where he died under the persecution of Emperor Decius. The efforts of Origen and others of the Alexandrine school to engage philosophy and faith provided an alternative approach to that of Gnosticism and eventually contributed to its decline.

However, the major factor that weakened the influence of Gnosticism was the sheer fact of numbers. What could be called the Catholic party, with its open invitation to all, was growing much faster than Gnosticism. When persecution came later to Egypt, many Christians fled outside of

Alexandria, and the faith spread with them into the countryside. In time, Christianity became identified with Egyptian identity and nationalism. In addition, women and men began to go to the desert areas of Egypt in search of a more ascetic and isolated life, parallel to the developments in Syria.

Most Christians lived in urban areas around the year 300, but there were movements into some rural areas as well. The greatest density and spread of Christianity were in Asia Minor and North Africa, and the declaration of Armenia as a Christian nation near the beginning of the fourth century led to its quick growth there. However, most Christians inside and outside the Roman Empire lived as minority communities.

Threads of Christian Tradition

Scripture

Until the late part of the second century, the Bible for Christians was the Old Testament (OT) in the Greek translation called the Septuagint (LXX). The Pentateuch was translated in the third century BCE initially for Greek-speaking Jews (Hellenists) in Egypt and eventually for those around the Roman Empire. The Septuagint was completed in the first century CE. This sacred text was the authoritative basis for preaching, pastoral care, theology, and spirituality, and for disputing with Jews and those considered heretics. Justin Martyr in *Dialogue with Trypho* treated every part of the OT as if it referred explicitly to Christ.

Christians also had the need to preserve in writing both the sayings of Jesus, which had been circulating only in oral form, and the events from Jesus's life, beginning with the passion narrative of the suffering and death of Christ. By the end of the first century the letters of Paul and some of the gospels were widely known among many Christians, but these writings were not yet regarded as authoritative scriptures. In the second century the Marcionites and Gnostics—in opposition to the stance of Justin Martyr and others—rejected the God of the OT as either being evil or a lower god. While both groups would eventually be considered heretics, their positions pointed to the need for the church to define the canon of the NT and to insist on the unity of both OT and NT.

From the many writings that were in circulation, a Christian canon began to emerge based on the following criteria: apostolic origin, content, conformity with the rule of faith, and the importance of the community that preserved a text, particularly through liturgical usage. The gospel of Thomas contained many sayings of Jesus found in the synoptic gospels but was rejected as a whole from the canon due to its Gnostic flavor and reinterpretations. Several "infancy" gospels that collected legends of Jesus's childhood were not accepted because they portrayed Jesus more as a magician or even, in one case, as a murderer of another child. The book of Revelation was under suspicion for some time due to its popularity among millenarian groups.

The gospels of Matthew, Mark, Luke, and John emerged in different Christian contexts and initially had restricted regional use. However, by the end of the second century they were fairly widely read, and by the end of the third century the four gospels with their accepted diversity were considered by most as canonical or authoritative. These gospels were originally written in Greek, but there were also some early Syriac translations. The theologian Tatian the Assyrian wove together the four gospels into a single text known as the *Diatessaron*. This single harmonized gospel circulated in Syriac in the late second century and became the preferred version through the Syrian Church in Asia for several centuries until it was replaced by the four full gospels. It is interesting to note here that "though the four Gospels were now generally accepted in the Church, the concept of the canon was not so rigid as to prevent some freedom in handling the text" (Rogerson et al., 244). A Syriac translation of most of the OT existed by the end of the second century and the entire NT by the end of the fourth century in the form of a paraphrase or "simple" translation known as the *Peshitta*. In terms of other translations, portions of the Bible were available in Latin in Roman North Africa by the year 300.

Returning to the question of the NT canon, a number of attempts were made to establish it during the third century: the Muratorian Canon around 200, the categorization of books by the theologian Origen around the middle of the third century, and the decision in 265 by Bishop Dionysius of Alexandria to exclude Revelation from Origen's category of accepted or received books. A further but not a final determination of the NT canon would occur in the fourth century.

Another important issue related to scripture is hermeneutics, or the theory and practice of interpretation. Origen of the school of Alexandria acknowledged that scripture has multiple levels of meaning. While not denying the literal meaning, he emphasized the spiritual one. Building upon the work of his teacher, Clement, Origen promoted the method of the allegorical interpretation of the language of symbols used in scripture to express the ultimate mystery for listeners of all times and places. The methodology of Origen and the Alexandrine school would influence others in the future such as Ambrose of Milan and Augustine of Hippo. However, another method of interpretation would be introduced by the school of Antioch in the fourth and fifth centuries. Origen was also a prolific commentator on both the Old and New Testaments. On the former he wrote a massive work called the *Hexapla*, in which he listed side by side in columns six texts of the OT, beginning with the original Hebrew and including the LXX, in order to identify the best translation.

The interpretation and use of scripture were and continue to be important for all other aspects or "threads" of Christian tradition, to be treated below. The liturgy broke open the scriptures and early Christian art provided visual expressions; many forms of the ministry focused on proclaiming, serving, and witnessing to the word of God; spirituality and spiritual movements were nourished and challenged by the Bible; scripture was an expression of theology itself and a primary source for further theological development; and in mission Christians brought the word of God across personal, cultural, religious, and/or geographical boundaries. Therefore, the Bible was a guide and resource for all aspects of church life and daily Christian living.

Liturgy, Sacraments, and Art

In the Acts of the Apostles we read that the early Jewish Christians "spent much time together in the temple, [and] they broke bread at home" (2:46). After the destruction of the Temple in 70 CE, the local synagogue and Jewish worship pattern continued to influence the development of new patterns of Christian liturgy. This liturgy included blessing, prayer, ritual eating, and reading of the word of God, which initially was drawn from the OT and then eventually included the letters and writings from which the NT would emerge.

Christians in the Roman Empire generally met and worshipped in private homes in the second and third centuries, although some separate buildings appeared in the second half of the third century only to be destroyed during persecutions in 303. There is evidence of a separate church building in Edessa by 200, which points to the freedom of Christians outside the Roman Empire. The best-preserved example of a house that was renovated into an identifiable building for worship is in the ancient fortress town of Dura-Europos in eastern Syria (close to the present-day Iraqi border). Along with one large space for the Eucharist, there was another room with a basin and frescoes that suggest it was used for baptisms.

In the early church, liturgies were characterized by improvisation within clearly established patterns. With time, some liturgical written documents emerged. "As Christianity grew, the natural tendency to regulate and record traditions, teachings, and worship developed" (Foley, 62). This is parallel to the concern to establish the NT canon, noted above. Several Christian "handbooks" with moral teachings and church rules also provide glimpses of the liturgies. The *Didache* of late-first-century and/or early-second-century Syria described fasting, baptism, the Lord's Prayer, and possibly an early Eucharistic Prayer. *Apostolic Tradition*, traditionally attributed to

Hippolytus of Rome but now under question, includes a Eucharistic Prayer and instructions for ordinations, the catechumenate, and other aspects of worship. While written for particular communities, such Christian writings often were shared with others, like the letters of Paul, and they were very influential in spreading common patterns of liturgy and church life. Liturgist Edward Foley puts this into the context of the meaning of the Eucharist at this time: "While there is some attention to the norms for procedures and materials for use in worship, these were clearly secondary to the emphasis on spiritual nourishment and the continuity between Christian prayer and Christian living" (ibid., 76).

At the beginning of Christianity worship was conducted in the common language of a local community. Greek was the official language of the Roman Empire, and it would remain the liturgical language of the church in the eastern part of the empire. Latin, which was becoming prominent around Rome, would first be brought into Roman churches when Victor from North Africa became the bishop of Rome in the late second century. Many churches in the western part of the Roman Empire would use both Greek and Latin into the third century, but Latin would eventually become the liturgical language in the West. As Christianity spread along the seacoast and the Nile River in Egypt, the Egyptian language was used in liturgy and theology by the third century in these areas outside the city of Alexandria (Irvin and Sunquist 2001, 91). As noted above, Syriac became the liturgical language of Christianity across Asia. Armenians would also soon be using their own language in liturgy.

In terms of early developments of sacraments, the catechumenate process, which sometimes lasted three years, included instruction in the essential elements of the faith, which were contained in early creeds. However, it focused more on conversion and Christian living than on an intellectual understanding of Christianity. Baptism included renunciation of sins, profession of faith, laying on of hands, baptism by immersion, the trinitarian formula, and anointing with oil. Adult baptism was the norm, but infant baptism started to appear at the beginning of the third century. Around this time some theologians began to associate the bestowal of the Holy Spirit with the anointing with oil, which later led to the development of the separate sacrament of confirmation and the understanding that baptism, Eucharist, and confirmation form the sacraments of initiation.

One of the main challenges for the early church was dealing with apostasy. How could individuals be readmitted to the Christian community who, during the time of persecution, had renounced Christ or purchased false certificates stating that they had offered sacrifices to the imperial gods? The church in North Africa eventually accepted a pastoral approach of readmission and penance based on particular circumstances. The church in Rome was sharply divided between those advocating the moderate approach, similar to North Africa, and those refusing any readmission. The latter group united under the leadership of the presbyter Novatian, who was eventually excommunicated. Its members founded and sustained their own communities and churches in various areas around the Roman Empire until the fifth century. However, the moderate approach based on penance and forgiveness was generally accepted around the Christian world.

Another crisis emerged when members of the Novatian communities sought readmission into the majority church, whose leaders referred to themselves as catholic or, later in the fourth century, as orthodox. Christianity had to deal with the question of the status of baptism received outside the network of catholic churches. Cyprian, the bishop in Carthage, insisted that these individuals had to be re-baptized within the church, whose bishops could trace their succession to the apostles and in turn secure the unity of the church itself. Stephen, the bishop of Rome, representing a moderate perspective from his local church, stated that those of the Novatian communities did not have to be re-baptized because the ritual of baptism with the trinitarian formula was valid in itself. They were admitted into the catholic churches through a ritual of laying on of hands to confer the Spirit upon them. The famous statement of Cyprian that "outside the church there is no salvation" surfaced within this intra-church context, but later it was applied to the followers of other religions or no religion.

We now shift our attention from ritual expression to Christian art. The earliest explicit examples are from the late second or early third centuries. Many are found in the catacombs around Rome on frescoes and sarcophagus relief sculptures. One of the oldest, rather clandestine symbols was the fish, whereby the first letters of the Greek phrase "Jesus Christ, Son of God, Savior" form the Greek word for fish, *ichthys*. Other early Christian symbols include the anchor, chalice, boat, and dove with olive branch. The painting "Jesus the Good Shepherd," from the catacomb of Callistus in the third century, is considered the earliest known depiction of Jesus in art. In addition to Jesus as the Good Shepherd, the church in Dura-Europos has well-preserved scenes of Jesus walking on water and healing the paralytic; these date from the first part of the third century. Scenes from the OT and NT are very common, although images from the passion and death of Jesus do not appear at this time. It is interesting to note that other third-century depictions from the catacombs outside Rome include "Jesus as Philosopher" and "Virgin and Child." Rather than offering a concise intellectual explanation of the faith, the use of symbols and artistic expressions captures the imagination of Christians and invites them to enter the mystery of their faith in another way, similar to Christian ritual and worship.

Ministry and Organization

The ministry, mission, and life of Jesus centered on the kingdom of God: "Repent, for the kingdom of heaven is close at hand" (Mt 4:17). The kingdom-centered ministry of Jesus, all Christians, and the entire church is often understood as being marked by the following characteristics: preaching (*kerygma*), serving (*diakonia*), witnessing (*koinonia*), and praying (*leitourgia*). Jesus shared this ministry with the twelve and the wider group of his disciples, who were considered companions and coworkers (Mk 3:14–15; Mt 10:1; Lk 9:1–12). The Acts of the Apostles describes the emergence of specific ministries in the earliest days of the church: the leadership of Peter and the twelve (Acts 1:15–26; 2:14) and James ("brother of Jesus") at the Council of Jerusalem (Acts 15:13–21); the appointment of the "seven" (Acts 6), including Stephen and Philip; evangelists at Antioch (Acts 11:19–20); prophets and teachers (Acts 11:27; 13:1; 21:9); elders/presbyters (*presbyteroi*) in Antioch, Derbe, Lystra, Iconium, and Jerusalem (Acts 11:30; 14:23); and elders/presbyters from Ephesus at Melitus (20:17), who are also called overseers (*episkopoi*) (20:28). The letters of Paul describe a wide range of ministries, such as teaching, preaching, healing, miracle working, prophecy, discernment of spirits, and the gift of the interpretation of tongues (1 Cor 12—14; Rom 12; Eph 4). Paul refers to *episkopoi* and deacons (*diakonoi*) (Phil 1:1), but never to presbyters. The pastoral letters describe the qualifications of good *episkopoi* and deacons (1 Tim 3), but the distinction between *episkopoi* and presbyters is not clear (1 Tim 5:17–22; Titus 1). At this very early stage one should not too quickly identify the ministries of *episkopoi*, presbyter, or deacon with later developments. No individual Christian was called "priest" in the NT, and it is not certain who presided over the Eucharist in the early communities with their varied structures.

The *Didache* describes the transition that took place at the turn of the second century. Prophets and traveling evangelists and charismatics served in the beginning as the regular presiders of the Eucharist, and then *episkopoi* and deacons begin to fulfill the roles of prophets and teachers. The seven officially accepted letters of Ignatius, the *episkopos* of Antioch, which were written at the beginning of the second century, are very important early Christian writings. They present for the first time the picture of the threefold office of bishop, presbyter, and deacon, or their Greek terms *episkopos*, *presbyteros*, and *diakonos*. In the ministry and order of the mono-episcopate, the bishop is the ordinary presider of the Eucharist and the single leader and source of unity for a local church, much like a pastor of a huge parish today. This structure becomes the model in the West over the next decades, although Rome didn't adopt it until the end of the second century. Deacons, according to Ignatius of Antioch, are "true servants" of the church who serve frequently as emissaries from one church to another and are subject to bishops and the presbytery. Unlike bishops and deacons who are defined according to function, for Ignatius presbyters are distinguished by the status of "being models of discipleship" and by acting "as a consultative body for the bishops" (Bernier, 51). It should be noted that the holders of these three offices could be and were normally married.

The *Apostolic Tradition* states that bishops were chosen by all the people and usually from the group of presbyters. This ancient document also describes the ordinations of bishops, presbyters, and deacons through the laying on of hands around the year 200, and for the first time the term *priest (sacerdos)* is used for a bishop as the usual presider of the Eucharist. "In the middle of the third century Cornelius, the bishop of Rome, found himself with approximately fifty thousand Christians out of a population of a million or so. . . . [There were] forty-six presbyters; seven deacons; seven sub-deacons; forty-two acolytes; fifty-two exorcists, lectors, and doorkeepers; hundreds of lesser ministers; and fifteen hundred poor needing daily care" (Bernier, 54). The deacons, as the "right hand" of the bishop, were each in charge of one of the seven districts of the city. As the church grew in size and complexity, the mono-episcopate tended to become more of a monarchical episcopate, increasingly concerned with administration, supervision, and the ordering of ministries. The term *laity* began to be used in the third century, but at this point it appears to be more a distinction regarding the level of education and one's role in the community than a separation due to ordination. Paul Bernier explains the relationship between the ordained and the community in this way: "Though we can see the beginnings of the process whereby the bishop and his presbyters and deacons were set apart from the masses, it is important to stress that the bishop at this time was still elected by the church at large and regularly consulted the community in matters of church and public life" (55). The underlying principle is that ministry in general belongs to the community.

The eventual network of episcopal leadership provided an organization of interconnection among local communities/churches. Bishops from neighboring churches gathered to consecrate a new bishop, and letters were exchanged between bishops. Bishops also provided a sense of historical connection with the first disciples of Jesus, such as Bishop Papias in the district of Phrygia (present-day Turkey) with the apostle John; Bishop Irenaeus in Lyons (present-day France) with Bishop Polycarp, who knew John as well; and bishops Anicetus or Victor of Rome tracing their link with Peter. The universality or catholicity of the church in the second and third centuries "was an organic concept, achieved not through adherence to precise formulations of ideas but through relationships in and among various communities" (Irvin and Sunquist 2001, 68). Ignatius of Antioch was the first in his *Letter to the Smyrnaeans* to use the term *Catholic Church* to refer to the universal and orthodox church.

The term *pope* was not used until the eleventh century. However, in a second-century dispute over the dating of Easter between the eastern and western parts of the Roman Empire, the bishop of Rome played a symbolic role in leadership among the churches in the West due to the prestige and riches of the city of Rome as the capital of the empire and the church's tradition that both Peter and Paul were martyred there. Callistus of the early third century was the first bishop of Rome explicitly to cite Petrine authority. While Rome was the only local church beginning to be recognized as having some particular leadership beyond itself in the West, the bishops and churches of Antioch, Alexandria, and, to a lesser extent, Jerusalem were very influential in the East, where Christianity was much stronger.

It is important to note the important role of women in ministry in the earliest phase of the church. Jesus was accompanied by women who shared in and supported his ministry, such as Mary Magdalene, Joanna, Susanna, and the women witnesses of the resurrection to the apostles. In the NT we hear of women leading house churches, such as Prisca (Rom 16:5; 1 Cor 16:19) and Nympha (Col 4:15), and possibly Phoebe (Rom 16:17), Chloe (1 Cor 1:11), Lydia (Acts 16:14–15, 40), Martha (Lk 10:38), and Mary, the mother of John Mark (Acts 12:12). We can assume that some women continued this tradition in the post-apostolic period. Paul speaks of some women as his coworkers and laborers for the gospel, such as Phoebe as a *diakonos* of the church of Cenchreae, and Junia as an apostle or traveling evangelist (Rom 16). He also refers to the four prophesying daughters of Philip (Acts 21:9), where prophecy was a recognized ministry. In the second century references to the preaching of Maximilla within the Montanist movement and the traveling evangelism of Thecla point to the continual role of women in ministry in Asia Minor. Furthermore, Tertullian disapprovingly notes that in the third century in Carthage women appealed to Thecla for the authority to preach and baptize. While the practice of women in official roles of ministry generally disappeared by the end of the third century in the West, the ministry of deaconesses described in the Syrian document *Didascalia Apostolorum* (*Catholic Teaching of the Twelve Apostles and Holy Disciples of Our Redeemer*) continued much longer in the East.

Spiritual, Religious, and Social Movements

Within a couple of decades after the resurrection the social context of the Jesus movement shifted from the Palestinian village to primarily an urban context. Sociologist Rodney Stark describes Antioch as "a city filled with misery, danger, fear, despair, and hatred . . . rooted in intense ethnic antagonisms and exacerbated by a constant stream of strangers . . . a city repeatedly smashed by cataclysmic catastrophes" (Stark, 160–61). Within that context Christians offered hope and meaning for life, formed communities across ethnic and socioeconomic lines, and extended their medical and physical care to fellow Christians and others. Contrary to a common perception that most Christians were from the lower classes, recent studies indicate that Christianity was based in the middle and upper classes (Stark, 30–31), with members of the lower class as well. Not only the poor and enslaved but many others who were dissatisfied with life and searching for more were drawn to the Christian community.

This was particularly true for women, who formed the majority of Christians. The inclusive love of the gospel upheld the human dignity of women more than the Greco-Roman, Persian, Egyptian, and Jewish societies. This was reflected in the Christian condemnation of infanticide (most often female), divorce, incest, marital infidelity, and polygamy—all of which dehumanized women in particular. Christian widows were cared for and respected rather than pressured to remarry, and some widows had recognized roles of ministry within the community (1 Tim 5:3–15). Christian women were given more freedom in choosing a spouse rather than being completely subject to pre-pubertal arrangements by others. As noted earlier in the discussion on ministry, women could exercise leadership and share responsibility in the Christian home and community, especially until the beginning of the third century. For these reasons a number of wealthy women were attracted to Christianity, thus providing Christianity with an avenue into the upper classes.

In contrast to Gnostic claims, Christianity was not an elitist religion. Political leaders could not kill the movement by killing or imprisoning its leaders. Rather, every man and woman, Jew and Gentile, free and slave was an equally full member of the community and each was to live out his or her spiritual faith in daily life. Some suffered and died because of their belief. In the Roman Empire sporadic and local persecutions around 250 CE turned into broader systematic attempts to wipe out Christianity. The martyr was considered the ideal Christian and martyrdom the highest spiritual victory, the model of dying to oneself for the sake of Christ. A "cult" or religious veneration of martyrs developed. The anniversaries of their deaths were celebrated, the places of their suffering were respected, and pilgrims would visit and pray at their graves.

The oldest written record outside of scripture of an individual martyr is of Polycarp, the eighty-six-year-old bishop of Smyrna in Asia Minor around the year 156. An eyewitness account of the death of Blandina, a slave girl and recent convert in Vienne (present-day southern France) in 177, describes how others saw "in the form of their sister, him who was crucified for them" (Eusebius *Church History* V.1.41). *The Passion of Perpetua* describes the martyrdom of a fairly wealthy African woman, Perpetua, and her servant, Felicitas, in Carthage, probably in 203. Incidentally, if the first part of this narrative was written by Perpetua herself, it is one of the earliest Christian texts written by a woman (Bevans and Schroeder 2004, 86). The letter of Ignatius of Antioch to the Romans, written during his journey to Rome for his martyrdom, is like a martyr's manual. The roll of martyrs included women and men, slave and master, the ordained and non-ordained. Those who survived imprisonment and/or torture for their faith were called confessors and were held in high esteem in the community. In third-century North Africa, for example, some were admitted as presbyters without ordination.

While "religious" movements are considered here as more external and institutional and "spiritual" movements tend to be more internal and fluid, the case of martyrdom in the early church illustrates the overlap between these two categories. The cult of martyrs was institutionalized and became a significant expression of Christian spirituality. Furthermore, between the daily spirituality and service of Christians and the radical spirituality of martyrs and confessors, various forms of ascetical practices emerged to promote self-denial and moral discipline. Tertullian called for a rigorous moral code and became associated with the Montanist (or New Prophecy) charismatic movement in North Africa, which encouraged severe fasting and even celibacy in preparation for the coming of the age of the Spirit. Beyond Montanism, celibacy was a more general form of asceticism adopted by some Christians, both men and women. Some young women who never married dedicated themselves to a life of virginity, and some married women either after the death of their husband or while they were still alive joined the ranks of these "consecrated virgins" who carried out the ministry of prayer and good works; sometimes several lived together in a house owned by one of them.

Most of those living such a dedicated life of celibacy did so "in order to devote themselves entirely to God, not to pursue self-fulfillment" (Irvin and Sunquist 2001, 142). However, there were some who considered any bodily pleasure contrary to the Christian life. Tatian the Assyrian, who held this extreme view, was condemned by other Christian leaders, but he is also associated with the beginnings of the broader ascetic movement of the second century in the Syrian wilderness that would spread across Asia. Around the same time, many men and women were moving to the desert areas of Egypt for isolated ascetic living. Ascetics sometimes were given the status of authority in churches that were not directly under the sphere of a bishop. Egypt and Syria would become the birthplaces of communal monasticism in the future.

As a final note for this thread of tradition—spiritual, religious, and social movements—we recall what was mentioned earlier in this chapter about charismatic, prophetic, and apocalyptic movements, particularly in Asia Minor and North Africa into the third century—that some individuals were reportedly performing signs and wonders. For example, Gregory the Wonderworker, who brought the gospel to the area of Cappadocia in Asia Minor and later became the bishop of Neocaesarea in the middle of the third century, was widely known for casting out demons and performing miracles.

Theological Developments

Men and women in the catechumenate, preparing for baptism and entrance into the church, learned the key doctrines of the church particularly through the use of short statements of faith called creeds. These teaching sessions and early creeds represent the beginning of the theologizing process in and among local Christian communities. In this context it is essential to note that theology was not only done in writing, but it also "was done as Christians preached, sang hymns, decorated Roman catacombs and churches, prayed with one another" (Bevans 2009, 208). In this way we are reminded of the strong ongoing connection between two threads of Christian tradition: liturgy, sacraments, and art; and theological developments. Keeping this broader scope in mind, we shall now turn to the written expressions of theological developments.

Looking beyond common perceptions, the emerging NT was in itself a collection of theological writings, with each author doing theology within and in response to his own community and context. Paul develops a theology of grace, church, the Spirit, and Jesus Christ. Each of the Gospels contains its own theology and Christology; for example, Matthew's theology was perhaps the most "Jewish," Luke's perhaps the most "Gentile," and the gospel of John the most explicitly theological. The other NT writings contribute their own theologies and perspectives. We see also the link and overlap between the threads of scripture and theological developments, which appear throughout this book.

In the second and third centuries most theological writings came not from western Europe, but rather from Antioch (Syria), Edessa (Oshroene), and Alexandria and Carthage (North Africa). We have already made reference to and drawn upon some of the earliest and most significant writings, such as the *Didache*, the seven letters of Ignatius of Antioch, and the accounts of the martyrdoms of Polycarp, Perpetua, and Felicity, and the martyrs of Lyons, particularly Blandina. In terms of Christology, Ignatius of Antioch insists on the true humanity of Jesus in response to the heresy of Docetism, which claimed that Jesus only seemed to be human.

A group of theologians called apologists wrote in defense of Christianity in response to attacks and misunderstandings. Justin Martyr, the son of Greek colonists in Samaria and a student of Greek philosophy, went to Rome, where he became a Christian and claimed that his new faith was the true philosophy. He used the Hellenistic philosophical concept of *logos* to describe God's Word as present throughout history and in people's minds and hearts in a partial way and now known in its entirety by Christians in the incarnate Word of Jesus Christ. Clement of Alexandria was converted by Pantaenus, the founder of the famous catechetical school of Alexandria and possibly associated with the beginning phase of Christianity in India. Like Justin, Clement saw continuity between Hellenistic philosophy and Christianity to the point of describing philosophy as preparation for the gospel. Clement's greatest student was Origen of Alexandria, who, in addition to the tremendous contributions he made to the study of scripture, used Platonic philosophy to describe God as absolutely transcendent and humans as spiritual beings who through sin strayed from contemplating God. In Jesus all people and creation can be drawn back to God.

In contrast to these three apologists, the theologian Tertullian considered Hellenistic philosophy opposed to Christian faith. Raised in the Romanized city of Carthage in North Africa and probably trained in Roman law, Tertullian was one of the first, if not the first, to write theology in Latin. He seems to have coined the term *trinitas* to describe God as well as other theological Latin terms that became standard in Western theology. Tertullian described God as a lawgiver and humans as sinners who broke the divine law and disturbed the world's order. Through the new law brought by Jesus, humanity can be saved by baptism and by obeying God's law.

The theology of Irenaeus was based more on his origins in Smyrna in Asia Minor than on his later context as a bishop in Lyons in the western Mediterranean area. Unlike Tertullian, he wrote in Greek. Rather than either embracing or rejecting Hellenistic philosophy, Irenaeus basically discounted it as a measure for Christianity. His theology was more pastoral and biblically rooted. Irenaeus described God as a shepherd, and humanity created in God's image as having fallen into the clutches of Satan through sin. However, Christ freed humanity from the devil's grasp so that humans may grow into the fullness of God's likeness until all will be recapitulated in Christ at the end.

Bardaisan was born of Persian parents exiled in Edessa and converted to Christianity as a young man. Some of his theology was written in hymnody, but he also wrote discursive works, such as against Marcionism, in which he maintained that God was one and not two. Like Origen, Bardaisan would later be labeled by some as a heretic. This was partially due to his very positive attitude toward the cultures of other peoples. In contrast, Tatian the Assyrian was noted for his extreme asceticism and for his opposition to Hellenistic philosophical thought, surprising considering he had been a student of Justin Martyr. However, he did praise the wisdom of his own Syrian culture and that of the Jews (Norris 2002, 19). Tatian was under suspicion because some of his ideas were similar although not identical with the Marcionites and Gnostics.

In *Christian Thought Revisited*, Cuban-born theologian Justo González identifies and traces three fundamental theological typologies throughout Christian history. According to this insightful schema, Tertullian represents Type A, which is mainly concerned with maintaining order and the law of God and which will be primarily developed out of Carthage and Rome and within Latin-speaking Christianity. Origen, Justin, and Clement represent Type B, which is mainly concerned with discovering the truth and which will primarily be developed out of Alexandria and within Greek-speaking Christianity. Irenaeus and Bardaisan represent Type C, which is mainly concerned with God in history and which will primarily be developed out of Antioch and Edessa and within Syriac-speaking Christianity (González 1999).

In connecting the threads of theological development with ministry and organization, it is interesting to note that Justin, Clement, Tertullian, Bardaisan, and Tatian were all lay theologians, while Origen was a presbyter and Irenaeus a bishop.

Mission, Cultures, and Religions

The mission of Jesus was centered on the kingdom of God. The Acts of the Apostles is a theological history of the movement from mission to the birth of the church. The early disciples were faithful to the Spirit, who led them in new directions. Years later, the Second Vatican Council recalled and reclaimed that the church, still on a pilgrimage, is "missionary by her very nature" (*Ad Gentes* 2; cf. *Lumen Gentium* 1). This fundamental identification of church and mission was very evident in the early church.

Outside the Roman Empire the spread and foundation of Christianity were through particular individuals who could be called evangelists or church founders: Addai the Galilean Jewish Christian in Oshroene, Tatian the Assyrian in Adiabene, Gregory the Illuminator in Armenia, Thomas and/or Pantaenus in India. The Christian merchants, who first brought the name of Christ to Armenia, represent many unnamed Christian merchants, migrants, and slaves who carried their Christian faith on their travels. The names of Tatian, Pantaenus, and Bardaisan point to the roles of Christian teachers, writers, and theologians in mission. Finally, ascetics left the Syrian wilderness and spread the good news in a life of witness and service along the trade routes across the Persian Empire. There is a report of Christians living as far east as present-day northern Afghanistan before the year 200, and by 225 "there were already more than twenty bishops in Persia, with jurisdiction from the mountains of Kurdistan in the east to the Caspian Sea in the west" (Moffett 1998, 79).

Within the Roman Empire the *Didache* described traveling preachers in the early days, but they probably became scarce by the end of the second century. As charismatic itinerant preachers disappeared, resident bishops like Ignatius, Polycarp, and Irenaeus became key figures in the spread of Christianity, each in his own way. The names of the apologists and teachers, who presented the faith in the academic sphere, can also be added here, and merchants from Asia Minor probably established Christian communities in Lyons before Irenaeus arrived (Irvin and Sunquist 2001, 75). Furthermore, the names of Polycarp and Ignatius, along with Perpetua, Felicitas, and Blandina, are among a thousand and perhaps as many as ten thousand Christians who were martyred. Their witness not only strengthened the Christian community, but we have evidence that their willingness to die for their faith drew others to Christ and the church. Tertullian captured this in his famous phrase in *Apology*: "We become more numerous every time we are hewn down by you: the blood of Christians is seed" (Tertullian 1950, 50, 12).

Alongside the human means of mission mentioned in the previous two paragraphs, the main reason for the rapid spread of the church was due to the witness and efforts of "ordinary" Christians. Not all Christians were openly and explicitly seeking converts; rather, they invited people to share their Christian faith through casual, informal witness and conversations. This began in the Christian home, the center of Christianity in the second and third centuries, but Christians also took it "to the streets." Michael Green, a twentieth-century theologian, describes it in the following way: "This must often have been not formal preaching, but the informal chattering to friends and chance acquaintances, in homes and wine shops, on walks, and around market stalls. They went everywhere gossiping the gospel; they did it naturally, enthusiastically, and with the conviction of those who are not paid to say that sort of thing" (Green, 173). "Gossiping the gospel" was both verbal and nonverbal, including, for example, the witness of Christian communities to care for those in need, whether they were Christian or not. And, as noted several times in this chapter, both women and men were participating fully in the life of the church and mission. The motivation of all of the agents of mission mentioned above in this thread of

Christian tradition, both outside of and within the Roman Empire, is based on the fundamental model and theology of mission in the early church that baptism is a call to mission.

In terms of the issue of culture, we see in the Acts of the Apostles how the gospel touched the many cultural and regional identities of Jewish people on Pentecost and then crossed into the worlds of the Samaritans, Ethiopians, and Gentiles. The Council of Jerusalem (Acts 15:1–29) officially stated that people did not have to become Jews, religiously and/or culturally, when they became Christians.

While peoples from different cultures were drawn to the church, the attitude regarding the relationship between Christianity and culture varied. As noted above, in the section "Theological Developments," early theologians like Justin Martyr and Clement of Alexandria, on the one hand, endorsed the continuity between the faith and Hellenistic philosophy; Tertullian of Carthage, on the other hand, stressed the discontinuity between them, as captured in his famous statement in *On Prescription against Heretics*, "What does Athens have to do with Jerusalem?" (Tertullian 1994, 7). Irenaeus of Lyons took a middle position. Beyond philosophy and regarding culture in broader terms, Bardaisan of Edessa, situated at the crossroads of east and west and north and south, "wrote of the ways of the Chinese, Indians, Persians, Arabs, Greeks, Germans, and Britons . . . [and] saw the means by which Jesus Christ, the First Thought of God, could bring about the redemption of all without the displacement of their various laws and cultures" (Irvin and Sunquist 2001, 126). These various perspectives provide a spectrum of the theological principles and tensions surrounding the translational character of Christianity and the phenomena of what we today call inculturation.

In daily life many Christians took a countercultural position. Tertullian counseled Christians not to engage in careers like stone masons and painters because their trade often involved making images used for idolatry. He also discouraged Christians from becoming soldiers, although there is evidence of a legion in the third century composed primarily of Christians (Norris 2002, 23). The ethical standard of the early Christian communities to uphold the dignity of women and the unborn and to care for widows and orphans generally went against societal norms and practices. At the same time, members of the early church used many elements from their societal context to express and live their faith. As one example, pre-Constantinian artwork on Christian sarcophagi included both the Christian symbols of the fish and the anchor and the Roman symbol D.M. (*Diis Manibus*) and the wreath. The well-known line from the second-century anonymous *Epistle of Diognetus* that Christians are "in the world, but not of the world" points to the underlying and ongoing dynamics and challenges of Christianity and culture.

In the encounter with other religions, the relationship of Christianity with Judaism was quite complex. On the one hand, for example, the long-established Jewish community of Trastevere in Rome provided the foundation for that early Christian community, and the influence of Jewish Christians continued well into the third century, which is a much longer time than previously understood. At the same time, many synagogue services at the end of the first century included a curse against Christians, and Christians were likewise demonizing Judaism. The Jews were striving to maintain the identity and integrity of Judaism, especially since many Hellenized Jews were becoming Christians. Christianity also was attempting to maintain its identity and integrity. Against what was considered the heresy of Judaizing, Ignatius wrote the following to the Magnesians: "It is monstrous to talk of Jesus Christ and to practice Judaism" (par. X).

Dissimilar to the situation north of the Mediterranean, it seems that in North Africa there was "little conflict between the two communities as late as the early third century" (Irvin and Sunquist 2001, 84). However, later in the third century anti-Semitism and the hostility between the two religions in general became more intense around the Roman Empire. Outside the Roman Empire, Christianity had also originally taken root in Jewish communities, such as in Oshroene and India, and it appears that their relationship remained positive for a longer time. For example, in Edessa "relations between Jews and Christians were relatively friendly, to the point where the two communities appear to have cooperated in such matters as Bible study and dealing with the city's rulers" (ibid., 61). Such differing perspectives were reflected in the area of scripture as well. Irenaeus insisted on keeping the Jewish scripture in the Christian Bible, while people like Marcion and some Gnostics rejected this idea.

Another connection with Judaism was the presence of God-fearers, Gentiles who were familiar with the monotheistic God of the LXX and the Jewish community of faith, but didn't become Jewish due to the requirements of circumcision and Jewish customs or for other reasons. However, this prepared many for accepting the message of Christ. Anglican bishop, missionary, and scholar Stephen Neill maintains that the influx and significance of this group of God-fearers makes it difficult to compare this period of church and mission with other times (1986, 25).

Regarding other religions, Christians generally rejected Greco-Roman religion as pagan and polytheistic. It is interesting, though, to note how Paul, in the midst of his condemnation of their religion while preaching in the Areopagus in Athens, refers to "an altar with the inscription 'To an unknown god'" (Acts 17:23). He implies that the Christian God is this 'unknown god' they are seeking. Clement and Origen of the Alexandrine school were knowledgeable of Buddhism and described it with "both praise and blame" (Norris 2002, 14). The Christians generally opposed the religion of Manichaeism, a dualistic religion with Christian roots founded by Mani in third-century Persia that spread over the next thousand years across Asia and into Europe.

Conclusion

During this period of the early church, until around the year 300, Christianity as a religion was born and took its first steps toward claiming and developing its own identity. Like the two disciples on the road to Emmaus, the first followers of Jesus were probably somewhat disillusioned and uncertain after the resurrection. However, the Acts of the Apostles provides a beautiful theological history of the movement from following the mission of Jesus to the eventual birth of the church as distinct from Judaism and inclusive of Gentiles. The message of Christ then spread out in all four directions to Asia Minor, Greece, Armenia, Mesopotamia, Syria, Persia, India, Egypt, North Africa, Spain, Gaul, and Italy.

Those small scattered Christian communities, which often had their beginnings in urban Jewish neighborhoods, became minority diaspora communities in many places and a larger percentage of the population in other areas, such as in Asia Minor and North Africa. These diverse local communities eventually formed regional networks based on relationships and communications among themselves and their bishops. Sometimes this extended between regions, as when dealing with the issues of the date of Easter and the process of the readmission of apostates. All of this was built on the principle of unity in diversity.

Within this context we have seen the early developments of six threads of Christian tradition: scripture; liturgy, sacraments, and art; ministry and organization; spiritual, religious, and social movements; theological developments; and mission, cultures, and religions. There are two basic movements at work at the same time. First, the local churches are striving to be faithful to the teachings of Jesus Christ; and second, they are adapting to their own particular contexts. This was a time marked by creativity and fluidity. However, as Christianity grows, there will be a need for more organization and some standardization, such as the canon of scripture, forms of ministry, and the pattern of liturgy.

We end with the following eyewitness account of a Christian community in the Roman Empire during this period. It comes from *The Apology of Aristides the Philosopher*. Original copies of this text exist in Greek, Armenian, and Syriac.

> When they see a stranger, they take him to their homes and rejoice over him as a very brother; for they do not call them brethren after the flesh, but brethren after the Spirit and in God. . . . And if they hear that one of their number is imprisoned or afflicted on account of the name of their Messiah, all of them anxiously minister to his necessity, and if it is possible to redeem him they set him free. And if there is among them any that is poor and needy, and if they have no spare food, they fast two or three days to supply to the needy their lack of food. Every morning and every hour they give thanks [*Eucharistion* in Greek] and praise God for His loving-kindness toward them. (Aristides 1925, 276–77)

2

The Age of the "Imperial Church"

ca. 300 to ca. 600

Around the beginning of the fourth century Christians were growing very quickly in number, particularly in North Africa and Asia Minor, to the point that perhaps as much as half of the populations of some of their cities were Christians. At this time Christianity also experienced a major shift in its political status in the Roman and Persian empires, which in turn greatly influenced its development in these areas. Some of the theological-cultural developments, such as Donatism and Arianism, were considered unorthodox and caused major divisions. While these latter two movements didn't last very long, other theological distinctions around Christological debates are identified with various Christian entities or streams that will continue to exist as living Christian communities much longer, some, such as the Coptic Christians of Egypt, until the present day. Another significant development was that the earlier trickle of women and men going into the desert and wilderness seeking a more ascetic Christian lifestyle became a steady flow. This led to the formation of a variety of monastic communities, which will become the primary agents of preserving, deepening, and spreading Christianity as far as Ireland, Ethiopia, and Central Asia during this three-hundred-year period. By the year 600, the church had built upon its initial foundations, but it had also experienced some divisions. Furthermore, it had become what Irvin and Sunquist called "the imperial church" (2001, 155–255). We fill out this historical backdrop in the first part of this chapter, and in the second half we continue tracing the six threads of Christian tradition that we introduced in Chapter 1.

Historical Context

Constantine and the Making of the Church

At the end of the third century, the Roman Empire was facing many challenges (see Map 2). Externally, it was struggling militarily against the

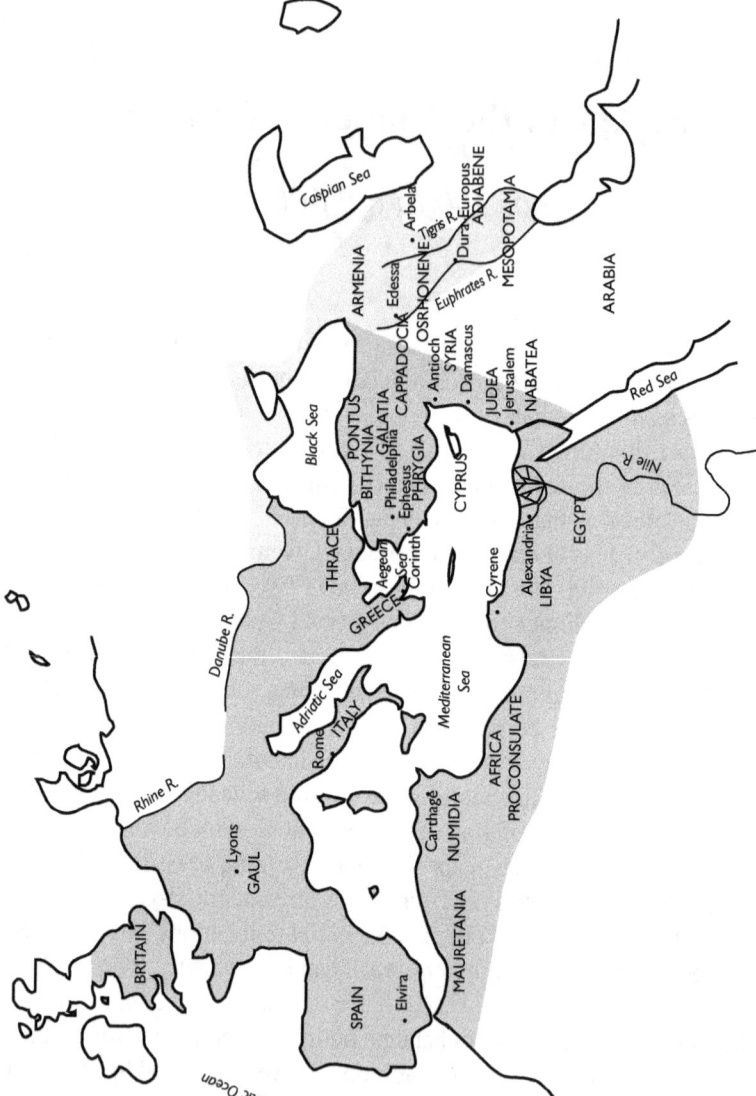

Map 2. Boundaries and Jurisdictions of the Roman Empire in the Year 300

Persian Empire, its longtime enemy to the east, and against the migrating and invading Germanic tribes from the north. Internally, the administrative infrastructure was breaking down and adding to the strain of heavy taxation. Also, the Roman gods and emperor cult, which were considered important for maintaining the well-being of the empire and the sense of political unity and loyalty, were declining in the face of new religions. Christianity, as one of these new religions, was growing rapidly and eventually seen as a political threat due to the refusal of Christians to worship the Roman gods. The empire at this point was divided into four regions, each with its own emperor or caesar, and one of them, Diocletian, initiated a major persecution against the Christians in 303.

Constantine in 306 became the emperor of the region of Spain, Britain, and Gaul (roughly present-day France), and six years later he was attacking Maxentius, the ruler of Italy and North Africa. Before a decisive battle in 312 in Rome, Constantine reportedly saw the sign of the first two letters of the name of Christ, the *chi-rho*, in the sky and heard a voice guaranteeing victory. With this symbol on their shields, Constantine's soldiers were victorious, and he became the sole emperor in the West. A year later, in 313, he formed an alliance with Licinius, the sole emperor in the east, and together they issued a ruling that became known as the Edict of Milan, which guaranteed religious freedom and returned confiscated properties and places of worship to Christians. Taxes would be used to build churches, and bishops would receive endowments from the state. The status of Christianity shifted from being persecuted to being legalized and, eventually, after about eighty years, becoming the official religion of the empire in 392 with the Edict of Constantinople. Other "pagan" religions would then be persecuted.

The personal conversion of Constantine is a subject of debate. He postponed baptism to his deathbed to avoid the consequences of post-baptismal sins. However, it is clear that Constantine associated belief in the God Christians worshipped with military and political success, and he also hoped that this religion would provide the needed unity in the empire, which he ruled as the sole emperor after 324. For political and possibly other reasons, Constantine did maintain some allegiance to the Roman solar god. When he set aside Sunday as the official day of worship, "it is not clear whether it was the Invincible Sun or Jesus Christ whom he intended to honor" (Irvin and Sunquist 2001, 162).

A second action that influenced the future shape of Christianity was Constantine's decision to establish a new eastern capital of the empire in the town of Byzantium, which was situated strategically between the Black and Aegean seas and closer to the eastern border. This city, renamed Constantinople (present-day Istanbul), became very rich and the eventual capital of the East Roman Empire. More important for Christianity, it was situated near the denser Christian population in Asia Minor, and it would become the center of the Byzantine Church (Greek East) for the next eleven hundred years. Constantinople soon was filled with beautiful new churches, and construction was begun on a huge cathedral, later renamed Hagia Sophia.

The third major impact that Constantine had on the shape of Christianity was that the Persian Empire, which to this point had allowed Christians freedom of worship, now turned against Christianity when it became first the tolerated and later the official religion of their enemy. The Christians in Persia faced stiff opposition from the officials of the state religion of Zoroastrianism, and their political loyalty was questioned. Tens of thousands of Christians died for their faith in the fourth century in the Persian Empire, perhaps more than those who died as martyrs in the earlier centuries in the Roman Empire.

North Africa and Donatists

Around the year 300, the church in Roman North Africa was quite strong despite or because of periodic persecution. "With some seven hundred bishops and numerous presbyters and deacons, they [Christians] were clearly a political presence no matter what their legal status might have been" (Irvin and Sunquist 2001, 167). Surprisingly, the turnaround in the relationship of the church and state in the Roman Empire did not bring the unity that Constantine wanted but rather a major division. One group of Christians rejoiced with this change and the freedom it brought and its members were willing to move beyond the memories of persecution. However, Christians in another group were very resistant to entering into any type of association with the political authorities, who had been persecuting them, and they were not willing to forget either their memories of the martyrs or those who had "betrayed" the faith during the times of persecution, particularly the traitors (*traditores*) who "handed over" the written scriptures for destruction during the persecution by Diocletian. This second group followed a strict moral adherence that had been pursued earlier by Tertullian of Carthage and in Rome and North Africa under Novatianism.

The initial crisis arose in 311, two years before the Edict of Milan, when Caecilian was consecrated a senior bishop of the important city of Carthage without the customary participation by the bishops of Numidia. Furthermore, Caecilian had a questionable past, since he had prevented Christians from bringing food to their relatives in prison, and one of the bishops who participated in the consecration was possibly a *traditor*. The Numidian bishops declared the bishop's consecration invalid, especially since a *traditor* had participated, and they elected Majorinus as bishop; he was soon succeeded by Donatus. This movement adopted the latter's name and its followers became known as Donatists. All churches of North

Africa were then forced to choose between the Donatists and the group known as Catholics. The Donatists said they were following Cyprian, an earlier bishop of Carthage, who had stated that the validity of baptism for salvation was dependent upon the unity of the Catholic Church, guaranteed through apostolic succession, and that sacraments performed by a person not in unity with the church were invalid.

In 313, just six months after the Edict of Milan, the Donatists brought their charge against Caecilian before Constantine. The emperor handed the matter over to Miltiades, the bishop of Rome, who called a local council of bishops. This local council decided in favor of Caecilian, but the Donatists dismissed the decision because one of the bishops who had ordained Miltiades was suspected of being a *traditor* and therefore the bishop of Rome was suspect. A broader council was convened in 314, and it also favored Caecilian and granted those in union with him official recognition with the associated political and financial support. However, as a compromise, the Donatists, who were very popular, were allowed to continue even without official recognition. Constantine, who wanted a united church for the sake of uniting the empire, initially used peaceful means, but in 317 he ordered the suppression of the Donatists for disruptive behavior. Their property was confiscated and their leaders arrested or exiled. The use of force was rescinded in 321. The relationship between the Donatists and the Catholics for the next century swung between peaceful coexistence and external violence.

The invasion of North Africa in 429 by the Germanic Vandals, who were Arian Christians (discussed in the following section), brought the Donatists and the Catholics closer together against a common enemy. A spirit of more cooperation between these two groups grew when the area was reclaimed under the rule of Constantinople, but both sides with time also found the Byzantine government to be oppressive. When the Muslims captured Carthage in 698, Christianity declined very quickly in an area where it had been very strong.

Arianism, Nicaea, and Chalcedon

Moving eastward from Carthage across the northern part of the African continent brings us to the Egyptian city of Alexandria, the second largest city in the Roman Empire, with its catechetical school and fast Christian growth. However, this intellectual environment provided the context for creating and/or further developing not only orthodox theology, but also heterodox teachings like Gnosticism.

During the post-300 period Arianism was the main controversy. Arius, for whom Arianism was named, was ordained a presbyter in Alexandria in 311. In order to protect the monotheistic belief of one infinite God, he began teaching that Jesus could not be God. The Logos was not eternal but the firstborn of creation, or as Arias preached, "There was a time when the Word was not!" In contrast to the theological emphasis of Antioch, where Arius was educated, on the human nature of Jesus Christ, the emphasis in Alexandria was on the divinity of Jesus Christ and the Logos. The people and Christian leaders of Alexandria were upset with the teaching of Arius and banished him from the city, but the ideas spread. Soon the eastern part of the empire was divided between those, particularly in Palestine and Asia Minor, who supported Arius, and others who supported the stance of Alexandria.

Constantine, who wanted Christianity to be a source of political unity and had already seen the divisive effects of Donatism, decided to call a general council to resolve the issue in his summer resort in Nicaea in 325. This was primarily an Eastern council with the majority from Asia Minor and North Africa. There seems to have been one bishop, named John, representing India and Persia, and an East Syrian bishop, named James (or Jacob), from Nisibis. The bishop of Rome was represented by just two legates. The Arian position was condemned, and Arius and some of his followers were sent into exile. The deacon and theologian Athanasius of Alexandria became the primary pro-Nicene champion. However, Constantine within a couple of years invited the exiled Arians back to their ecclesiastical positions and pushed for reconciliation between the two theological perspectives. With the exception of Athanasius, who had become the bishop of Alexandria, most of the churches in the eastern part of the empire favored a moderate Arian position, while those in the western part strictly maintained the stance of Nicaea. The Council of Constantinople in 381 modified the Nicene Creed in the basic form that is still used today. However, diverse Christological understandings continued to develop within the different "streams" of Christianity.

The Council of Chalcedon in 451 endorsed the formulation that there are two natures and one person of Christ, which would be accepted by the church of the Latin West (western part of the Roman Empire) and most of the Greek East (eastern part of the Roman Empire). Another position, known as Monophysite (one nature), maintained a Christology of one person and one nature. Cyril of Alexandria was the primary spokesperson of this understanding, which would continue to be held by Christians in Armenia, West Syria, Egypt, Nubia, and Ethiopia. A third Christology, known as Dyophysite (two natures), was defined as two persons and two natures. It represented the school of Antioch and was followed by Christians in East Syria and Persia. This latter understanding, associated with Nestorius, the bishop/patriarch of Constantinople, was called Nestorianism and considered heretical by others. (We use the more neutral terms *East*

Syrian and *Persian* for this stream of Christianity throughout this book.) It is important to note that the Chalcedonian definition was a compromise, "thereby setting forth a middle way that combined insights from both sides [Alexandria and Antioch]" (Irvin and Sunquist 2001, 158).

Egypt, Ethiopia, and Nubia

Outside the theological and philosophical "hotbed" of Alexandria, another very significant movement for the Christian tradition was brewing in the desert areas of Egypt. In the previous chapter we noted that men and women had started moving there in search of a more ascetical Christian life. With the official toleration and acceptance of Christianity and the end of persecution and martyrdom, it seemed that "the Christian movement had lost something of its spiritual edge, something of its dynamic power" (Irvin and Sunquist 2001, 210). As a result, many Christians added their number to the initial trickle of ascetics, and others came seeking spiritual direction from them. The hermit Anthony (ca. 251–356) became widely known through his biography, *The Life of Anthony*, written after his death by Athanasius of Alexandria (ca. 295/300–373). Seeing the need for some organization of the lives of the individual ascetics, the Egyptian ascetic Pachomius (292–346) wrote a rule for a communal order early in the fourth century. Within a few years after the death of Pachomius the number of monks and nuns living according to his rule reached tens of thousands. Some visitors to these Egyptian communities adopted this rule for other orders, and many forms of monasticism around the Christian world trace their roots to Egypt. This list includes Basil of Caesarea, Melania the Younger, John Cassian, Martin of Tours, Patrick of Ireland, Benedict of Nursia, and Radegunde of Gaul.

While Egypt was contributing to developments in the broader Christian world in terms of theology and monasticism, a national Christian identity was also being shaped. Politically, there was a growing tension with the authority of Constantinople; economically, there was a growing feeling that the rich agricultural production of Egypt was being exploited by the East Roman Empire; culturally, the Egyptian (Coptic) language was used in liturgies and in translating scripture; and, theologically, the Chalcedonian definition of the nature of Christ that was supported by Constantinople would eventually lose prominence to the non-Chalcedonian Monophysite definition of Coptic Christianity in Egypt. The bishop of Alexandria sometimes played a political role along with the important ecclesiastical one.

South of Egypt beyond the borders of the Roman and Persian empires was the city of Axum, capital of the Kingdom of Ethiopia or Abyssinia. Ethiopia traces its Christian roots to the Ethiopian eunuch in Acts (8:27) and the apostle Matthew, but the first historical evidence of a Christian community is found in the fourth century and linked with the name Frumentius. He was one of two Syrian-Christian youths sold into slavery to the royal court of Axum, where their ship unfortunately docked after the commercial agreement with the Roman Empire had been broken, unbeknownst to the ship's captain. The two young people gained favor in the court and eventually earned their freedom. Frumentius traveled to Alexandria to request that Bishop Athanasius send a bishop to Ethiopia. Instead, Athanasius made Frumentius a bishop and sent him back. Frumentius is credited with the conversion of the royal court of Axum and translating certain portions of scripture into the Ethiopian language of Ge'ez. Later in the fifth century Syrian monks following the rule of Pachomius spread the Christian faith in the rural areas of Ethiopia, which eventually developed its own form of monasticism. Ethiopian Christianity would continue to associate itself with Alexandria as the ecclesiastical authority.

In Nubia (in present-day Sudan), between Egypt and Ethiopia, there were some Christian communities in the fifth century—probably through the efforts of Egyptian monasteries. More intentional missionary efforts occurred the following century through the initiative of Theodora of the East Roman Empire sending the priest Julian from Constantinople. Eventually, four north Nubian kingdoms became Christian. Ecclesiastically, they affiliated themselves with Alexandria rather than with Constantinople.

East Syria, Persia, India, and Armenia

In Chapter 1 we saw how Christianity grew rapidly across Syria and Persia under favorable conditions. However, Christianity's shift in status—from being persecuted to being tolerated and then finally favored—in the Roman Empire initiated by Constantine led to the eventual persecution of suspected Christian "Roman sympathizers" in the rival Persian Empire. Beginning in 339, heavy taxes were levied against Christians, their churches were destroyed, and they were forced to perform the Zoroastrian rites of worshipping the sun. The estimated number of Christians who died for their faith in the Persian Empire in the mid-fourth century runs into the tens of thousands or higher (Irvin and Sunquist 2001, 196). In this context the East Syrian monastic communities that developed strongly from the early ascetic movements in the Syrian wilderness "provided safe havens where worship and prayer could be carried on, texts could be protected, and theological ideas could be debated" (ibid., 197). Aphraates (or Araphat), called the Persian Sage, and Ephraem the Syrian were two major theologians of East Syrian Christianity during this time period.

The period from the late fourth century into the fifth century was a time of relative peace between the Roman and Persian empires as the Romans focused their military resources toward the invading Germanic tribes from the north. The shah of the Persian Empire issued a decree of toleration for Christians in 409, and the first national council of the Persian (East Syrian) Church occurred the following year. This synod of 410 and a later one in 424 confirmed acceptance of the Council of Nicaea, and they recognized the bishop of Seleucia-Ctesiphon, capital city of the Persian Empire, as the *catholicos* (leader) of the Persian Church with authority equal to that of the other patriarchs, such as the bishops of Rome, Alexandria, and Constantinople.

However, changes were on the horizon. First of all, persecution of Christians recommenced in the Persian Empire in the fifth century, and it included forcing Christians to live in segregated communities in a system called *melet*. The appointment of the *catholicos* had to be confirmed by the shah. Zoroastrians were forbidden to become Christian, but Christian communities and monasteries continued to spread the faith as they could. Second, after the Council of Chalcedon in 451, the Persian Church with its Dyophysite or Nestorian Christological definition grew distant from the rest of Christianity theologically. In 489, the famous theological school of Edessa in eastern Syria was closed due to the movement from western Syria toward the Alexandrine-Monophysite position theologically and toward Constantinople politically (see "East Roman Empire" below). The school reopened in the Persian city of Nisibis, where it eventually had over a thousand students; its subjects of study included medicine, scripture, and Greek philosophy and logic. Also, the monasteries became educational institutions not only for theology and spirituality, but the monks also translated Greek medical texts and trained physicians. By the end of the fifth century the Persian Church had developed in a distinctive way—institutionally, socially, and theologically. Geographically, it was establishing itself further along the Silk Road in central Asia and western China by the end of the sixth century (Norris 2002, 40).

In this chapter we return to the ancient Christian roots in India. The first clear historical evidence of an established Christian community there is from the middle of the fourth century. The Persian Christian Thomas of Cana, of possible Armenian descent, came with a group of settlers around the year 350 to the area of Cranganore on the Malabar coast (in the present-day state of Kerala). Perhaps they were escaping the Christian persecutions in the Persian Empire, described earlier. It is possible that Thomas sponsored a bishop, priests, and deacons, who were sent by the *catholicos* of the Persian Church (Irvin and Sunquist 2001, 203). However, in the fifth century the bishop of Rewardashir in southern Persia had direct authority over the Christians in India. While the majority of Christians probably belonged to the foreign Persian merchant communities, reports that Christians were assigned a specific caste indicates that they were recognized as part of Indian culture and that probably Indians were becoming Christians (ibid., 204). In the sixth century an Egyptian monk, known as Cosmos the Indian Navigator, encountered Christian communities celebrating the Eucharist (in Syriac) along the Malabar coast and present-day Sri Lanka.

Chapter 1 introduced Armenia as the first Christian nation around the beginning of the fourth century. In the next century the creation of an alphabet provided these Christians with the means to translate the scriptures and theological texts into Armenian and to celebrate the liturgy in their own tongue rather than in Greek or Syriac. These developments shaped and strengthened their distinctive national Christian identity. In the mid-fourth century Eustathius started ascetic communities in Armenia that were also committed to serving the poor and needy (Wilken, 104). Persia took over Armenia in the fifth century and attempted to force its people to adopt the Zoroastrian religion. The consequential and violent political and religious confrontation led to the death of thousands of Armenians. After years of struggle Persia eventually allowed the Armenians to live their Christian faith. Theologically at the Synod of Dvin (ca. 506–508), the Armenian Church rejected the Dyophysite Christology represented by the invading Persians and tended to accept the Monophysite Christology of the Alexandrine school, although they "never allied themselves with churches that officially took Monophysite positions" (Norris 2002, 39).

Latin West

We now return to Rome, where we started this chapter, with Constantine. The invasion of Germanic peoples was the driving force not only for the political, economic, and social transformation of the western part of the Roman Empire, but also its religious and ecclesiastical future. Already in the third century Goths had invaded Asia Minor and carried off Christians as slaves to the north, where they established an independent kingdom in a former territory of the Roman Empire and became Christian themselves. Other Germanic peoples soon followed this pattern. The western capital of the empire (the eastern capital was Constantinople) was moved from Rome to Milan in 354 to better defend the northern frontier, and then to Ravenna by the beginning of the fifth century because it was easier to defend. The Visigoths sacked Rome in 410, while the Vandals moved into Spain and into North Africa. Attila led an army of Huns into Italy around 450. As many as 150,000 Vandals migrated into North Africa, over 100,000 to Gaul, and thousands of others into Spain and northern Italy. These Germanic peoples established kingdoms, became Christian, learned Latin, and settled down as farmers and administrators together with the Roman residents and landowners. By contrast, the Angles, Saxons, and Jutes, who invaded the former Roman territory of Britain, were not Christians at that time. By the year 600, Germanic kings were ruling Spain, Gaul, and Italy, including Rome. Churches and monasteries became the vehicles for basic civic services and preserving the "classical" Roman culture. Ecclesiastically and theologically, it is probably better at this point to refer to this stream of Christianity as the Latin West rather than to use a reference to the declining western part of the empire.

The Christian history of the Germanic tribes traces back to the Arian bishop of Nicomedia, who consecrated Ulfilas (Wulfila) around the year 340 as the bishop among the Goths, who received the Christian faith from monks and priests from the eastern part of the Roman Empire. The greatest achievement of Ulfilas was the creation of a script for the Gothic language and the translation of most of the Bible. "With the translation of the scriptures, Christianity quickly spread among the Goths, and from them to other Germanic tribes" (Irvin and Sunquist 2001, 179). Their strong sense of tribal solidarity contributed to the phenomena of mass conversions, since a common religion was important for their communal identity and unity. Furthermore, the Arian form of Christianity brought by Ulfilas was very compatible with their traditional worldview, which included intermediaries between the divine and human. However, something happened to change the theological and political situation. Clovis, a young king of a Germanic people known as the Franks, was baptized around the year 500, and three thousand soldiers quickly followed suit. Clovis's decision was greatly influenced by his Christian wife, Clotilde. Although she was Arian, Clovis became a Christian of the Catholic (non-Arian) affiliation. Alliances developed between the Frankish aristocracy and the Roman landowners in the neighboring Visigoth Arian kingdom. This contributed to the rapid success of the Franks in expanding their political realm under what would become known as the powerful Merovingian Dynasty. This also marked the shift of the Germanic peoples from the Arian to the Catholic belief.

Monasticism had a major impact on shaping Christianity in the Latin West. In the sixth century Radegunde, who had been married to a Frankish king, founded a convent in Portiers and was known for her hospitality and her teaching. A few decades earlier Benedict of Nursia founded a men's monastic community in Italy and, with his sister Scholastica, a women's community. In the preceding century Patrick had returned to Ireland, the place of his earlier enslavement outside the Roman Empire, to announce the Christian message. Although he probably was not a monk himself, monasticism from the beginning was a central characteristic of the Irish Church. Brigid of Kildare with seven other women formed the first Irish women's monastic community, which men soon joined to form a double monastery of women and men. In particular, the Benedictine and Irish monks and nuns played a very significant role in spreading and deepening the Christian faith throughout Europe.

Throughout this time of turmoil and change the bishop of Rome was regarded as the highest ecclesiastical authority in the Latin West. For example, Constantine called upon the bishop of Rome to settle the conflict associated with the Donatists, as noted above. However, the authority of the bishop of Rome was diminishing in the eastern part of the Roman Empire in favor of the bishop of Constantinople. This was influenced by the shift of political and economic power on the Mediterranean from Rome to Constantinople, which is treated in the next section.

East Roman Empire

As mentioned earlier, another major influence that Constantine had on the course of Christianity was the establishment of a new capital of the eastern part of the Roman Empire in Byzantium, renamed Constantinople. The city grew quickly in political, economic, and ecclesiastical prominence. It became the center of the Byzantine Church (Orthodox Church) or what can be called the theological and ecclesiastical Greek East stream of Christianity.

As the western part of the Roman Empire was collapsing, the eastern part would strive to restore the prestige of the Roman Empire and to establish the integration of church and state envisioned by the Edict of Constantinople in 392. This was highlighted under the sixth-century rule of co-emperors Justinian and his wife, Theodora. Justinian is known for the complete codification of the existing corpus of Roman law, called the *Codex Justinianus*. He completed this work in 529, which was the same year that he closed the last non-Christian school of philosophy in the East Roman Empire, the famous Academy in Athens. Justinian also promulgated a set of new laws that included the treatment of aspects of church life that had earlier been under the purview of ecclesiastical authority. These latter two actions indicate a greater synthesis of church and state. Externally, Justinian reached a truce with the Persian Empire and was then able to devote military resources to regaining lost lands of the empire. His armies defeated the kingdoms of Germanic peoples in North Africa, Sicily, and Italy (including Rome and Ravenna). Rather than appointing a co-emperor of the western part of the empire, Justinian appointed agents of the emperor of Constantinople in Carthage and Ravenna. There was political tension between the Romans and Goths, on the one side, and the new rulers from Constantinople, with their soldiers drawn from many different peoples. "The bishop of Rome continued to pay nominal allegiance to Constantinople's emperor, who, by tradition and canon law, had to approve his appointment as pope" (Irvin and

Sunquist 2001, 244). These points of unease and tension between the East and the West were further highlighted by the linguistic divide. By the end of the sixth century few in Rome spoke Greek and few in Constantinople spoke Latin.

While Justinian was successful in many ways, the East Roman Empire had to deal with divisive internal theological issues around the Chalcedonian and non-Chalcedonian Christological definitions, described above. The differences were even present in the co-emperors Justinian and Theodora, with the former officially supporting the Chalcedonian position and the latter strongly promoting the non-Chalcedonian (Monophysite) one. Justinian "was the first Roman emperor to engage in theological dispositions or render theological decisions on matters of the faith and practice apart from councils or bishops," in that he "actually wrote and published his own treatises, which he sought to enforce as church doctrine" (Irvin and Sunquist 2001, 245). Theodora devoted much of her energy to religion in the empire. She promoted her theological position by turning a palace in Constantinople into a monastery for five hundred monks and nuns of the non-Chalcedonian persuasion and by sending a missionary named Julian to the kingdom of Nubia (in present-day Sudan) and several non-Chalcedonian bishops as missionaries to the small Arab nation of Ghassanid. Jacob Baradeus, who had been a monk in Theodora's monastery, was ordained a bishop and traveled around Syria for some thirty-five years establishing what would become known as the Jacobite (or West Syrian) Orthodox Church, of which small communities exist today.

During the period of 300–600, Christianity grew dramatically both within the changing reality of the Roman Empire and beyond. It moved from being primarily a diaspora movement to becoming affiliated with empires and kingdoms in many situations. The enriching diversity was represented by Irish, Ethiopians, Nubians, Germanic peoples, and Indians. At the same time, Christianity struggled with the tension caused by theological differences, but there was a common faith and identity. The church moved beyond and built upon the "baby steps" of the first several centuries in further clarifying and developing the Christian tradition.

Threads of Christian Tradition

Scripture

As seen in Chapter 1 the early church was very concerned with determining the official canon of scriptures. The decisive moment for the New Testament (NT) came in the fourth century through the person of Athanasius, the outstanding pro-Nicene theologian and bishop of Alexandria. In his

Paschal Epistle (367) he listed twenty-seven books as the NT, which is the accepted canon today although the order has changed for the seven "catholic Letters"—James; 1 and 2 Peter; 1, 2, and 3 John; and Jude. Due to his prestige, the NT canon of Athanasius was immediately accepted in the Greek East. The promotion of his list by Jerome and later by Augustine paved the way for its adoption in the Latin West as well. At first, the Syriac-speaking churches did not include the minor catholic Letters and Revelation. However, the Jacobite (West Syrian) Church in the sixth century decided to include these books; the Persian (East Syrian) Church never accepted them. It is interesting that today "in the Greek Orthodox Churches Revelation is not normally read in public worship" (Rogerson et al., 246–47), though it is in their NT canon.

The question of the Old Testament (OT) canon among Christians was more complicated. In addition to the protocanonical books of the original Hebrew Bible, the Greek Septuagint (LXX) translation also contains what were called deuterocanonical books—Judith; Tobit; Wisdom of Solomon; Sirach; Baruch; 1 and 2 Maccabees; and additions in several other books. The monumental Latin translation of the OT and NT, the Vulgate, used the books found in the LXX (although often the translation was made from the original Hebrew and not the Greek), but there was a distinction between "canonical books" of the Hebrew Bible and "ecclesiastical books," which were less authoritative but useful as spiritual guides. Later, Augustine did not accept these categories but rather accepted all the books of the Vulgate of equal authority. Although there would be some doubts through the years about the status of the deuterocanonical books, the Vulgate became the OT canon for the Latin West. This would only receive official recognition at the Council of Trent in the sixteenth century in response to the Protestant Reformation, which did not accept the deuterocanonical books as canonical. The LXX, including the deuterocanonical books, represented the OT canon for the Greek East. The Syriac translation, the *Peshitta,* used the Hebrew Bible, but later Syriac texts basically followed the same canon as the LXX. However, the Persian (East Syrian) Church did not make this adaptation to the LXX.

The translation of the Vulgate has traditionally been attributed solely to Jerome, but it is acknowledged today that a number of women who were learned in Greek and Latin—Marcella, Paula, Melania the Younger, and Eustochium—"no doubt helped Jerome in his daunting task; and they certainly supported him with their wealth as well" (Bevans 2009, 230). In addition to Greek, Latin, and Syriac Bible translations, we noted in the first part of this chapter that all or parts of scripture were also translated into Coptic (Egyptian), Ge'ez (Ethiopian), Armenian, and Gothic. Some parts of scripture were also translated into Georgian (north of Armenia), where the Christian movement began in the fourth century (Norris 2002, 38, 48). These translations allowed the people to hear the word of God in their own language and contributed to a closer link between faith and culture, to a national Christian identity, and to the spread of Christianity.

In the previous chapter we noted the importance of the allegorical methodology of the Alexandrine school to interpret the Bible as symbolic language about the ultimate mystery of the Divine. Rather than looking for this spiritual meaning, another method was developed to uncover the literal meaning of scripture in the fourth and fifth centuries in Antioch, the other important theological center. One of the leading figures, Diodore of Tarsus, in his biblical commentaries "insisted on a grammatical analysis of the text in order to reach its historical meaning" (González 1994, 94). Two of the most famous proponents of this literal-historical approach were John Chrysostom (ca. 347–407) and Theodore of Mopsuestia (ca. 350–428). The work of the latter was developed in the school of Nisibis and became very important for the Persian Church. However, while the Arians used the literal sense of scriptures in their argumentation, the wider church moved more to the allegorical principle and the criterion of the "rule of faith." Ambrose of Milan (ca. 338–397) and Augustine of Hippo (354–430) developed the allegorical methodology in the Latin West. Although the great biblical scholar Jerome (ca. 347–419) initially followed the Alexandrine school, his interest in the literal sense grew later in life. The literal-historical approach will be influential for the eventual development of a more nuanced historical-critical approach. At the end of the sixth century, biblical scholar Gregory I (known as Gregory the Great, 540–604)—a rich aristocrat turned monk and eventual bishop of Rome—drew upon both literal and allegorical interpretations, but "the most profitable and accessible way to interpret Scripture was as a vast moral allegory" (ibid., 96). For him, the "study of the Bible is intended primarily to appeal to the heart and will of the reader, with the practical aim of promoting love of God and care for humanity" (Rogerson et al., 277).

The Bible was of course important for the other threads of Christian tradition. For example, the focus of the Alexandrine school on allegorical exegesis pointed to the explicit importance of scripture for the spiritual life. The majority of Christians who were illiterate became familiar with the Bible through liturgy and art. Scripture was divided for lectionary purposes for the Eucharist and was often the subject of the preaching by bishops and presbyters. Bible stories, images, and characters were frequently the subjects for Christian paintings in churches. During the time of persecution, the sacred manuscripts of scripture were sometimes destroyed, and any Christian who handed them over to the persecutors, as in North Africa, earned the title of traitor. After Constantine, special places for proclaiming the word, such as an ambo, and special cabinets for storing the scriptures when not in use, were installed in churches. The scriptural books themselves became works of art. The monasteries became the places for copying, preserving, and studying scripture. The monastic tradition of the spiritual reading (*lectio divina*) of scripture led to prayer and the edification of the soul. Scripture continued to be a main source for theology and mission, especially through the monks and nuns.

Liturgy, Sacraments, and Art

At the beginning of the chapter we noted the significance of Constantine's actions in initiating a shift that shaped the history of Christianity. This is very evident in its liturgy, sacraments, and art. Moving into the public sphere and growing in number in the Roman Empire contributed to Christianity's adaptation to some aspects of Greco-Roman society, to its move toward more standardized liturgical forms, and to the rise in infant baptisms. At the same time, liturgist Edward Foley raises the point that every liturgical change during this period "was not necessarily a result of Constantinian leadership. . . . Many developments in the fourth century had their roots in the third century and even earlier" (Foley, 80).

Keeping in mind this dynamic of both external and internal factors, we begin to paint the picture of liturgy during this period by looking at architecture. While a number of enlarged and renovated house churches continued to be used for liturgy, Christians (particularly in the western part of the Roman Empire) adapted the form of the Roman basilica to create a building for public worship. A basilica had a long, rectangular shape and an apse on one end and the main entrance at the other. An episcopal throne and a free-standing altar of wood or stone were situated in the apse, and the congregation usually stood in the nave. Eventually the laity would not be allowed in the sanctuary area. Partly due to the religious meaning of the sun for other religions in the Mediterranean area—such as the cult of Mithras, which was very important for Constantine—many church buildings were orientated toward the east and the rising sun. Sometimes other structures were built for baptisms or for remembering the martyrs; these were called baptisteries and *martyria*, respectively. They borrowed from the Roman style of round burial mausoleums. "The Christian belief in baptism as a participation in the death and resurrection of Christ contributed to the architectural resonance between martyria and baptistries" (Foley, 89). This points to continuity with the meaningful relationship between Christian life and martyrdom in the early church, particularly in the Roman Empire.

While the rectangular basilica design became prominent in the western part of the Roman Empire, the centralized, domed design was preferred in the eastern part. These two architectural forms reflect not only cultural and historical differences, but also theological and spiritual ones. For example, "Byzantine architecture and iconography contribute to a sense that in such spaces one experiences worship as a participation in the heavenly liturgy" (Foley, 90). It is noteworthy that both the Greek (*ekklesia*) and Latin (*ecclesia*) terms for the Christian community became more widely used by themselves to describe both the community and the place where they gathered. The fifth and sixth centuries are considered the Imperial Age or Golden Age, especially under Justinian, for the development of basic characteristics of the Byzantine rite, such as ritual splendor, chanting, and processions.

The tremendous growth in the number of Christians, the relationship between the emperor and the church, and theological controversies and developments were factors contributing to the formation of a more complex Eucharist and the need for more direction. "Thus, the era of improvisation gave way to one of approved texts" (Foley, 103). At first, liturgical bibles had markings in the margin to indicate the beginning and end of readings for the Eucharist, but by the end of the fifth century separate lectionaries began appearing. Around this same time, martyrologies and liturgical calendars provided a list of days for remembering and celebrating martyrs' deaths and Christian feasts. Liturgical prayers and prefaces also began to appear in pamphlet form. In terms of eucharistic theology, the Latin West placed emphasis on the words of institution from the Last Supper as the "moment of consecration," while the Greek East "will continue to honor the role of the Holy Spirit in the sanctification of the Eucharistic elements, both in its theologies and structures of its prayers" (ibid., 123). The Arian Eucharist was very similar to that of the Latin West, except for the doxology; the Arians prayed "to the Father, through the Son, in the Holy Spirit," rather than "to the Father, and the Son, and the Holy Spirit" (Irvin and Sunquist 2001, 180).

While Greek continued to be used in liturgy in some places in the Latin West, Latin was becoming the exclusive liturgical language in that part of the world. Greek continued as the liturgical language in most of the Greek East. Worship was also celebrated in Syriac, Armenian, Ge'ez, and Egyptian/Coptic among communities within and outside the Roman Empire.

At the beginning of this time period the Eucharist was closely linked with what it meant to be church. It was not considered a separate sacrament, but rather a culmination of the sacraments of initiation, including baptism and confirmation. A rich tradition of mystagogical catechesis on the "mysteries"—what today we would call the liturgy—occurred either after or before the rites of Christian initiation. This catechetical instruction often "followed the outline of the baptismal creed used by that particular church"

(Irvin and Sunquist 2001, 235). While the Nicene Creed was used by most churches, many in the Latin West continued to use a creed developed in second-century Rome that later became known as the Apostles' Creed.

In the fourth century adult baptism was the norm, and this would continue as Christianity spread into new areas. However, by the beginning of the seventh century infant baptism became more common as children began to grow into the faith. "As a consequence, the linkage between Eucharist and initiation will largely disappear, and rather than a sacrament of 'unity,' increased attention will be given to the role Eucharist plays in individual holiness and salvation" (Foley, 125). The form of baptism will shift from full immersion for adults to pouring water over the foreheads for infants and, by the end of this period, to sprinkling replacing immersion even for adults. The unity of confirmation with the sacraments of initiation begins to disappear as those who were baptized as children received confirmation later by traveling bishops, and a separate word for confirmation begins to be used in the fifth century in Gaul. Obviously, the extended catechumenate process—through which adults prepared for becoming members of the church—becomes less common over this three-hundred-year period.

Penance experienced a new development through Irish monasticism. As the monks and nuns went to their abbots and abbesses for spiritual guidance, local people were drawn to the monks and nuns for the same. With time, these private conversations became moments for the confession of sins and absolution. "The monk and nun counselors would then propose 'tariff penances'—particular prayers or sets of prayers to be said to 'atone' for the matters that were confessed" (Bevans 2009, 231). Similar to the specific "penance" allotted to breaking specific items of the monastic rule, the monks gradually developed handbooks called penitentials to assist "confessors" in assigning a particular penance for a particular offense in order to offer a standard guideline and avoid overly austere penances. Often absolution was given upon the completion of the penance. This practice spread with the Irish monks and beyond. What we now know as the sacrament of penance "moved away from its roots as a public, communal, and unrepeatable event to become private, individual, and repeatable" (Bellitto, 140). The role of confessor would be taken on by priests in the future.

Blessed oils were sometimes used during prayers for healing. In Spain and Gaul links are made between blessings with oil and the healing power of the Holy Spirit. The anointing of the sick often accompanied penance when a person was near death. Ordination rituals started to become more elaborate. In contrast, Christian marriage rituals were not developed much more, although in some places the blessing by the *episkopos* or *presbyteros* began to replace the blessing by the bride's father.

As for the artistic element of the Christian tradition, we already discussed the importance of architecture in relation to liturgy above, for both the Latin West and the Greek East. The iconography, which drew from the imperial and religious contexts in both of these regions, "began to depict Christ more as an emperor, philosopher, magician, or a competitor to the ancient gods than as Good Shepherd" (Foley, 92). One of the oldest (548) and influential architectural and iconographic examples of the Greek East is found in San Vitale in Ravenna, the Byzantine seat of power in northern Italy after 554. Mosaics also reflected Arian and non-Arian theologies, and sometimes were later "fixed" according to the changing theological "tide." In contrast to this rich artistic tradition the Persian churches had no images and "empty wooden crosses were the only adornments in most Syriac churches" (Irvin and Sunquist 2001, 199).

After the fourth century in the Latin West and Greek East distinctive Christian music began to develop through a process of both adaptation and innovation. It is interesting that Ephrem composed hymns in Syriac to be sung by women (Wilken, 148). Scriptural liturgical books, as noted above, and some other ritual books became works of art. Finally, there was also a shift from household utensils to liturgical vessels. "Gold and silver became the preferred materials, the hand of the artisans was more evident, and the sacredness of the vessel itself was emphasized" (Foley, 119).

Ministry and Organization

In the Roman Empire the end of persecution, the mass movement toward Christianity, and the link between church and state led to a more complex and institutionalized church organization. Bishops (*episkopoi*) exercised more leadership both within the church and in society. "There were assignments given them [bishops] by the emperor; episcopal courts given civic recognition; bishops often called upon to ensure domestic tranquility" (Bernier, 78). Furthermore, they considered preaching and teaching their primary responsibilities, and many of the great theologians at this time were bishops. At the beginning of the fourth century every local community continued to have one bishop-pastor, and the laity had a voice in choosing them. However, after the regulations of the councils of Nicaea and Chalcedon, fellow bishops and presbyters played the more prominent role in selecting bishops, which had already been happening earlier in some areas, such as the selection of the senior bishop of Carthage. This very strong sense of episcopal collegiality was also evident in the number of shared letters, regional and metropolitan synods, and more than seventy-five councils in the fourth century.

The senior bishop among the other bishops in a metropolitan area became more prominent, and significant patriarchates developed first in Alexandria, Antioch, Carthage, and Rome, and later in Caesarea, Constantinople, Milan, Armenia, and Seleucia-Ctesiphon. The bishop of Rome was the highest ecclesiastical authority in the Latin West, and by the end of the sixth century he sent a *pallium*, a white vestment worn over the shoulders, as a sign of Rome's authority to newly appointed bishops in the West. Gelasius I (492–496) did much to clarify that the bishops of Rome were independent of the surrounding political structures; Gregory I was the first to use the term *servus servorum Dei* (servant of the servants of God) for the papal ministry, and he was very concerned about the spiritual life and mission of the church.

Other patriarchs recognized the primacy of Rome as the church of Peter, but not in terms of supremacy. With the continual political decline of the western part of the Roman Empire, the bishop (and emperor) of Constantinople played a stronger ecclesiastical leadership role in the Mediterranean area. By 520, the bishop of Constantinople was called the ecumenical patriarch by some in the East, and despite some protest from the West, this title became quite common after 600. It is significant that the first eight general ecumenical councils (some called by an emperor) were all held in the Greek East. The term *pope* was first generally used as a title for the bishop of Alexandria in the third century, and the Coptic patriarch of Alexandria continues to bear the title of pope until today. The title of pope started to be used occasionally for the bishop of Rome in the late fourth century; however, the word for papacy only occurs in the eleventh century.

In regard to ministry, deacons (*diakonoi*) in the third and fourth centuries were more important than presbyters (*presbyteroi*) due to their involvement in daily church matters. The leader of deacons in Rome, the archdeacon, often became the bishop of Rome, even into the ninth century (see Bernier, 82). While male deacons worked alongside the bishops, deaconesses were responsible for women in the church and had taken over the responsibilities of the previous order of widows, particularly with assisting at baptisms and visiting the sick. Deaconesses were more plentiful in the Greek East than in the Latin West, but they would disappear in both areas in the sixth century. At this time the male diaconate also was beginning to be reduced to the final step to the presbyterate.

While the diaconate grew and then declined during the period of 300–600, the presbyterate developed in the opposite way. At the beginning, as we saw in Chapter 1, presbyters served in an advisory role to the bishop. However, with the growth in the size of the local Christian communities, the presbyters were given "a semi-autonomous sacramental and pastoral role conferred by the bishops in areas where people could not get to the cathedral church for Sunday Eucharist" (Bernier, 98). Both bishops and presbyters were more identified with their sacramental "priestly" roles, and presbyters were now called priests. This ministry was understood less as a functional role and more as a state of life, but both bishops and priests were ordained for serving a particular local community.

The value of celibacy began to emerge due to several factors. First, Gnosticism, Montanism, and pre-Platonic philosophy tended to consider the material world (including the human body) and sexual activity negatively. Second, most monasticism that was spreading quickly at this time promoted the Christian ideal of a "state of perfection" and abstinence from the things of this world. Third, the ministry of bishop and presbyter/priest was linked with the cultic purity of the Old Testament. The local Spanish Council of Elvira (ca. 300–310), which is famous for very strict disciplinary rulings, proposed that bishops and other ordained persons not marry, and if already married, not engage in conjugal relations, especially around the time when they are ministering at the altar. By the end of the fourth century the idea of a celibate clergy was growing in the Latin West, but it wouldn't become permanent church law until the twelfth century. The Greek East until today allows married clergy. The shift in the understanding of ordination and the initial consideration of celibacy in the West led to a larger distinction between those ordained and the laity.

The monastic movement was a very significant element of this thread of ministry and organization within Christian tradition. In Irish Christianity, which spread far beyond Ireland, the abbot or abbess generally had more authority than the bishop. However, under the more influential Benedictine monastic model on the European continent, the monks were under the authority of the local church, but they were very significant in rekindling the pastoral ministry focus of the local bishops and priests. A number of influential bishops like Martin of Tours, Patrick of Ireland, and Augustine had been monks themselves and/or promoted monasticism in the local church. Scholastica, Brigid, and Radegunde reflect the importance of women in ministry through the monastic movements. Irvin and Sunquist state that Radegunde of the Franks "continued to play an important role in bringing Christian values to bear upon the society" (2001, 238). In the Greek East and Syrian East, monastic communities also became a setting for various forms of witness and ministry. One must remember that most of the monks were not priests at this time, so the groupings according to ministry and identity could be understood as threefold: ordained, lay, and monastic.

Another area of ministry during this period was the development of what we call hospitals today. Early Christian communities, particularly in the Roman Empire, were known for their care of those in need. By the third century care of the poor was seen as the primary responsibility of the bishop. In the fourth century Christians started to construct buildings for the specific purpose of attending to the needs of the unfortunate. Later some monasteries provided healthcare. Basil of Caesarea as a bishop established institutions to provide medical care for the sick and lepers; these would later be called *basileias* after Basil in the Byzantine world. "These hospital-like complexes founded in the Christian East more closely resemble modern hospitals than anything in pagan antiquity or in the Latin West" (Wilken, 161).

In terms of the history of canon law, the earliest collections of canons included some of the rulings of general and regional councils and letters of the bishops of Rome and/or significant bishops of the Greek East. Such collections by Dionysius Exiguus, a monk in Rome in the fifth century, and by John Scholasticus, a priest and later patriarch of Constantinople in the sixth century, played a role in the development of canon law in the Latin West and Greek East, respectively. However, initial attempts to establish general rather than regional collections of canon law as "law" would come through the efforts of political leaders like the Byzantine emperor Justinian in the sixth century in the Greek East, and much later through the Carolingian rulers Pepin and Charlemagne in the ninth century in the Latin West.

Spiritual, Religious, and Social Movements

As a result of the changes initiated with Constantine, the spiritual and religious expressions and experiences became more public in the Roman Empire and overlap with the thread of liturgy treated earlier. In 321, Constantine made Sunday a holiday on which Christians could legally take off work to attend the public celebration of the Eucharist. Although celebrated on different days in the Latin West and Greek East (and later Ireland), Easter became the major feast. In the fourth century the celebration of Holy Week began in Jerusalem, and the forty days of Lent was instituted for the spiritual development of Christians, especially for the catechumens in their final days before receiving the sacraments of initiation at Easter. The Roman celebration of the Sun-God around the winter solstice on December 25 became the official celebration of Christmas under Constantine for the Latin West, while the Christians of the Greek East had probably already been celebrating the birth of Christ on January 6 to supplant the imperial celebration of the winter solstice. This feast of the Epiphany will later be distinguished as the celebration of the visit of the three wise men. It seems that the custom of midnight mass on Christmas began in Bethlehem and eventually came to Rome, while Advent started in Spain and Gaul in the fourth century and was later promoted by Gregory I as the time of preparation for Christmas for the broader church. These examples illustrate how liturgical and spiritual expressions and movements find their roots in different regions and streams of Christianity.

Even though the persecution of Christians ended in the Roman Empire, except for cases like the Donatists, the earlier veneration of martyrs grew as the commemorative liturgies became more elaborate with vigils, readings, and chants, and churches were built on their burial sites. Communities venerated the relics of martyrs and later of those considered saints due to their lives of virtue and/or asceticism. The wooden cross was also venerated, and as noted above, this was the only image found in East Syrian churches. Persecution and martyrdom during this time period shifted to the Persian Empire, including newly conquered Armenia, and affected spirituality and daily life. Marian devotion became stronger after the Council of Ephesus in 431 declared Mary the Mother of God (*Theotokos*) and not just the mother of the human Jesus.

The most significant spiritual, religious, and social movement during this three-hundred-year period was monasticism. Growing out of the earlier ascetical movements of thousands of individuals going to the mountains of Syria and the deserts of Egypt, a wide variety of communal monastic expressions emerged around the Christian world at this time. We already have noted the significance of Anthony, Athanasius, and Pachomius for the initial developments in Egypt, and the subsequent influence on the birth of other monastic movements through such founders as Basil of Caesarea and Melania the Younger in the Greek East; Martin of Tours, Benedict of Nursia, and Radegunde of Gaul in the Latin West; John Cassian for both the East and the West; and Patrick of Ireland outside the Roman Empire. Other monks following the rule of Pachomius brought the monastic tradition to Ethiopia. While tracing their roots to Egypt, each of these monastic traditions developed its own characteristics according to its own context, theology, and founding charism. The strict asceticism of Irish monasticism was shaped by the traditional mobile clan culture of Ireland, and the highest form of asceticism was "wandering for the sake of Christ." With his classical Roman education Benedict emphasized moderation, balance, and stability in one community. The central task of the Benedictine is prayer (*ora*)—regular common prayer, as well as personal prayer and reading (*lectio divina*)—and work (*labora*)—manual work is dignified activity that also leads to sanctification. The Irish and Benedictine monks and nuns lived a countercultural life, and they had a big influence on the life and faith of the local people.

In contrast to their Egyptian counterparts, the early Syrian ascetics stressed mobility and mission, which influenced the nature of East Syrian monasticism that extended across the Persian Empire to India by the fourth century. The East Syrian monastic movement included black-robed "religious" monks and white-robed "secular" monks, although this distinction appears to have been quite fluid. This East Syrian holistic understanding of salvation, body and soul, was evident in its most famous theological center in Nisibis, Persia. "Including the study of medicine and Greek logic and philosophy, its curriculum was centered around the study of the Bible within a strict monastic-like environment" (Bevans and Schroeder 2004, 103). This nondualistic perspective is evident in the writings of Ephrem the Syrian, the most significant theologian of Nisibis. He advocated for virginity and asceticism not because of a negative attitude to the material, as noted earlier with neo-Platonic and Western thought, but rather for the positive purpose of "marriage with the Bridegroom, the goal of wakefulness, and the ideals of Paradise" (Holt, 37). Ephrem and other East Syrian theologians understood the entire process of Christian life as divinization (*theosis*). The Syrian monk Pseudo-Dionysius, who is treated in the following section, contributed much toward the development of spiritual and mystical theology and practice in both the Greek East and Latin West. At the same time, *The Book of Steps*, written by an anonymous Syrian probably living in the Persian Empire, highlighted the spirituality of those working for the social concerns of the world, and this mitigates the impression "of early Syriac spirituality as being overly focused on severe forms of renunciation" (Wiseman, 92).

The development, growth, and impact of monasticism were phenomenal in terms of geographical spread, contextual diversity, and Christian commitment. Monasticism was mentioned above throughout the various sections of the historical background of this chapter. Irvin and Sunquist accurately capture part of this significance by stating: "Monasticism became one of the most important vehicles for cross-cultural spiritual fertilization among churches in the world" (2001, 213). However, its influence extends beyond spirituality. The virtues of these monastic communities included service to others and hospitality. The communities in Armenia served the poor and needy, those of Macrina cared for orphan girls, and Basil more and more saw the link between contemplation and service (see Wilken, 105). Monasticism helped to shape not only ministry and organization, but also the threads of scripture and liturgy, sacraments and art. It will also be treated in the final two threads.

Theological Developments

The earlier section "Arianism, Nicaea, and Chalcedon" outlined the main theological developments necessary for understanding the various historical contexts and the other threads of tradition. We shall now examine the theology of this period, as a thread in itself, in more depth.

The council held in Nicaea in 325 was probably the most significant event for the church and Christian theology in the period from 300 to 600 for the following reasons. First of all, while scripture continued to be the norm for theology, the teachings of Nicaea "represented a move *beyond* the scriptural formulations for an understanding of the identity of Jesus in terms of Hellenistic culture" (Bevans 2009, 219). Second, the council initiated a process of developing the Christian doctrines of Christology and Trinity over the next several hundred years. Third, the Council of Nicaea was the first of twenty-one ecumenical or general church councils, which today "together with the pope [are] the primary authority in the church" (ibid.).

Nicaea was responding to the teaching of Arius, educated in the school of Antioch, who out of concern for protecting the transcendence and oneness of God denied that Jesus Christ was God. The Alexandrine school, with its emphasis on the divinity of Jesus Christ, strongly opposed Arianism. In the words of the Alexandrine theologian Athanasius, "What has not been assumed has not been redeemed." This controversy extended beyond theologians and into the marketplace, where, according to Gregory of Nyssa, merchants and others vehemently discussed whether Jesus Christ was subordinate to God the Father or not, since this issue affected their spirituality and faith (Bevans 2009, 220). In an attempt to foster unity Constantine presided over this first general council, promulgated the decrees, and is credited with proposing the use of the term *homoousios* (same substance) to describe the relationship of the Son to the Father. The council accepted this formulation and incorporated it into the Nicene Creed in professing that Jesus Christ was "begotten, not made, consubstantial with the Father." The use of *homoousios*, a Greek philosophical term, in a Christian creed was a radical move.

However, the Christological controversy did not end with the Council of Nicaea. While denying the divinity of Jesus Christ, Arianism did maintain Jesus's humanity, which was in danger of being denied after Nicaea. Many bishops of the Greek East and Constantine himself later took more moderate positions regarding Arianism for theological and/or political reasons. The Second Ecumenical Council held in Constantinople in 381 refined and affirmed the Nicene Creed, and the Fourth Ecumenical Council in Chalcedon in 451 endorsed the formulation of the two-natures-and-one-person Christology. However, the challenge for balancing the two elements—human and divine natures—of an orthodox doctrine of Christology would only be resolved at the Seventh Ecumenical Council, Nicaea II, in 787. In retrospect, the first Council of Nicaea "represents the great moment of clarification for the doctrine of the Trinity, and it is the beginning of the refinement of the church's doctrine about Jesus" (Bevans 2009, 221).

At the same time, as noted in the section "Arianism, Nicaea, and Chalcedon" and throughout the historical overview above, other Christological formulations—Monophysite (one nature) and Dyophysite (two natures)—were developed and are still held by Christian communities, such as the Coptic and Assyrian churches today. We realize now that these differences were perhaps based more on culture, linguistics, and to some degree politics than on theology. "Adding to the theological complexity of these fifth-century controversies in the East was the fact that much of what was being argued was in translation" (Irvin and Sunquist 2001, 200). The Syriac terms for *nature* and *person* did not have an identical meaning with the Greek ones. In the post–Vatican II age of ecumenism and reconciliation, Mar Dinkha IV of the Assyrian Church (Nestorian Church) and Pope John Paul II signed the *Common Christological Declaration* in recognition of their unity in a common Christology in 1994.

Having reviewed the major theological issues of this time period, we now survey its major theologians. Beginning with the Greek East, we have already spoken of Athanasius of Alexandria in terms of his influential *Life of Antony* and his role as champion of Nicaea's "one substance" doctrine. He paid a high price for the latter. With the shifting support for or opposition to the Nicene formula by emperors, he was exiled at least five times for a total period of sixteen years during his forty-five years of service as bishop. Four other theologians of the Greek East and supporters of Nicaea, who lived in Cappadocia (present-day eastern Turkey), were Basil of Caesarea, Gregory Nanzianzen, Gregory of Nyssa, and Macrina. The first three were bishops who were very influential in the Council of Constantinople and beyond in laying the foundations for orthodox trinitarian theology, including the full divinity of the Holy Spirit. Macrina, the sister of Basil and Gregory of Nyssa, was well versed in philosophy and theology and involved in the theological discussions with the other three. Basil also wrote a very important monastic rule, and Macrina was leader of a women's ascetic community.

An anonymous Syrian monk of the late fifth and early sixth centuries, under the pseudonym of Dionysius the Areopagite (known today as Pseudo-Dionysius), developed "the first systematic articulation of Christian mystical doctrine" (Irvin and Sunquist 2001, 248), which had a major influence in both the Greek East and Latin West. He insisted that God can only be known through who God is not (for example, God is not unjust), that is, through the negative way (*via negativa*). Second, he developed the three stages of the spiritual journey toward Christian perfection and full union with God—purgative, illuminative, and unitive. Also, his celestial hierarchy laid the foundation for the future theology of angels.

Upon his return from the first Council of Nicaea, James (or Jacob) established a theological school in Nisibis and appointed as its first director the deacon Ephrem (309–373), who would become the preeminent East Syriac theologian of this period. He was more interested in symbols and mysteries than in doctrine, and most of his theology is written in poetry and hymns rather than in prose. Ephrem wrote about the full divinity of Jesus, the importance of human divinization (*theosis*), and the Eucharist as life-giving medicine. He had a strong Mariology and used female images for the Holy Spirit. Ephrem is the only officially named doctor of the church from the non-Byzantine East, or "perhaps we could say he is the only fully (West) Asian doctor" (Bevans 2009, 223). Another important East Syrian theologian was Aphrahat (also known as Aphraates, ca. 270–345), nicknamed the Persian Sage. He was a monk, and possibly a bishop, in a monastery near the city of Mosul on the Tigris River in present-day Iraq. Aphrahat had a strong trinitarian theology and shared much of the teachings of Nicaea. He depicted the Holy Spirit "as a Mother brooding over her creation and a female dove descending upon Jesus at this baptism" (Irvin and Sunquist 2001, 197). Finally, Jacob of Serugh, an excellent representative of later Syriac theologians, used symbolic rather than philosophical terms and poetry as his form, including hundreds of verse homilies (*memre*).

In the Latin West, Hilary of Poitiers was the first bishop in the West to acknowledge the danger of Arianism, and he responded to it as a theologian. He is the only doctor of the church who was married. Ambrose, born in Trier in present-day Germany, was a catechumen and governor of Milan when he was chosen as that city's bishop. "He was a pioneer in using hymnody in liturgical celebrations, and his work *On Duties* is perhaps the first comprehensive survey of Christian ethics" (Bevans 2009, 226). However, he is most widely known for his support of Monica, and his role in their conversion of her son, Augustine.

After receiving a classical education in Carthage and leading a rather dissolute life, Augustine initially joined the Manichean religion (founded in third-century Persia) but later went through a conversion experience in 386, was baptized, and became a monk. He soon became the bishop of Hippo, and more important, probably the greatest theologian of the Latin West until Thomas Aquinas. The best way to highlight his major contribution from the huge quantity of theological writing is to focus on his response to two major controversies of his time and context. The first was Donatism, which was described in the section "North Africa and Donatists" above. Theologically, the Donatists within their strict moral framework held that Christians should not be involved with the world, that the church and state should be completely separated, that the holiness of the church was identified with the holiness of its members, and that baptisms and other sacraments performed by a person not in unity with the church were invalid. In response, Augustine held that the church is not a refuge from the world but rather exists for the sake of the world and that Christians should be involved in building a more Christian society. He also maintained that the holiness of church is not identical with the holiness of members, and therefore the validity of sacraments is not dependent on the moral standing of the minister of the sacrament, or what would be developed in sacramental theology as *ex opere operato* (literally, "from the work done"). Augustine's theology of the holiness of the church is the beginning of the "ecclesiasticization" of salvation, that is, the act of baptism becomes more important than the internal appropriation of the faith.

The second controversy that engaged Augustine's response was Pelagianism. Pelagius, an ascetic and exegete from Britain, had traveled in the East, where he acquired a positive attitude toward human nature. Later in Rome he was shocked by the moral corruption in the church there, and he preached a moral reform based on human willpower. Pelagius's teaching emphasized (but not exclusively) justification by works, illumination by the Spirit, and inspiration more than redemption. Augustine, with his negative view of human nature and his insistence on divine grace, held that human depravity demanded radical conversion and encounter with God's grace, that is, justification by faith. In this context he developed the idea of original sin and its debilitating effect upon human free will. This theology reinforced the practice of infant baptism. Augustine's negative attitude toward human nature and culture was very much influenced by the unbelievable event of the sack of Rome by the Goths in 410.

Before closing this section, it is necessary to note another contribution made by monasticism in the Latin West. The Irish monks copied manuscripts of church documents and the writings of pre-Christian authors, thereby preserving the patristic literature and the classical literature of the Western empire that was collapsing. In a similar way the Benedictines preserved the classical manuscripts of Western society, and they collected "scriptural and 'patristic' passages around particular theological themes in works called *catenae* (from the Latin for 'chains') and *florilegia* ('bouquets' of quotations)" (Bevans 2009, 232).

Mission, Cultures, and Religions

In the early church, as seen in Chapter 1, the main model of mission was the informal witness and "gossiping the gospel" of ordinary Christians. While monasticism was becoming the primary model of mission during this period of 300–600, the pattern of ordinary Christians witnessing to their faith certainly continued in the Persian Empire and across Asia, where Christianity was restricted and sometimes persecuted. "Wherever they went, whether merchants or artisans, clergy or laity, they carried the gospel with them. Supporting themselves by the labour of their own hands, or filling in appointments as secretaries, physicians and stewards in the households of the nobles and princes of those lands to which they went, they were one and all missionaries of the Cross" (Stewart, 17). Historian Samuel Moffett noted that "there were times when Christian physicians became even more of a Christian influence on Persian culture than the theologians" (1987, 481). The importance of medicine within this holistic approach of mission was also reflected in the curriculum of their theological school in Nisibis and the writings of Ephrem the Syrian. The East Syriac monks also provided health care within their holistic understanding and practice of mission that included religious and secular roles. We have an account of seven East Syrians—two laypersons, a bishop, and four priests—who carried out mission work among the Huns by preaching, baptizing, and developing a written script for their language. The two laymen remained for thirty years among the Huns (ibid., 484). Through these various models of mission, the East Syrian Church engaged other cultures across central Asia and into southern India.

In terms of other religions, the relationship of Christianity to Judaism in Persia appears to have been complex and intense for several reasons. Jewish Christianity continued for a longer time in the Persian Empire than in the Roman one, and East Syrian Christianity was culturally close with Judaism, particularly in Mesopotamia (present-day Iran and Iraq). Ephrem's *Hymns on a Pascal Feast* is unfortunately very anti-Jewish. Christianity and Judaism were so close that this conflict was, as described by Bevans, "the result of an inter-family squabble, which is often the most bitter kind" (2009, 223). At the same time, East Syrian theologian Aphrahat dialogued with rabbis, and his "theological writings suggest a great deal of Jewish influence, both in the methods of his arguments and the content of his thought" (Irvin and Sunquist 2001, 197). His major work, *Demonstrations*, does not have an anti-Jewish tone. Aphrahat was probably a convert from Zoroastrianism, for whom the world is caught in warfare between good and evil. "In this context, Aphrahat described Christianity as the power against such evil and Christ as the light that withstands the fire, drawing upon central Zoroastrian symbols" (Bevans and Schroeder 2004, 133). The mission theology of this East Syrian minority community often "was expressed in terms of struggle, fight, battle and war" (Philip 1997, 11).

Within the Roman Empire, Christianity was growing numerically and engaging new Germanic peoples. The Frankish king Clovis on behalf of his people raised the following two objections and questions to Bishop Remigius. If we abandon our gods (Wotan, Thor) for Jesus, who belongs to another race, will they not abandon us? And, if Jesus allowed himself to be crucified, how could he possess divine power? The first question reflects the Germanic traditional worldview that culture and religion are inseparable and that religion brings blessing only to one's own people. Conversion to Christianity required a belief, not in a tribal God, but in a God of all tribes. The second question comes from a worldview in which God is far above the human situation and there are intermediaries between God and humanity. For this reason the Arian belief in Jesus Christ as a creature of God fit very well into the traditional worldview. As described above in the "Latin West" section, most Germanic peoples received and/or chose the Arian teaching, but Clovis and his people were baptized within the Catholic (non-Arian) understanding. Many peoples became Christian through such mass baptisms and the growing practice of infant baptism. The agents of mission included mission-minded bishops like Martin of Tours, Patrick of Ireland, Ulfilas of the Goths, and Remigius of Reims; Christian political leaders like Justinian and Theodora of the East Roman Empire; theologians and teachers like Athanasius of Alexandria, Ephrem the Syrian, and Augustine of Hippo; and individuals like Frumentius (captive servant) and Julian (priest).

However, the primary mission agents who deepened the faith of those who were only superficially or culturally Christian were the men and women of the monastic movement. As noted in the section "Spiritual, Religious, and Social Movements," there was great diversity and richness in the various forms monasticism took in different local and regional contexts. We focus on the two monastic movements that were particularly influential in terms of mission in the Latin West.

Irish monasticism was effective in deepening the faith commitment of local people, in part through the practice of spiritual counsel and the eventual development of practice of private confession. Furthermore, its highest form of asceticism as *peregrinatio pro Cristo* (wandering for the sake of Christ) provided the motivation for going out in groups of twelve as new monastic communities; Columba founded a community on the Scottish island of Iona, and Columban founded monasteries in Luxeuil (present-day eastern France) and later in Bobbio (Italy).

The Benedictines also were agents of deepening the faith through their close interaction with the local people. Like the Irish, they were concerned with true Christian conversion, but the Benedictines were more concerned with church organization, and they were dependent on kings and political leaders. While the Irish and Benedictine monks and nuns were motivated primarily for their own spiritual perfection, and not explicitly for mission itself, they implicitly through a process of witnessing and osmosis were the primary agents of mission in extending and deepening the Christian faith during this time.

One example of explicit mission was initiated by Gregory the Great, the Benedictine monk who became the bishop of Rome. He sent forty monks under the leadership of Augustine of Canterbury (as he would become known) from the church in Rome in mission to England. Gregory sent a letter through Abbot Melitus instructing the monks to follow an approach of adaptation and persuasion with the Germanic peoples. The letter, which was recorded in 731 by Bede the Venerable (*Ecclesiastical History* 1.30), reads in part:

> The temples of the idols among that people should on no account be destroyed. The idols are to be destroyed, but the temples themselves are to be aspersed with holy water, altars set up in them and relics deposited there. For if these temples are well-built, they must be purified from the worship of demons and dedicated to the service of the true God. In this way, we hope that the people, seeing that their temples are not destroyed, may abandon their error and, flocking more readily to their accustomed resorts, may come to know and adore the true God. And since they have a custom of sacrificing oxen to demons, let some other solemnity be substituted in its place.... For it is certainly impossible to eradicate all errors from obstinate minds at one stroke, and whoever wishes to climb a mountain top climbs gradually step by step, not in one leap.

This instruction set the tone for an accommodational approach to the cultural-religious world, similar to what has been called inculturation in recent years. Those elements considered idols are to be removed, but the traditional sacred places and rituals are to be transformed into Christian places and rituals. And this can be considered a pastoral "step by step" process.

Conclusion

During this period from 300 to 600, the church shifted from being the early church to becoming what Irvin and Sunquist call the "imperial church"; from being a minority and restricted diaspora to becoming a majority and favored religion within the Roman Empire; and from being in opposition with the state to becoming an integral part of the western and eastern parts of the Roman Empire. Christianity was shaped by and shaped these two political, social, economic, and religious contexts. "Constantine's embrace of Christianity in the fourth century was the first step toward a great synthesis of religion, state, and culture in the Roman world" (Irvin and Sunquist 2001, 155). However, Christianity did not develop as an "imperial church" outside the Roman Empire. Rather, it found itself in various forms of acceptance and compliance within different contexts—ranging from the strong national-cultural-religious identity in Armenia to the restricted and persecuted situation in the Persian Empire.

On the one hand, the church was becoming more institutional and standardized, particularly in external forms, but on the other hand, it became more institutionally divided during this three-hundred-year period, particularly around theological issues. Donatists and Arians were exiled in the name of the church. However, much-longer-lasting divisions occurred due to issues of Christology. In distinction to the Chalcedonian definition of the two natures and one person of Jesus Christ, national churches that identified orthodox belief with the one-nature formula of the Alexandrine school included the Egyptian (Coptic), Ethiopian, Nubian, Armenian, and Jacobite (West Syrian) churches. At the same time, those who followed the two-nature teaching of the Antiochene School found themselves exiled further east into the Persian Empire, where the East Syrian or Persian Church would develop its own identity across Asia. Meanwhile, the Latin West and Greek East would agree on the Chalcedon teaching, which was a compromise between the schools of Alexandria and Antioch, but they would grow apart on other issues, particularly the tension caused by Constantinople replacing Rome as the imperial capital. This latter point reminds us that the developments of the different streams of Christianity were not determined by theology only; rather, these different streams within their theology were shaped by different political, economic, sociocultural, and linguistic contexts.

Within this diversity the survey of the threads of Christian tradition point first of all to the fact that each of the different streams of Christianity is attending to the six threads. Second, there are some basic patterns emerging, such as the canon of the Bible, forms of ministry, and the Eucharist. Third, monasticism is a fine example of how an expression of the thread of spirituality developed in a rich diversity as it crossed into other contexts and affected the other threads in those contexts, particularly mission, cultures, and religions. New challenges would await Christianity in the seventh century.

The eyewitness account from this period comes from Egeria, who was probably a nun from Spain. Her diary accounts of several years of pilgrimage at the end of the fourth century through Sinai, Egypt, Palestine, and Mesopotamia (including Edessa) provide wonderful descriptions of architecture, monastic living, and liturgy, including the following excerpt describing the earliest celebration of Holy Week in Jerusalem.

> When seven weeks have passed, there remains one paschal week that they call here Great Week; then the bishop comes in the morning into

the major church at the Martyrium. A chair is placed for the bishop at the back of the apse behind the altar, and there they come one by one, males with their "fathers" and females with their "mothers," and all repeat the Creed back to the bishop. (Ch. 46; McGowan and Bradshaw, 191)

In her diary we get a glimpse of a common Christian faith and tradition across the diversity of the churches of the Latin West, Greek East, East Syrian, and Coptic Egypt.

3

New Challenges and New Beginnings

ca. 600 to ca. 1000

At the end of the sixth century much of Christianity around the Mediterranean had reached a certain stage of standardization and a close relationship with the state, although differences and tensions between the Latin West and Greek East were beginning to show. On the other hand, Christian diversity had become more institutionalized and distinctive in such areas as Egypt, Nubia, Ethiopia, West Syria, Armenia, Persia, and India. The most significant external challenge at the beginning of the seventh century was the birth of a new Abrahamic religion, Islam. Within a relatively short time Muslim military and political forces overthrew the Persian Empire, spread across North Africa into Spain, and seriously threatened the East Roman Empire. At the same time, new opportunities also emerged as the East Syrian Christians brought their faith across the Silk Road to Central Asia and the heart of China. Back in the West, Charlemagne in 800 reestablished the Holy Roman Empire, which would expand to include the Saxons and Scandinavians. Despite the advances of Islam, the Greek East remained strong in the faith and spread it among the Bulgars, Slavs, and Russians. Monasticism continued to be the primary means of mission all across the Christian world at this time. Following Irvin and Sunquist, we refer to this four-hundred-year period as "new challenges and new beginnings" (2001, 257–381).

Historical Context

Muhammad and the Birth of Islam

From any historical perspective "the Prophet Muhammad stands among the most important persons who have ever lived" (Irvin and Sunquist 2001,

260). He came from Arabia, between the Roman and Persian empires. Organized into tribes, most of the people were herders or Bedouins, but the Arab merchants also played a big role in trade among people between Ethiopia and Armenia. Linguistically and culturally the Arabs were close to the Jews. Some Arabic people were Christians, and there was occasional violence between the Christians and Jews. Muhammad was born in 570 in the city of Mecca, with its popular temple and place of pilgrimage called Ka'bah, which housed 360 images of Arabic and non-Arabic deities, including icons of Jesus and Mary. "From the pages of the Qu'ran it is clear that Muhammad had firsthand knowledge of Christianity, although we have no indication in Arabic, Syriac, or Greek sources of there being an organized church with bishops and clergy in Mecca or Medina" (ibid., 264).

In 610 Muhammad began receiving spiritual visions, through which he was to recite the exact words he heard (*Qur'an* means "to recite"). The heart of the message was that people were to turn away from idolatry and to worship and submit to the one God of Abraham, Allah (*Islam* means "to submit"). Many in Mecca opposed his words because his message threatened the significant income associated with Ka'bah. About eighty followers of the Prophet fled across the Red Sea to Ethiopia, where they received asylum and hospitality because of their common monotheistic beliefs. With the growing persecution in Mecca, Muhammad accepted the invitation of the city of Yathrib (later called Medina) and fled by night in 622, marking the first year in the Islamic calendar and called the *Hijrah* (migration). The Prophet organized the rapidly growing believers of this new religion in and around Medina militarily and politically to fight polytheism and idolatry. Jews, Christians, and Zoroastrians, as monotheists, were not forced to become Muslim, but Jews and Christians had limited legal status as *dhimmi* (protected people). The basic Muslim foundations of Muslim practice, called the five pillars, were developed in Medina. At first Muslims prayed in the direction of Jerusalem, but in the second year they prayed in the direction of Mecca. Muhammad began to receive revelations related more to social and community life. After several years of battles and treaties between Mecca and Medina, Mecca was captured in 630, the religious images were removed from Ka'bah, and soon most of Arabia was united under the Prophet. He died two years later.

Since Muhammad died with no male descendent, he was succeeded by a *caliph* (deputy or successor). Within the next twenty years one official copy of the Qur'an was authorized, and until today it cannot be properly translated into a language besides Arabic, because it is considered the direct revelation of the word of God. By this time Jews and Christians no longer were "protected" people, and by 650 they had to leave the Arabian Peninsula. The Muslim state *dar al Islam* (house of Islam) would grow quickly into a large empire stretching from Spain to Central Asia, so that as many as half of the Christians in the world would be living under Muslim rule within a hundred years after the Prophet's death (see Map 3).

Persia, Armenia, and Islam

As noted in Chapter 2, the East Syrian Church had developed its own distinct and separate identity—with a Dyophysite Christology, its own patriarch, and the Syriac liturgy, and within its particular political, social, and religious context. At the same time, East Syrian Christians "shared much more with other Christians than has often been acknowledged, such as their ecclesiastical structures, their confession of the Nicene faith, and their understanding of the role of Jesus Christ in the salvation of the world" (Irvin and Sunquist 2001, 307).

At the beginning of the seventh century Christians in Persia were still living under a legally restricted status in the segregated *melet* neighborhoods, and they didn't have a patriarch in Selucia-Ctesiphon for over twenty years (605–628) because the government wouldn't approve the church's choices. At this time the armies of the East Roman and Persian empires were fighting again. At first the Persian forces pushed forward, capturing Edessa, Antioch, and Jerusalem. The Persian army continued through Asia Minor, and by 617 it was near Constantinople. However, the East Romans launched a successful counterattack, and they were in original Persian territory within five years.

It is very interesting that at that point the Persian court turned to the newly approved patriarch, Yeshuyab II, to negotiate a peace between the Persian and East Roman empires and between Byzantine and East Syrian Christians. The patriarch was successful in both cases. (We will return several times to Yeshuyab II, because he was one of two outstanding East Syrian patriarchs during this two-hundred-year period.) Major changes were on the horizon in the political scene. A Muslim army defeated a Persian one in 636 and completed the defeat of the Persian Empire six years later. At first, the Persian Christians were actually in a better situation under Muslim rule than they had been in the Persian Empire, because now they were freed from the domination of Zoroastrianism and official persecution. This will change with time.

Similar to the *melet* system of the Persians, Christians were designated as *dhimmi* under Muslim rule. No matter what theological and other differences they had among themselves, all Christians in a particular region were grouped as one minority group under one leader or patriarch; their common belief in the Trinity put them all in error from the perspective of the strict monotheistic teaching of Islam. However, in contrast to those considered

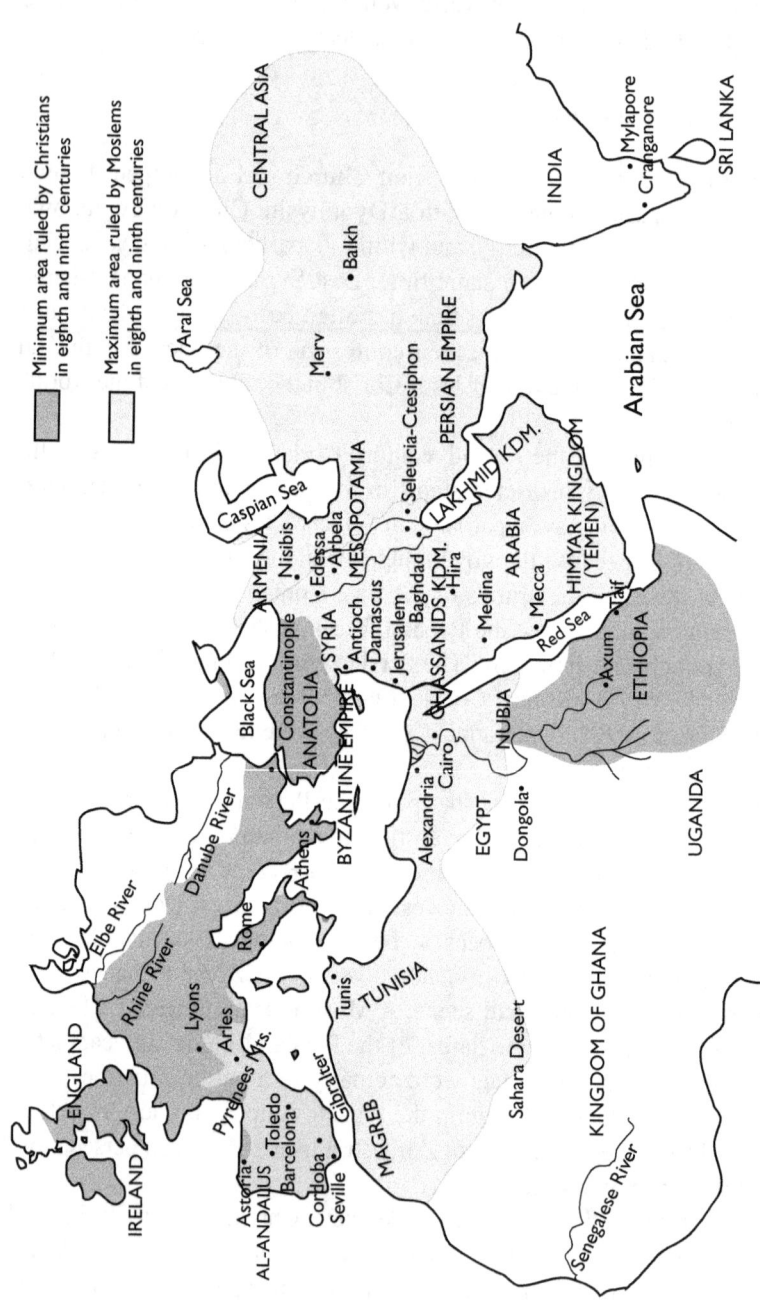

Map 3: Arabic-Islamic Empire and the Christian World, about the Year 900

idolaters, Christians were allowed to practice their religion. While there were certainly exceptions, in general Christians were encouraged but not forced to become Muslims. In fact, over time many Christians did choose the Islamic faith.

Christians were forbidden to share their faith with Muslims, and any Muslim who became Christian could be punished with death. Christians and other non-Muslims could suffer this same fate it they disrespected either the Prophet or the Qur'an. Christians were allowed to use their own places of worship, although they couldn't build new ones. However, some churches were converted into mosques. Christians were not allowed to ring church bells or to display crosses in public. They were able to use wine for the Eucharist, although alcohol was forbidden for Muslims. "Christians and other minority peoples were not permitted to serve in the military, carry weapons, or ride horses. Only mules and donkeys were allowed them for their transportation needs. Christians and Jews were also required to wear special identifying articles of clothing, although it appears this rule was unevenly enforced" (Irvin and Sunquist 2001, 274–75). Christian men could not marry Muslim women, but Muslim men could marry Christian women with the general understanding that the children were to be raised as Muslims. All adult Christian males (priests and monks exempted) had to pay a high head tax. "At times this tax was enough of an incentive itself to lead Christians to convert" (ibid., 275). It is important to note that this general description of Christian life under Muslim rule eventually applied to roughly 50 percent of all Christians.

At first, the Persians were under the caliphate of the Umayyad Dynasty, with its capital in Damascus (western Syria). The Arab Muslims initially lived outside the cities in military camps, but by the end of the seventh century the number of Muslims grew and they moved into the cities. Arabic became the official language at the beginning of the eighth century. A few years later the Abbasids Caliphate gained power; it shifted the capital to Baghdad in 762. Life became more difficult for Christians, but they survived and actually increased in number at times. The East Syrian Christians were accustomed to facing hostility and even persecution. They served important roles for the government and society as translators and educators. Christian schools were the major educational institutions in Persia, where they translated and taught classical Greek texts for almost two centuries under Muslim rule. The "first truly Arab academy" was established in Baghdad in 830 to prepare Muslims in philosophy and science (Irvin and Sunquist 2001, 277). Christians assisted in developing the curriculum of this school, which had as one of its major goals translating the Greek classics into Arabic. As noted in Chapter 2, Christian schools continued to excel in medical teaching due to their access to Greek medical knowledge. Caliphs often retained Christian physicians. Alongside Jews and Manicheans, Christian merchants were very significant in this new Islamic world, especially for trade with China and India. Last but not least, the East Syrian monasteries continued to grow and became very important for the church as they "provided many of the resources for the pastoral, medical, and educational needs of the Christian communities" (ibid., 276).

In the eighth century the East Syrian patriarchs also moved to the political capital of Baghdad, and they were now appointed directly by the Muslim ruler. Many of these patriarchs were associated with bribery and corruption. An outstanding exception, together with Yeshuyab II of the previous century, was Timothy I. As a person of integrity and administrative competency, he was responsible for extending and/or strengthening the East Syrian Church in Tibet, India, and Yemen, and among the Turks. Back in Baghdad, Timothy I in 781 had a two-day conversation on interreligious issues with the caliph Al Mahdi. (This is treated in detail below in the thread "Mission, Cultures, and Religions.") After 850, the Abbasids began to lose power and stability, and this change was mirrored in the church, with corruption and abuse appearing more frequently among patriarchs, bishops, and monks. Official and local persecutions of Christians occurred at this time, including the destruction of some churches, monasteries, and cemeteries.

We now turn our attention briefly to Armenia, the nation caught between empires. At the end of the sixth century its denizens were politically under Persian rule, religiously free to live their Christian faith, organizationally united under their own patriarch (*catholicos*) in Etchmiadzin, and theologically grounded in a Monophysite Christology. When Arab Muslim armies entered Armenia in the seventh century, they encountered strong resistance and a mountainous terrain difficult for their horsemen. Armenia remained a buffer kingdom; it paid tribute to the caliph but remained free of direct Muslim rule and was able to build new churches. Politically, Armenia extended its rule into Georgia and the Caucasian region in the ninth century, but its fortunes changed in the following century. "Until a Muslim army finally sacked their capital early in the tenth century, forcing the catholicos into exile, the Armenian churches experienced few of the disruptions encountered in other areas where Arab rule dominated" (Irvin and Sunquist 2001, 281). The Byzantine armies gained control of Armenia for some time later in the century.

India, Central Asia, and China

Even though the East Syrian Christians were under various degrees of restriction and persecution "back home" under Persian and then Muslim rule, they continued to reach out across Asia. Patriarch Yeshuyab II is credited with probable responsibility for establishing India as a metropolitanate, and with clear responsibility for initiating the first official mission to China. This latter action led to extensive mission among the Turks and other peoples in Central Asia. With Yeshuyab II as the reference point, Samuel Moffett wrote that the East Syrian Church became "for much of the next seven hundred years in truth as well as in name the Church of the East, the church of Asia" (1998, 257).

India had been under the metropolitanate of Rewardashir in southern Persia, but after the latter broke its relationship with the patriarch, India was designated as a metropolitanate itself within the Persian Church in the seventh century. In the eighth century Timothy I reminded the metropolitanate to send the name of the proposed new metropolitan to him for approval before submitting it to the local king. Other correspondence from the patriarch contains information regarding a monk accompanying a group of immigrants to India and Timothy's permission for intermarriage between Persian and Indian Christians. Two Armenian brothers who came to India in the ninth century as missionaries were given land by Indian authorities to build several churches. Through Christian merchants and others from India, Christianity had reached Sri Lanka, and possibly Java, the Malay Peninsula, and the coast of China.

Samarkand was the capital of the province of Sogdiana on the far northeastern border of the Persian Empire (see Map 1, in Chapter 1). Following the Silk Road eastward beyond Samarkand was the vast multireligious and multicultural area of Central Asia. Christians encountered Zoroastrians, Manicheans, Buddhists (from India), traditional religions (including shamanism), and later, Muslims. Early Christian presence was through merchants and monasteries in or near cities and towns along the Silk Road. The monasteries provided lodging, religious services, and medical care for travelers and local people. Christian burial inscriptions in cemeteries "indicate permanent Christian communities along the Silk Road from Persia to western China" (Irvin and Sunquist 2001, 312). There were two signs that Christianity was spreading into the rural areas already in the sixth century: (1) a request to the East Syrian patriarch for a bishop from a king among the Huns; and (2) crosses tattooed on the foreheads of Turkish prisoners, who learned this practice from their Christian neighbors. In the eighth century Samarkand received metropolitan status, and some religious literature was translated from Syriac into the local Sogdian language. Around this time Patriarch Timothy I sent a bishop and some monks to a Turkish people who had become Christian, and he consecrated a bishop for the Tibetans. The extensive correspondence of the mission-minded Timothy describes his "interest in assisting the growing number of churches, monasteries, and episcopal sees across what are now the nations of Uzbekistan, Kazakhstan, and Tajikistan" (ibid., 313). A letter from the bishop of Merv (in present-day Turkmenistan) to the patriarch around the year 1000 states that the king of the Kerait Turks and some two hundred thousand members of his tribe in northern Mongolia were ready for baptism. In this case Christian merchants had played a role in giving Christian instructions and bringing them a copy of the gospel (ibid., 314).

In terms of China, there is evidence of intentional missionary presence in the sixth century in the person of Mar Sergis in Lint'ao along the Silk Road, about three hundred miles west of the Chinese capital of Chang'an (Norris 2002, 40). The T'ang Dynasty, considered one of the greatest in China's long history, came to power at the beginning of the seventh century after some years of political instability. With it came favorable conditions for international trade and exchange. The capital, Chang'an (present day Xi'an), near the eastern end of the Silk Road, was the largest city in the world at that time with an estimated population of two million, and the imperial library was one of the largest with some 200,000 volumes (see Map 4).

As many as one hundred thousand non-Chinese merchants came through the port city of Kuang-chou (Canton) every year at the height of the T'ang Dynasty (Irvin and Sunquist 2001, 315). Mechanical woodblock printing on paper started in China before the eighth century. Alongside the traditional ideology of Confucianism and a strong Taoist religion, the Chinese were open to the foreign religions of Buddhism, Manichaeism, and Zoroastrianism. While there may well have been Persian and Armenian Christian merchants in China earlier, Patriarch Yeshuyab II initiated the first intentional mission to China, as noted above, These East Syrian monks, led by Alopen, arrived in Chang'an in 635. As Buddhists had already translated many of their religious writings into Chinese, the Christians were asked by the emperor to translate some Christian texts.

After reading these Christian Chinese sutras, a term and style used by Buddhists, Emperor T'ai-tsung granted Christians an edict of toleration in 638 to spread the gospel freely. He also ordered the construction of a monastery, with his portrait copied on its wall. Such a ruling was probably also associated with the economic hope that support of Christians would bring more Christian merchants (Wilken, 242). This imperial proclamation along with the history of the first 150 years of Christianity in China was recorded in the year 781 on a large black stone stele—three meters high and one meter wide—and erected in public at what may have been (Morris, 254–255) the second Chinese Christian monastery in the area of Lou Guan Tai, about forty-three miles from Chang'an. This stele would later be buried and hidden for hundreds of years, only to be recovered in the seventeenth century. The original stele now stands in a museum in Xi'an and a duplicate at its original spot in Lou Guan Tai. Some of these first Chinese Christian sutras were discovered near the cities of Dunhuang (Tunhuang) and Turfan in western China at the beginning of the twentieth century in caves where they had been hidden and protected with thousands of Buddhist manuscripts for almost a thousand years. These valuable Christian sutras, which reflect the interreligious encounter of Christianity with Buddhism and Taoism, and to a lesser degree with Confucianism, are treated below under the thread entitled "Mission, Cultures, and Religions."

Christianity continued to experience favor under the rule of T'ai-tsung's son, and perhaps as many as a dozen more monasteries were built. A 2006 discovery of another inscription points to the presence of a Christian community in Luoyang, the eastern capital of the T'ang Dynasty (Tang and Winkler, 143). With the change of rulers came a strong pro-Buddhism movement accompanied by anti-Christian persecution (683–712), but this was followed by a time of restoration and full support of Christianity (712–781). During this latter period, others came from Persia to further the growth of the church in China, including Bishop Chi-Lieh, who was also part of an official embassy from the Muslim Arabs on two occasions. The East Syrian Christians served as diplomats and interpreters. The stele monument describes I-ssu, a married Persian priest-monk, serving as a military commander and lieutenant governor for China. He was also described as a "white-robed" monk-scholar and a person of financial means who supported the monasteries and gave donations to the poor in Chang'an. In terms of scholarship and translation, Central Asian bishop and missionary Ching-ching (Adam in Syriac) was identified as the author of the text on the monument and the translator of some thirty works into Chinese, including scripture, which were later found in the caves of Dunhuang.

In the mid-ninth century, when Christians were facing serious internal and external problems in Persia, as noted above, the church in China was likewise facing persecution again. A Chinese imperial decree issued in 845 drastically reduced the number of monasteries and deported foreign religionists. It also forced 250,000 Buddhist monks and nuns and 3,000 Christian monks, nuns, and priests back into secular life. If this latter number refers to Chinese nationals, one gets an indication of the possible growth of Christianity among the Chinese themselves. The first period of Christianity in China received its final blow with the fall of the T'ang Dynasty in 907.

Despite the challenges and persecutions during this period from 600 to 1000, it was a moment of Christian growth across Asia. Around the high point, in 800, it is estimated that there were approximately ten million Christians from Antioch to China, and the majority were East Syrian Christians (Norris 2006, 133).

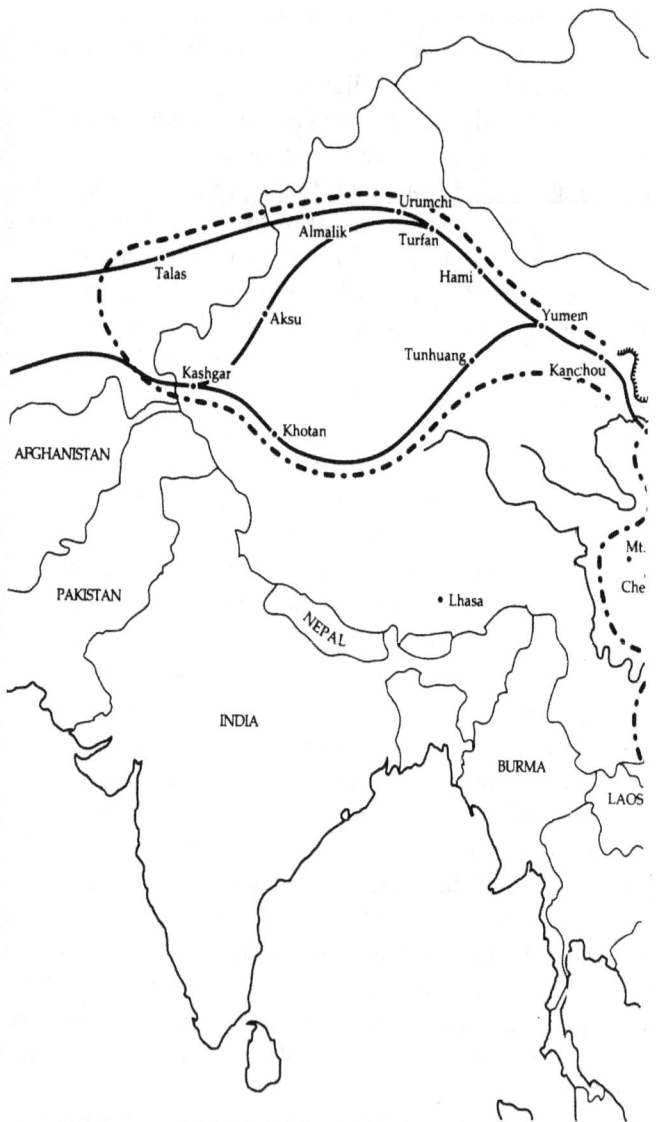

Map 4: East Asia and T'ang Dynasty China at approximately the Year 800

East Roman Empire

Justinian, a key figure in Chapter 2, marked the end of an era. He was "the last to rule over a unified Roman imperial world" and "the last to speak Latin as his governing language in the East" (Irvin and Sunquist 2001, 355). In 620, Greek became the official language of politics and of the streets. The bishop of Constantinople was being called the ecumenical patriarch. The East Roman or Byzantine Empire was becoming more clearly a separate entity. As noted above, it was involved in a major war with the Persian Empire in the first part of the seventh century, but soon both empires were much more concerned with the fast advance of Arab Muslims. The East Roman Empire lost Damascus and all of Syria in 634; Jerusalem and Palestine in 636; Alexandria and Egypt in 642; and North Africa, Sicily, and parts of Asia Minor over time. The Muslim Umayyad Dynasty made Damascus its capital in 661, and its forces reached Constantinople in 669. A new period in the history of the Byzantine Empire began when Emperor Leo, with the timely assistance of a Bulgar army, and later his son, were able to push back the Islamic forces and add "internal strength by a profound military, economic, and administrative reform of the state" (Schmemann, 199). However, by the ninth century the East Roman Empire was reduced to Greece, part of Asia Minor, the southern end of Italy, and some islands in the Mediterranean; Constantinople, however, remained the center of the church of the Greek East and a major Christian center for others.

At first, living under Muslim rule in Syria and Palestine did not change daily Christian life very much, because the Muslims were more attentive to their internal issues. With time, however, Christians found themselves moving into a more restricted *dhimmi*-like environment, as described above for Persia. The bishops of the Jacobite (West Syrian) Church, with their Monophysite Christology, lost much of their power, although their monasteries, like those of the East Syrians, played an influential role in passing on Greek classics to the Arab world. The Jacobites grew quickly in what had been the Persian Empire during these first years under Muslim rule. A smaller group, called Maronites, had been founded around the fifth-century monastery of Maron in northern Syria. They held what was then considered a non-Chalcedonian Christology, developed a Syriac liturgy, and were under their own patriarch by the end of the seventh century. Due to the Arab invasion the Maronites moved to the mountains of Lebanon, where they developed a very close and lasting association with Lebanese culture and history. The third major Christian group in Palestine and Syria comprised those with the Chalcedonian Christology and aligned with the patriarch of Constantinople. A number of them fled to the Byzantine Empire and further west. While there was generally stability for those who remained, occasionally Muslims who accepted the Christian faith and Christians accused of disrespecting Muhammad were put to death and added to the list of Christian martyrs.

The Greek East faced internal tension caused by the iconoclast controversy, which emerged in the eighth century. Those who became known as iconoclasts (icon breakers) held that the longstanding use of icons for spiritual purposes was actually a form of idolatry. On the other side, iconodules (icon devotees) maintained that icons were not the objects of worship in themselves. While the iconoclasts were influenced by the surrounding Muslim prohibition of images, much of the motivation was linked to a growing cult and center of power around the emperor. The primary targets of iconoclast action and persecution by the emperors and their armies were the monks and nuns, who didn't pay taxes and raise children to serve the empire, and "engaged in criticism of imperial excesses" (Irvin and Sunquist 2001, 361). Empress Irene, who was an iconodule herself, called the Seventh Ecumenical Council in 787 in Nicaea, which affirmed the orthodoxy of the veneration, not worship, of icons. The controversy continued after Irene's death but was finally resolved in 843. Further references to the iconoclast controversy and the primary theological response by John of Damascus are treated in several of the threads of tradition in the second half of this chapter.

After reaching a political stalemate with the Arab expansion, the East Roman Empire turned more attention to the Slavs and Bulgars, who were migrating, invading, and resettling in their northern territory. The Slavs had already been entering the empire during the time of Justinian, and many became Christians more through a process of osmosis in a Christian land than through explicit mission outreach. In the early ninth century the Slavs formed an independent kingdom called Moravia (present-day Slovakia). South and west of Moravia was Bulgaria—the independent kingdom of the Bulgars, a Turkish people—which had been growing in the eighth and ninth centuries and included many Greek Christians within its boundaries. In response to a request from King Rastislav of Moravia for Christian teachers, the emperor of Constantinople sent two brothers, Cyril and Methodius, as missionaries in the name of the Byzantine state and church. These efforts would eventually take root among the Bulgars, whose king (Boris) and family had been baptized by a bishop from Constantinople.

The third new kingdom that had a significant impact on the East Roman Empire during this period was that of the Russians. Following a similar pattern as above, the Christianization of Russia involved the inseparable link between political and religious identity for both parties. The baptism of the Russian king Vladimir in 988 and his marriage to Anna, the sister of the Byzantine emperor, were followed by the baptism of Russian royal family and many members of the army. Churches were built and bishops appointed. Constantinople sent artisans, teachers, monks, and nuns to Russia. A Russian national Christianity developed by drawing upon its Byzantine roots, a Syriac liturgy, and its own cultural and religious riches.

Africa, Iberian Peninsula, and Islam

Using the birth and spread of Islam as the starting point for this chapter, we have looked at the situation of Christianity east and north of the Arabian Peninsula. We now turn our attention westward across the continent of Africa. At the beginning of the seventh century Alexandria was still one of the largest and wealthiest cities in the world. Still, Alexandria and Egypt in general felt economically drained, theologically misunderstood, and ecclesiastically harassed by Constantinople. Therefore, many initially considered the Arab conquest in 642 a liberation. However, similar to Syria and Persia, the situation of Christians in Egypt became more restricted to the point that there were riots and resistance against Muslim rule in the eighth century. Christians also suffered financially. "The number of reports of destitute Christians unable to pay their taxes suggests a situation that was different from that of either Persia or Syria" (Irvin and Sunquist 2001, 292). At the same time, new monasteries for men and for women were still being built in rural and desert areas, and "many of the distinctive traits of Coptic Christianity took on the shape they still have today" (ibid.).

The Christians of Nubia (within present-day Sudan) had received the Monophysite Christology initially through Theodora of Constantinople, and they looked to the patriarch of Alexandria for leadership. Politically, in the seventh century Nubia had become an independent kingdom stretching from Aswan to Meroë (see Map 1, in Chapter 1). Nubians were the first to defeat the Arabs in battle. Later, Nubia made a treaty whereby the Arab Muslims would not attack it as long as Nubia delivered three hundred slaves to the Arab Muslims on an annual basis. During the seventh through tenth centuries Christianity flourished in Nubia. Although not as great in number as in Egypt to the north or Ethiopia to the south, archaeology has uncovered evidence for many monasteries as well in Nubia.

Ethiopia, or the Kingdom of Axum, was not attacked by Arab Muslim forces primarily because it had offered safety and hospitality to the group of early followers of Muhammad in flight from Mecca. The leader of the Ethiopian church continued to be appointed by the patriarch of Alexandria, although this became more difficult at times with Egypt under Muslim rule. The monastic movement generally remained strong.

Having followed the Nile River, we move to what had been Roman North Africa, or what the Muslims called the Maghrib (Arabic for "the place of sunset"). After several defeats the Arab forces won the final battle in 702 and established a capital in Tunis (present-day Tunisia), near Carthage. Many of the Berbers (barbarians or Germanic Vandals) became Muslim, and many Latin Christians fled north of the Mediterranean. By the tenth century only a few Christian communities remained in the Maghrib. The Arab-Maghrib coalition established trade across the Sahara to the Kingdom of Ghana, some of whose people eventually became Muslim. "This means that West Africa first encountered the story of Jesus . . . in its Islamic form, along with Islam's criticism of the Christian religion" (Irvin and Sunquist 2001, 298–99).

The next step in the Muslim advance was the Iberian Peninsula. Before their arrival, an Arian Visigoth minority had ruled over an indigenous Catholic majority. However, in 587 the Visigoth king was baptized Catholic and a strong national Spanish church identity developed, with the bishop of Seville and later the bishop of Toledo having primacy. Two years later, at the Third Council of Toledo, the Spanish bishops and theologians added *filioque* ("and the Son") to the creed—that is, that the Holy Spirit proceeds from the Father and the Son—in order to strengthen the equality of the Father and the Son and combat any trace of Arianism. Over a hundred years later, in 711, the Muslims defeated the Visigoths quite easily. Since the Muslim Empire was becoming so expansive, an independent kingdom was established in 755 in the Iberian Peninsula, except for the areas that will eventually become the kingdoms of Castille and Aragon, which remained under Christian rule. Following the pattern in other areas, the situation for Christians became more difficult with time. A strong intellectual center developed in Spain, particularly in Córdoba, where Muslims, Jews, and Christians studied and worked together.

Latin West

The Frankish military leader Charles Martel halted the Muslim advance from Spain at the battle of Tours in 732, and the Latin West was not so affected by Islam as other parts of the Christian world. At this time the church was already under the influence of the Frankish kingdom. Although episcopal appointments had to be confirmed by other bishops, Frankish nobility selected bishops from their own aristocratic class, who in turn owned large tracts of land and supported the secular authority. The Frankish Merovingian Dynasty came to an end in 751, when the palace mayor Pippin the Short deposed the king, defeated the Lombard kingdom in northern Italy, and put several major cities, including Ravenna, under the pope's authority.

"The alliance between Rome and the Franks had assumed a new dimension" (Irvin and Sunquist 2001, 334). This culminated when Pope Leo II placed a crown on Charlemagne's head and declared him the Roman emperor on Christmas Day of the year 800. Charlemagne was surprised by this presumption on the part of the pope to be able to name an emperor, rather than the army, and fourteen years later Charlemagne didn't involve the church when his son was made co-emperor. Some claim that Charlemagne put the crown on his own head in 800 (Norris 2002, 74). However, notwithstanding the ambiguity of the situation (cf. Irvin and Sunquist 2001, 336–37), the alliance between church and state became closer and the Carolingian Empire or Dynasty was born. The East Roman Empire considered this elevation an insult to its position, adding to the tension between the Latin West and Greek East.

Charlemagne led a number of fierce military campaigns against the Saxons, who lived on the northeast border of the Frankish land. Extreme measures to subdue the Saxons included the choice between baptism and execution. One of the few voices of critique was that of the theologian and imperial adviser Alcuin. Under Charlemagne, Latin became the official language to be taught in schools and to be used in all church matters. He also ruled that *filioque* be added to the Latin text of the Nicene Creed out of similar concerns as those raised in Spain years earlier. While the pope considered it orthodox, this addition would not be used in the creed in Rome until the eleventh century, after it had become more widely accepted throughout the West. The *filioque* clause was considered heretical by the Byzantine Church, since it seemed to compromise the person of the Father and divide the Holy Spirit between two sources.

Throughout this period of forced baptism, bishops chosen by and from nobility, and church-state alliances, the monastic movement continued to be "not only the major missionizing factor but in many cases the major civilizing force among western European people" (Irvin and Sunquist 2001, 342). The Irish and Benedictine monks and nuns, introduced in Chapter 2, met in England—the former coming from the north and engaging the Welsh and Britons of their own traditional Celtic background, and the latter from the south led by Augustine of Canterbury and successors practicing the accommodation promoted earlier by Gregory the Great among the Germanic Anglo-Saxons. The newly formed Anglo-Saxon monasticism and church, after a debate at a synod in Whitby in Northumbria in 663/664, chose to be more connected institutionally with Rome and the pope, characteristic of the Benedictines. In the eighth and ninth centuries the Anglo-Saxon monks and nuns, such as Boniface and Lioba (Leoba), became important agents of mission on the continent, alongside Frankish monks and nuns. While Latin was the common church language, the vernacular languages were preserved and the church accommodated itself in some ways to the local cultures.

As the Carolingian Dynasty ended at the beginning of the tenth century, the social-economic-political feudal system was well established. A new line of kings with Saxon roots took power in the eastern part of the empire (roughly present-day Germany), including Otto I, who appointed bishops and made them part of the feudal system. By the end of the tenth century Christianity through mass movements had been accepted in Bohemia, Poland, Hungary, and Scandinavia, and priests, monks, and nuns would follow to deepen the faith.

During the period of 600–1000, Christianity faced new challenges and new beginnings. The challenges included the rapid spread of Muslim religion and political rule; changing church-state relations, whether in China, Armenia, or Europe; forced and mass conversions to Christianity; and theological controversies over monothelitism, iconoclasm, and the *filioque* clause. New beginnings included the first period of Christianity in China; the foundations of inculturated Slavic, Russian, and Anglo-Saxon faith; and interreligious conversations, such as the one between Timothy I and the caliph Al Mahdi and another among the scholars of the Abrahamic religions in Córdoba. We now trace the challenges and beginnings through the six threads of tradition.

Threads of Christian Tradition

Scripture

Determining the canons of the Old and New Testaments was no longer a major concern during this period of 600–1000, even though the East Syrian Church continued to accept a narrower version, as noted in Chapter 2. Timothy I reported receiving a Syriac translation of Origen's *Hexapla* (Cochrane, 80). As Christianity spread across Asia, Christian literature, including some scripture, was translated from Syriac into Chinese, Garshuni (Arabic with Syriac script), and Sogdian in present-day Uzbekistan and Tajikistan (Irvin and Sunquist 2001, 277, 322). The latter is very significant since the Sogdian language served as the lingua franca along the Silk Road for both Arabic-speaking and Chinese-speaking people at this time.

Portions of the Christian scriptures were translated into Arabic in Judea and Sinai (Wilken, 312–13) and in Syria and Persia; and the entire Bible was translated into Arabic in Spain by the ninth century (Irvin and Sunquist 2001, 279, 303). Furthermore, Psalms and four Gospels were translated into the Slavic language, building upon the work of Cyril and Methodius (ibid., 368), and the Northumbrian theologian Alcuin (ca. 735–804) revised the Latin text of the Vulgate. It is very interesting that the main source for the *Heliand*—a sung version of the gospel for the Saxon people of Central Europe—was Tatian's *Diatessaron*. This harmonized gospel of the second century, treated in Chapter 1, was used but then set aside after a couple centuries by Syriac-speaking Christians in western Asia, only to resurface years later in Europe (Norris 2002, 99).

Gregory the Great, whom we covered in the previous chapter, "laid the foundation for the mediaeval exegesis" (Rogerson et al., 277). This form of the allegorical and mystical method of the Alexandrian school would be used within monasticism for several hundred years. Furthermore, reading the Bible through the monastic lens meant that the Bible "was usually interpreted as a call to monastic renunciation and contemplation" and read "in the context of prayer and worship" (González 1994, 96). Biblical study could be directed to the spiritual challenges of this time, since it wasn't necessary to use the scripture to respond to the challenges of theological issues and heterodoxy that had characterized much of the previous five hundred years of Christianity.

The famous biblical commentator Bede the Venerable (673–735) wrote many biblical commentaries and treatises for his fellow monks. While the rule of faith was the guide for Bede and his contemporaries, the interpretation and application of the scriptures was determined by older commentaries to the point that "the words of predecessors are incorporated in the work of later writers, sometimes without acknowledgement" (Rogerson et al., 279). The extensive commentaries of the ninth-century monk and archbishop Rabanus Maurus (d. 856) followed this pattern of quoting older sources, but he also included some material from the Antioch school of literal exegesis.

Highlighting the monks Gregory, Bede, and Maurus points to the primary role of the monasteries during this early part of the Middle Ages in maintaining the study of scripture and in developing the use of scripture in spirituality, prayer, and liturgy in the monasteries. Notwithstanding this creativity, the main contribution of the monasteries was that of preservation. They were responsible for copying the scriptural manuscripts and preserving in their commentaries the interpretation of past scholars. In the section "Theological Developments" in Chapter 2 it was noted that many interpretations of scripture and theological writings of the patristic period were preserved in collections called *catenae* (chains) and *florilegia* (bouquets).

"It is estimated that over half of the [biblical] commentaries of the Fathers have been preserved though *catenae,* including passages from [those considered] heretical writers otherwise doomed to possible oblivion" (Sloane, 258). The catenae of the Greek East, which were produced from the end of the fifth century until the eleventh century, are particularly valuable because the scripture and commentaries are preserved in the original Greek. Several significant Syriac *catenae* were written in the seventh and ninth centuries. The beginning of the scriptural *catenae* of the Latin West is associated with Bede, and "by the end of the ninth century virtually every book of the Bible has its commentary pieced together from the Fathers" (ibid.). While one needs to study these collections with a critical eye for accuracy and interpretation, the *catenae* and *florilegia* preserved some materials of the Christian tradition that would have been otherwise lost. Another genre, called a gloss, began in the ninth century as notes from earlier Christian scholars were added either between the lines or in the margins of a biblical text. There was also a renewed interest in learning Hebrew. The new production or development of these various types of collections and commentaries in the Latin West would decline in the tenth century but begin to surface again in the eleventh and twelfth centuries. This may have been due to "the closure of monastic schools as monks concentrated on liturgy and worship, and their libraries were used only by a few scholarly Abbots" (Rogerson et al., 65).

Liturgy, Sacraments, and Art

In Chapter 2 liturgical developments in the Latin West and Greek East reflected the interaction between the church and the society of the Roman Empire around the Mediterranean. In this chapter the liturgy in the Latin West focuses on the interaction of the church with the Germanic peoples farther to the north. Their history of Christianity in the fourth to sixth centuries was characterized by an initial communal and rather superficial acceptance of the Christian faith, a political and theological interplay between Arian and non-Arian (Catholic) beliefs, and the beginning of a deeper understanding and practice of Christianity primarily through the influence of the rural monastic communities. During the seventh to tenth centuries the future of the church in the Latin West was linked with the political and religious developments of the Frankish kingdom, which hoped that a unified liturgy would contribute to political unity. Toward this purpose Pepin and Charlemagne tried to impose the Roman liturgy on the Frankish Church, which had been using diverse "Gallican" styles of worship.

However, instead of an imposition of the Roman liturgy, a new hybrid of worship emerged by "mixing the sobriety of the Roman style with the dramatic elements" (Foley, 137). Even Charlemagne commissioned Alcuin to gather and add local Frankish customs. In terms of music, Roman chant was adopted by Frankish musicians, but Celtic and German songs also became Christian hymns. Due to the Germanic magico-religious worldview that tended to assign sacredness to objects, the Eucharist started to be "treated like a tool for achieving spiritual ends . . . more a noun than a verb, more a thing to be reverenced that an action in which one was to be engaged" (ibid., 179). A theological debate regarding the real presence of Christ in the Eucharist surfaced in the ninth century (see ibid., 172–76), but it will become a dominant issue in the next time period. Under Charlemagne, Latin did become the official language of theology, liturgy, sacraments, and church administration, while preaching was done in the vernacular. This new Franco-Roman or Germanized liturgy was adopted eventually throughout Europe and became the predominant liturgy of the Latin Church during the Late Middle Ages. However, an older Mozarabic rite and an Ambrosian rite still continued to be used in Toledo, Spain, and Milan, Italy, respectively, even until today.

New church architecture in the Latin West reflected the growing separation between the laity and clergy, the common practice of infant baptism, and the introduction of private masses (Eucharists) and secondary altars. This last development was due to several factors. First of all, rather than Eucharist only on Sunday (or Saturday and Sunday), daily mass was common in the West by the seventh century, probably due to the practice in monastic communities. Second, while praying for the dead was part of ancient Christian practice, the emphasis of Augustinian theology on the salvation of souls influenced the importance given to celebrating the Eucharist for the dead. Third, the practice of mass stipends developed whereby a monetary gift was given to celebrate a mass for a particular intention, often in exchange for the "tariff" or penance given during private confession. More masses needed to be celebrated to respond to these requests. Fourth, an earlier arrangement of the priest and the people both facing east, the direction of the rising sun and a symbol of the resurrection, in basilicas where the apse faced east, started to become more common in the eighth century in all basilicas and churches (see Foley, 142). Thus, "by 1000, altars placed at the wall and priests standing with their backs to the congregation were the norms" (Bellitto, 117). Also appearing at this time were full missals that were practical for private masses. They included material from lectionaries, sacramentaries, and rubrical instructions.

While the Latin West was moving in the direction of unity though uniformity, the Greek East continued to promote unity in diversity. The most striking example during this period was the development of the Slavic liturgy through the initial efforts of Cyril and Methodius, described above. Pope Hadrian II had invited the two Greek brothers to celebrate the Slavic liturgy in Rome, but the opposition of the Frankish bishops would eventually suppress these inculturated efforts among the Slavs; still, the Slavic liturgy would flourish among the Bulgars and was used during the early years of Christianity in Russia. In contrast to the Latin West, the Greek East used leavened bread and prohibited the eating of milk products during Lent. Under Charlemagne, the Creed was added after the Gospel, as it had been in the Greek East already in the sixth century.

As Arabic became the common daily language of Christians living in Islamic lands, Coptic continued to be the liturgical language in Egypt, as Syriac was throughout Mesopotamia and Persia. For the latter, the most common rite was the Liturgy of Saint James, "which tradition credits with first being celebrated by the brother of Christ himself" (Irvin and Sunquist 2001, 284). The Maronites and Jacobites used Syriac in liturgy. Nubia, which was not under Islamic rule during this period, in its liturgies used both Greek, due to early connections with Constantinople, and Coptic, due to their ecclesial link with Alexandria and the significant number of clergy who emigrated or fled to Nubia from Muslim rule in Egypt (ibid., 294). As we move further east across Asia and outside Muslim rule, the Christian communities of India also continued to use Syriac in their liturgies due to their ancient ecclesial association with the East Syrian Church, while they also adapted to their local context. For example, "in their eucharist they utilized rice cakes and palm wine, indigenous elements available where bread from wheat and wine from grapes were not" (ibid., 310). Syriac was the initial liturgical language in China, but Chinese was beginning to be used in worship by the end of the eighth century (ibid., 320). Along with the Eucharist, the East Syrian Church also practiced baptism and priesthood ordination.

As for the other sacraments within the Latin West, infant baptism became the most common in areas where Christianity was the religion of the majority, while adult baptism was still relevant among people for whom the Christian faith was new. Confirmation, like the Eucharist earlier, was seen more and more as a distinct sacrament and less as a part of the sacraments of initiation. As for penance, the individual confessional practice introduced by the Irish was highly valued, but it was experiencing some abuse; for example, the practice of substitution, whereby a wealthy landowner hired others to carry out his penance. Around the eighth century "bishops and councils began to recommend confession for grave sins before the reception of communion, and some diocesan canons even made confession obligatory for everyone one to three times a year regardless the seriousness of their sins" (Martos, 339). The anointing of the sick became more associated with the anointing of the dying.

During the time of Charlemagne polygyny was forbidden and "marriage was made monogamous for the first time among the Germanic people" (Irvin and Sunquist 2001, 338), although the practice of concubinage continued for both men and women. While marriage had earlier been considered only a civil matter, marriages in Frankish territories were considered legally valid only with a clergy's blessing. This, however, wouldn't become common in Rome and other parts of Europe for some time. Furthermore, while remarriage after divorce was strictly forbidden under Charlemagne and later councils in France and Germany, remarriage was allowed under certain circumstances around 1000 throughout the Latin West. Ordination ceremonies became more elaborate. Since, as mentioned above, objects were considered more sacred, the rite of the anointing of the hands was added to priesthood ordination, because priests would be touching consecrated altars, vessels, and the Eucharist (Foley, 178). "Minor orders" were developing as stages leading to priesthood, and permanent deacons were less common.

In terms of art we already discussed architecture in the Latin West. Liturgy, architecture, and art were interrelated and very significant features of the Greek East. For example, the decision of Prince Vladimir of Kiev in 988 to choose Byzantine Christianity among other options was greatly influenced by the overwhelming experience of worship by members of his delegation in the beautiful church of Hagia Sophia in Constantinople (see Norris 2002, 92–93). The biggest event regarding Christian art during this period revolved around the iconoclast controversy, described in the first part of this chapter, regarding the devotional use of icons and images. This controversy, which lasted over one hundred years and led to persecutions, was associated with political and social factors, but it also raised theological and pastoral issues regarding art and images. While the church of the Latin West also had to deal with some minor iconoclastic movements, in general it "regarded both iconoclasm and iconodulism as extremes to be avoided" (Irvin and Sunquist 2001, 363). In terms of East Syrian Christians, they "typically did not allow images in their churches" (ibid., 307), but Sogdian Christian art has been uncovered from around the eighth century (see Wilken, 240–41), when Christianity was quite well established in this part of central Asia under the metropolitanate of Samarkand.

Ministry and Organization

As noted in Chapter 2, monasticism continued to have a major impact on church organization and ministry. Rural parishes were springing up and growing rapidly in the Latin West due to the influence of monks and nuns already in the sixth century, and "the great monasteries and monastic families must have appeared as the true image of what the church should be" (Bernier, 103). Abbots sometimes had more authority, influence, and resources than bishops. The important contribution by women to the ministry and mission of the church was made primarily by those in the monastic communities. They are represented by women like Hilda, who was the foundress and abbess of the double monastery of Whitby and the site of the decisive seventh-century synod in Northumbria, and Lioba (Leoba), who worked collaboratively with Boniface among the Frankish people in the following century.

As more priests were needed to minister in the rural areas that were distant from the urban bishops, the lives of these local clergy were modeled after the life of a monk. They were eventually required to pray the divine office (breviary), and they began to use monastic dress. Under Frankish rule priests and bishops were often married but were expected to avoid sexual relations and possibly to live in different residences after ordination. Most other churches didn't expect this abstinence. However, most agreed that bishops, priests, and deacons would not marry if they were unmarried at ordination and would not remarry upon the death of their wife.

Feudalism was the second major influence on ministry and church organization in the Latin West. Some landowners built churches or chapels on their land, and they assumed the right to control the community and to choose the local priest, who was often uneducated and not approved by the bishop. Charlemagne, in an attempt to protect the rights of the bishop (and ultimately the pope) and to appease the influential landowners, developed a tithing system to provide financial support for the priest and local Christian community and the bishop. This system basically fell apart in the ninth century, which led to corruption and civil interference on the local level. Similar dynamics were at work on the episcopal level. Bishops were often selected from the aristocracy by the Frankish nobility, and the confirmation of these appointments by other bishops normally followed. The nobility supported the churches and some monasteries with land grants and endowments, and some bishops were landowners themselves. The church unfortunately became more associated with wealth and political influence. "The hierarchy of the church itself was fully integrated into the land-based economy of the Frankish realm" (Irvin and Sunquist 2001, 333).

On a broader level, the bishops of larger cities in the Latin West became known as archbishops, and they had some authority and jurisdiction over neighboring bishops, called suffragan bishops. These archbishops often presided over local and regional councils and synods, settled disagreements between bishops and abbots, and made decisions on appeals in cases regarding both civil and canon law (see Bellitto, 8–9). Regarding the latter, Carolingian rulers Pepin and Charlemagne tried to promote a more uniform set of canon law but with limited long-term success at this time.

The pope became the sovereign ruler of the papal states in 744, and the crowning of Charlemagne in 800 established a strong link with the Holy Roman Empire. On the negative side, this papal alliance added to the tension between the Latin West and the Greek East, and the papacy would struggle to maintain its independence and spiritual authority. "Some of the papacy's darkest days occurred in the centuries from about 850 to 1050" (Bellitto, 62). On the one hand, the Franco-Roman Church attempted to address abuses, establish more order, and safeguard the church. On the other hand, the organization and ministry of the Latin West took on the hierarchical shape from feudalism, and with that came new challenges; for example, the gap between laity and clergy grew wider. However, the influence of the laity will emerge again in the next time period.

While the Latin West had a more institutional understanding of the church, the Greek East continued to have a more spiritual one. There was a close identification between the Byzantine Church and the state, as seen with the rule of Justinian and Theodora and the choice of the monk Methodius for the diplomatic-missionary outreach to Moravia. However, the church experienced little civil interference and control. Monasteries were not dependent on the state or nobility. Bishops until today are chosen from the monks, not from the aristocracy. The bishop of Constantinople, recognized outside of the Latin West as the ecumenical patriarch, maintained the practice of episcopal collegiality, which was declining in the Latin West under the pope's growing power and authority.

As noted above, as many as half of the Christians in the world were living under Muslim rule by the middle of the eighth century. The basic pattern of church organization and Christian life within this context was described above in the section "Persia, Armenia, and Islam." Monasteries continued to be important centers for Christian organization, ministry, and stability in many of these areas. The East Syrian Church shared similar ecclesiastical structures with the wider Christian world (Irvin and Sunquist 2001, 307). Patriarchs Yeshuyab II and Timothy I played a major role in church-state relations and in organizing the church in the face of challenging political situations and intra-church divisions. Timothy I "was a tireless organizer, writing letters, making appointments, and overseeing affairs of churches spread thousands of miles apart" (ibid.). Yeshuyab II probably is the one who established India as a separate metropolitanate. The patriarchs of Alexandria and Armenia also contributed greatly to the organization of the church in their respective areas and beyond (in the case of Alexandria).

Spiritual, Religious, and Social Movements

The social influence of the monastic movement during this time period is evident throughout both the survey of the geographical/cultural movement of Christianity and all of the threads of Christian tradition. There were seventeen thousand abbeys and priories in Europe by the eighth century (see Bernier, 103). The desire for unification and uniformity in the Latin West included the choice of the Benedictine over the Irish form of monastic life.

Monasticism contributed greatly to this development spiritually, socially, economically, and in terms of education. However, many monasteries eventually became entangled with wealth and power. The French Benedictine monastery of Cluny became the center for monastic reform in the tenth and eleventh centuries by refocusing on communal prayer and liturgy.

Monasticism continued to attract many people in the Greek East, where the number of monks and nuns was approximately one hundred thousand in the eighth century (Irvin and Sunquist 2001, 366). In contrast to the situation of strong political and social influences upon monasticism in the Latin West, the monastic communities of the Greek East in the eighth and ninth centuries were able "to focus more on the devotional life and spiritual contemplation" and to emphasize even more "the austere dimensions of spiritual life" (ibid., 365). The monasteries had little institutional affiliation with the local bishops and dioceses. Partially due to their tax-free status, the monastic communities grew in wealth, which sometimes led to corruption, similar to the situation of the Latin West. From a religious perspective, the Greek monastery of Mount Athos was the center of monastic renewal in the tenth and eleventh centuries. Its greatest teacher at this time, Simeon the New Theologian, is credited with further developing spiritual understanding of deification (*theosis*) and the practice of hesychasm—"stilling and focusing the mind in order to behold the inner light" (ibid., 366)—traditionally focused on reciting the Jesus Prayer. The spirituality of the Greek East was at the same time sacramental-liturgical in such a way that "mysticism and the everyday sacramental life of the Church are bound together rather than separated" (Sheldrake, 69). Finally, there is "an aesthetic dimension at the heart of Eastern spirituality" (ibid.), which is expressed and experienced through its liturgical music, religious poetry, and well-known icons. The deep meaning associated with icons for monastic and popular spirituality is illustrated by the way the iconoclast controversy sparked public riots and persecution.

Monasteries were very important centers of spirituality, education, and evangelism in many areas where Christians were living under Muslim rule. Of particular importance were the monasteries of Kenneshre on the Euphrates River for the Jacobites, Mar Saba outside Jerusalem for the Chalcedonian Greek East, and Gundishapur in present-day Iran for several Christian communities (see Irvin and Sunquist 2001, 283). East Syrian monasticism had communal prayer seven times a day, and along with the regular spiritual and educational dimensions of its lifestyle, it also continued the study and practice of medicine. Since the sixth century the monks had a tonsure whereby the unshaved section on the head was crown-shaped. Isaac of Nineveh, a seventh-century bishop, mystic, and writer of the East Syrian Church, described the spiritual life as "one of progression moving through stages from bodily passions to spiritual wonder" and at times as a state of ecstasy (ibid., 284). Outside of the monasteries, Christians living in Muslim territory sustained their faith through the liturgical, sacramental, and communal life of the church that was permitted in public.

Let us return to the Latin West for another key development in spirituality during this time period. As seen in "Liturgy, Sacraments, and Art," the Germanic religious-cultural worldview also influenced Christian spirituality through a process of assimilation. For example, the traditional Celtic feast of Samhain corresponded to the feasts of All Saints and All Souls (see Sheldrake, 83), and churches were often built on traditional worship sites (similar to the instructions of Gregory I to Augustine at the end of the sixth century). Past Christian saints "quickly appropriated the place in popular life that had been earlier occupied by local gods and spirits," and monks and nuns sometimes used "signs and wonders to demonstrate the superior spiritual power of the gospel" (Irvin and Sunquist 2001, 350). "There were blessings for plows, weapons, and battlefield wounds; prayers against thunder and lightning, famine, illness, and difficult pregnancies; and relics to ward off toothaches and blindness" (Bellitto, 167). Relics of saints or the true cross "created sacred Christian spaces in people's lives and brought the great memory of saints and holy events into the everyday world where people lived" (Irvin and Sunquist 2001, 350). On the negative side, the trafficking of relics sometimes led to magical practices and financial preoccupation in monasteries. The spirituality associated with relics went beyond the popular level. "By the end of the ninth century nearly every church altar in the West had a relic associated with it" (ibid.). Christians began to go on pilgrimages across Europe to visit and pray in the churches with the more well-known relics, and pilgrims began traveling to the church of Santiago de Compostela in northwestern Spain in the tenth century. Of course, pilgrimages to Jerusalem had already begun in the fourth century.

The Frankish laywoman Dhuoda in the ninth century wrote the *Manual* as a spiritual guidebook for her son. She is "one of the very few women in the first millennium of the church's history from whom we have something written by herself . . . [and she represents] the countless, anonymous Christian women of the first millennium who strove to bring up their children in accord with the teaching of Scripture and of the church" (Wiseman, 105–6).

Theological Developments

We begin our treatment of theology with the Greek East. Patriarch Sergius of Constantinople before the Arab advance introduced a proposal that became known as monothelitism (one will)—the two natures of Jesus Christ acted together under one will—in an attempt to bring together the

Chalcedonian and non-Chalcedonian positions for theological and, more important, political reasons. Martin I, the bishop/pope of Rome, in 649 called a regional council that condemned monothelitism. The East Roman emperor, who had ruled in favor of the one-will formulation, had Martin I brought to Constantinople in chains and tried, tortured, and sent into exile. This incident highlights again the strong identification of church and state in the Byzantine Empire and the growing antagonism between the Latin West and the Greek East. Monothelitism was intended to mend the division between the Chalcedonians and non-Chalcedonians, especially in Syria and Egypt, but the only reportedly non-Chalcedonian group that accepted the teaching was the Maronite community. However, the East Roman emperor in 680 called the Sixth Ecumenical Council, Constantinople III, which condemned monothelitism and extended the Chalcedonian definition to include the "two wills" with the "two natures" of Jesus Christ.

Later, the Greek East was dealing with the divisive iconoclast controversy, mentioned several times already in this chapter. John of Damascus, an Arab Christian theologian and doctor of the church, defended the use of icons by appealing to the incarnation. "As the fullness of God was revealed in Jesus' flesh, so God's presence and the presence of the saints are revealed through their images or 'icons'" (Bevans 2009, 233). The treatise *On the Triune Nature of God* by an anonymous author appeared in 755; it is the first known Christian theology written in Arabic. This text, which used both the Old Testament and the Qur'an as references, appears to have been a pastoral guide for Arab-speaking Christians in their Muslim context.

The text from the two-day interreligious exchange between the East Syrian patriarch Timothy I and the Muslim caliph Al Mahdi in 781 is another example of the theology developing within the Muslim context. Quite a number of original works and translations of Christian theology and apologetics were written in Arabic from the ninth to the eleventh centuries (see Wilken, 307–15). On the other side of Asia, the East Syrian monks and scholars—like Alopen and companions and later Ching-ching (Adam)—who worked in China in the seventh and eighth centuries certainly translated and possibly wrote the first theological treatises in Chinese. These are studied in more detail in the following section.

The years 600–1000 were not characterized by much theological development, debate, or creativity in the Latin West, especially in comparison with the preceding and following time periods. It was more a period of preservation, as noted earlier in "Scripture." However, several persons and developments need to be noted. Bede the Venerable (673–735) recorded the important Christian history of England, and theologian Alcuin of York (735–804) developed the script and pronunciation of Latin and protested the use of force by Charlemagne to baptize the Saxons. Two theological debates surrounding the *filioque* addition to the Nicene Creed and the eucharistic presence were mentioned earlier in this chapter and will resurface in Chapter 4.

Mission, Cultures, and Religions

During this period of 600–1000 monks and nuns of the monastic movements were the primary agents of mission in the many varied contexts where Christians encountered other cultures and religions. We begin with the East Syrian Church, which can be considered the most missionary church during this time period (see Bevans and Schroeder 2004, 111). Despite the restricted conditions imposed upon Christians under Persian and Muslim political authority in Persia, Christianity not only survived but continued to spread across Asia to China.

Two East Syrian patriarchs, mentioned throughout this chapter, were particularly significant for mission. Yeshuyab II was a peacemaker and initiated the first official mission to China. Timothy I promoted the growth of the church beyond Persia to the areas of Tibet, Yemen, India, and to the Turks, including the present-day nations of Uzbekistan, Kazakhstan, and Tajikistan. Timothy I is considered "one of the most missionary-minded church leaders of the first one thousand years of the Christian movement" (Irvin and Sunquist 2001, 285). As for relating to other religions, Timothy I in 781 had a noteworthy two-day interreligious exchange with the caliph Al Mahdi, during which they discussed the Muslim and Christian understandings of revelation, Muhammad, the Trinity, and Christology. In response to the final question regarding the truth, the patriarch used the image of people of different religions searching for a pearl by feeling around on the ground in darkness and not being sure if what they hold in their hand is a piece of glass or the actual intact pearl. The patriarch concludes, "God has placed the pearl of His faith before all of us like the shining rays of the sun, and everyone who wishes can enjoy the light of the sun" (Coakley and Sterk, 242). On a negative note, the patriarch affirmed the common Muslim and Christian hatred of the Jews. However, the positive aspect of the official approach of Timothy I was that "the defence of Christian faith with a mild rejection of Muslim understanding and strong praise of Muhammad is one high point in the dialogue" (Norris 2002, 82). Other Christian apologetic works, such as those of Abraham of Tiberius and Theodore Abū Qurrah in the ninth century, present a more negative view of Islam (see ibid., 82–83).

Under the section "India, Central Asia, and China" we noted how Christian merchants for years were important implicit bearers of the Christian life and message across Asia. In a more explicit way the East Syrian monks brought the Christian message into parts of China in the sixth century and to the capital city of Chang'an in the seventh. Of the Christian Chinese texts from this period the *Jesus-Messiah Sutra* most clearly reflects the interaction of Christianity with Buddhism, Taoism, and Confucianism, whereby Christian beliefs were maintained and yet somehow reinterpreted within the context of other religious beliefs. For example, Christianity replaced the Confucian hierarchy of obedience—with the emperor considered supreme, followed by the parents—with obedience shown first of all to God, and then to the emperor and parents. Another example of interreligious interaction is the Christian monk Ching-ching (Adam), who was "so famed for his knowledge of Chinese language and literature that even Buddhist missionaries came to him for help in translating their own sacred books" (Moffett 1998, 300). Adding to this situation of interreligious cooperation, two famous Buddhists, who would become founders of two major schools of Buddhism in Japan, were living in the same Buddhist monastery in China around the time when these joint translations of seven volumes were being done (see Irvin and Sunquist 2001, 320). One wonders what sort of mutual exchange occurred in this context. Around this same time, in 781, the large stele record of the first 150 years of Christianity, described earlier in this chapter, was erected outside of Chang'an. It is noteworthy that the public display of this monument marking Christian presence and interaction with major Asian religions in eastern Asia occurred in the same year that Timothy I was engaged in an interreligious exchange with Islam in western Asia. We noted above that this first period of Christianity in China comes to a close in the ninth and early tenth centuries with the decline of the T'ang Dynasty.

While Christianity was encountering new cultures and religions in mission across Asia, many Christians from Persia to the Iberian Peninsula were encountering a new religion and culture at "home," as they found themselves living under Muslim rule. In general, they lived as *dhimmi* under varying restrictions. In Syria, Palestine, and Persia, Christians eventually adopted Arabic as their common language but continued to use Syriac or Greek, depending upon their ecclesiastical affiliation, in liturgy. As noted above, some Christian writing and bible translations emerged in Arabic in these areas. The percentage of Muslims increased greatly in these areas—from 20 percent to 50 percent over the ninth century in present-day Iraq, and nearly 70 percent in present-day Iran during the same time period (see Norris 2002, 81–82). Much of this was due to the large number of Christians who were becoming Muslims for a variety of reasons (cf. ibid.). At the same time, it seems that Christian monasticism may have somehow influenced "the development of a distinctive form of Islamic mystical and ecstatic experience known as Sufism" (Irvin and Sunquist 2001, 283).

In Egypt, Arabic became the language of common usage, while Coptic remained the liturgical language. Moving westward from Egypt, Christianity would basically disappear across North Africa except for a few isolated groups. In Spain, some Christians adopted Arabic, while others maintained their Latin culture. The translation of the entire bible into Arabic and the first translation of the Qur'an into Latin occurred in Spain. Before the Muslim invasion in Spain, strong anti-Jewish attitudes were already present. A council in Toledo in 694 ordered that all Jews be sold into slavery and their property be confiscated by the state. Even though this ordinance was not carried out completely, life had become very difficult for Jews in Spain. Under Muslim rule Jews were given equal legal status with Christians, so that by the ninth century "a lively Jewish intellectual and cultural life was thriving in several cities of Spain" (Irvin and Sunquist 2001, 303).

Mission during 600–1000 in the Latin West continued to be marked by mass conversions of tribes, like the Germanic ones earlier, with a strong communal worldview whereby religious and social identities were inseparable. The peoples of Bohemia, Poland, Hungary, Denmark, Sweden, Norway, and Iceland were baptized en masse. The conversion of Iceland in the year 1000 is "one of the best illustrations of this tribal form of Christianity in the West" (Irvin and Sunquist 2001, 379), in that it involved an open debate in the Icelandic assembly and an all-night, shamanistic-type divinization by the non-Christian president of the assembly (see ibid., 380). Unfortunately, some of the other mass "conversions" were coerced at the point of the sword, as Charlemagne did against the Saxons. Theologian Alcuin protested this action to no avail. Whether the mass baptisms occurred through peaceful or forceful ways, "these nominal Christians would then wait for the arrival of bishops, priests, monks and nuns to offer them a further understanding and witness of this new faith" (Bevans and Schroeder 2004, 126).

In Chapter 2 we highlighted the mission efforts of the men and women of the Irish and Benedictine monastic movements. In Chapter 3 we have seen that Benedictine monasticism grew in prominence and was joined by many Anglo-Saxon monks and nuns as the primary agents of mission to those baptized in mass movements. While Anglo-Saxon monasticism adopted the identification with Rome and the more accommodational approach from the Benedictines, the former adopted the value of "wandering for the sake of Christ" from Irish monasticism, not as a form of asceticism but more for the sake of mission in itself. The most well-known Anglo-Saxon monk was Wynfrith of Crediton, later known as Boniface (ca. 675–754), the Apostle of Germany. He contributed greatly to the reform of the Frankish Church, and his life commitment to mission ended at the age of eighty with his martyrdom and that of fifty companions in Frisia. Boniface also "called on women to share explicitly in mission on a wide scale for the first time in the post-Constantinian period" (Bevans and Schroeder 2004, 125). He felt such a sense of partnership in mission with the learned nun Lioba (Leoba) that he asked that they be buried in the same tomb. Although the monks did not honor this request, it "can be seen as a powerful symbolic statement regarding the collaboration and equality between women and men in mission" (ibid.).

The section "Mission, Cultures, and Religions" in the previous chapter ended with the letter of Pope Gregory I of Rome to Augustine and the Benedictines en route to England on mission, in which Gregory outlined an accommodational approach. While the Benedictine and later the Anglo-Saxon monks and nuns didn't necessarily have a high regard for Germanic society, they decided, at least initially, to adapt some aspects of tribal cultures according to Gregory's "step by step" approach. Furthermore, despite the attempts of Charlemagne to impose Roman culture on the Germanic peoples, with time they "both appropriated Christianity within their traditional world view and reshaped Christianity in the West" (Bevans and Schroeder 2004, 132), as noted above, for example, in the threads of liturgy and spirituality. An anonymous monk in the ninth century wrote the *Heliand*, a powerful poetic version of the gospel from the Saxon worldview intended to be sung in mead halls. The prophets were called "soothsayers," the disciples "warrior-companions of Jesus," and Jesus himself the "best of healers" and the "chieftain of clans." The *Heliand* demonstrates again that "while northern Europe had become Christian, its Christianity had become in turn very much Germanized" (Bevans 2009, 236). As the Hellenistic-Roman phase of Christianity ended, "Christianity had been saved by its cross-cultural diffusion" (Walls 1996, 19).

Due to the close identification of religion and state in the Byzantine Empire, the spread of Christianity can continue to be understood as a rather benign form of "imperial mission," exemplified in the outstanding work of Cyril and Methodius. These two brothers developed a Slavic liturgy and a Glagolitic script for the Slavic language. Although these noble efforts received the blessing of Pope Hadrian II, they were sabotaged by the rival Frankish kingdom of the Latin West with its own political and religious motivations. However, the seed for an inculturated Slavic Christianity would thrive among the Bulgars. The conflict surrounding Cyril and Methodius highlights not only the political rivalry between the Frankish (Holy Roman) and Byzantine empires, but also a different understanding of church, mission, and culture. The Greek East was "stressing cultural particularism and the formation of a more independent church," while the "Germanized" Latin West was "stressing cultural uniformity and membership in a universal church" (Bevans and Schroeder 2004, 128). However, in both situations mission in general had the advantages and disadvantages of having the support of a political state. This, of course, was not the situation for the many Christians who lived under Muslim rule.

The primary role of monks and nuns in mission had begun to taper off by the year 1000. Monasticism in the Latin West and the Byzantine Empire was challenged by wealth and corruption. Apparently, the East Syrian (see Moffett 1998, 361) and Ethiopian (see Irvin and Sunquist 2001, 297) monastic movements were also less active in explicit mission toward the end of the first millennium. Although there were strong spiritual renewal movements within the monasticism of the Latin West and Greek East, their contribution to explicit mission would not be as significant as it had been at its height.

Conclusion

We entitled this chapter—and this period—"New Challenges and New Beginnings." Certainly, the rapid spread of Islam was a major challenge to Christianity, and yet many Christians continued to live out their faith under a situation of restriction similar to the challenge faced by the early Christians of the Roman Empire (Chapter 1) and later Christians in the Persian Empire (Chapter 2). The witness of Arabic-speaking Christians and the existence of Arabic Christian writings cannot be forgotten as part of the Christian response to this changing context. Furthermore, in spite of this challenge at home in Persia, the East Syrian Church experienced new beginnings across Central Asia and China. As a reminder, around the year 800 there were approximately ten million Christians between Antioch and China, with the majority being of the East Syrian Church (Norris 2006, 133). And this was a time of great interreligious exchange—from Christianity engaging Buddhism, Taoism, and Confucianism in the heart of China, to a Christian patriarch carrying on a conversation with a Muslim ruler in Baghdad. Between those two points many Christian monks and merchants traveled alongside believers of other religions on the Silk Road.

In the face of changing political and cultural situations in Europe, the Latin West experienced a new beginning as the Germanic peoples both appropriated the Christian faith and reshaped it, for example, in the areas of liturgy and spirituality. At the same time, they preserved scripture and theology. Feudalism had a very strong influence, particularly on the shape of ministry and church organization. More important, we can trace the impact of monasticism throughout Christianity. Missiologist David Bosch maintains that "it was because of monasticism that so much authentic Christianity evolved in the course of Europe's 'dark ages' and beyond" (1991,

230). We have seen in this chapter how the women and men of monastic movements around the world were involved either implicitly or explicitly in preserving and developing every aspect of the Christian tradition and in deepening and spreading the Christian faith. However, monasticism was facing new challenges as we come to the end of this period.

Through the process of engaging other cultures the Christian faith had spread during the first millennium from Antioch to India and China; from Egypt to Ethiopia and Nubia and across North Africa; from the Middle East to Asia Minor and Armenia; from Ireland to Europe and England; from Constantinople to Moravia, Bulgaria, and Russia; and from Rome across western and central Europe to Scandinavia. Even though Christianity was receding in certain areas around the year 1000, we can still say that Christianity "had become a global religion" (Wilken, 355), as "global" was understood at that time. This happened through the process of encountering new challenges and new beginnings.

We end this chapter with an excerpt from the *Jesus-Messiah Sutra*, one of the oldest Chinese Christian texts. They are the final verses (from a torn manuscript) of the retelling of the passion and death of Christ for the seventh-century Chinese context:

> The evil ones brought the Messiah to a place set apart, and after washing his hair led him to the place of execution called Chi-Chu [Golgotha]. They hung him high upon a wooden scaffold, with two criminals, one on either side of him. He hung there for five hours. That was on the sixth cleansing, vegetarian day. Early that morning there was bright sunlight, but as the sun went West, darkness came over the world, the earth quaked, the mountains trembled, the tombs opened and the dead walked. Those who saw this believed that he was who he said he was. How can anyone not believe? Those who take these words to heart are true disciples of the Messiah. As a result . . . [break in text]. (Ch. 5, par. 44; Palmer, 168)

4

New Political Horizons

ca. 1000 to ca. 1453

At the beginning of the second millennium Europe was divided into feudal states, and the Church of the Latin West provided cohesion and leadership. When Muslim rule was weakening on the Iberian Peninsula but obtaining a tighter hold in Palestine, the pope of Rome with his growing authority was the one person capable of calling Europe together for a crusade. These military campaigns would eventually be led against not only Muslims but also against those considered nonbelievers and heretics in Europe. Another victim of the crusades was the relationship between the Latin West and Greek East. In the midst of the crusades and the church's alignment with wealth and power, a variety of grassroots religious movements swept rapidly across Europe, calling Christians and the institutional church back to the core values of the gospel.

Christianity across Asia was also caught in the midst of changing political situations. Genghis Khan arose in central Asia to establish the Mongol Empire, which would eventually stretch from the Pacific to the Mediterranean, and Christians experienced religious toleration and even full participation in society. In the thirteenth century, Christians in Asia formed what "was geographically the largest Christian Church of the Middle Ages with its centre in Baghdad" (Tang and Winkler, 5). However, in 1295 the Mongol Empire embraced Islam, and a new phase of Christian persecution began in Asia. A later political revival of the Mongol Empire under Tamerlane would lead to even harsher circumstances for the church in Asia. Back in the west, the powerful Muslim Ottoman Dynasty took over in Turkey and eventually captured the city of Constantinople in 1453, ending the thousand-year-old history of a Christian empire. Russia would pick up the mantle of leadership for the church of the Greek East. In light of the strong impact of all of these political changes on Christianity, we follow Irvin and Sunquist in naming this period "new political horizons" (2001, 383–506).

Historical Context

Controversy, Crisis, and Crusades in Christendom

The Anglo-Saxons had begun using the term *Christendom* in the tenth century to describe the joint social-political and religious identification in Europe under the Roman Catholic Church. This situation led to confusion and corruption. Lay political leaders appointed bishops and priests, who in turn took oaths of fealty to feudal lords. Some even paid for these ecclesial appointments. The Gregorian reform, which extended beyond the pontificate of Gregory VII (1073–1085), tried to separate spiritual and temporal authority. This became known as the Investiture Controversy. Compromises were eventually reached, for example, at the Concordat of Worms in Germany in 1122, whereby bishops would be chosen according to ecclesial canonical procedures but would still take oaths of loyalty to political rulers. Those holding ecclesiastical offices were forbidden to pay for those positions. "The compromise recognized that there were two centers of authority within a Christian society, a situation that was to continue to bring conflict in the West in successive centuries" (Irvin and Sunquist 2001, 390).

The much older version of Christendom, the Byzantine Empire, had expanded its territory into Syria and Armenia. However, a new Turkish Muslim Dynasty gained power and took a number of cities in Armenia, Georgia, and most of Asia Minor. They then conquered Jerusalem and severely restricted the passage of Christian pilgrims to the city. The Byzantine Empire was threatened not only by the Muslim forces, but also by the Normans in Italy and other tribes from the north. The new Byzantine emperor Alexius Comnenus sent an appeal for military assistance to the pope in 1095, and Urban II called the first crusade several months later. This was not what Emperor Comnenus expected.

This emperor's request came at a time when relations between the Latin West and Greek East were strained. In 1054, Pope Leo IX had sent three envoys to Constantinople to settle current problems caused by the imposition of Latin rites on Greek Christians in southern Italy and the opposite scenario in Constantinople. Of course, these were based on longstanding theological, liturgical, cultural, and political tensions. After a number of diplomatic miscues, the Roman delegation excommunicated the Byzantine patriarch, who in turn excommunicated the Roman delegation. Disturbing as this was, this "event was more symbolic of the distance that had grown between the two communions, however, than it was a permanent stage of institutional separation or schism" (Irvin and Sunquist 2001, 392). The decisive blow of separation between the Latin West and the Greek East occurred when the western crusaders sacked Constantinople in 1204.

Let us now turn to the beginning of the crusades. The papacy, on the one hand, attempted to prevent feudal authorities from interfering with ecclesiastical authorities. However, on the other hand, it did not want to separate the sacred and the secular in a Christian society it viewed as united under the spiritual leadership of the pope. Preventing Christians from going on pilgrimage to Jerusalem under the new Muslim rule was considered a denial of Christian access to the sacred, and it needed to be addressed by Christendom. The call of Pope Urban II in 1095 initiated a series of crusades. For their participation, crusaders were granted an indulgence from punishment in the afterlife for sins they had confessed. The first crusade succeeded in reclaiming Nicaea, Edessa, Antioch, and Jerusalem from Muslim control. However, relationships with Muslims, Jews, and Orthodox (Greek East) Christians were severely damaged, as Muslim civilians were massacred, the synagogue in Jerusalem was burned, and the Orthodox patriarch in Antioch was replaced by a bishop of the Latin West. Meanwhile in the western Mediterranean area, the reconquest of the Iberian Peninsula from Muslim domain, which had begun with the capture of Toledo in 1085, continued with Frankish military assistance. Five Christian kingdoms were established by 1200—León, Navarre, Castile, Aragón, and Portugal. The last Muslim kingdom on the Iberian Peninsula would be conquered in 1492.

After Muslim forces recaptured Damascus and Edessa, Pope Eugenius III called a second series of crusades in 1146. This effort was promoted by Bernard of Clairvaux, a very effective preacher of the newly founded Cistercian monastic community. The king of France and the emperor of Germany, representing the two major political entities formed from what had been the Holy Roman Empire, led armies to the Holy Land. This crusading movement also included military campaigns in Spain and approval for the German rulers to attack the Wends, a tribal people in northern Europe who were not Christian. The crusades had military success on the Iberian Peninsula, and the Wends were conquered and, sadly, were forced to be baptized. Muslim forces defeated the western crusaders, reestablished their authority over most of Syria, and recaptured Jerusalem in 1187 after over eighty-five years of Christian rule.

A third series of crusades, called in response to the fall of Jerusalem, drew responses from the German emperor and the kings of France and England. The efforts of the latter two led to a truce with the Muslim ruler whereby parts of Palestine were under the authority of the Latin West and Christian pilgrimages to Jerusalem were again permitted, even though the Holy City remained under Muslim rule.

The fourth crusade, called in 1198, was a disaster in many ways. The French crusaders turned to the rich trading city of Venice for financial assistance, and their combined efforts turned into a crusade for wealth, with the eventual pillaging of the city of Constantinople in 1204. One can say that "the sack of Constantinople would go down in history as one of the most ignominious episodes of a long and inglorious period in East-West relations" (Irvin and Sunquist 2001, 405). In addition, the crusades themselves are considered by Christians to be the "worst débâcle, arguably with the exception of the European Holocaust" (Norris 2002, 108).

In order to combat the threat of heresy back in Europe, the Catholic Church discontinued its practice of calling upon civil authorities to judge those considered heretics and in 1229 instituted a central ecclesiastical court system, called the Inquisition, to investigate and determine guilt or innocence regarding charges of heresy. The Inquisition process consisted of private trials and methods like physical ordeals. Those who admitted heresy and embraced appropriate beliefs could be reconciled into the Christian community, while those who were found guilty and refused to recant could be handed over to the state for punishment, which included burning at the stake.

As we move into the fourteenth century, religion and politics continue to be tightly interwoven within a Christendom understanding, but changes were occurring in the Latin West. The feudal economy based on the land and the exchange of goods and services was shifting to a new, urban-based, commercial economy. "The older political system of feudalism, in which relations were shaped by the exchange of oaths of fealty and sealed through symbolic exchange of gifts, was likewise giving way to a new urban political reality in which associations of artisans and traders played a significant role" (Irvin and Sunquist 2001, 384). On the bigger scale, national identities and languages were forming under the monarchies of the English, French, Germans, and Spaniards. There was constant conflict between these nations, most notably the Hundred Years' War between the English and the French. Famine and disease, especially the bubonic plague (black death), also seriously affected social life. "It is estimated that one-third of the fifty to seventy million people who lived in the West died from the epidemic in the middle years of the fourteenth century" (ibid., 477). The church also faced many challenges in the fourteenth and first half of the fifteenth centuries: corruption within the church, conflicts between the papacy and France, the schism in the papacy itself, and calls for reform by John Wycliffe in England and John Hus (Huss) in Bohemia.

Spiritual Renewal in the Latin West

The preceding section is not a complete representation of Christianity in the Latin West. While the church was involved with politics and the crusades, at the same time Christianity was being renewed religiously and spiritually. Initially, this renewal consisted of reformed and/or stricter monastic movements, beginning with the Cluny reform, mentioned in the preceding chapter, and followed by the founding of the Carthusians, Cistercians, Canons Regular, and Premonstratensians. These well-intentioned reforms were generally initiated by the aristocracy. "Beginning in the twelfth century, the renewal moved more and more into the hands of the town and city dwellers and of the peasants, reflecting the changing of the guard in the social order as well" (Bevans and Schroeder 2004, 140). These various movements, including groups of penitents, were attempts to live the *vita apostolica* (evangelical life), based on the Gospels and the life of Christ, and not on the institutional church.

A fairly wealthy merchant named Waldo of Lyons had a conversion experience at the end of the twelfth century that led him to give much of his property to the poor and to begin itinerant popular preaching. A French translation of the scriptures became a central element of his activity, which attracted a small group of people. The local bishop banned these followers of Waldo since they had no official church affiliation. Not wanting to separate themselves from the Catholic Church, they appealed to Pope Alexander III for formal recognition, but he simply referred them back to the local bishop. This group, known as Waldensians, refused to stop preaching, and they were then excommunicated as heretics. Their life was centered on prayer, Bible study, preaching, pacifism, and voluntary poverty. A growing number of Waldensian communities formed in France, Austria, and northern Italy, where they still exist today in isolated areas of the Alps. On June 22, 2015, Pope Francis, the first pope to visit a Waldensian house of worship, while in Turin, Italy, asked for forgiveness for "the non-Christian and even inhuman attitudes and behaviour" of the Catholic Church toward the Waldensians.

Another group that developed across southern France and northern Italy at this time was the Cathars or Albigenses. Their roots probably can be traced to groups from Bulgaria and Armenia that exhibited some Manichaean and possibly Gnostic teachings and followed a strict moral code. Cathar teaching included a sharp dualism between the spiritual realm of good and the material realm of evil, which led to rejection of the incarnation and sacraments, since both were associated with material existence. Cathars also distinguished the learned, or a type of elite, from regular members. While many men and women were drawn to the Cathars due to their voluntary poverty and call to a deeper spiritual life, some nobility supported the Cathars as an alternative to the authority of Catholic hierarchy. Particularly due to the latter issue, a crusade was called against the Cathars. It is estimated that tens of thousands of civilians, both Cathars and Catholics, were massacred in this military campaign (Irvin and Sunquist 2001, 414). The Inquisition also was directed against the Cathars.

While the Waldensians and Cathars for different reasons and under different circumstances had conflicts with the official church, other mendicant movements within the evangelical renewal found acceptance. The priest Dominic de Guzman of Caleruega had grown up in a noble family in the region of Castille, recently liberated from Muslim rule, and he lived near the region of southern France where the Cathars were quite strong. In contrast to a crusading approach, Dominic adopted a life of voluntary poverty and itinerant preaching, and he soon had others from the diocese of Toulouse following him. The Fourth Lateran Council of 1215 forbade the acceptance of any new orders, because the council was afraid of possible heresies among the wide variety of new movements. However, at the time of Dominic's death in 1221, the Order of Preachers (the Dominicans) was accepted under the existing rule of Augustine. There were about twenty thousand members by the beginning of the fourteenth century. The First Order of Friars had been joined by women very early on; they became the Second Order, cloistered nuns committed to prayer, hospitality, and education for girls. In 1285, the Order of Preachers officially promulgated an Order of Penance, which eventually became a Third Order for laity who wanted to affiliate themselves with the Dominican movement while continuing to live in their single or married state.

Around the same time, in central Italy, the layman Francis of Assisi renounced his social status and embraced a life of austere poverty and penitential preaching. Many quickly joined him. Although the church was hesitant to acknowledge new orders, as noted above with the Dominicans, the simple rule of Francis was accepted around 1209–1210 by Pope Innocent III for the First Order of Friars Minor (Franciscans). Clare of Assisi was one of the first to join the movement of Francis, and she founded the Second Order of Franciscans, or Poor Clares, a cloistered community of women aligned with the mission of Francis. While her community was originally under the Benedictine rule, two days before her death in 1253, the pope accepted the rule of Clare based on this Franciscan vision, and it was the first rule for religious life written by a woman. Parallel to developments within the Dominicans, the rule for the Order of Brothers and Sisters of Penance (Third Order) for laypersons was written around 1221. The Franciscan movement in all its forms touched the hearts of many who were searching for the evangelical life. There were about forty thousand Friars Minor by 1300, although the number was halved by 1385, due primarily to the bubonic plague.

Another significant movement was that of the Beguines. During the twelfth century, individual women particularly in Belgium began living a more intentional spiritual lifestyle while continuing to live in their homes as single, widowed, or married women and supporting themselves through manual labor. They wore a uniform dress of gray, similar to the early Franciscans. In the following century, groups of Beguines became unofficially affiliated with individual monks and clerics and spread into Germany. In 1223, Pope Gregory IX gave them quasi-legal recognition as laywomen, not nuns, but some were suspected of heresy. Later they received official civil and religious recognition and began to live in beguinages—a closed circle of cottages, including a church and building for dispensing charity. They were under direct clerical authority but were never an official religious order. As suspicion continued to grow from the official church, many of the Beguines joined and contributed greatly, particularly through their mystical writings, to other women's communities, such as the Cistercians. There was also a male counterpart of the Beguine movement called Beghards.

Asia

From Chapter 3 we know that there were as many as ten million Christians in the year 800 from Antioch to China, the majority being of the East Syrian Church. Around the year 1000 the number of Christians living within a Muslim majority in Syria, Palestine, Mesopotamia, and Persia had declined, but in the eleventh century Christians in Persia experienced more freedom than they had in the preceding centuries. While the first period of Christianity in China ended in the tenth century, Christianity continued to grow across Central Asia, particularly among the Uighurs, Kerait Turks, and some Mongol tribes. However, while many people of the northern tribes in Central Asia were Christians, as well as Muslims, Buddhists, and Manicheans, the majority followed their traditional shamanistic-type religion.

At the end of the twelfth century a Mongol warrior, who became known as Genghis Khan (*khan* as a title for ruler), began uniting a number of tribal armies and forming what would become the expansive Mongol Empire. One of the neighboring peoples who early on came under his rule was the Keraits, many of whom were Christian. He gave Sorghaghtani, an apparently Christian woman he took from the Kerait ruling families, to one of his sons as a wife, and she became the mother of several important future Mongol leaders, including Hulagu and Kublai Khan. During the time of Genghis Khan, Christian monks and priests served as scribes, and other Christians worked as governors, administrators, and interpreters. Franciscan friars later reported seeing a church tent with East Syrian wooden gongs in the khan's camp. "From various sources it appears that the Mongol ruler's wives and daughters were actively practicing their Christian faith" (Irvin and Sunquist 2001, 454).

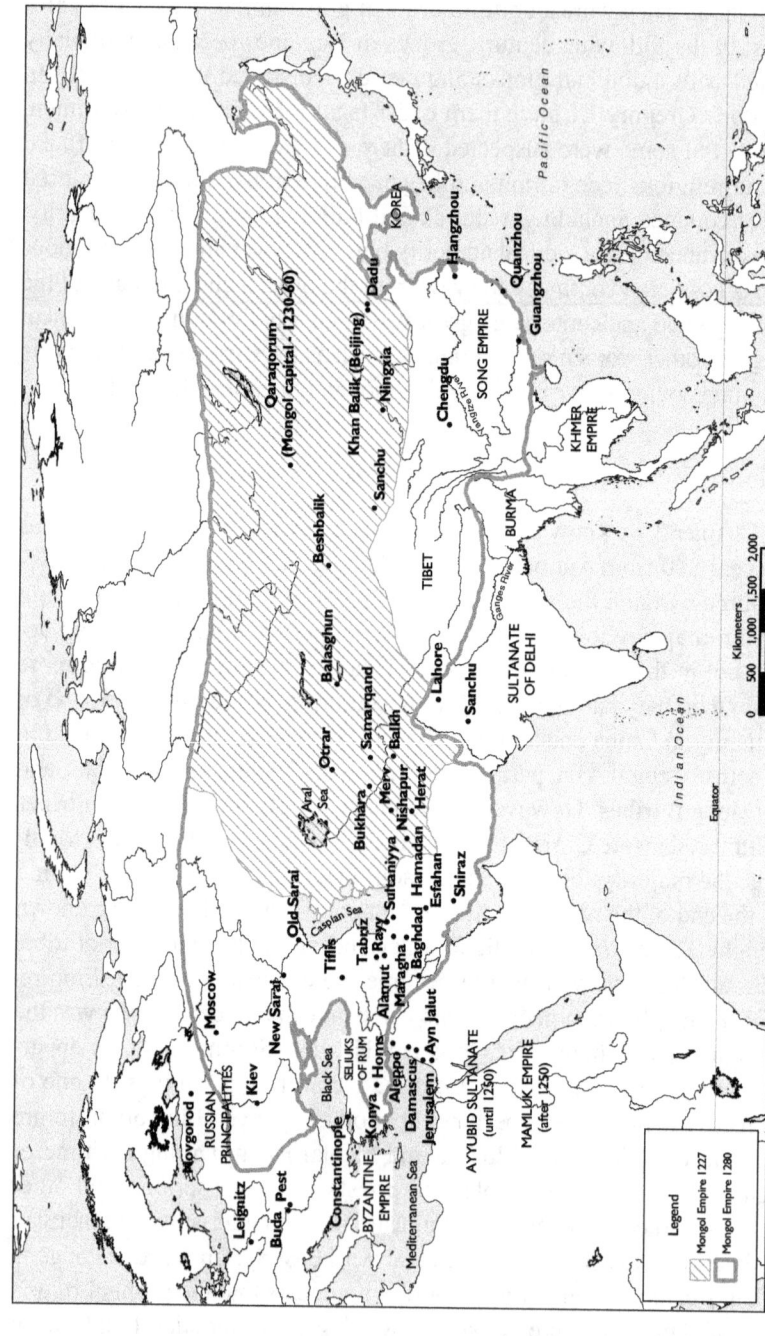

Map 5: The Mongol Empire in 1227 and 1280

The growing military forces of Genghis Khan extended the boundaries of the Mongol Empire to Beijing in China, the Indus River in India, and to eastern Persia and the Caspian Sea, so that the empire had to be divided into four regions before the death of Genghis Khan in 1227. Mongolian armies continued on a path of destruction and conquest across Russia, through Poland and Hungary into Austria, and later to Baghdad, Persia, and Mesopotamia (see Map 5). By 1280, Mongol rule "for the first and only time in history . . . gave Asia a continental unity, a short-lived but immensely powerful trans-Euroasian empire" (Moffett 1998, 405).

Several groups of Franciscan friars on diplomatic missions from the Latin West met the khan in the eastern part of the Mongol Empire. John of Plano Carpini led the first band with a letter from the pope to the Mongols with an invitation to baptism and a request to end the Mongol attacks on other nations. The khan refused on both accounts. The second attempt, headed by Franciscan William of Rubruck, aimed to procure the military assistance of the Mongols against Muslim forces. The khan again declined this request. However, William of Rubruck engaged in an interesting interreligious debate. Upon his return to Europe, the Rubruck written record of his journey "is the earliest accurate description of the Asiatic heartland, its people, and its religions to reach the West" (Irvin and Sunquist 2001, 413).

In 1260, Kublai Khan was selected as the great khan. He moved the capital of the empire from Karakorum (near the present-day city of Kharkhorin in Mongolia) to Khanbalik (near present-day Beijing). His brother, Hulagu, became the ilkhan (lesser khan) in the west with Baghdad as the capital. The next thirty-five years provided a window of opportunity for Christians in the vast Mongol Empire. "Muslims still vastly outnumbered Christians in the Persian world and violence was still a constant threat, but under the Mongols a generation of Christians had greater freedom than they had experienced in Persia in almost a thousand years" (Irvin and Sunquist 2001, 460). An attempt was made to reestablish the network of bishoprics across Asia and into India and China. Under Kublai Khan in China, Christians served as physicians, advisers, and astronomers in the court; a number of churches and monasteries were built in China; bishops were appointed to the metropolitanate of Khanbalik; and an East Syrian physician was appointed the head of a newly formed government department to handle issues related to the growing Christian population (see Bevans and Schroeder 2004, 162). When the father and uncle of Marco Polo came to the imperial court in China around 1265, Kublai Khan sent a letter with them back to the pope requesting a hundred Christian scholars. Unfortunately, they wouldn't arrive for almost thirty years and after the death of Kublai Khan. When Marco Polo himself visited (around 1275), he reported that there were significant Christian communities along the Silk Road, smaller communities of Persian and Armenian Christians in southeastern China, and even a small Chinese group in the coastal city of Fuzhou who may have been the remnants of Christians or Manicheans from the T'ang Dynasty (see Irvin and Sunquist 2001, 465–66).

Two East Syrian monks, Rabban Sauma and Mark, who had met in China, were sent as official envoys from Khanbalik to Constantinople and Europe to secure allies to fight against the Muslim forces. Mark, of Uighur descent and born in Shaansi province, became Patriarch Yaballaha in Baghdad of the entire East Syrian Church in 1281. Rabban Sauma, now a bishop, was later sent on to Paris and Rome to continue the original diplomatic task. His historic meeting in Rome with the cardinals and pope is treated under the thread "Ministry and Organization" below.

The thirty-five-year window of favorable conditions and opportunity for Christianity closed with the death of Kublai Khan in 1294 in the eastern part of the Mongol Empire and the ascension to leadership of the Muslim ilkhan Mahmud (Ghazan) the following year in the western part. A new wave of persecution of Christians began as the empire shifted in a decidedly Muslim direction and was much less tolerant of other religions. The last synod of the East Syrian Church was held in 1318.

Franciscan John of Monte Corvino, who arrived in China after the death of Kublai Khan, was the first in a series of Franciscans who baptized people and began building churches of the Latin West until they were expelled in 1369 after the Chinese forced the Mongol rule out of China. At this time a Turkish Muslim military man from the area of Samarkand, by the name of Timor Lenk (or Tamerlane), led a bloody conquest to reestablish the empire of Genghis Khan. He massacred tens of thousands of Christians and destroyed the social-economic infrastructure. The spread of the bubonic plague also contributed to the decline of Christianity. "Fourteenth-century grave inscriptions along the Silk Road witness the spread of the black death" (Norris 2002, 118).

By the end of the fifteenth century, across this vast area "only a handful of churches clustered in northern Mesopotamia remained of the East Syrian tradition" (Irvin and Sunquist 2001, 495). The Saint Thomas Christians of southern India, who were outside the spheres of the Mongol Empire, continued to grow; also, "evidence indicates the presence of East Syrian Christian communities in Ceylon (Sri Lanka), Burma, Siam (Thailand), Java and quite possibly also in Annam (Vietnam), the Malay Peninsula and Sumatra" (Bevans and Schroeder 2004, 162). Some Christians most likely had also been in Korea by the late eleventh century and again during the Mongol period of the thirteenth century, and in Japan as soldiers during the Mongol expansion (Morris, 256, 261).

Egypt, Nubia, and Ethiopia

As we have seen throughout this chapter, Christianity in Africa was also affected greatly by the changing political horizon. The situation for Christians in Egypt had been relatively calm through the twelfth century. Some held low-level government jobs, and others were doing well financially. Old churches could be repaired, and new ones could be built. However, the situation changed with the rise to power of the Muslim Mameluke Dynasty in Egypt in 1250. It established control throughout Palestine, Syria, and parts of Armenia, and "tens of thousands of Christians and Jews were sold into slavery from the cities in Syria and Armenia" (Irvin and Sunquist 2001, 470). The Mamelukes also persecuted the Coptic Christians in Egypt. The codes and structures of *dhimmi* were reestablished, newly built churches and monasteries were destroyed, and many Christian peasants were forced off the land. This was a time of trial and crisis for Coptic Christians.

Farther south, in Nubia, Muslim influence grew after the year 1000 due to economics and some military expeditions, but Christians still had religious freedom. However, the new Mameluke Dynasty put more restrictive demands on the Nubians. Muslim immigration and military pressure pulled Nubia more and more under the Egyptian sphere of influence, until the Mamelukes in 1323 appointed a Muslim ruler in the northern region of Nubia and it did not allow the patriarch in Alexandria to send more priests to Nubia. "The last evidence of Christian communities in the region comes from the mid-fifteenth century" (Irvin and Sunquist 2001, 472).

At the beginning of the second millennium Ethiopia was rather weak politically and religiously. In the twelfth century the Zagwe Dynasty promoted territorial and economic expansion, which also contributed to the growth of the church. A monastery, established in 1248 in the southern region of Ethiopia on the island of Lake Hayq, became a center of education and mission outreach. A new political dynasty emerged, and there was a revival of the religious identity of Ethiopia called the Solomonic Revival. According to the text of *Kebra Nagast* (*Book of Kings*), which surfaced in the thirteenth century, the Ethiopian queen of Sheba, after returning home from visiting King Solomon (see 1 Kgs 10:1–13), gave birth to their son, Menelik. According to *Kebra Nagast*, during a return trip to Jerusalem Menelik was given the Ark of the Covenant, which he brought back to Ethiopia. Accordingly, "the royal line that descended from Menelik is directly related to King Solomon, and through him is a member of the royal house of Israel's greatest king, David" (Irvin and Sunquist 2001, 474). *Kebra Nagast* reaffirmed the strong identification of Ethiopian Semitic culture and religion with the Old Testament and Judaism, and it provided a distinct political and religious identity in the face of the growing influence of the

Mamelukes to the north. Ethiopian monasticism, which was "traditionally nationalistic in its orientation," embraced the Solomonic Revival and spread "the unique Ethiopian Christian identity throughout the countryside" (ibid., 475). Monks and nuns became the primary pastoral agents.

At the beginning of the fifteenth century the Coptic Christian minority was struggling to survive in Egypt, and Christianity had practically disappeared in Nubia. The faith was strong in Ethiopia, however, although it was bounded on three sides by a strong Muslim presence. Men and women of the First and Second Order Franciscans had come to North Africa. A number were martyred—five friars in Morocco in 1220 and an entire community of Poor Clares in Tripoli (present-day Libya) in 1289. One Franciscan apparently traveled with Muslim traders into West Africa, but there is no evidence of a lasting Christian influence from this effort (see Irvin and Sunquist 2001, 475). It is also possible that some traders from isolated Christian Berber tribes in North Africa may have been responsible for bringing the Christian message and symbols "that have been found in the art of native Nigerians" (Norris 2002, 125).

Byzantium, Russia, and the Greek East

In "Controversy, Crisis, and Crusades in Christendom" we traced the split between the Latin West and Greek East through the diplomatic fiasco in 1054 and the sack of Constantinople. A Latin emperor and patriarch were installed, and the clergy of the city were forced to use the Latin rite. The Latin rule ended in 1261 when the Byzantine emperor Michael Palaeologus recaptured Constantinople while the Western troops were away on another military campaign. However, the Byzantine Empire would never be the same as before. The sack of Constantinople in 1204 had other ripple effects. Bulgaria and Serbia had earlier separated themselves from the political rule of Constantinople but had maintained ecclesiastical affiliation with Constantinople. Within a couple of decades after 1204 both churches gained recognition as autocephalous (self-heading) churches among the other patriarchs in the East.

Back in Constantinople, the war of swords between the Greek East and Latin West was replaced by the war of words. At the Second Ecumenical Council in Lyons in 1274, the Byzantine emperor sent a letter with the three representatives from the Greek East agreeing to submit to western doctrines and policies, including papal primacy. However, most of the bishops of the Greek East refused to accept such an understanding, which fueled papal resolve to enforce union between the two churches. The Greek East turned its focus to a theological debate of the western addition of the *filioque*— "the Holy Spirit proceeds through the Father *and the Son*"—to the Nicene

Creed. The Greeks or "unionists," who wanted a peaceful compromise with the West, argued for the acceptance of the western phrase. However, the Greek "non-unionist" camp held to the traditional Orthodox position that the *filioque* idea violated their belief that God the Father is the single cause within the Trinity.

New political problems were also on the horizon. While the Muslim Mamelukes based in Egypt were in power farther south, a new Turkish-Muslim dynasty, known as the Ottomans, came to power in Asia Minor in the fourteenth century. Rather than advancing westward toward the Mongol Empire, they conquered Greek territories. The Byzantine emperor appealed to the pope for military aid, but to no avail. The Ottomans soon controlled Bulgaria, Serbia, and Macedonia. Their advance was then delayed temporarily while they responded to the military threat of Tamerlane from the east.

As noted in Chapter 3, a Russian national Christianity had developed by blending its Byzantine foundations with its own cultural and religious riches. The Mongol Empire then absorbed Kiev and Russia through a brutal conquest, but at the beginning there was generally religious tolerance. Christian clergy were not taxed, new churches and monasteries were built, and funds could be collected for the patriarch in Constantinople. The city of Moscow grew in importance to the point that the metropolitan of Kiev moved to Moscow in 1310. Later in the fourteenth century military forces from Moscow defeated the Mongols in battle. Although the Mongols conquered the city two years later, the earlier victory "made Moscow the symbol of nationalist hopes among the Russian people" (Irvin and Sunquist 2001, 501). The other rising political entity in Russia was the independent Kingdom of Lithuania. The patriarch of Constantinople eventually established another metropolitan in Lithuania, which would then be in competition for prominence with Moscow. However, after the king of Lithuania became a Roman Catholic in 1386 and joined his kingdom with Poland in the west, Moscow was clearly the center of Russian Orthodox Christianity.

Mongol power began declining, and Russian nationalism increased. A growing tension regarding the appointment of the metropolitan of Moscow by Constantinople climaxed when the Russian Church appointed its own metropolitan in 1448, marking "a decisive turning point in the life of the Russian church" (Irvin and Sunquist 2001, 502). This did not represent a break with the Orthodox faith of the Greek East, but rather the "need for a self-governing church and the difficulties facing the patriarchate in Constantinople" (ibid.). The city of Constantinople fell to the Ottoman Turks after a long siege a few years later, in 1453. Because of the longstanding dependence by the Byzantine Church on the emperor and the state, this event was catastrophic for Orthodox Christians in the eastern Mediterranean area. But Russia would now carry the "baton" of leadership for the church of the Greek East.

During 1000–1453, with its many changing political horizons, Christianity experienced a number of high and low points. Asia Minor had been one of the strongest centers of Christianity from the beginning. In 1050 it had 373 bishoprics, and the population was practically 100 percent Christian, mostly of the Orthodox (Greek East) Church. In 1453, at the fall of Constantinople, there were only three bishoprics left, and Christians represented only 10 to 15 percent of the population (see Jenkins 2008, 23–24). It is estimated that the total number of Asian Christians decreased from around 21 million in 1200 to 3.4 million in 1500; and over the same period "the proportion of the world's Christians living in Africa and Asia combined fell from 34 percent to just 6 percent" (ibid., 24). "After fifteen hundred years the Christian movement thus found itself in a rather lopsided situation. The majority of the world's Christians resided in the European West" (Irvin and Sunquist 2001, 504). However, we must remember that Christian kings ruled in Ethiopia and Russia, the Indian communities of Saint Thomas Christians were growing, and occasional spiritual renewal and/or mission movements reenergized and challenged Christianity. We now examine the development of the six threads of tradition during these four-and-a-half centuries.

Threads of Christian Tradition

Scripture

The reforms within monasticism during the eleventh and twelfth centuries in the Latin West revived the monastic allegorical approach toward the Bible. Bernard of Clairvaux of the Cistercians "brought the tradition of monastic biblical interpretation to its high point" (González 1994, 96). While he did attend to the literal and historical meaning of the scriptures, the main purpose for reading the Bible was spiritual—to assist persons in their yearning for union with Christ. Bernard and those who followed him likewise read the Old Testament allegorically, "in such a way as to find Christ in every single page" (ibid.). Another way of interpreting the Bible emerged in the twelfth and thirteenth centuries in the newly developing cathedral schools and universities. While there had not been many theological controversies in the previous time period, scripture was now used again to settle intellectual disputes, as it had been in the fourth and fifth centuries, by developing the literal historical approach of Antioch described in Chapter 2. "One could say that while traditional monasticism read the Bible in quest of wisdom, the scholastics [of the cathedral schools and universities] read it in quest of knowledge" (ibid., 97).

The cathedral schools returned to the ninth-century practice of developing glosses of the scriptures—writing bits of information on the meaning of the texts from earlier writers in the margins and between the lines of the verses of scripture and sometimes adding original comments. In the early twelfth century Anselm of Laon produced a gloss of the entire Bible. This became known as the *Glossa ordinaria* and was used as a standard reference tool. Peter Lombard compiled an excellent work, *Magna glosatura*, on the Pauline material and the psalter. He also further developed the methodology of disputation in teaching—whereby study was done by addressing questions from the biblical text—by arranging the questions in a systematic theological format in his famous four-volume work, *Sentences*.

The masters of the cathedral schools wrote scriptural commentaries based primarily on the glosses that with time offered standard interpretations. The commentaries "were generally intended as an aid to preaching and teaching; therefore, their tone is often homiletical and hortatory" (González 1994, 97). One of the main challenges facing these authors was addressing the conflict between the literal and spiritual methods and goals of biblical interpretation. "On the one hand, the 'literal' sense must govern all interpretation and must never be ignored, while, on the other hand, the 'spiritual' was considered to be more valuable, for it dealt with permanent truth rather than with transitory events or things" (ibid., 98). Hugh of St. Victor Abbey near Paris represents one of the best early efforts to revive interest in the literal-historical sense and to bridge the gap between the two approaches. This involved studying the Old Testament in Hebrew and consulting with Jewish scholars (see Rogerson et al., 67).

The study and use of scripture received new attention when people during the popular movements searched for the *vita apostolica* (evangelical life). The Waldensians and Cathars centered their lives and worship on the Bible. Francis of Assisi was against scholastic efforts and in favor of a simple understanding of the scriptures, but Franciscans later went to universities to seek education for their penitential preaching. On the other hand, Dominicans from the beginning considered systematic theological education necessary for doctrinal preaching and were quickly drawn to the universities. Two major developments in biblical study occurred through the mendicant orders. First of all, interest in the literal-historical sense and the demands for preaching led to the desire for more information and the compilation of dictionaries and concordances of words from scripture. Second, the challenge of interpreting the Bible was aided by the return of Aristotelian works to the West through the Latin translations of the Arabic versions that had preserved Aristotle's thought.

Two Dominicans were key figures in the area of biblical studies: Albert the Great, who studied Aristotle and "insisted on the importance of the literal sense in order to establish the intention of the author" (Rogerson et al., 287); and Thomas Aquinas, who addressed the above-stated challenge of the relationship of the literal and spiritual meanings of the Bible by maintaining that a proper understanding of the former is necessary for an appropriate use of the latter. The literal sense is the full original meaning of the author, while the spiritual sense is an interpretation of the further unfolding of the meaning of God's message through history. For Aquinas, the use of scripture to find the spiritual meaning "is quite legitimate and even necessary, for without it the text would remain in the past, and not directly apply to different circumstances." But at the same time, "only the 'literal' meaning has final authority, in the sense that it requires acceptance by all and can thus serve as the basis for theological argument" (González 1994, 98). Aquinas and other scholastic academics used scripture as proof texts in theological debates through the exercise of disputation (*disputatio*), mentioned above. Philosophy would replace the Bible as the foundation, or handmaid, of theology in the West.

In contrast, the Franciscan scholar Bonaventure of Bagnoregio considered scripture the primary authority for theology. He used Platonic philosophy and the allegorical method to draw symbols of the faith from the Bible. He did this based on the understanding that "God is known by love rather than by reason, so that the purpose of Scripture is to open the mind to the mystical knowledge of God rather than to form the basis of a process of logical deduction" (Rogerson et al., 288). The Franciscans were concerned primarily with the spiritual renewal of the common people, and the Dominicans with heresy and defense of church teaching. Another Franciscan biblical scholar, Nicholas of Lyra, drew heavily upon Hebrew scholarship, particularly of Rashi, for his work on the Old Testament, and his widely accepted commentary on the entire bible would become the first one printed. Martin Luther's extensive use of this commentary was expressed in the common phrase *Si Lyra non Lyrasset, Luther non saltasset* (Had Lyra not played, Luther could not have danced).

Cistercian Joachim of Fiore divided salvation history into the three ages of the Father, the Son, and the Holy Spirit, and in the final stage the church of the hierarchy, sacraments, and law would be replaced by a "spiritual church." This vision later influenced the Spirituals, a group of Franciscans calling for a stricter observance of Francis's ideals. Although Joachim's apocalyptic message and use of scripture, especially the book of Revelation, had a popular following, it did not affect scholarly endeavors. "But it marks an important departure in the history of biblical exegesis, because the biblical text was made to signify, not the teaching of the Church as already universally accepted, but supposed future events with implicit criticism of the Church in its present state" (Rogerson et al., 289).

In terms of church reform and scripture, we move to the important figure of John Wycliffe in the fourteenth century. In response to the church's state of corruption and crisis, Wycliffe's call for renewal was based upon the primacy of scripture and upon the belief that every person can find salvation in the gospel, that is, without the necessity of the church as a mediator. This highlighted the importance of a vernacular translation of the scripture. Wycliffe organized the first translation of the entire Bible into English for the common people. A revised version of Wycliffe's Bible became very popular among those who were loyal to the church and those who were in favor of reform. However, Wycliffe and his followers faced strong official opposition. Two centuries earlier the Waldensians, who had French translations of scripture and promoted Bible study among common people, had also been banned by the church. The visions of Wycliffe and Waldo of Lyons were precursors of what would emerge during the reformations (covered in the next chapter). It is interesting to note that parts of scripture were also translated into Dutch with the bishop's approval in the early fifteenth century to serve lay Roman Catholic communities known as the Brothers and Sisters of the Common Life (see Bellitto, 171–72).

There was fear in the Latin West that the popular use of vernacular translations of the Bible, unaccompanied by proper instruction, could too easily lead to heresy. In contrast, new translations were appearing in Asia. East Syrian monks had translated scripture and other religious writings into the Uighur language using the famous Sogdian script (Irvin and Sunquist 2001, 452), and Franciscan John of Monte Corvino translated the New Testament and psalter into the language of the Ongut Turks. The Ethiopian Bible in Ge'ez also underwent a thorough revision in the fourteenth century (see Norris 2002, 134).

Liturgy, Sacraments, and Art

In terms of liturgy, the theological discussion of the real presence of Christ in the Eucharist, which initially surfaced in the ninth century, received much attention during the Late Middle Ages. To a great extent, this was in response to the Cathars, who taught that everything in the material realm, including the Eucharist and other sacraments, was evil. The term *transubstantiation* was officially used for the first time at the Fourth Lateran Council in 1215 "as a strong assertion of the saving presence of the Lord in the Eucharist in opposition to the anti-materialistic claims of the Cathars" (Macy, 103).

Later on, theologians attempted to provide a more precise explanation of transubstantiation. Drawing upon the rediscovered philosophy of Aristotle, Thomas Aquinas used the philosophical concepts of "accidents" (the characteristics of a thing that can be perceived by the senses) and "substance" (the essence of a thing, which cannot be perceived by the senses). With this understanding Aquinas and others proposed that before the consecration the accident of the bread was a certain kind of bread and the substance was bread, but after the consecration the substance was the Body of Christ while the accident remained the same. Aquinas's formulation was not fully consistent with Aristotle's philosophy, and he realized that there were weaknesses in this theological proposal, but he was striving to talk about a divine mystery in human terms. "Transubstantiation was a faith explanation, not a logical proof of Christ's eucharistic presence" (Foley, 230). An alternative explanation was given by Franciscan theologians Alexander of Hales and Bonaventure, as well as others. Rather than starting with philosophy, they maintained that the Eucharist was fundamentally a sacrament or symbol. Although *transubstantiation* was accepted by most theologians by the end of the fifteenth century as the term to describe the change that occurs during the Eucharist, it "does not mean, however, that all theologians understood transubstantiation in the same way" (Macy, 141).

While the active debate on the real presence of Christ in the Eucharist was happening in the cathedral schools and universities on the academic level, a different understanding of the Eucharist was developing on the popular level. The celebration of the feast of Corpus Christi (Body and Blood of Christ) started in France with the strong endorsement of the Beguine Juliana of Cornillon and received papal approval in the thirteenth century. A public procession of the consecrated host enhanced the feast in the fourteenth century. This was a spiritual experience of being in union with Christ, and it also pointed to the growing belief that just seeing the Eucharist, whether during a procession or the elevation of the host during mass, was already an opportunity for blessing. The Fourth Lateran Council required Catholics to receive communion at least once a year, especially during the Easter season. Also, the congregation was no longer allowed to share from the cup.

Christ's presence in the Eucharist began to be understood in terms of "flesh and blood," even in a literal sense with miracle stories of bleeding hosts. Foley points out that "such stories were so popular and powerful in the medieval mind . . . [because they] resonated with the Germanized imagination that was prone toward the physical and had a penchant for . . . a 'magico-religious' interpretation of sacraments" (231). Another illustration of this was the popular belief that attending ("hearing") mass—whether or not one received communion—not only had spiritual benefits ("fruits"), but also magical ones, in that one would not age or suffer sudden death on that day and one's house or barn would not be struck by lightning (see Foley, 234).

The practice of giving stipends to have masses celebrated for the dead increased significantly at this time due to the spread of church preaching and popular understanding regarding purgatory. Also, the fourteenth century epic poem *Divine Comedy* by Dante Alighieri provided intriguing and popular depictions of purgatory. Some people left significant amounts of money for masses to be celebrated after their death in order to avoid longer time in purgatory, and consequently some priests dedicated all their time celebrating masses for such purposes. Some theologians and bishops and the Lateran Council spoke out against the problems that were often the consequences of such practices. Such abuses will be strongly criticized and the concept of transubstantiation will be disputed during the reformations of the sixteenth century. This is already anticipated in the Middle Ages by Wycliffe and Hus, who were critical of any eucharistic theology and practice they considered nonbiblical and/or contrary to the true heart of Christian faith.

The introduction of the Latin Roman rite among non-Latin-speaking communities and the growing marginalization of the laity from active eucharistic participation "provided a climate appropriate for the development of prayer books for lay use during and outside the Eucharist" (Foley, 216). These books contained psalms, litanies, offices of the dead, meditations, and/or allegorical interpretations of the mass. For example, the *Lay Folks Mass Book* appeared in France in the twelfth century and later was translated into other languages (see ibid., 216–17).

There were two developments regarding religious music in the Latin West. First, choirs assumed the prominent role for singing liturgical music in Latin, and wonderful musical compositions were written for them during this time period. Second, while the role of worshippers decreased in singing the official parts of the mass, new religious music composed in vernacular languages was often sung during processions, pilgrimages, and town fairs, and after sermons, which were normally in the vernacular. Also, the singing of congregational refrains in Italian was "closely connected to the preaching of Franciscans and other penitent groups . . . [and] in special services of the laypeople who formed confraternities" (Foley, 208).

In "Controversy, Crisis, and Crusades in Christendom" and "Byzantium, Russia, and the Greek East," we pointed out how the imposition of the Latin rite on Greek East Christians, and vice versa, throughout this period of 1000–1453 was an expression and tool of political and cultural rivalries. In terms of the liturgy itself, outside of the obvious language difference, the Latin West omitted the "alleluia" during Lent and used unleavened bread, while the Greek East kept the "alleluia" throughout the liturgical season and used leavened bread. The Latin rite also forcibly replaced the Old Spanish liturgy in some areas of the Iberian Peninsula that were freed of Muslim rule. It is interesting that the Franciscan John of Monte Corvino celebrated the Eucharist in the Ongut Turk language, not in Latin, in the eastern part of Asia (see Bevans and Schroeder 2004, 151–52).

The East Syrians were continuing their practice of celebrating liturgy in Syriac and other languages across Asia. For example, the traditional East Syriac psalter was used in three or four daily religious services in nonmonastic communities and traditionally seven times a day within monastic communities (Tang and Winkler, 362). The psalter was also in the Pahlavi (Middle Persian), Sogdian, and New Persian languages and the Uighur script (ibid., 363).

In the Latin West theologian Peter Lombard accepted the opinion that there were seven sacraments. They were defined in terms of matter and form, that is, the materials or gestures used, and the spoken words or their meaning. For example, the necessary matter of baptism was the water poured or bathed in, and the form was the trinitarian formula. By the fourteenth century infant baptism was the norm, and infants were to be baptized by the pouring of water within a week of birth to avoid the possibility of dying in the state of original sin. Baptisms were no longer done during the Easter vigil although the font and water were blessed at that time. By the thirteenth century, confirmation as a distinct sacrament was administered by bishops throughout Europe, except in Milan and some dioceses in Spain (see Martos, 222). Children normally received the Eucharist for the first time between the ages of seven and twelve.

Private confession became an official sacrament of repentance or penance in the Latin West, and the Fourth Lateran Council declared that Roman Catholics were to receive this sacrament and communion at least once a year. Some penitents were allowed to make a financial payment instead of doing the prescribed penitential act, which opened the door for abuse, which will be addressed in the sixteenth century. The related issue of indulgences will be treated under "Spiritual, Religious, and Social Movements" below. Anointing became more focused on forgiveness of sins than physical healing, and it was usually done before death. It became known as the last anointing, or extreme unction. Marriage was recognized as a sacrament in the Latin West, and the Christian wedding ceremony went through a very significant development in the Middle Ages. The elements in the ceremony "still largely mirrored the civil practices for legal reasons, but now they were imbued with religious significance and, indeed, sacramentality" (Bellitto, 145). The expression of free consent and the instruction by the priest were the only parts of the ceremony that were not done in Latin. Lastly, priesthood ordination was generally recognized as a sacrament by the end of the twelfth century.

Alternative understandings and practices of the sacraments in the Latin West included the following. The Waldensians celebrated both baptism and Eucharist. While rejecting sacraments in general, the Cathars had a baptism ritual without water, but with the laying on of hands, and instead of the Eucharist they "held a simple meal of bread and water that resembled those of other ancient ascetic communities" (Irvin and Sunquist 2001, 413). Wycliffe did not accept the concept of transubstantiation, but he did accept the practice of sacraments in general as meaningful for worship.

Shifting to art, the Romanesque church architecture—with massive thick walls, small windows, and heavy "barrel" vaults and arches—spread around Europe in the eleventh and twelfth centuries. However, in the twelfth century a new Gothic style emerged with lightweight masonry, pointed arches, ribbed vaults, flying buttresses, and stained-glass windows. In terms of liturgy and ecclesiology, "Romanesque churches often appeared more as 'strongholds' against the outside world [while] Gothic churches . . . through their open structures radiated a divine presence to the surrounding environment that was shaped around the cathedral" (Foley, 194). "The cathedrals themselves with their high ceilings and amazing vaults and stained glass . . . put Christians in touch with their God" (Norris 2002, 119). At the same time, the architecture also reflected the shifting role of the congregation in the liturgy toward viewing rather than responding and participating; "ordinarily believers were kept at a distance from the sacred action of the priest" (Foley, 201).

Ministry and Organization

In Chapter 3 we saw that the church in the Latin West at the end of the first millennium had become quite ensnared within its political and economic context. Attempts at church renewal initially came through the Cluny Reform and other monastic movements, and then through the papacy. In the tenth century political factions in Rome competed in the process of selecting the pope, and lay leaders appointed bishops and priests in Europe. In response, a strong institutional papacy developed during the eleventh and twelfth centuries, providing the church the means to free itself from much of this political control and interference. The Gregorian reform, under the leadership of Pope Gregory VII (1073–1085), together with several of his immediate predecessors and successors, strove to address this situation through the Investiture Controversy, described earlier, and to improve the quality of clerical ministers and pastoral care. Another change at this time was with the College of Cardinals. The cardinals—bishops, priests, and deacons—had been a body of Roman-based advisers to the pope. In the eleventh century Pope Leo IX began appointing cardinals from other geographical areas, and later Pope Nicholas II gave the cardinal bishops not political powers but the right to elect the pope, with the other cardinals and the clergy of Rome providing their assent, and to act as an advisory council to the pope on important issues.

Externally, the growing authority of the popes in European society was manifested in their ability to call multiple crusades both to the Holy Land and in Europe. Internally, with the growing centralization of the institutional church, the ecclesial bureaucracy (*curia*) doubled in size during this time, and eventually the Inquisition system was introduced to safeguard the church from what were perceived as heresies and internal threats. In the twelfth century the Italian jurist Gratian compiled and classified four thousand canonical rulings into a single set of canon law, which would become the standard for the Roman Catholic Church until 1917.

After a period of 250 years with no ecumenical councils, four were held at the pope's residence in the Lateran over a period of less than a hundred years, from 1123 to 1215. These were the first ecumenical councils in the West. The Lateran councils stipulated reforms of ordained ministry, such as the appropriate selection and education of clerics, and the prohibition of ordained persons from managing property, serving in the army, or accepting money for sacraments. The councils also established the requirement of priestly celibacy, marking the official end of married priesthood in the Latin rite of the Catholic Church, even though some still violated this church law until the Council of Trent. As for the understanding and practice of the priestly ministry in the Middle Ages, "it was the priests who were the primary mediators between God and humankind in almost every aspect of Christian life. . . . But their priesthood was conceived almost entirely in terms of sacramental, liturgical, cultic ministry" (Martos, 503). The role of bishops was primarily seen in terms of church administration.

While this was a time when hierarchical thinking strongly influenced church organization and ministry and the gap between laity and clerics was growing, as noted in the liturgical developments earlier, "a vibrant laity was involved in apostolic acts, confraternities, pilgrimages, religious festivals, and a wide range of other activities" (Bellitto, 36). The underlying motivation and dynamic of this spiritual and ministerial renewal were described earlier in the "Spiritual Renewal in the Latin West" section as a search for the evangelical life. Furthermore, the various movements—characterized by voluntary poverty, itinerant preaching, and the desire for spiritual/moral betterment—represented a strong call for church reform, primarily from the laity. In this way they were all responding to the message of Francis of Assisi to "repair my church." In terms of persons officially recognized as canonized saints during the Middle Ages, "the number of clerical saints dropped while the relative percentage of lay saints rose" (ibid., 38).

In contrast to the institutional attempts at church reform initiated by popes, bishops, and councils, the "popular" reform (and ministerial) movements provided the opportunity for many women to participate. Clare of Assisi developed a new model of cloistered life; the Beguine community was an alternative model of ministry for women; thousands of women were part of the penitent and Third Order movements; Waldensian women preached in public; the outstanding example of Elizabeth of Hungary inspired other women, who founded women's communities dedicated to hospital ministry; some women were also recognized as mystics, healers, and miracle workers.

The fourteenth century was a period of renewed conflict between the pope and the French king over issues of spiritual and temporal authority. In addition, due to political instability in central Italy and the church's desire for French economic and military support, the papacy was moved to Avignon in southern France for about seventy years. Although Avignon was within the boundaries of the papal states, "for all intents and purposes it put the pope within the sphere of French political influence" (Irvin and Sunquist 2001, 481). The papal curia expanded in size and in wealth. The mystic Catherine of Siena, having served as a peacemaker between feuding city-states, played a significant role in persuading Pope Gregory XI to return the papacy to Rome in 1377.

After Gregory's death the next year, a situation known as the Great Western Schism arose whereby there were two popes and two colleges of cardinals, with the French supporting one and the English and Germans behind the other. The Council of Pisa in 1409, rather than clarifying the situation, added a third pope into the picture. The Council of Constance (1414–1418) finally resolved the situation by deposing all three popes and electing Martin V as the sole pope. This council also gave voice to an idea already circulating in the West for some time, particularly in the renowned University of Paris, called conciliarism—by which a general council, independent of the pope, had more authority than an individual pope. This was a more common understanding in the Greek East. Without denying the specific merit of the Council of Constance in resolving the papal schism, the general principle of conciliarism would not be accepted in the West. The Council of Basel-Ferrara-Florence-Rome (1431–1445) reaffirmed papal authority and prestige. Looking ahead, the accepted principle of collegiality as held in the twentieth century was that an ecumenical council in union with the pope has the highest teaching authority.

Returning to the Middle Ages, the now unified papacy and the institutional church would still be caught in the webs of corruption, power, and wealth. Reformer John Wycliffe "opposed what he saw to be excesses of papal power and wealth, and advocated clerical poverty," and reformer John Hus argued that "because of the papal schism, all claimants to the papal throne were unworthy" (Irvin and Sunquist 2001, 488–89). More radical calls for church reform will appear in the time period of the next chapter.

It is interesting to note that while the Latin West was concerned about the training of priests, the Saint Thomas Christians of India had developed a Malpanate system as an adaptation from the Hindu guru-disciple model, whereby prospective candidates for priesthood would live with and learn from an elderly and experienced priest, who taught them such subjects as scripture, liturgy, and Syriac (see Anathil, 27–29). The young clerics, who normally were married men, studied for a parish and not for a diocese, and the community was responsible for their training. This will change with the arrival of the Portuguese in the sixteenth century. In terms of church structure, the East Syrian patriarch of Persia continued to appoint the Metropolitan bishop in India, but an Indian archdeacon, as the right hand of the bishop, supervised the daily functioning of the church. Archdeacons in the Latin, Byzantine, and other rites did not have such authority.

The last area of church organization to be treated here is the relationship among the various streams of Christianity. First of all, in the twelfth century the Maronites in Lebanon, who were introduced in the last chapter, formally affirmed their union with Rome, which they never considered to be in doubt. Their patriarch attended the Fourth Lateran Council in 1215. The Maronite Catholic Church is considered today an Eastern rite Catholic community with Antiochene origin.

Second, we know from the historical section of this chapter that the East Syrian monk-bishop Rabban Sauma had visited Rome as part of his diplomatic mission on behalf of the Mongol Empire in the thirteenth century. During his first visit to Rome, Bishop Sauma was welcomed by the cardinals since the pope had just died. He then went to Paris to meet with the French king. Upon his return to Rome, Sauma had a very interesting encounter with the newly elected pope, Nicholas IV. The East Syrian bishop presided over the Eucharist in the Syriac rite; the western observers acknowledged the similarity with their own rite. Sauma received the sacraments of confession and the Eucharist from the pope. "The entire tone of the narrative is one of respectfulness and even excitement as the two ecclesiastical traditions encountered one another" (Irvin and Sunquist 2001, 463). A few years later the East Syrian patriarch wrote that "the patriarch of Rome (the pope) had the place of honor among all the patriarchs of the Christian world" (Bevans 2009, 257). Around this same time, Bar Hebreus, as the *maphrian* or leader of the Jacobite (West Syrian) Church, "made contact with the East Syrian patriarch Denha and sought to resolve disputes between the two churches in order to present a united witness before the Mongol ilkhan" (ibid., 464).

Third, about 150 years later the participants of the Council of Basel-Ferrara-Florence-Rome, intending to mend the break between the Latin West and the Greek East, agreed upon a "Decree of Union." Invitations to consider this union were also extended to Coptic, Ethiopian, and Jacobite churches. While there was some ecumenical openness and promise, the council's goal would not be attained. The "Decree of Union" was "dictated almost entirely by Latin theological interests and concerns" (Irvin and Sunquist 2001, 486). The patriarchs of Alexandria, Antioch, and Jerusalem rejected the council's decisions in 1443, and Constantinople fell to the Ottoman Turks ten years later.

Spiritual, Religious, and Social Movements

The spiritual and religious renewal of monasticism in the Latin West had begun with the Cluny reform of Benedictine life in the tenth century and by the mid-twelfth century there were one thousand Cluniac monasteries. Male and female communities of Carthusians and Cistercians, founded in the eleventh and twelfth centuries, continued the process of monastic renewal, and their houses quickly grew in number. The Cistercian abbot Bernard of Clairvaux was a prominent spiritual leader and writer. The next step in religious renewal came with the foundations of Canons and Canonesses Regular, which integrated clerical reform, contemplative-monastic observance, and a more active spirituality of service. "Many of the new communities of men and women ministered to the poor, nursed the sick, or cared for pilgrims" (Sheldrake, 75). A notable example, Norbert of Xanten, who was a friend of Bernard of Clairvaux, founded the Canons Regular of Prémontré, known today as Premonstratensians or Norbertines. A Second Order of nuns and later a Third Order of laypeople are also associated with the Norbertines.

This shift in the development of orders outside the strictly contemplative models emerged within a wider context. An evangelical awakening had begun stirring on the grassroots level—a spiritual search for the *vita apostolica* (evangelical life) beginning with the gospel and not the institutional church. Many Christians were "hungering for something that they didn't find in the church, which was often corrupted by power, wealth, clericalism and militarism" (Bevans and Schroeder 2004, 140). This spirit of change was very much influenced by contemporary social movements—the growth of the economy, cities and universities. The growing literate merchant class in the urban areas "partly explains the proliferation of new forms of Christian life and diverse spiritual practices outside the traditional (largely rural) monastic cloister" (Sheldrake, 77), and "the university in the city was an institution that acted as a bearer of religious life and spirituality for the Western world" (ibid., 82).

A wide variety of religious and spiritual renewal movements surfaced during this evangelical renewal. They were often characterized by voluntary poverty, itinerant preaching, and calls for spiritual and moral change. A number of the most significant movements were described in the "Spiritual Renewal in the Latin West" section earlier—Waldensians, Cathars, Franciscans, Dominicans, Third Orders, and Beguines. Reading scripture was central for the spiritual life of the Waldensians and worship for the Cathars. The mendicant orders of the Franciscans and Dominicans, in their many forms, replaced Benedictine monasticism as the prominent form of religious life in the Latin West. Additional mendicant orders founded in the thirteenth century were the Carmelites, Augustinians, and the Servites. Clare of Assisi developed a renewed version of women's cloistered communities (see Bevans and Schroeder 2004, 144–46). The Third Orders and the Beguine movement were radically new forms of Christian spirituality and life for the laity, especially for women. Later in the fourteenth and fifteenth centuries federations and congregations of women developed as Third Order Regulars of Franciscan Sisters, who combined semi-cloistered life and intentional apostolic activity. "These developments were among the first to break new ground in the transition from what was considered 'secular' to 'religious'" (ibid., 149).

Another spiritual and religious movement, which became known as *devotio moderna* (modern devotion), traces its origins to a Dutch deacon named Gerard Groote in the fourteenth century. After a conversion experience he critiqued clerical materialism, endorsed a Christ-centered discipline, and supported church reform. Some women and men established lay communities known as Brothers and Sisters of the Common Life "to balance prayer life, spirituality, work, and family" (Bellitto, 171). "Groote emphasized scripture as the basis of a person-centered educational method, the importance of individual moral formation, and the inculcation of a strong sense of community" (Sheldrake, 108). Of the many literary works written by members of this spirituality, the most well-known until today is the *Imitation of Christ*, attributed to Thomas à Kempis. The evangelical piety of this movement will have a significant influence during the period of reformations, particularly within Protestant Pietism.

"One of the most striking elements of Western spirituality in the period of 1150–1450 was the rise of devotions, and a devotional mentality" (Sheldrake, 98). With growing literacy rates among lay urban Christians, there was a significant increase in the production of handbooks of prayers, books for spiritual guidance, structured meditations on the life of Christ, and collections of the lives of saints. Devotional spirituality was expressed through pilgrimages (for example, the Holy Land, Rome, Compostella, and Canterbury), processions (such as the feast of Corpus Christi), veneration of religious statues or icons, visits to shrines with the relics of saints, and attendance at religious dramas (such as English mystery plays). Other devotional practices that were introduced at this time included the Christmas crib, the Rosary, and the Stations of the Cross. Except for commemorating the saints and martyrs, which had existed since the early years of Christianity, these devotions reflected a growing focus on the humanity of Christ, and they "expanded into an emphasis on the suffering and Passion, on devotion to Mary, the source of Christ's humanity, and on liturgical and mystical devotion to the Eucharist" (ibid., 99).

Another practice that influenced popular spirituality was indulgences. Before this time indulgences were related to shortening designated penances a person was to do before death. However, popes in the Middle Ages declared that crusaders, and later those who financially supported the crusades, could receive a "plenary" or full indulgence, that is, freedom from punishment after death for sins that were confessed. This was based on an understanding that the pope and bishops could dispense indulgences from the church's "treasury of spiritual merits." While several theologians raised questions and concerns, the practice grew to the point that indulgences could be "earned" by performing certain spiritual devotions or by giving a financial donation to the church. Eventually, it was understood that indulgences could benefit the souls in purgatory. "Once this happened the popularity of indulgences increased even further: people could use them to shorten the temporal punishment of their relatives in purgatory, and bishops could use them to build and repair churches and monasteries, schools and hospitals" (Martos, 350). This system was vulnerable to much misunderstanding and abuse, and it will be critiqued and reformed during the reformations, to be treated in the next chapter.

While there was a proliferation of movements, devotions, and other spiritual practices on the popular level, there were a number of major mystical writers, the majority of whom were women. Hildegard of Bingen stood out in the twelfth century. She wrote not only in the area of mystical theology, but she also produced a nine-volume work in science and an important book on the history of pharmacy in the West. She founded a Benedictine monastery in Bingen, and "from there she undertook a number of 'preaching tours' of Europe, advocating both monastic and ecclesiastical reform" (Bevans 2009, 251). Of the many mystical writers in the fourteenth century, we mention a few. Catherine of Siena of the Dominican Third Order was known not only for persuading the pope to return to Rome from Avignon, but also for her spiritual visions and mystical writing. The Englishwoman Julian of Norwich received a number of revelations, including the maternal image of God in Christ's passion. The Beguine woman Mechthild of Magdeburg lived with fellow mystics and women of great learning, Mechthild of Hackeborn and Gertrude of Helfta, in the same Cistercian monastery. The German Dominican Meister Eckhart through his teaching and preaching attempted to foster within people an inner spiritual experience of God. He was one of the first theologians to write in German.

Turning our attention outside of the Latin West, we return to the form of meditation in the Greek East called hesychasm (holy silence). In the fourteenth century a monk from the monastery of Mount Sinai was spreading a teaching about particular meditation techniques. A controversy regarding hesychasm arose, "provoked in part by the exaggerated language used of experiences of union with God" by some monks of Mount Athos (Sheldrake, 100). Mystical theologian Gregory Palamas very ably defended hesychasm in a council held in Constantinople in 1341. As a point of comparison, the Greek East spirituality of hesychasm had a very positive view of the body as a tool in prayer, in contrast to the negative view in the West. Also, the practices of hesychasm provided a degree of cohesion and unity for the Greek East as the Byzantine Empire was disappearing. "After the fifteenth century the unity of the Eastern Orthodox world rested on a common spirituality more than it did on imperial politics or ecclesiastical institutions" (Irvin and Sunquist 2001, 499). As a final note, the religious significance of the Solomonic Revival in Ethiopia was described in the "Historical Context" section above; it also included a renewed interest in the traditional Ethiopian Christian devotion to Mary that in the fourteenth century was "identified with monastic resistance against corrupt Ethiopian kings and clergy" (Irvin and Sunquist 2001, 475).

Theological Developments

While theology in the Latin West had basically been in the state of preservation from 600 to 1000, the Middle Ages was a time of creativity. A pioneer of such theology was Anselm of Canterbury of the eleventh century. He is important for understanding that theology involves both faith and reason, for formulating the "ontological proof" of the existence of God, and most significantly, for developing the "satisfaction theory" of redemption, by which God was incarnated to satisfy the grave offense of Adam and Eve. By drawing upon medieval feudal culture and its understanding of law, "this argument became a source of significant penetration of the gospel among the Frankish people" (Norris 2002, 103). Anselm's work on the incarnation, *Cur Deus Homo (Why God Became Human)*, is still considered a theological classic. However, some of his contemporary theologians didn't accept this formulation. In particular, Peter Abelard proposed the "exemplar theory" of redemption, whereby people can be redeemed if they change and accept the love of God as shown in the prime example of the cross. Furthermore, in *Sic et Non (Yes and No)*, Abelard "demonstrated not just the validity of reasoning in theological work but its *necessity*" (Bevans 2009, 243). He is partially responsible for developing the theological method of the *quaestio* (question), that is, after seriously examining and critiquing different opinions one can then propose one's own *sententia* (sentence). While Anselm and Abelard were doing theology in the schools or universities, Bernard of Clairvaux and Hugh and Richard of St. Victor Abbey are key examples of "monastic theologians" who opposed the use of dialectics and advocated that theology "could be done only out of wonder" (ibid.). One other notable theologian of the twelfth century was Peter Lombard, whose contribution to biblical studies and sacramental theology was noted earlier. His most important theological work was his *Four Books of Sentences* (opinions), which "was probably the most comprehensive and clearest treatment of the entire context of theology" in his time (ibid., 244).

As we enter the thirteenth century, "the stage is set in Europe for what is still considered one of the greatest periods in the history of theology, East or West" (Bevans 2009, 245), called high scholasticism. The major figures were members of the new mendicant communities. Dominican Albert the Great, in addition to his biblical and theological studies, was very influential due to his excellent commentaries on the works of Aristotle, recently translated and retrieved in the West from Arabic texts. His student and fellow Dominican Thomas Aquinas would be the one to elaborate on the importance of Aristotelianism for theology and to harmonize it with Christian faith. Aquinas's voluminous writings included philosophical works, scripture commentaries, sermons, poetry, and excellent systematic works, particularly the *Summa Theologiae* and *Summa Contra Gentiles*. He developed the *quaestio* method of theologizing more explicitly and was familiar with the work of Spanish-born Jewish philosopher Moses Maimonides and Iranian-born Muslim thinker Avicenna (Ibn Sina). "All in all, Aquinas was an extraordinary man and rightly called the era's most significant theologian, if not the most significant theologian in the church's history" (ibid., 246).

Aquinas's greatest contemporary was Bonaventure, who had studied under fellow Franciscan Alexander of Hales. Along with his biblical commentaries, Bonaventure's many writings included two biographies of Francis of Assisi, the classic spiritual work of *Journey of the Mind to God*, and a fine theological survey entitled *Breviloquium*. He was not as positive about the work of Aristotle as was Aquinas. "Bonaventure's theology was ultimately more contemplative, more Augustinian, and more in the 'monastic' style" (Bevans 2009, 248). Two other authors can be mentioned here as well. First, we earlier talked about the importance of Dante's *Divine Comedy* in terms of the idea of purgatory. In addition, the *Divine Comedy* "ranks, say some scholars, with Anselm's *Why God Became Human* and Aquinas' *Summa Theologiae*, as one of the three greatest works of theology in the Middle Ages in the West, and summarizes masterfully the moral, religious, and cosmological views of the entire age" (ibid., 249). It is important to note that Dante was greatly influenced by the writings of Aquinas and Bonaventure. Second, the name of the Third Order Dominican mystic Catherine of Siena reappears here. *The Dialogue*, her major work written in Italian, expresses the ideas of Aquinas on redemption in a more experiential way. She is one of four women to be named a doctor of the church (the others are Teresa of Avila, Thérèse of Lisieux, and Hildegard of Bingen).

Aquinas had a more positive attitude regarding the relationship of reason to faith than Bonaventure. This difference became more accentuated after their deaths between the Dominican school and the Franciscan school, to the point that Franciscans for a while were not allowed to even read Aquinas (Bevans 2009, 254). Two important Franciscan critics of Aquinas were John Duns Scotus and William of Ockham. The former held that humans could not know God at all with their mind only, and the latter rejected the use of reason for theology even more strongly. The theology of Ockham—characterized by a strong distrust of reason and an emphasis on scripture and faith only for salvation—will be developed later by Martin Luther.

"It is important not to give the impression that what was going on in theology in the twelfth and thirteenth centuries was simply an intellectual exercise" (Bevans 2009, 250–51). Many theologians included a mystical component in their theology—Bonaventure was very explicit in this regard, while Aquinas was more implicit. In addition, there were a number of theologians who wrote what we would call today mystical theology. A number of them were introduced in the preceding section on "Spiritual, Religious, and Social Movements": Hildegard of Bingen, Catherine of Siena, Julian of Norwich, Mechthild of Magdeburg, Mechthild of Hackeborn, Gertrude of Helfta, and Meister Eckhart. From a contemporary perspective, Bevans notes that the mystical theology of the Middle Ages "was for many centuries sidelined in the history of theology," but now "it is making a difference in the way that theology is done today" (ibid., 253–54).

Looking outside the Latin West, the theologians of the Greek East focused their energy on issues related to reunion and differences with the Latin West, while Gregory Palamas made a great contribution in resolving the hesychasm question. East Syrian theologian and Arabic Christian writer Elias of Nisibis was engaged in interreligious issues with Muslims, which will be treated in the following section. Several centuries later, eminent theologian and East Syrian patriarch Ebedjesu bar Berika wrote a number of works, including one on systematic theology, *Book of the Pearl on the Truth of Christian Doctrine*. While the theological writings among the Coptic Church were more about preservation than creativity, "it is important to note that theology was still being done in North Africa in the midst of Muslim rule" (Bevans 2009, 257). Another significant theologian in a predominantly Muslim context was Bar Hebreus (Gregory Abu'l Faraj) of the Jacobite (West Syrian) Church. His forty major works in the thirteenth century covered the areas of history, philosophy, theology, spirituality, and medicine. This is particularly impressive since he did this while also being the head of Jacobite Church. In the following century theologian Gregory of Datev defended the theology of the Armenian Church.

Mission, Cultures, and Religions

During this time period monasticism was replaced by the mendicant movement as the primary model of mission in the Latin West. The various movements emerging out of the search for the *vita apostolica*—Norbertines, penitents, Waldensians, Cathars, Beguines, and *devotio moderna*—represented important responses of mission, especially by laypeople. However, the pluriform Dominican and Franciscan movements played the prominent role.

The Dominicans emphasized scholarship, doctrinal preaching by clergy, and in general the *apostolica* aspect—that is, the apostolate dimension. On the other hand, the Franciscans emphasized martyrdom, penitential preaching by laity, and in general the *vita* aspect—that is, witnessing to and imitating Christ's passion through austere poverty. In Europe, the Dominicans attended to those considered marginal in terms of the faith, while the Franciscans attended to the wide strata of society, especially in urban areas. Outside Europe the Dominicans reached out to the Cumans, Prussians, and Greek East Christians, while the Franciscans attended to the Mongols, Lithuanians, and people in the Holy Land. The women in the Second Orders of both movements complemented the men through the prophetic witness of cloistered life. In addition, Dominican convents in Bavaria and Italy "developed the solid Dominican intellectual tradition" (Bevans and Schroeder 2004, 155), and Clare of Assisi insisted that the Poor Clares depend upon God's providence for daily needs rather than on endowments and patronage, and asserted that they are spiritually not recluses from the world, but rather that their life and prayer should include the needs of all people, especially the poor (see ibid., 145). The women and men of both Third Orders and confraternities from the "secular perspective" contributed to the holistic dimension of mission "in addressing the need for deepening and correcting the Christian faith in Europe, as well as responding to certain social and medical needs" (ibid., 158). Catherine of

Siena and Elizabeth of Hungary are two outstanding examples of women and precursors of members of Third Orders who shared in the mission of the mendicant movement.

In terms of the attitude toward other religions, the crusades reflect the general negative attitude and violent approach of Western Christians toward Muslims and Jews in Asia Minor and the Middle East. On the Iberian Peninsula, Muslims were expelled from areas reconquered by Christian forces, mosques became churches, and Muslim prisoners of war could be sold into slavery. Jews were likewise considered to be infidels, and many moved farther north into Europe. Violence against the Jews "became more frequent as their numbers grew in northern European cities" (Irvin and Sunquist 2001, 409–10). The Fourth Lateran Council stipulated that Jews and Muslims were to wear distinctive dress and were forbidden to hold public office. However, there was also a subaltern, more positive attitude toward other religions.

As "children of their time," both mendicant orders to some extent participated in crusade preaching, but in general they offered alternative approaches to Muslims, with the Franciscans following a more experiential approach of witness and example and the Dominicans a more rational intellectual-philosophical approach. As for the former, Francis set an example when he crossed the battle lines near the city of Damietta in Egypt and met with the pious sultan Al-Malik al-Kamil, who was already familiar with Christianity through his many Christian subjects who had a certain degree of autonomy and possibly representation in his court. After several days of conversation, the sultan granted Francis safe passage to the Holy Land. This experience shaped the two-pronged approach to mission that Francis included in the 1221 rule for the friars—Christian presence and witness or open and explicit proclamation. This is captured in the popular saying attributed to Francis, "Preach always, and, if necessary, use words."

Dominic likewise had an encounter that shaped the understanding of mission for himself and the Dominicans. After an all-night conversation with a Cathar, Dominic was able to convince him of the error of his thinking, and hereafter Dominic was convinced that the best way to approach someone considered a heretic or a person of another religion was through rational disputation. In the thirteenth century the Dominicans joined the intellectual and interreligious exchange in Spain, which had been occurring among fine Jewish and Muslim scholars, like Maimonides (Moses bin Maimon) and Averroes (Ibn Rushd) in the famous university in Córdoba. We pointed out earlier that Aquinas was influenced by Muslim and Jewish writers, and his work *Summa Contra Gentiles* "was itself a missionary treatise meant to help Dominicans in Spain explain their faith to Jews and Muslims" (Norris 2002,

130). The Dominicans, in order to engage and eventually convert Muslims and Jews, established schools in Spain for learning Arabic and Hebrew.

Ramón Llull, an outstanding person within this context, is considered "not only one of the greatest missionaries in Christian history but as perhaps the first theologian who reflected systematically on the church's mission" (Bevans 2009, 250). After some years of frivolity in court life, he experienced a deep Christian conversion and applied his academic talents toward mission to the Muslims. "Based on a belief that the conversion of non-Christians could be accomplished through reason and debate, one of his most famous works is a conversation about the gospel among a Christian, a Muslim and a Jew" (Bevans and Schroeder 2004, 151). Llull convinced the king of Aragon to assist in founding a school for training missionaries. He interacted with both the Dominicans and Franciscans, and eventually he became a Third Order Franciscan. In the early fourteenth century Llull was martyred on his third missionary trip to North Africa, at the age of eighty.

Several authors outside the Latin West who lived in Muslim-controlled areas also had a gentler approach toward Muslims. The East Syrian theologian Elias of Nisibis in the eleventh century maintained that Christians profess the same doctrine of monotheism as in the Qur'an. In the following century Paul of Antioch in letters to his Muslim friends quoted from the Qur'an in a favorable way as he upheld that "the central Christian doctrines of Trinity, incarnation, and union with God did not contradict Muslim conviction about the oneness of God" (Norris 2002, 112).

Interreligious relations were quite favorable in Asia before the turning point in 1295, as noted under "Christianity in Asia" above. Franciscan William of Rubruck, during his stay in the camp of the great khan Möngke, was invited to an interreligious debate including representatives of Muslims, Buddhists, Manicheans, and East Syrian and Latin West Christians. "The participants were enjoined on pain of death to show respect for one another's religions" (Irvin and Sunquist 2001, 458). On the following day the khan explained to Rubruck that "the Mongols believed in one God who had given different ways to various peoples like different fingers on one hand" and they "have been given a mission by God to unite the entire world under their laws" (ibid.). In terms of the interaction of Christians with other cultures, the East Syrians had adapted very much to Mongol culture—too much according to the perception of Rubruck from the West (see Norris 2002, 120–21). Some Franciscans around the year 1335 were accommodating to the Mongol nomad lifestyle. "Garbed in Mongol dress, they [Franciscans] traveled around with their portable altars and few possessions in wagons like those used by the pastoral nomads" (Bevans and Schroeder 2004, 152).

Conclusion

In this chapter on new political horizons we have seen how changing political situations greatly influenced Christianity everywhere, with the probable exception of the Saint Thomas Christians in southern India. Besides facing these external challenges, the church faced internal corruption, crisis, and controversy. At the same time, this was a period of much development in the threads of tradition. Several ways of interpreting scripture were expounded, and popular movements promoted the use and study of the Bible; creative advances were made in eucharistic theology, liturgical music, and church architecture; attempts for reform were made by popes, patriarchs, councils, monasteries, and the laity; evangelical renewal sparked the birth of new movements and devotional spirituality; monastic, scholastic, and mystical theology blossomed in the Latin West; itinerant preachers called for conversion of mind and heart; and there were occasional glimpses of peaceful interreligious interaction. However, within each of these threads were the seeds of future tension, abuse, and corruption, many of which will receive attention during the period of the reformations.

In Chapter 3 we saw that monasticism had a major influence on each of the threads during the period from 600 to 1000. During the period from 1000 to 1453 the women and men of the multiform mendicant movements had a significant impact on the developments in biblical interpretation, theology of the Eucharist, ministry, spiritual/religious renewal, Western theology, mission, and approaches to other religions.

At the end of the first millennium Christianity appeared to be a global religion—stretching from Scandinavia and Russia to the Sahara, from the Atlantic to the Pacific. It is estimated that there were over twenty million Asian Christians around the year 1200 (Jenkins 2008, 24). However, by the mid-fifteenth century, with the fall of Constantinople (present-day Istanbul) and the deep impact on Christians under Mongol and Muslim rules, the vast majority of Christians lived in Europe. This will begin to change as we move into the next time period with the initial spread of Christianity among the people of the Americas, Asia, and sub-Saharan Africa.

At the end of the study of a period during which the mendicant orders had a major influence, we close with an excerpt from the biography of Francis of Assisi written by Thomas of Celano.

> Then with great fervour of spirit and joy of mind he began to preach repentance to all, with simple words but largeness of heart edifying his hearers. For his word was like a blazing fire piercing through the inmost heart, and it filled the minds of all with wonder. (par. 23; Celano 1908)

5

Conquest, Reformation, and Indigenous Growth

ca. 1454 to ca. 1600

In 1454, Christianity found itself in a lopsided situation whereby the majority of Christians lived in Europe (see Map 6). Irvin and Sunquist refer to the next 150 years of the Christian movement as "two major transformations" (2012, 1–163). The first transformation is linked with Europe's conquests of new lands and peoples in Africa, America, and Asia. The Portuguese by 1482 built a fort at Elmina (in present-day Ghana) that temporarily housed enslaved Africans destined for overseas. The discovery made by Christopher Columbus in 1492 opened the door for Europe to enter America. In 1498, Vasco da Gama arrived in Kozhikode (or Calicut) in India, initiating a new phase in the history between the West and Asia. Some Christians raised empathetic voices on behalf of the conquered peoples. Many indigenous, particularly in America, became Christian. "Through these various colonial expansions, a major transformation of Christianity was under way, one that would take the rest of the modern era to complete" (ibid., 7).

The second major transformation of Christianity occurred within Europe through a number of reformations. In Germany, Martin Luther in 1517 posted ninety-five theses challenging many current church practices. Ulrich Zwingli called for reform in 1518 in Switzerland, and this was followed by others, most notably John Calvin. In 1534, the English parliament declared its monarch the head of the Church of England. Within a relatively short span of time, initial foundations were laid for Lutherans, Anabaptists, the "Reformed" faith, Anglicans, and Unitarians. The transformation due to these reforms represented "the internal fragmentation of the unified European church that had for so long provided its peoples with a common culture" (Irvin and Sunquist 2012, 71). The Roman Catholic Church also underwent its own reforms. Many Christians faced serious challenges within various

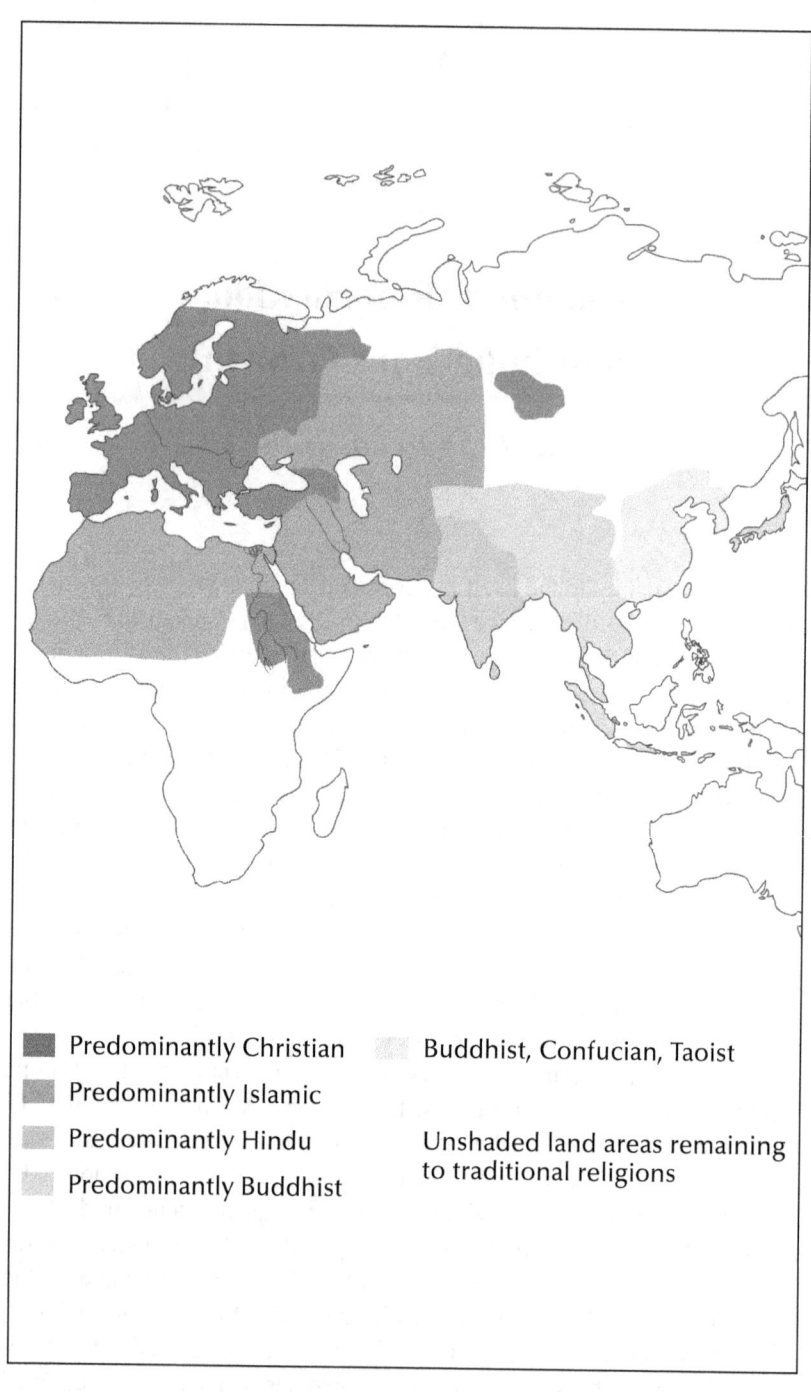

Map 6: Approximate boundaries of Eurasian religions in approximately 1450

Muslim empires, while the Orthodox Church continued to grow in Russia. The subtitle for this chapter, "ca. 1454 to ca. 1600," is taken from Frederick Norris's (2002) treatment of this general period: "Conquest, Reformation, and Indigenous Growth" (137–74).

Historical Context

America

The defeat of the Muslim forces in Granada in 1492 and the eventual expulsion from the Iberian Peninsula of the Muslims and Jews who refused to be baptized marked the end of the *reconquista* (reconquering) from Muslim rule that had existed for over 750 years. Then "Spain turned its crusading spirit toward the *conquista* of the 'pagans'—the 'new' peoples who were discovered by Columbus that same year" (Bevans and Schroeder 2004, 174). Columbus, following an apocalyptic vision, saw "himself as a powerful actor in God's global drama" (Norris 2002, 143).

Another event that added fuel to the fire of this conquest was the massive enslavement of sub-Saharan West African peoples. While slavery had existed in a variety of forms throughout human history, the "magnitude of this enslavement and forced movement of people makes it one of the worst tragedies in human history" (Bevans and Schroeder 2004, 173). The trade triangle consisted of (1) manufactured goods from Europe to Africa; (2) enslaved peoples from Africa to America (South, Central, and North); and (3) cotton, sugar, and tobacco from America back to Europe. Some estimate that over a 350-year period, ten to twelve million enslaved persons arrived in America; one or two million died in the "middle passage" across the Atlantic and possibly another twelve million even before getting on the ships, that is, during their capture and transport from their villages to the African coast or during their stay in Elmina or the other twenty Portuguese holding forts along the coast of West Africa. Furthermore, "the role that religion played in authorizing and sustaining it [slavery] poses a challenge to the very heart of the Christian movement" (Irvin and Sunquist 2012, 41). Slavery and Christianity influenced each other in America, Africa, and Europe.

When the Europeans arrived in the Caribbean and America in the fifteenth century, the large indigenous population south of the Rio Grande River (approximately 60–65 million people) was about 15 percent of the total world population. While many lived in tribal communities, there were two large urban civilizations—the Incas in Peru and the Aztecs in Mexico—and the former Mayan Empire still had a strong influence in what is now Central America. The smaller population of five to ten million peoples north of the Rio Grande did not live in such urban contexts but in smaller settlements and/or as nomadic people within a broad region.

With the two navigational powers of Spain and Portugal laying claims to the "new lands," after the "discoveries" of Columbus and then Pedro Álvares Cabral of Brazil, the pope drew a line from the North Pole to the South Pole to determine the domain of each in a ruling called the "Bulls of Donation." Out of a primary concern for mission, the pope also created a royal patronage (*patronatus*) arrangement, whereby these two Catholic nations were given the right and responsibility for bringing the Christian faith to the indigenous peoples, which included naming bishops and establishing dioceses. This C of Christianity was combined with the other two C's of commerce and civilization in the Christendom mindset. The conquistadores would announce the following statement, from the *Requerimiento* (requirement) document of 1510, to the indigenous either inaudibly or in a language they normally did not know: "Accept God, pope, and king, or suffer the consequences." The Europeans established an *encomienda* system of properties, whereby the settlers would have the responsibility to teach the faith to the indigenous on their land and the right to their labor. This was indentured labor at best and slavery at worst.

While most priests arriving on European ships followed the conquest mentality, many friars from the mendicant orders raised voices against it. On behalf of Dominicans on Hispaniola (present-day Dominican Republic and Haiti), Antón de Montesinos preached a sermon before Christmas of 1511 condemning the *encomienda* system and the inhumane treatment of the indigenous: "You are all in mortal sin! You live in it and die in it! Why? Because of the cruelty and tyranny you use with these innocent people" (Gutiérrez, 29). In response, the Spanish government the following year enacted the Burgos Laws, which became a key policy document upholding the *encomienda* structure and forbidding any appeal to the pope. Millions of indigenous died during these centuries of conquest due to armed conflict, hard labor, dietary changes, new sicknesses, and social disintegration. In some cases smallpox was deliberately given to them with blankets. The most extreme depopulation occurred on Hispaniola, and "in some areas of Mexico there seems to have been nearly a ninety percent decline in the indigenous tribes by the end of the sixteenth century" (Norris 2002, 143–44).

Bartolomé de Las Casas, who was a priest and owner of an *encomienda*, went through a major conversion of heart in 1514 after witnessing the cruel treatment of the people and hearing the protest by the Dominicans. Las Casas devoted over fifty years of his life to speaking and writing against the *encomienda* system on both sides of the Atlantic. He became known as the Defender of the Indians. He influenced the writing of *Sublimis Deus* by Pope Paul III in 1537 in defense of the indigenous and the promulgation of the "New Laws" (*Leyes Nuevas*) in 1542–1543 by King Charles V to address the major *encomienda* abuses. In America, Las Casas addressed these injustices as the bishop of Chiapas (in present-day Mexico).

The Society of Jesus (Jesuits), founded in 1540 by Ignatius of Loyola as part of the Catholic Reformation, was subject directly to the pope and therefore not officially under the *patronatus*. In order to separate the indigenous from the *encomienda* system, the Jesuits developed a plan initiated by some Dominicans and Franciscans to establish independent indigenous settlements, called reductions (*reducciones*), which were intended to promote what was considered the best of both cultures, such as the study of both Latin and the vernacular language.

In spite of the many aspects of violence in the conquest, the Amerindians "began to become Christian, undergoing baptism and seeking to follow what they considered to be Christian ways of life" (Irvin and Sunquist 2012, 250). Normally, a village or town had a church and a small community of friars at its center and included some European settler families and many indigenous. Several important regional church councils were convened in Lima (Peru) and Mexico to address particular aspects of sixteenth-century Christian life in America—such as sacraments, spirituality, organization, and culture.

A particular event that shaped Christianity in Mexico was the appearance of the Virgin of Guadalupe, La Morenita, with indigenous features and symbolism, to the peasant Juan Diego in 1531. In contrast to the dominant tabula rasa attitude toward non-Western cultures, this phenomenon became a lasting popular expression of the adaptation of indigenous spirituality and culture within Christian faith.

Africa

Around 1450, Islam was the prominent religion in North Africa, Egypt, and Nubia, and it had begun already in the thirteenth century to spread over trade routes by land as far as the Senegal River in West Africa and by sea as far as Mozambique in East Africa (see Irvin and Sunquist 2012, 35). In the fifteenth century Portugal began to establish its presence on the islands of Madeira and Cape Verde (off the northwest coast of Africa) and then in trading centers in Guinea and farther along the coast of West Africa. As mentioned above, the Portuguese initiated a slave trade with the existing local African kingdoms, which captured people for enslavement from neighboring kingdoms or tribes.

Farther south along the coast at the mouth of the Kongo River, the Portuguese and Christianity had a different type of encounter. Within ten years after the initial amicable cultural exchange in 1483, the Portuguese sent Franciscan friars, and King Nkuwu of Soyo, a client kingdom under the Kongo Kingdom, was baptized. Although he would later renounce his Christian faith, his son and successor, Afonso, kept it and strove to spread Christianity, unfortunately often with force. Out of his desire for an African clergy, Alfonso sent his son Henrique to Portugal to study for the priesthood and in 1520 he became the first sub-Saharan African bishop. With the death of Alfonso, the Soyo Kingdom weakened, but the Portuguese strengthened their political control in order to maintain the slave trade. Although the support of the church in Europe would eventually discontinue, missionaries of the new Capuchin order would find a Kongolese form of Christianity when they returned years later in 1645. The Portuguese established a neighboring colony in Angola, and the Jesuits followed by developing Christian villages there. The colonists also established a permanent settlement in Mozambique and a trading relationship with Zimbabwe.

In addition to this early phase of Christianity in sub-Saharan regions, Christianity developed in new ways among the enslaved Africans overseas. The slaves brought their West African religion as a resource to survive cruel conditions and they merged it with the Christianity they received. "The larger plantations often had a religious cult house, coexisting as a parallel religious expression with the prescribed Iberian Catholicism" (Irvin and Sunquist 2012, 45). Enslaved women and men had roles of leadership in terms of ritual and social organization. Some became leaders "of the first revolts by the enslaved that occurred in Colombia, Cuba, Haiti, and Brazil" (ibid.). Almost 40 percent of those brought across the Atlantic on slave ships were taken to Brazil.

Having described the newer faces of African Christianity, we turn to Ethiopia—the home of Christians who had experienced political support and religious freedom since the fourth and fifth centuries. In the fifteenth century they were feeling more constrained by the Muslim rule around them. However, over a period of thirty-five years the powerful Ethiopian emperor Zar'a Ya'iqob "reorganized the government, enforced a greater uniformity in religious belief and practices, and strengthened Ethiopia as an island Christian nation in the sea of Islam" (Irvin and Sunquist 2012, 46). In the sixteenth century the neighboring Muslim Kingdom of Adal (in present-day Somalia) defeated the Ethiopian forces and tens of thousands of Christians became Muslims. The Portuguese helped the Ethiopians to defeat the Muslims some fourteen years later. However, this collaboration led to ecclesiastical conflicts between two ancient churches. Portugal insisted on appointing a Latin patriarch in Ethiopia, and the Jesuits were assigned the task of bringing the Ethiopian Church under the authority of Rome. They did not have much success at the beginning, but Ethiopia would have to continue to engage European political and religious colonialism.

Asia

At the beginning of the fifteenth century the Chinese, who had been trading and migrating in Asia for centuries, were at the height of their overseas expeditions under the Ming Dynasty, extending their reach from Japan and Korea in the east to Arabia and Madagascar in the west. However, following the death of the Ming emperor in the 1420s, the Confucian *literati* (scholars) regained control and dismantled this external outreach from China. Muslim merchants, who had been establishing trading colonies by sea across Asia for centuries, were still active and had brought their trade and religion as far as Indonesia and the Philippines by 1500. In the sixteenth century a grandson of Tamerlane who ruled a small Muslim kingdom in Central Asia defeated the Muslim sultan of Delhi, signaling the beginning of the Mughal Empire that would extend from Afghanistan to central India. The Portuguese presence in Asia began with the arrivals of explorers Vasco da Gama in 1498 and Pedro Álvares Cabral a few years later in the port city of Kozhikode (Calicut) in southwest India. Within twenty years the Portuguese had taken control of key trading ports and the maritime trade routes in the Indian Ocean and were moving into the South China Sea. Like the Muslims, the Portuguese also carried their religion with them. Within this context "the modern histories of Africa and Asia were determined as much by matters of religious beliefs as they were by material economy and military might" (Irvin and Sunquist 2012, 55).

When the Portuguese landed in Kozhikode, they encountered the ancient Saint Thomas Christians, who at this time were "a small but important minority community of less than 100,000" (Irvin and Sunquist 2012, 55). They maintained their use of Syriac in liturgy and enjoyed religious toleration, economic prosperity, and caste social identity under the Hindu Vijayanagar Empire of South India. At first the Portuguese were welcomed as trade partners and liberators from Muslim control, but soon the Saint Thomas Christians and other Indians were irritated by the behavior of the soldiers and the aggressive colonial intentions of Portugal. Also, the Franciscan friars arriving on the ships were intent on shifting the affiliation of the Indian Christians from Baghdad (Chaldea) to Rome, similar to the pattern noted earlier for Ethiopia. Some of the Saint Thomas Christians joined the Roman Catholic Church, while others remained aligned with the East Syrian Church. A breaking point occurred at the Synod of Diamper in 1599 under the leadership of Portuguese Archbishop Aleixo de Menezes, who tried to force all Christians under Rome. Afterward, an inquisition was declared against those who refused, and Syriac documents and records were destroyed. "The issues that divided the two sides were always as much cultural and linguistic as they were theological" (ibid., 60). Within a different context, the Portuguese had captured the trading port of Goa (north of Kerala) from the Mughul Muslims, and a Portuguese Roman Catholic community, including a few Hindu and Muslim converts to the Christian faith, developed there.

In contrast to the conquest in America, the Portuguese in Asia developed unlinked coastal strongholds, there was no inland invasion, and there were very few settlers. At the same time, a number of the Asian peoples were organized in larger, unified political entities—such as India, China, and Japan—that could more successfully resist foreign invasion. In this way the work of the European missionaries was not shaped so much by the conquest when they got outside of the coastal Portuguese strongholds, like Kozhikode and Goa.

As seen in their reductions in America, the Jesuits demonstrated a more positive attitude toward human nature and culture. Francis Xavier was the first Jesuit to arrive in Asia. After six months in Goa, he traveled to the southeast Fishery Coast (in the present-day state of Tamil Nadu) to teach the Christian faith to peoples of a low caste who had been baptized by the Portuguese with little or no catechesis. During a short return to Goa he ministered to the marginalized and spoke against the immorality of the Portuguese. Xavier then traveled further east, teaching the faith in the port of Malacca (in present-day Malaysia) and on several islands of Indonesia. Dominicans, Franciscans, and other Jesuits baptized many in Flores, Timor, and other parts of Indonesia.

Through his acquaintance in Malacca with Yajiro, a Japanese refugee who later was baptized, Xavier decided to go with him to Japan. Buddhism had come to Japan from Korea in the seventh century and integrated itself with the indigenous religion of Shintoism. In the sixteenth century Japan was divided politically and religiously into rival kingdoms under local feudal-like lords (*daimyos*) with their *samurai* warriors, Buddhist abbots, and armies of monks. Due to the advice of Yajiro and his own positive experience of Japanese society, Xavier decided to focus on getting a favorable hearing among the *daimyos* and Buddhist monks, rather than the emperor or the common people, and to adapt the Christian message accordingly—a major shift from the tabula-rasa method. After twenty-seven months in Japan, Xavier had baptized about a thousand, including several *daimyos* and Buddhist monks. His intention to go next to China ended with his death on an uninhabited island off the Chinese coast in 1552.

Alessandro Valignano, the official Jesuit visitor for the Far East, came to Japan in the 1580s and played a key role in further developing the accommodational approach throughout Asia. The mission work of other Jesuits to spread the gospel message in the interior areas of China, Vietnam, India, and Japan will be treated in the next chapter.

While the Portuguese entered Asia from the west, the Spanish came from the east, using the basic conquest pattern of America. The Philippines, named after King Philip II of Spain, was an archipelago of seven thousand islands and many diverse tribal cultures. Muslims arrived there through trade in the tenth century. The Spanish explorer Ferdinand Magellan landed on the island of Cebu in 1521 with five ships. Magellan was killed when he and some soldiers got involved in a local conflict. A second Spanish expedition arrived about twenty years later in Cebu under the leadership of Miguel Lopez de Legazpi; it was accompanied by five Augustinian friars. This encounter turned violent, and the indigenous were defeated. Legazpi moved to the island of Luzon, conquered the local people, and built a walled city in the harbor of Manila. The Spanish conquered much of the Philippines within the next eleven years. At the same time, the first bishop of the Philippines, Domingo de Salazar, often interceded on behalf of the indigenous people.

In contrast to the American context, Irvin and Sunquist make the following observation regarding sixteenth-century Asia: "The Catholic Church was in the first stages of a transition from a conquering and crusading mode, as was still seen in the Philippines, to a missionary mode, where representatives of the Western church beyond its traditional homelands were more than royal agents" (2012, 69).

Age of Reforms in Europe

Of the two major transformations in Christianity during this time period, the focus so far has been on the first—the developments in America, Africa, and Asia. We now attend to the second major transformation—the age of reforms in Europe.

At the beginning of the sixteenth century "Europe was in the throes of a cultural transformation that brought about the end of the unified church and culture of Christendom and the beginning of modern European nation-states, whose overseas colonial expansion was to prove critical to national economic development" (Irvin and Sunquist 2012, 71). The royal patronage of the church by Spain and Portugal in the colonies reflected the broader trend of using national political power over the papacy and religion in Europe. In intellectual and social spheres a humanist movement—beginning in fourteenth-century Italy and later called the Renaissance—was marked by great accomplishments in the arts and humanities; a return to the study of ancient texts, including scripture in its original languages; and an interest in vernacular languages of Europe. Francesco Petrarch, Dante Alighieri, Thomas More, and Desiderius Erasmus were key figures in European humanism who shaped the cultural transformation of Europe and influenced the reformations. In particular, Erasmus, who was very concerned with reforming Christian life and the institutional church, had a major impact on Martin Luther.

The young German theologian and Augustinian friar Martin Luther, agonizing over whether his sins were ever truly forgiven, came to the conviction that salvation and forgiveness did not depend on the mediation of the church or the merits gained by an individual, but rather solely on the merits of Jesus Christ. This shaped Luther's doctrine of justification by faith alone. In 1517, he nailed to the church door of Wittenburg Castle—the normal place for community announcements—a list of ninety-five theses challenging such practices as indulgences (see Chapter 4). Luther and his colleagues proposed that scripture and liturgy be in the vernacular, and that laypeople and preaching have a bigger role in worship. Although Luther did not initially intend to break with Rome, the movement developed in that way. Some members of the German imperial assembly sided with Luther, while Emperor Charles V and other princes supported Rome. Luther's party became known as Protestants and Lutherans, although they "preferred to speak of their position as being 'evangelical' since they looked to the Good News ('evangel') as the final source of authority" (Irvin and Sunquist 2012, 86). From a global perspective, Luther considered the Church of Ethiopia a forerunner of Protestantism because this ancient church had embodied the gospel message outside of Roman Catholic papal authority and had practiced elements of the faith that Protestants would later adopt, such as communion under both species, vernacular scriptures, and married clergy (see Daniels 2017b).

Theologian Philip Melanchthon in 1530 presented the case for this evangelical position to the emperor and assembly in a statement called the Augsburg Confession, which continues to be the fundamental confessional statement for Lutherans. Due to the newly invented printing press, Luther's pamphlets and books were distributed quickly through Europe, including Scandinavia. In Switzerland, the priest Ulrich Zwingli in 1518 opposed the sale of indulgences and accepted an invitation to become a public preacher by the civil council of Zurich. With his understanding that scripture was the fundamental source of church authority, he found no basis for church doctrines like the universal role of the pope, celibate priesthood, and mandatory fasting during Lent. Zwingli emphasized the need for moral and spiritual regeneration. This movement spread and laid the "foundations for an enduring Reformation tradition in Switzerland" (Irvin and Sunquist 2012, 91).

Another group in Switzerland, the Swiss Brethren, opposed Zwingli's practices of infant baptism and association with secular authorities. They proposed what would develop into the broader Anabaptists' understanding of church, which "was much more egalitarian than either Zwingli or

Luther had allowed" (Irvin and Sunquist 2012, 92). A statement of faith by the Swiss Anabaptists, known as the Schleitheim Articles, was written and distributed in 1527. The Anabaptist movement spread, but its members often faced the threat of imprisonment, torture, exile, or death in Swiss, German, and Austrian territories. Many Anabaptists found safety in Moravia, which a century earlier had protected the United Brethren, inspired by the popular preacher John Hus. Jakob Hutter, who sought refuge there, developed the community practice of holding everything in common, and like other Anabaptists, his followers "refused to participate in the use of violence and believed in separating themselves as much as possible from the political life of established Christendom" (ibid., 96). A small group of radical Anabaptists, who preached the imminent return of God's reign and the direct inspiration of the Holy Spirit, made Münster in western Germany their center. This movement experienced a quick and violent end. "Evangelicals [Lutherans] and Roman Catholics alike considered the integration of religion and political life to be divinely mandated, and thus Anabaptists were by definitions enemies of the state" (ibid., 98). Despite this opposition, Menno Simons in Holland and northern Germany was able to organize the spreading Anabaptist congregations under a new identity known as Mennonites.

Another major figure of reform, John (Jean) Calvin, around 1533 was forced to leave France under suspicion of being an evangelical sympathizer. He spent the rest of his life in Switzerland, where he led an endeavor to shape Geneva according to his vision of a Christian city and to what was called the Reformed faith. The latter was described in Calvin's most important written work, *Institutes of the Christian Religion*. He insisted on justification by grace through faith, like Luther, and added a very strict moral code and the teaching that God's election for salvation was not universal. While Calvin and Luther shared many points, the differences "were significant enough usually to prevent the followers of the two reformers from being in communion with each other" (Irvin and Sunquist 2012, 103). These movements were considered a threat to the unity of the Roman Catholic Church in France, but a small evangelical group, called Huguenots by their opponents, gathered in southern France. Some of the first executions of evangelicals were carried out in the 1520s in the provinces that would later form the Netherlands, Belgium, and Luxembourg. With independence in 1609, there was a Reformed north region (Netherlands) and a Roman Catholic south region (Belgium). A few years earlier, in 1598, King Henry IV had legalized the Reformed faith in France.

Developments in England during this time were not associated with theology and church reform but rather with King Henry VIII. The king asked the pope to grant an annulment of his marriage to Catherine of Aragon under complex circumstances related to canon law and European politics. While the pope was delaying his decision, the English Parliament in 1534 declared that the English ruler was also head of the Church of England (Anglicans) and therefore could oversee all church matters. Henry confiscated the properties of the monasteries and introduced other changes. After his death, during the reign of Edward, the government took a more evangelical turn, including the introduction of a new *Book of Common Prayer*. Things then went back and forth. Queen Mary moved back toward the Roman Catholic Church, and several hundred Protestants were executed. Then Queen Elizabeth slowly reinstated the former changes made under kings Henry and Edward. "Over the course of the next four decades a distinct Anglican theological tradition blossomed, one that drew upon both Catholic and evangelical strands of faith but was expressed in the vernacular of English life and culture" (Irvin and Sunquist 2012, 109).

John Knox was a central figure for the reform in Scotland. After being freed from his captivity by the French for his evangelical leanings, Knox eventually returned to Scotland when the context was more conducive for spreading the Reformed faith. In 1560, with five others, he drew up the Scots Confession, which relied heavily on Calvin and Geneva.

At this time some were questioning central Christian doctrines such as the Trinity and Christology. Two Italian theologians, Lelio Sozzini and his nephew Fausto, developed what could be considered the Unitarian formulation that God is not three persons and Jesus Christ was human and not divine. This position attracted persecution from many sides, and so Fausto and others escaped to Transylvania. Later the Reformed churches in that area divided into Unitarian and Calvinist affiliations.

"While it was certainly fueled by anti-Protestant polemic, and so could be called a Counter-Reformation, nevertheless Catholic efforts to reform the church in this context of a general religious renewal might well be called a reformation in its own right (hence the term *Catholic Reformation*)" (Bevans and Schroeder 2004, 173). One of the earliest efforts was through Francisco Ximénez de Cisneros, a humanist and Franciscan, who was appointed by Queen Isabella of Spain in 1492 as her personal chaplain and adviser. Later, as a cardinal, his pastoral reforms in Spain included requiring standard education for priests and preaching during mass. This anticipated several institutional reforms addressed later during the Council of Trent, held in three sessions over the years from 1545 to 1563. The greatest attention for council reform was focused on priests and bishops, which included insistence on establishing seminaries. In response to issues raised by the reformers, Trent affirmed that grace is the foundation for justification by both faith and good works, that both scripture and church tradition are sources of faith, and that the church could grant indulgences but with moderation. The differences in terms of sacraments and ministry will be described later in the relevant threads. Another major resource for the Catholic Reformation was the renewal of older religious orders and the foundation of new ones, such as Jesuits, Ursulines, Capuchins, and later the Vincentians and Daughters of Charity.

The age of reforms was a time of tension. The evangelicals (Lutherans) and Reformed Christians were in conflict with the Roman Catholics. The Anabaptists and Unitarians were harassed and persecuted by all three. Anglicans and Roman Catholics were at odds from the beginning. Military conflict broke out in 1546 between the armies of Lutheran princes and those of Emperor Charles V. The Peace of Augsburg in 1555 specified that no Lutheran territories would be forced to become Roman Catholic and that no more territories would become Lutheran. This was based on the understanding that the religion of the ruler would be the religion of the churches in that area. Also, early incidents of Catholic-Protestant conflict began to occur outside Europe, for example, in the area of present-day Rio de Janeiro, Brazil. However, it is important to remember that the age of reforms was also a time of Christian renewal. "Both the Protestant and the Roman Catholic wings of the revival strove to lift the level of the masses of Christians more nearly to New Testament standards" (Latourette, 17).

Orthodox Churches within the Empires

Following the classification of Irvin and Sunquist, the "Orthodox churches in the fifteenth and sixteenth centuries were organized into several communions" (2012, 126). Those holding the non-Chalcedonian Monophysite Christology included the Ethiopians, Copts, Jacobites (West Syrians), and Armenian Orthodox; those of the non-Chalcedonian Dyophysite (Nestorian) Christology and of the East Syrian Church included small mountainous communities in Persia and the Saint Thomas Christians; those of the Chalcedonian Christology and the Church of the Greek East were living in Western Asia, Eastern Europe, and Russia. The Ethiopians and Saint Thomas Christians were treated earlier. We now review the situation of the Orthodox Christian churches within Muslim and Russian domains.

There were four Islamic empires within the period from 1454 to 1600: the Ottoman Empire in Western Asia and parts of Eastern Europe; the Safavid Dynasty in Persia; the Mughal Empire in India; and the Mameluke Dynasty in Egypt. The Ottomans recognized two Christian *dhimmi* communities: the Greek-speaking Orthodox under the ecumenical patriarch and the Armenian Orthodox (and Roman Catholic and East Syrian communities) under the Armenian patriarch (now in Istanbul). There was also a Jewish *dhimmi* community (Irvin and Sunquist 2012, 128). Christians endured hardships related to church repair, travel, dress, and taxes. In Persia the remaining small East Syrian communities in present-day eastern Turkey and northern Iraq and Iran "had little opportunity to regroup under the Safavid rulers" (ibid., 133). Due to some initial Franciscan efforts, some of these Christians would eventually form the Chaldean Catholic Church under a Rome-appointed patriarch. Along the Silk Road and even in China there were still some small Christian communities in the sixteenth century (Norris 2002, 158). In Egypt the Copts played an important role in the society under the Mamelukes. Their situation worsened when the Ottomans took over in 1517, but the long-serving Coptic Pope Gabriel VII managed to rebuild several important monasteries.

After 1453 the Russian Church was no longer dependent upon the ecumenical patriarch of Constantinople (Istanbul). Ivan III, the Grand Duke of Moscow, overthrew the remaining Mongol rulers in 1480 and took the title of tsar over the new independent state. Upon his marriage to the niece of the last Byzantine emperor, Russia took on that political and ecclesial mantle, and Moscow became known as the Third Rome. "More than any other institution, the church was seen as the heart of Russian national unity and the foundation for rebuilding Russian society" (Irvin and Sunquist 2012, 135). In the 1550s, Ivan IV (the Terrible) defeated the mostly Muslim Tartars and then established a reign of terror against all those considered his opponents, including the monk Philip who spoke out against Ivan's killing of innocent people. As a final indication of the new ecclesial status, the first patriarch of Moscow was consecrated in 1589 and confirmed in 1593 during a synod in Constantinople.

Turning southward, Ukrainian Christianity had blended Byzantine Christianity with Russian society. In the sixteenth century Jesuit missionaries from the newly formed Polish-Lithuanian Commonwealth came into Ukraine. The Union of Brest in 1596 brought some Russian-speaking churches from Ukraine and Lithuania into communion with Rome as the Roman Catholic Ukrainian Church. Parallel to developments in Ethiopia and southwest India, people with an ancient Christian heritage were accepted as, according to a later understanding, an Eastern rite of the Roman Catholic Church. They were allowed to continue to have married clergy and to use their ancient liturgical rites.

The period of 1454–1600 was determinative for the future of Christianity. First, the majority of the world—Africa, Asia, and America—experienced new Christian beginnings. Second, reforms in Europe created new Christian diversity that sparked both renewal and conflict. "At the end of the sixteenth century Christianity was both fragmented as never before and spreading as never before. . . . Christianity was becoming global in new ways" (Irvin and Sunquist 2012, 163). We now trace the development of the six threads of tradition during this century and a half.

Threads of Christian Tradition

Scripture

Within the Roman Catholic Church the "traditional monastic reading of scripture, as a source of wisdom and edification rather than of knowledge and doctrine, was typical of the monastic revival that centered in Spain" (González 1994, 99) around such persons as Teresa of Avila and Ignatius of Loyola. At the same time, some theologians, like Dominicans Domingo Báñez and Francisco de Vitoria, followed the scholastic method of using the Bible as a resource for theology when they addressed issues related to the indigenous peoples of America. Later, many Catholic theologians used this scholastic approach for doctrinal and polemical purposes to refute teachings of the Protestant reforms. In this context, the Council of Trent had two key pronouncements regarding scripture. First, the council decreed that in matters of faith and morals the Bible was to be held "in equal devotion and reverence" with church tradition. With this understanding, "theologians who disagreed on the meaning of a biblical text were to settle their differences, not exclusively or even primarily by examining the text itself, but by searching the tradition" (ibid., 100).

The second pronouncement of Trent was that the Latin Vulgate edition of scripture was the only authentic authoritative version. This was to counteract the use of original Hebrew and Greek texts and the many vernacular translations used to ground reform teachings. As an example of the former, humanist Lorenzo Valla, through his fifteenth-century comparative study of Jerome's Vulgate and the original Greek text of the New Testament, began to "question the adequacy of that time-honored Latin text" (Irvin and Sunquist 2012, 75). In terms of the latter, the council—out of fear that vernacular translations would lead to heresy—declared that vernacular translations needed to include explanatory notes, while Protestants were willing to publish scripture without them.

While the pronouncements of Trent would in general hamper Catholic biblical scholarship, noteworthy Catholic works of the sixteenth century included a polyglot Bible by Benito Arias Montano with texts in Hebrew, Greek, and Syriac, and a sixteen-volume commentary on the New Testament by the Jesuit Alfonso Salmerón. After the fall of Constantinople many Greek manuscripts and scholars found their way to the West and contributed to the renewal of Greek studies. Also, the Syriac version of the New Testament that was published in Vienna in 1555 and circulated through Europe "had been brought to the west by a delegation of Maronite Christians from Syria some forty years earlier" (Rogerson et al., 302).

The humanist Erasmus "can be taken as the starting point for all the main developments in the study of the New Testament in this period" (ibid., 296). Rather than his biblical interpretation, however, it was the first published critical edition of the Greek New Testament in 1516 that "marked a new age in biblical scholarship" (González 1994, 101). His significance was initially recognized and appreciated by Cardinal Ximénez, but these sentiments shifted among Roman Catholics due to the later anti-Protestant developments. However, Martin Luther welcomed and built upon the writings of Erasmus.

The various schools "of biblical scholarship and interpretation merged and took new forms with Martin Luther" (González 1994, 101). He was a biblical theologian who was familiar with the monastic practice of reading scripture for wisdom and edification, the scholarly work of Erasmus and others, and the use of the Bible as a source of theology and knowledge. With his principle of *sola scriptura* (scripture only), it is important to note that the word of God for Luther extended beyond the scripture to the redemptive action of God through Jesus Christ and history. While Luther used the monastic allegorical approach to read the Bible for illumination, he insisted on the literal sense for theological debate. John Calvin was even more consistent on this latter point. It was absolutely necessary to critically study the original text within its historical context before applying it to contemporary questions. Calvin drew upon his extensive knowledge of the biblical languages and patristic writing as well as the secular knowledge of classical authors, philosophy, and natural science (see Rogerson et al., 85–86). The other reformers also insisted on the primacy of scripture. However, the literalism of the Anabaptists "had serious political and ecclesiastical implications" (González 1994, 103), in that they held that the practices of the contemporary church should follow that of the New Testament to the letter.

The centrality of scripture during the reforms prompted vernacular translations, which spread rapidly in Europe due to the printing press with moveable metal type—an invention that revolutionized society. Luther published a German version of the New Testament in Wittenberg in 1522 that "can be studied not only as an important religious document, but also as the printed book that created the modern German mother tongue" (Norris 2002, 153). Cranmer oversaw the publication of an English translation of the Bible in 1537, and about twenty years later John Knox collaborated with Calvin in printing a more popular English version, known as the Geneva Bible. Several French translations were published in the sixteenth century, but "the vernacular Bible has never had the influence on the language of the French people as it had in Germany and England" (Rogerson et al., 303). As noted above, the Roman Catholic biblical translations into these European languages included explanatory notes.

In sixteenth-century America the Bible was not available in an indigenous language, but occasionally excerpts were translated and, as an outstanding exception, Franciscan ethnographer Bernardino de Sahagún translated the four Gospels into the Nahuatl language of Mexico. It should also be noted that women would not have the opportunity to study the Bible in South America for a long time (see Irvin and Sunquist 2012, 31). In the Asian context Yajiro had translated the gospel of Matthew into Japanese even before he accompanied Francis Xavier to Japan, and the Jesuit visitor Alessandro Valignano later promoted the translation of scripture into Japanese. In the ancient churches of the Saint Thomas Christians one would "typically find a copy of the Syriac Bible, often in gold leafing on an elaborately carved stand" (ibid., 57). A Slavonic translation of the entire Bible was completed by 1500 but wasn't widely available in Russia until 1582 with the arrival of the printing press. Augustinians working in the Persian Gulf translated the four Gospels into Arabic at the end of the sixteenth century (ibid., 157).

The following statement captures key developments of the thread of scripture during this period. "Three things were achieved which constitute a breakthrough in the use and understanding of the New Testament: the recovery of the Greek text; the wide diffusion of vernacular translations, made possible by the invention of printing; and the liberation of interpretation from the rigid control of ecclesiastical authority" (Rogerson et al., 316). On a popular level the evangelical movement in its various forms made reading and hearing the Bible a central characteristic of Christian life.

Liturgy, Sacraments, and Art

Different practices of sacraments and catechesis emerged as the church encountered new peoples and contexts in the "new world." In the beginning in the Americas baptism was done en masse followed by some catechesis. Later, the First Council of Lima in 1551 affirmed that the indigenous people were to be catechized before baptism in the vernacular language. The Third Lima Council of 1582–1583 recognized the need for catechetical materials in local languages and called for a catechism in three languages—Spanish, Quechua, and Aymara. Unfortunately, a more formal catechumenate process didn't develop at this time, perhaps because the Council of Trent didn't propose it, so "this movement for pre-baptismal catechesis dwindled toward the end of the sixteenth century" (Bevans and Schroeder 2004, 178).

The First Lima Council stated that local people were not allowed to receive the Eucharist and were to attend a church separate from the Europeans. "As late as the end of the sixteenth century, indigenous Americans were generally only admitted to the Eucharist on Easter and only if they convinced the priest that they had a clear understanding of the sacrament" (Irvin and Sunquist 2012, 27–28). In 1550, the Spanish government ordered the friars to teach the indigenous Spanish language and customs. The First Council of Mexico in 1555 forbade a person who was not fully European from ordination, and this ruling was extended to the entire Spanish Empire in America in 1578. The king of Spain had applied this for some time against *mestizos* (mixed Spanish and indigenous heritage) as well. The ban against the indigenous being ordained was officially lifted only in 1772. Interestingly, Las Casas, as the bishop of Chiapas, proposed denying the sacraments to anyone who held an *encomienda*. He was soon forced to return to Spain.

The situation was quite different in Asia. A Catholic seminary was established by the Franciscans in Goa for candidates of all ethnicities by 1541. Within a few years it was under Jesuit supervision. Three Indian seminarians from this seminary assisted Francis Xavier with translating and teaching the Christian message in the local Tamil language. Unfortunately, one of the early Jesuit seminary rectors caused most of the Indian and other non-Western candidates to run away, because he considered them incapable of attaining an academic Portuguese education. Years later, Xavier as the newly appointed Jesuit provincial of the East, dismissed that rector and invited the Indian seminarians to return. The first Indian was ordained a Catholic secular priest in 1558. In Japan, far away from the Portuguese influence in Goa, Xavier had founded a Christian community that was more accommodated to the Japanese society and culture. Continuing with this approach Valignano established the first seminary in Japan in 1580 where the students could receive communion on a regular basis. He also revised the original Japanese catechism of Xavier and Yajiro into a 1581 version that reflected "a relatively significant degree of sensitivity to the indigenous culture and society" (Irvin and Sunquist 2012, 160).

The reformations in Europe also produced much change in the areas of liturgy and sacraments. While the Protestant reformers held differing understandings of the Eucharist, their critique centered around two points. First, they questioned the theology of transubstantiation, a term with differing understandings from the beginning (see Chapter 3). Luther believed in the real presence of Christ's Body and Blood along with the substance of the bread and wine, and this became known as consubstantiation. Zwingli held that Christ's presence in the Eucharist was spiritual and a sign, not the real presence. He focused on Christ's presence in the community rather than in the elements. "John Calvin, who held something of a middle ground between Luther and Zwingli, believed that communicants really shared in the Body and Blood of Christ, but that presence was not on the altar, but in heaven" (Foley, 284). In response, Trent reaffirmed that the substances of the bread and wine were changed into the Body and Blood of Christ. The Catholic Church also continued to venerate the Eucharist in the tabernacle.

Second, Luther and the other reformers were unanimous in their critique of the relationship of the Eucharist to sacrifice and the subsequent role of the priesthood. They held that the Eucharist was not a sacrifice offered to God but rather a commemoration of the one sacrifice on the cross and the redemption that God offers us through it. This theological affirmation was also a critique of the pastoral practice of indulgences, stipends, and "buying" masses. The last was "founded on questionable approaches to the doctrine of eucharistic sacrifice [that] supported an image of salvation more akin to magic than one of sustained personal conversion and commitment" (Foley, 286–87). In other words, salvation through the one sacrifice on the cross cannot be "earned" through human "works." The Protestant reformers embraced the idea of the priesthood of all believers rather than the role of a priest to offer the sacrifice of the mass. They developed non-eucharistic liturgies focused on the Bible and preaching. Following Knox, the Eucharist was to be celebrated only four times a year, while in England, "Anglican worship varied between newer, more Protestant forms and older more medieval forms" (Martos, 285).

The Council of Trent continued to speak about the "sacrifice of the mass" and the role of ordained priests in offering the Eucharist, but it also addressed abuses related to eucharistic practices and other concerns cited by the reformers. "As a consequence, the training of clergy was greatly improved, regular preaching was encouraged at Sunday worship, and the people received better preparation for receiving the sacraments" (Foley, 244). To promote the appropriate celebration of mass liturgically and theologically, Trent established a liturgical commission that produced a common breviary in 1568 to assist the daily prayers of priests and a Roman Missal or official sacramentary in 1570 with the prayers for mass. Older rites such as the Ambrosian rite in Milan and the Mozarabic rite in Spain could continue. "These Catholic reformations did not end the private Masses, which left the problem of the overlooked communal aspect of the Mass unresolved in most places" (Bellitto, 123). While Protestants celebrated liturgy in the vernacular, Catholics continued to celebrate mass in Latin although the vernacular was to be used in preaching, teaching, and catechesis.

The strong emphasis on faith over works by Luther, Calvin, and others challenged the role of sacraments as a means of receiving grace. Although the reformers had varying understandings, they generally accepted the sacraments of Baptism and Eucharist as scripturally warranted. The Eucharist, also known as the Lord's Supper by Protestants, was discussed above. In terms of Baptism, Zwingli defended infant baptism, not as a sacrament of grace, but as an important sign of the covenant with God. The Anabaptists only baptized adults and only under the scripturally based form of immersion. Other reformers accepted both infant and adult baptisms as the reception of the gift of faith (Luther), a sign of being among the elect (Calvin), or as a symbol of God's redemption and an expression that Christians should follow Christ (Zwingli). In terms of other sacraments, the Anglicans at the beginning kept the practice of private confession. Luther and Calvin, while acknowledging the benefit of being reassured of God's pardon, denied the sacramental nature of Penance and the need of a priest as a mediator. The Anabaptists replaced private confession with acknowledgement of one's sins before the congregation.

Responding to these reforms, the Council of Trent affirmed the sacramentality of Penance as part of the broader recognition and renewal of seven sacraments. To reinvigorate the sacraments of initiation—Baptism, Eucharist, and Confirmation—it authorized the publication of a catechism as an instrument for religious instruction from Baptism through Eucharist and Confirmation. Catholics "still received the Eucharist infrequently, but sometimes more often than simply making their Easter duty" (Bellitto, 149). Penance manuals were developed after Trent to assist the confessor and penitent and to emphasize continual spiritual development rather than a quick dispensation of sins. Although few received the sacrament of extreme unction or anointing, according to the Council of Trent it "was the completion of penance and indeed of the whole Christian life" (Martos, 392). The idea of marriage as a sacrament was to be emphasized more during marriage preparation. In response to the Protestant emphasis on the priesthood of the baptized, the Catholics reaffirmed orders as a sacrament with an indelible mark. While Protestants rejected ordination as a sacrament in a strict sense, they "recognized the need for some sort of ceremonial initiation into the ministry" and this could be considered "still a sacrament in the broad sense" (ibid., 509).

A core issue underlying the differences between the Protestants and Catholics was justification by faith and good works. "Disagreement repeatedly came back to the question of whether any activity on humanity's part (including the act of receiving grace) is a necessary part of the total event of justification" (Irvin and Sunquist 2012, 121). In terms of the role of the church for salvation, "Roman Catholics insisted on the church being empowered by Christ to be the channel of grace, while Protestants on all sides (Lutheran, Reformed, and Anabaptist) argued for a more immediate relationship with Christ for grace" (ibid.). However, Irvin and Sunquist maintain that from today's perspective on the doctrine of justification, "the two sides shared far more in common than either side was willing to admit" (ibid.).

We turn our attention beyond Roman Catholic and Protestant Christianity. The remaining East Syrian communities under Muslim Persian rule, along with the new Chaldean Catholic group, continued "to use the ancient Syriac liturgy in worship and maintain Orthodox practices" (Irvin and Sunquist 2012, 134). Christians in Russia and Ukraine celebrated their Orthodox liturgies. While Rome had appointed a Portuguese archbishop in both South India and Ethiopia with a hope that Christians would conform to the Latin rite, many continued to follow the ancient ecclesial traditions. In Ethiopia, Ge'ez continued to be the language of the scripture and worship, although many no longer understood that language. Those of the Saint Thomas Christian tradition continued to celebrate liturgy in Syriac, a language that even many of the priests no longer understood. Their marriage ceremony included elements from the Hindu wedding ceremony as well as "images from the biblical book the Song of Songs" (ibid., 57).

In terms of art, church architecture reflected the differing Catholic and Protestant characteristics. The reconstruction of St. Peter's Basilica in Rome marked the transition to the energetic baroque style that became "the architectural symbol of the post-Tridentine Roman Catholic Church" (Foley, 247). Building St. Peter's required over eighty years, with Michelangelo serving as the architect for some time. In contrast to the baroque style, many Protestants preferred something "less distracting." While generalizations are difficult to draw among the various forms of Protestantism, tabernacles were usually removed and simpler altars normally received less emphasis than the more elaborate pulpits. Reform communities using existing churches sometimes removed statues and iconography or created new artwork considered theologically correct. "Most centrally planned Protestant churches were more austere . . . and the Roman Catholic emphasis on the visual elements of worship was rejected by the major segments of the Reformation" (ibid., 257). Instead, Protestants developed the auditory with an emphasis on music in liturgy. "Regarding the presence of images in the church, Zwingli had argued for their validity and allowed for those such as a cross, while rejecting others such as images of saints" (Irvin and Sunquist 2012, 90). Anabaptists took a stronger stance against images and often worshipped in homes or common buildings rather than in churches.

In the Americas the Christian message was presented not only in catechesis but also through paintings, art, and music, as it continued to be in Europe. It is noteworthy, but not surprising, that in the different church context of Asia, "Japanese artists were beginning to paint Japanese-styled Christian religious paintings of the Madonna and child, the crucifixion, and other scenes" (Irvin and Sunquist 2012, 160). Several important developments were occurring in the religious architecture and art of Russia in the fifteenth and sixteenth centuries. Their grandiose cathedrals can remind one "of the European Renaissance mixed with Russian and Asian hues" (ibid., 142), and the towers of St. Basil's in Moscow "represented Persian, Turkish, Kazak, and Indian motifs, which were woven in to represent the expansion of the Orthodox Church throughout Asia" (ibid., 140, 142). Russia was also developing its own style of Orthodox iconography. In contrast, the churches of the Saint Thomas Christians had no images and were built in the Hindu pagoda style with a cross on top. "The floors of churches were 'painted' with cow dung in the manner of the pagoda, and they had lamps and umbrellas in the local style" (ibid., 57). Most Ethiopian Orthodox churches were built in the round with concentric circles within—the outer circle for laity, the next for priests, and the inner circle for the eucharistic elements (see ibid., 51). Diversity within this thread of liturgy, sacraments, and art increased dramatically during this 150-year period.

Ministry and Organization

Similar to the preceding thread, the age of reforms also had a major impact on the developments of church organization and ministry. In the mid-fifteenth century the Catholic Church focused on defending itself from the many political pressures being asserted over it by reaffirming the primary authority of the pope after the Great Western Schism and by officially condemning conciliarism. "Despite continued rumblings for change during the fifteenth and early sixteenth centuries, the history of the church continued to be one where greater interest was given to ecclesiastical power than to spiritual welfare" (Bernier, 150). The reformers strove to recover the communitarian and decentralized vision of the early church with greater participation of the laity and greater emphasis on scripture. Papal authority was a central controversial issue.

Representing new forms of ecclesial organization, the Lutherans, Reformed, and Anglicans had the support of local civil authorities, and the first two of these streams "share a much stronger evangelical commitment to the authority of scripture" (Irvin and Sunquist 2012, 123). The fourth stream of Anabaptists, later called the Radical Reformation, normally held scripture as their guide to "recovering what they considered to be the authentic church" (ibid.) and they were independent of civil magistrates. This fourth stream developed into three groups: (1) Mennonites (also influencing a seventeenth-century movement in England that birthed the Baptists); (2) communities focused on the Holy Spirit and imminent return of Christ's reign, which didn't have such a lasting existence during this period but did "provide a link in the long tradition of Holy Spirit churches that today identify themselves as Pentecostal or Charismatic, as well as many indigenous Spirit churches around the world" (ibid.); and (3) evangelical rationalists, from which the Unitarians developed.

As for the Catholic Church, Archbishop (and later Cardinal) Francisco Ximénez de Cisneros at the beginning of the age of reforms supervised the Spanish Inquisition that was initially directed against possible relapses to former beliefs by Muslims and Jews who had become Christian (called *conversos*). Later it was directed against spiritual teachings that were considered challenges to the authority of the church and heresies of the evangelical movements from Switzerland and Germany. Heroic figures like Dominican prior general Thomas Cajetan and lay diplomat (later cardinal) Gasparo Contarini "attempted conciliation with the German reformers, only to be attacked by both sides" (Bevans and Schroeder 2004, 173). The Council of Trent was too late for any type of dialogue between the reformers and the Roman Catholic Church.

On the one hand, Trent was a Counter-Reformation event—defending the Catholic Church by reaffirming the central authority of Rome and the papacy. Popes after Trent were more administrators than pastors, but they did not repeat the sometimes scandalous papal behavior of the earlier part of the Middle Ages. Sixtus V in 1588 was successful in reorganizing the ecclesial bureaucracy (curia) into fifteen congregations—six dealing with temporal affairs and nine with more spiritual ones. On the other hand, the council was also a reformation of genuine renewal. "Trent ordered an end to the practice of church benefices, or the income received from offerings or endowments assigned to particular churches or chapels being used for the support of persons other than clerics or members of religious communities" (Irvin and Sunquist 2012, 122). To address the situation of frequent absenteeism by bishops, the council mandated that they had to reside in their dioceses. Furthermore, they were to avoid extravagant lifestyles, improve preaching in the parishes, and have more regular meetings with fellow bishops, the priests of their diocese, and officials in Rome (*ad limina* visits). The goal of the bishops "was to make the parish the center of life, and attempt to balance liveliness with uniformity and orthodoxy" (Bellitto, 18). Much Catholic reform focused on appropriate seminary training of priests. The celibacy requirement was also to be more strongly enforced. All of these measures—intended to address abuses and weaknesses—solidified what can be called the sacerdotalization of ministry (see Bernier, 175), and contributed to the gap between the ordained and the laity.

While the Roman Catholic Church was affirming the ministry of the pope and reforming the ministries of priests and bishops, the Protestant reformers were basing their understanding and practice of ministry on the concept of the priesthood of all believers. "Ordained ministry for Calvin, as for Luther, was an office that belonged to the whole church and not an individual priest. The church conferred on some the ministry of word and sacrament as a matter of good order, doing so through the laying on of hands by the elders" (Irvin and Sunquist 2012, 103). The internal call of the Spirit to an individual was to be confirmed by an external call from the congregation. Within the Reformed stream, elders and deacons were elected from the people to govern local congregations. These elders and deacons formed regional conferences or colloquies that were to meet four times a year. Representatives from the regions formed a national synod that met once a year. "In effect, the Reformed Churches had moved beyond the conciliar theology of the past to embrace a new form of collective episcopacy. The structure was intended to provide oversight of churches, ensure lay participation, and create a vehicle for ongoing work of reform" (ibid., 105). The Lutherans and Reformed, along with the Roman Catholics, did not allow women to be ordained. Women did have more leadership possibilities—although not full equality with men—among the Anabaptists, who were very egalitarian.

The organization of the church in the Americas was based on the European model. Furthermore, the friars, priests, and bishops were under the authority of the colonial powers—stated very clearly in the Burgos Laws as a response to the prophetic preaching of Montesinos. "By the middle of the sixteenth century bishoprics and diocesan structures were fairly well established throughout the entire continent" (Irvin and Sunquist 2012, 25). The parish structure followed tribal groupings but the indigenous peoples could not worship with the Spanish and *criollo* (European descendants born in America) congregations (see ibid., 26). As we had seen above with the prohibition of ordination for the indigenous, ethnocentrism and prejudice were present within the church as well. By contrast, church organization and ministry were much more accommodated to the non-Western Asian context due to the influence of Francis Xavier. The seminary in Goa trained Asian and African priests. Alessandro Valignano, building upon the founding work of Xavier in Japan, "believed that Japanese could and should be educated to lead the Japanese Catholic Church" (ibid., 161), including becoming priests and bishops. For this reason he established two colleges, two seminaries, and a system of church elders in Japan. As in the past, councils and synods greatly affected church organization. We already noted the roles of the Council of Trent, the First Council of Mexico, the First and Third Councils of Peru, the Synod of Diamper, and the national synods of the Reformed churches.

Let us conclude this thread by looking briefly at several churches under the general Orthodox category used in the first part of this chapter. "An East

Syrian patriarch in Baghdad was still to be appointed; but he was little more than a figure" (Irvin and Sunquist 2012, 54). However, the Saint Thomas Christians maintained their dependence for episcopal appointments from the East Syrian Church, also known as the Assyrian or Chaldean Church. With the arrival of the Portuguese, they divided into Roman Catholic and East Syrian communities. "The St. Thomas Christians, along with all eastern Christians at the time, allowed their priests to marry (although not their bishops), but they also had orders of monks and nuns who were celibate" (ibid., 57). The organization of the ancient church of Ethiopia consisted of a patriarch, or *abuna*, appointed from Alexandria, as well as many priests, monks, nuns, and hermits. The church of Ethiopia never developed episcopal ministry. "Consequently, the power of a foreign patriarch was greater, and the church was much more localized through the leadership of local monasteries and charismatic monks and priests" (ibid., 50). Ethiopian Christians resisted attempts to bring them under Rome at this time.

Church organization of those living as a minority (*dhimmi*) under Muslim rule was described in the section "Orthodox Churches within the Empires." Patriarchs played a significant role. An exchange in the 1570s between Lutheran theologians in Tübingen and Patriarch Jeremiah II in the Ottoman Empire "can be considered the first bilateral dialogue between Protestants or evangelicals and the Orthodox" (Irvin and Sunquist 2012, 130). The Russian Orthodox Church officially separated administratively from the Greek Orthodox with the first consecration of its own patriarch in 1589 with the (somewhat hesitant) participation of the ecumenical patriarch. The organization and situation of the Ukrainian Church was also presented earlier.

Spiritual, Religious, and Social Movements

Two strands of spirituality fed into the major spiritual and religious movements of this time period in the West. First is the "modern devotion" begun by Gerard Groote and the subsequent founding of the lay communities of Brothers and Sisters of the Common Life (presented in Chapter 4). Groote emphasized the importance of scripture, individual moral formation, and community. "In general, the evangelical piety and lay emphasis of the movement had a significant influence on both Protestant and Catholic Reformations" (Sheldrake, 108). Second, Christian humanism influenced this age of reforms, with Erasmus being the most influential figure. Erasmus, who "never wavered in his commitments to the Catholic faith and the hierarchy," called for "an inner spiritual discipline that went beyond the external aids of religious life, such as relics, fasts, and even the church's sacraments" (Irvin and Sunquist 2012, 80).

Luther, who was influenced by both the Brothers of the Common Life and Erasmus, "rejected a two-tier view of holiness (where special lifestyles were 'superior') in favor of the holiness of the everyday life of work, family, and citizenship" (Sheldrake, 111). Furthermore, for Luther, "spirituality is not so much something one does as rather what is done for one by God, followed by an inevitable change in one's personal behavior" (Wiseman, 141). Calvin's spirituality is (1) mystical and a union of love; (2) corporate and communal; and (3) social and a public matter. "A moral and spiritual life touched all elements of existence—public and personal" (Sheldrake, 114). Anabaptist spirituality was marked by radical simplicity and refusal to cooperate with civil authority and structures. For Anglicans, the *Book of Common Prayer* was to promote a personal spirituality that "was shaped by living and worshipping as part of a community both ecclesial and civic" (ibid., 117). The renewing spirituality of these four streams of Christianity share an emphasis on scripture and a desire for "a religion of the heart in place of formalism and an over-reliance on externals" (ibid., 109). This spiritual yearning and desire for church reform led to an energetic birth of a variety of religious movements throughout Europe, as described in "Age of Reforms in Europe" above and throughout this chapter.

In opposition to monasticism and Catholic religious orders, Luther and Calvin "envisioned a church in which all members of the laity would have access to the spiritual benefits that were found in monastic discipline" (Irvin and Sunquist 2012, 103). Both understood that "every human being is called by God to a particular work in life, be it administering justice, fixing wagons, or raising a family" (ibid.). This spirituality and work for the glory of God has been called worldly asceticism. The disciplined life in smaller communities of the Anabaptists, who were striving to live a life of radical discipleship, reflected the witness of monastic movements in their beginnings. However, the Anabaptists "placed a great deal more emphasis than did monasticism on the need to bring the gospel to the common people . . . putting them in many ways in the tradition of the Third Order Franciscans, the Beguines, and other spiritual renewal movements among the laity from earlier centuries" (ibid., 93). Within these new religious movements we see the emergence of a spirituality of intentionally seeing God in everyday experience, which is also reminiscent of the earliest years of Christianity.

In the Roman Catholic Church, "Catholic Reformation spirituality had two major elements: the foundation of new religious orders and the development of new forms of lay Christian life and devotion that were interwoven with daily life" (Sheldrake, 122). In terms of the former, some of the older orders renewed themselves, for example, the Capuchins as a reformed branch or order of the Franciscans. The order that clearly embodied the Catholic spirituality of this age was the Jesuits. Their founder, Ignatius of

Loyola, had been influenced by the "modern devotion," and by Erasmus's writings and followers. After a religious conversion and a period of receiving spiritual guidance at a monastery, Ignatius "learned the lessons of discernment as he slowly outgrew a tendency to excessive asceticism" (ibid., 124). From this experience and over the next twenty-five years he wrote the famous *Spiritual Exercises*, for which the "theme of 'finding God in all things' suggests a growing integration of contemplation and action" (ibid., 126–27). Rather than advocating for doctrinal change, Ignatius sought to "promote religious and moral reform" (Ormerod, 294). Furthermore, in comparison with the earlier monastic and mendicant orders, the Jesuits were an "activist" congregation. Around the same time, the laywoman Angela Merici visited hospitals and cared for orphans in her home. Even though Trent attempted to restrict nuns to cloistered life, Merici in 1535 founded the non-cloistered Ursulines, "the first women's order established solely for education" (Irvin and Sunquist 2012, 113). They would become a major Catholic mission congregation in the future.

Another contribution from religious communities was the reform and mystical writings of the Carmelite order in Spain. In terms of spirituality, Teresa of Avila "may be viewed as the most important figure of this period" (Norris 2002, 160). She initiated the Carmelite reform back to its contemplative origins and in her book *The Interior Castle* she describes her spiritual journey in terms of progression through various "rooms" of the soul—a work considered a spiritual classic by many. She later formed a new women's community called the Discalced (barefoot) Carmelites. Fellow Carmelite mystic Juan de la Cruz (John of the Cross) was another key figure in this movement. His spiritual writings include *Ascent of Mount Carmel* and the poem "Dark Night of the Soul." It is interesting that, like a number of their Protestant contemporaries, both "were writing in a European vernacular language (Spanish in their case), and not just in Latin, indicating the growing importance of use of the vernacular languages for spiritual and intellectual life in Europe, and charting reforms in new vernacular directions" (Irvin and Sunquist 2012, 115).

The spiritual enrichment of the laity was the second major component of spirituality during the Catholic Reformation. Sodalities were established eventually across most of Europe. They were not only for devotional purposes, but "were intended to inculcate a broad lay spirituality that combined personal spiritual development, collective support through meetings, and a significant amount of charitable action" (Sheldrake, 131). Along with more regular and better prepared Sunday preaching, parish missions were held for several days or a week by visiting priests, including Jesuits who adapted the Ignatian spiritual exercises for laypeople. "Such missions also reinforced the local parish as the primary context for sustaining lay spirituality" (ibid.,

132). With Trent's reaffirmation of the real presence of Christ in the Eucharist came more eucharistic devotions such as weekly benediction and forty hours of adoration. Pope Pius V did much to reinvigorate the practices of Marian devotion and praying the Rosary.

Catholic spirituality was reshaped in the encounter with the indigenous in the Americas. The clearest case was the transformation of the Spanish devotion to Our Lady of Guadalupe to La Morenita through appearances to Juan Diego at Tepeyac, a sacred mountain of the Aztecs. The original story began in 1531, just ten years after the conquest started, but it would be preserved in written form only in 1648. This new religious expression and experience of the Virgin of Guadalupe drew from two worldviews. "In Diego's experience the two devotional streams met and merged (*encuentro* in Spanish) into one, creating a new mestizo ('mixed') spirituality" (Irvin and Sunquist 2012, 33). In relation to social change, since only 10 percent of the colonists were women before 1570, many sexual relations and/or marriages of European men with Amerindian and African women led to the formation of new racially mixed people and contributed to the new face of Christianity in America. Returning to the point of spirituality, the *mestizo* spiritual and religious movement is part of the more general pattern of the coming together of Native American cultural-religious worldviews and practices with Roman Catholic spiritual practices. "Roman Catholic devotions to the saints and to Mary was more readily embraced by indigenous peoples, and later by Africans brought to America" (ibid., 31–32).

While Christian spirituality developed on a grassroots level in the Americas, the indigenous of the Americas and Africa were not allowed to join European religious orders for most of the sixteenth century. One exception was Martin de Porres, who was of mixed European and African descent. As a Dominican (lay) brother, he became well known for his knowledge of herbal medicines and his medical skills, which he used both in the monastery and with the poor on the streets of Lima. In sharp contrast with other religious orders, almost 17 percent of the Jesuits in Brazil were indigenous by 1600, but they also held African enslaved persons (see Irvin and Sunquist 2012, 24). Female religious orders at the beginning did not normally originate from Europe but rather were founded in the Americas and were usually contemplative communities. However, some began to offer education for girls who were relatives of the nuns and later for daughters of the royalty. Due to the efforts of Valignano, the first four Japanese were admitted to the Jesuits in 1578, less than thirty years after Xavier's arrival in Japan; the total number of Japanese Jesuits reached twenty within five years; the first Japanese Jesuit priest was ordained in 1602 (Ross, 55, 65, 87). While there were no women religious orders in these earliest years of

Christianity in Japan, in the 1580s there were groups of consecrated Japanese women and confraternities of Christian women for charitable works.

In 1480 the Orthodox monasteries owned about one-third of the land in Russia, and "monks became more concerned with crops, servants, and the price of agricultural goods than living the self-denying life of Christ" (Irvin and Sunquist 2012, 137). The monk Nilus of Sorka led a reform movement to return Russian monasticism to its more spiritual purposes, which included opposition to monastic landownership. His followers were known as the Non-Possessors. On the other side, Abbot Joseph Volotsky proposed that wealth and strict discipline were the best ways to serve the social needs of the poor. Joseph's group became known as the Possessors. In the end, the Non-Possessors were driven underground by the tsar and most church leaders. Turning to Egypt, monasticism faced challenges under Muslim rule. Coptic pope Gabriel VII organized the rebuilding of several monasteries, of which St. Anthony's prepared well-educated leaders and future Coptic popes into the nineteenth century.

Theological Developments

As we begin our treatment of this thread in the Americas and Asia, the following observation from Stephen Bevans offers us an important reminder.

> While our focus here will be on theology that has been preserved in writing, we must never forget that most of the theological reflection of this time was expressed in architecture (e.g. the marvelous churches in the colonial Philippines), art (the magnificent altar pieces in Latin American cathedrals), music (witness the recently discovered music of anonymous Bolivian composers), popular devotions to Mary and the saints, or catechetical lessons in indigenous languages. (2009, 259)

In terms of writing, Las Casas produced a massive amount of theological and legal work (including fourteen volumes in Spanish). Against the opinion of the majority of theologians, he argued for the acknowledgment of the personal and religious freedom of the indigenous of America and for the salvation of those who do not profess explicit faith in Christ. We also have a significant amount of theological material from indigenous Christian voices and expressions. Felipe Guamán Poma de Ayala, an indigenous person from Peru, wrote a book to the king of Spain describing the injustices done against "Christ's poor" and calling for the conversion of Christians (see Bevans 2009, 260–61). A set of early-sixteenth-century material from Mexico, called collectively Testarian manuscripts, consists of catechisms and prayer books "that use indigenous pictographs to represent the doctrinal and ethical teachings of the missionaries" (ibid., 261). These writings, often by indigenous Christians, sometimes included original pictographs to capture new Christian teachings, and they were further interpreted to some degree in the commentary in local languages. Finally, two texts written by Mexican-born Spanish priests described the apparitions of the Virgin of Guadalupe that occurred in 1531. The first version (1648) in Spanish was for the elite, while the 1649 version in the local language of Nahuatl was the more popular version. In both the oral and written forms "we have the first indigenous reflections on Mariology—or perhaps even on the doctrine of God—in the Americas" (ibid.).

With mission work beginning a bit later in Asia, Xavier and Valignano signaled a more positive theological attitude toward culture in Japan. The more accommodational approach included the Jesuits' use of a Japanese name for God rather than the Latin *Deus*. The appearance of Japanese-styled Christian religious paintings represents a response. This theological perspective will be developed in much more detail after 1600.

In Europe, theology was developing among the reformers. While Luther's theology was more pastoral than academic, "what always anchors his theologizing is the insight that grace has been freely given through the work of Jesus Christ, and only by faith in him (*sola fide*, 'by faith alone') can we grasp that faith and be saved" (Bevans 2009, 264). This key issue of justification was discussed earlier in regard to sacraments. Also, scripture was of primary importance for Luther and other Protestant reformers. Calvin's *Institutes of the Christian Religion* is considered a theological classic. While his teaching on "double predestination" is not the central point of his theology, it is an important part. "Like Augustine before him, Calvin saw this doctrine more as a consolation for Christian life than as a threat" (ibid., 266). However, this became a controversial issue among Catholics and fellow Protestants. For example, Knox presented predestination in terms of the nature of God, rather than the doctrines of grace and salvation. Anglican theologian Richard Hooker wrote *Of the Lawes of Ecclesiasticall Politie*, "one of the most important theological works of the Elizabethan period" (ibid., 267).

Catholic theologians Thomas Cajetan and Johann Eck both met with Luther, but the theological differences weren't resolved. The Council of Trent was not concerned with reconciliation with the reformers. The Catholic Church took more of a defensive stance, although important reforms were also introduced, particularly regarding bishops and priests. All the bishops and abbots at the council were Europeans, and they did not treat the questions and developments coming from Latin America and Asia. Bishop Juan de Zumárraga of Mexico City unfortunately died before he could travel to the council. A number of Catholic theologians at the council from the prominent University of Salamanca in Spain included Domingo de Soto, Andrés de Vega, and Melchior Cano. Two important spiritual writers, mentioned earlier, were Teresa of Avila and John of the Cross. Both were named doctors of the church, and Teresa in 1970 was the first woman declared so. Finally, influential theology was also being produced in artistic and musical forms by persons like Michelangelo Buonarroti, Leonardo da Vinci, and Giovanni Pierluigi da Palestrina.

Mission, Cultures, and Religions

The term *mission* had been understood basically in a theological sense to talk about the sending of the Son and the Spirit. Now the Jesuits began using it in a general sense of carrying out what the pope requested and then in a more specific sense of being sent on mission "directed toward non-Christians and non-Catholics and Catholic Christians, as well" (Bevans and Schroeder 2004, 173–74). The term *missionary* was first used by the Jesuits to describe the agents of mission and the expansion of the church.

The situation of mission was very different between the Americas (and the Philippines) and Asia. The context of the conquest in America—including the systems of the *requerimiento* and *encomienda* and the death of many indigenous people—strongly affected the mission approach. While many priests collaborated with this official imperial approach of mission, others defended the indigenous. For example, the Dominican friar Bartolomé de Las Casas took a strong prophetic stance. It is important to note that he was not a lone voice, since "approximately one-third of the bishops in the Americas until 1620 likewise defended the human rights and freedom of the indigenous people" (Bevans and Schroeder 2004, 177). One of the unsettling aspects of the life of Las Casas was his initial support of African slavery in order to alleviate the situation of the indigenous peoples. Later he changed this stance to the degree that he "came to oppose the African slave trade, but not the holding of people of African descent in bondage" (Irvin and Sunquist 2012, 23). This illustrates how prejudices from being a child of one's time influences even a prophetic figure like Las Casas. Other friars and members of religious orders, such as Franciscans, Jesuits, and women's congregations, also pursued respectful methods, such as through the Jesuit "reductions," schools for girls, and "Christian" villages. But paternalism and some complicity with the conquest were still evident. In general, attempts by the church to pursue a less violent approach toward the indigenous population became more difficult in the face of an even stronger "Hispanization" program after 1550 by the colonial government.

However, the Third Council of Lima was still promoting the path of gentle persuasion in 1582–1583.

Mission in Asia happened in a context of colonization, but not with the same intensity as in the Americas. As the first Jesuit in Asia, Xavier experienced conversion from his European ethnocentrism through his encounter with the Japanese, and he then set the tone for the Jesuit accommodational mission approach in Asia. Several Japanese Christians were also key figures. The Japanese ex-criminal Yajiro, whom Xavier met in Malacca, not only translated Matthew into Japanese but more important encouraged and advised the Jesuit missionary. "Yajiro deserves much of the credit for being the early pioneer in this method of missionary adaptation" (Irvin and Sunquist 2012, 64). Another important Japanese Christian was the first Japanese Jesuit, a (non-ordained) brother who took Lourenço as his name in the religious community. As a nearly blind traveling minstrel, he "was very significant in spreading the Christian message in a Japanese form through the composition and singing of Christian songs and in debates with Buddhist monks and other educated persons" (Bevans and Schroeder 2004, 185).

Valignano developed the accommodational model into what he called *il modo soave* (the sweet or gentle way). Under his leadership the Jesuits in Japan developed the following: (1) recruits (*irmao*) for the Jesuits, some of whom would be ordained; (2) men living in a community (*dojuku*) combining the monastic tradition of Christianity and a Zen Buddhist lifestyle, who committed themselves to the ministry of the word; and (3) local elders (*kambo*) of the Christian communities. "Many of the *kambo*, along with the women and men of the confraternities established by the Jesuits, would become the backbone of the Japanese church when the missionaries and priests were killed or deported and the Japanese church would go through a long period of persecution [starting in 1614]" (ibid., 186).

The relationship of mission and culture is evident in the above pattern. The tabula-rasa approach was dominant within the conquest mentality in the Americas. Liturgy and scripture were usually in Latin. A number of friars tried to learn local languages and some customs. An outstanding example was the Jesuit José de Acosta, who "took the Peruvian Amerindian culture seriously and made the theological decision that many of its features needed little change" (Norris 2002, 166). Another Jesuit, José de Anchieta, learned the Tupí and Guarani languages in Brazil and wrote the first dictionary and grammar for the former. Reductions attempted to respect and preserve aspects of the indigenous culture and to blend it with what the Jesuits considered the best of European culture. The Virgin of Guadalupe event and phenomenon was an accommodational moment in America that traces its origins to the indigenous people, not to the missionaries. In "unofficial" ways, American and African cultural-religious worldviews have blended with or existed alongside European Christian beliefs and practices until today. While noting the tragedies, complexities, and opportunities within the context of colonialism and mission, Irvin and Sunquist note that "it took less than a century for most of Spanish and Portuguese America to become at least nominally Catholic, making it the most rapidly Christianized continent in the history of the Christian movement" (2012, 32).

In contrast to the attitude toward non-Western cultures in America, Xavier and Valignano charted an accommodational approach toward Japanese culture in terms of dress, diet, architecture, and social behavior, which was extended throughout Asia. There was little adaptation in liturgy, which was normally in Latin, and "Western instruments such as harpsichords, viols, and even organs were used in churches" (Irvin and Sunquist 2012, 160). However, the Jesuits translated scripture, the catechism, and prayers into the local language, and they used a Japanese name for God. Regarding Europe, Foley makes the interesting point that the "Protestant Reformation can, in one sense, well be understood as a radical move toward inculturation, whereby certain cultural or contextual sensibilities engaged the traditional theologies and worship practices of the church, and something new emerged" (Foley, 289).

In terms of other religions, the church in Europe took an adversarial stance. In the same year that Islam was finally driven out of the Iberian Peninsula, "the Spanish crown ordered all remaining Jews, perhaps as many as 100,000, expelled from Spain." This led to "an exodus of Jews to other cities in Europe and across the Mediterranean" (Irvin and Sunquist 2012, 78). Europeans likewise despised the traditional religions of the indigenous peoples of Africa and the Americas. However, this encounter raised new theological questions. Theologians de Soto and Las Casas were open to the possibility of salvation for those who didn't profess faith in Christ. At the same time, we have noted throughout this chapter that the people of these "new" lands found ways to somehow integrate their ancestral religions with Catholicism so that a "highly complex cultural and religious mix was forged in the Americas" (ibid., 45).

In India an initial period of toleration toward Hinduism ended with an order in 1540 that all the Hindu temples in Goa were to be destroyed. In Japan, Xavier entered into conversation with Buddhists monks. One of them who became Christian, Ashikaga Gakko, became an important bridge for teaching the Jesuits about Japanese culture and Buddhism and for explaining "Christian faith to those asking questions, usually elite Japanese, in terms of their culture and their faith" (Norris 2002, 150). Valignano rewrote the original Japanese catechism in narrative form, rather than in a question-and-answer format, and "the section on cosmology reflects sensitivity to

Japanese concepts" as the Jesuits "were concerned to communicate the necessity for a creator, a created order, and ethical responsibility to this creator" (Irvin and Sunquist 2012, 160). Valignano also borrowed the term *dojuku* (a certain Buddhist lifestyle) to name a Christian monastic-type community.

Several points can be added from the current understanding of mission. First of all, mission was not only occurring in the so-called new lands. The activity of the Jesuits explicitly, and the Protestants implicitly, would be understood today within the scope of mission. Second, the Anabaptist stance on nonviolence and the communal sharing of goods continues to be a prophetic message. Third, the Italian-founded order of Misericordia did hospital work in India and provided for the dying, sick, poor, and imprisoned, which included taking care of the burial of the poor and caring for those condemned to death (see Irvin and Sunquist 2012, 61). Finally, many unnamed individuals of different ethnicities around the world were contributing to mission in their local contexts.

Conclusion

The significance of the two major transformations within Christianity from 1454 to 1600 is captured in the chapter's title: "Conquest, Reformation, and Indigenous Growth." This diversity combined with growth led to division and prejudice, on the one hand, and revival and creativity, on the other. Interest in scripture and preaching grew, and both Martin Luther and Ignatius of Loyola were "exploring a different vision of the spiritual life" (Sheldrake, 110). New developments in terms of sacraments, liturgy, church organization, ministry, and theology brought renewal and challenges. Various approaches to mission and other cultures and religions emerged in differing contexts.

Beyond the continuity and changes among the "new peoples" in America, Africa, and Asia, and among the "old peoples" of Europe, the Christian faith and tradition were also developing among Christians living in Russia, the Ukraine, in areas under Muslim rule, and in places like Ethiopia, as described below:

> Worship consisted in recited prayers (sung or chanted), readings from the Psalms, and music provided by bells, drums, and the human voice. Dance was part of the worship, as was a procession of priests carrying censors in the right hand and crosses in the left. . . . As with other Orthodox churches, the bread and wine were mixed and then served with a small spoon, followed by some water. . . . [Infants] were baptized at

the entrance of the church with water poured over the infant and were then given Communion. There also developed in Ethiopia a practice of annual rebaptism, which was practiced in regional centers in large baptismal pools. (Irvin and Sunquist 2012, 51–52)

Their sacramental and liturgical practices reflect both similarities and differences in relation to other streams of Christianity at this time, and they point to some elements (drums and dances) that will surface in sub-Saharan Africa in the twentieth century.

6

Global Religious and Secular Encounters

ca. 1600 to ca. 1800

The breakthrough event of people circumnavigating the earth for the first time in the sixteenth century ushered in an understanding of the world as global. The subsequent missionary movement and European political and economic expansion would continue hand-in-hand during the period from 1600 to 1800. "The long-range impact of this association would be both to link Christianity to Western colonialism and later to imperialism in significant ways, but also to transform Christianity from a mostly Western religion to a truly global or world religion" (Irvin and Sunquist 2012, 165).

The seventeenth century also saw the beginning of secularization. Civil leaders in Europe tried to restrict the public role of the church. A contributing factor was the Thirty Years' War in Europe, which was based on political, economic, and religious (interdenominational) rivalries. At the same time, the movement of European humanism, mentioned in the last chapter, was attracted to the worldview of science and rationality, and the Enlightenment supported the growing understanding of individual freedom. "Notions of political and intellectual freedom by the end of the [eighteenth] century had begun to collide, with religion, and state-dominated forms of Christianity in particular, often relegated to the side of authoritarianism and tyranny" (Irvin and Sunquist 2012, 318). On the other side, movements of religious awakening attempted to revive spiritual life in Europe and North America, particularly among Protestants.

Outside Europe, religious and secular encounters took new turns by the end of the eighteenth century. An energetic period of Catholic mission in Asia came to an end with the suppression of the Jesuits in 1773 and a church decision not to allow Chinese Christians to practice ancestor veneration. North America experienced both awakenings and revolution. Dutch colonial rule was reshaping the southern part of Africa. With the weakening of the Ottoman Empire, Orthodox churches "began to experience new shoots of self-rule and independence" (Irvin and Sunquist 2012, 318). The title of this chapter is taken from the title of Irvin and Sunquist's section on the seventeenth century: "Global Religious and Secular Encounters" (ibid., 165–315).

Historical Context

Asia

As noted in Chapter 5, Jesuit missionary Francis Xavier shifted from a tabula rasa to a more accommodational approach to mission in Japan. This latter methodology was developed by Alessandro Valignano, the official Jesuit visitator, into what he called *il modo soave* (the sweet or gentle way). In Portugal he had to confront "the crown and the altar" understanding so that he could choose and prepare forty-one new Jesuit missionaries to follow *il modo soave* and remain independent of the *patronatus* system.

Following Xavier, Valignano promoted the use of Japanese for prayers and the catechism, training Japanese men for priesthood, and adaptation of many Japanese customs by missionaries. Christianity grew so quickly that there may have been 300,000 Christians by 1614. While still a minority among an approximate total population of twenty million, "it is no exaggeration to say that Christianity was becoming the dominant religion in the south, and had the overall political climate continued as it had been there is no reason to believe that Christianity would not have become a major religious presence throughout Japan" (Irvin and Sunquist 2012, 181). However, anti-Christian laws and persecutions began in 1614. Fortunately, church elders and women and men in many confraternities "would become the backbone of the Japanese church when the missionaries and priests were killed or deported" (Bevans and Schroeder 2004, 186). Perhaps as many as five thousand Japanese died as martyrs and many more suffered and went into hiding. The first century of Christianity in Japan came to an end in 1639. However, many "hidden Christians" will surface when missionaries return to Japan in the nineteenth century.

Michele Ruggieri and Matteo Ricci, both protégés of Valignano, initiated the Jesuit mission efforts in China at the end of the sixteenth century (see Map 7). Because foreigners were not allowed to live in the Chinese Empire, they learned Cantonese Chinese in the Portuguese enclave of Macao, off the south coast of the mainland. When finally allowed to enter China, they at first adopted the dress and lifestyle of Buddhist monks, but then Ricci decided that Confucianism provided the more appropriate doorway of influence into Chinese culture. He studied Confucian classical literature and, after a time, was recognized as a member of the Confucian scholars

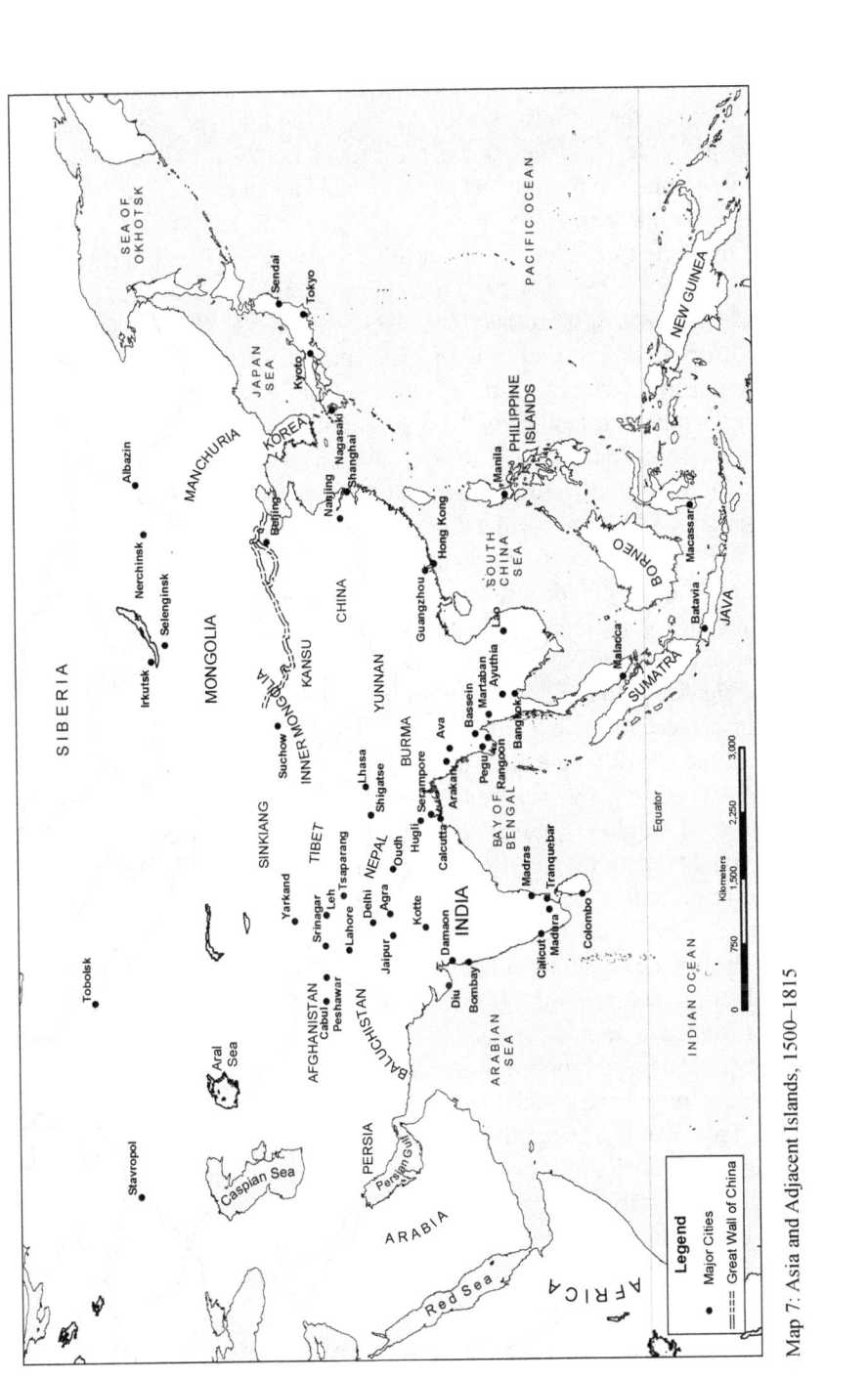

Map 7: Asia and Adjacent Islands, 1500–1815

(*literati*) and received the Chinese name of Li Madou. Furthermore, Ricci's knowledge of clocks, sundials, map making, and mathematics was valued by the *literati* and eventually the emperor's court. In 1601, Ricci and three other Jesuits were finally allowed to live in the imperial city of Beijing. Later, another Jesuit scholar, Johann Adam von Bell, was so highly regarded as an astronomer in Beijing that he was named the director of the important Astronomical Bureau.

In those first decades sixteen Jesuit priests joined Ricci, who died in 1610. By 1650, they had baptized about twenty-five hundred Chinese, including *literati* and ordinary Chinese. A number of Chinese Christians were instrumental in promoting Christianity. Xu Guangxi, who became an adviser to the emperor, shared in the scientific work of the Jesuits and was influential in establishing the first Catholic community in Shanghai in 1608 (see Irvin and Sunquist 2012, 173). Yang Tingyun interpreted Christian faith in light of Confucianism. "His interpretation of Jesus in light of the history of Chinese civilization provided a more universal framework for understanding salvation than the Western Jesuits had provided" (ibid.). Xu Candida, the granddaughter of Xu Guangqi, founded thirty Christian communities, two groups of women catechists, and a couple of orphanages.

Jesuit Robert de Nobili arrived in the state of Tamil Nadu, India, in 1606. He discovered that being Christian implied becoming Portuguese, a foreigner (*paranghi*). In line with Valignano and Ricci, he strove to accommodate the Christian message to Indian life. He learned the languages of Tamil and Telugu and was the first European to learn Sanskrit, the sacred language of Hindu scriptures. While the missionaries in this part of India had worked only with lower-caste Indians, de Nobili planned to approach upper-caste Indians by studying the sacred texts and living the austere lifestyle of an Indian holy person (*sanyyasi*). In this way he was able to interact with the Brahmin and other high-caste persons, but due to strict social discrimination among castes, de Nobili was no longer able to associate with lower-caste Indians or fellow Europeans. In order not to lose sight of the lower castes, he founded one group of missionaries to work with them, while a second worked with the upper castes. "Even though the number of Brahmin converts to Christianity was small, de Nobili succeeded in witnessing the Christian faith to them in a way that has not been duplicated" (Bevans and Schroeder 2004, 190).

While Dominicans, Franciscans, and Augustinians worked in Vietnam in the sixteenth century, the real birth of Vietnamese Christianity began with the arrival of the Jesuits in the seventeenth century. Alexandre de Rhodes was the central figure. Building upon his excellent linguistic skills, he developed a simplified system for writing Vietnamese still used today. One of the first written works was the catechism, in which de Rhodes accommodated Christian faith and theology to the Vietnamese context. He developed lay leaders and catechists, including many women. They can be considered cofounders of Christianity in Vietnam (see Bevans and Schroeder 2004, 191). The first of many Vietnamese Christians was martyred in 1644. de Rhodes was expelled the next year due to his conflict with the *patronatus* system. He continued the *soave modo* approach in the Moghul Empire in present-day Pakistan. There were approximately 300,000 Christians in Vietnam in 1650, but persecution soon followed. The first of several waves of Vietnamese Catholics seeking religious freedom settled in the Chanthaburi province of Thailand around 1707 and became the foundation for a future Catholic community there.

The stories of two other missionaries illustrate other underlying factors in Asia. Miguel de Apresentacão, of the Shona people of East Africa, had been taken as a prisoner to Goa (on the west coast of India). He later became a Dominican in Lisbon, was ordained, and chose to continue missionary work in India. One report states that "while respected as a teacher and priest, the African experienced opposition from other members of the order solely because of the color of his skin" (Irvin and Sunquist 2012, 207). Joseph Vaz, a Brahmin from Goa who became Roman Catholic, was ordained in 1676 but not allowed to join a religious order at that time. During his work in Ceylon (present-day Sri Lanka) he had serious conflict, including imprisonment, in the area governed by the Dutch East India Company, which, like the British East India Company, considered any missionary activity an obstacle to its commercial goals. Disguised as a migrant worker, Vaz founded many Catholic communities and composed catechetical materials in the Sinhalese and Tamil languages. He was eventually accepted by a Buddhist king in Ceylon.

In the seventeenth century a complex set of factors shaped a long confrontation known as the Rites Controversy between the accommodational and tabula-rasa approaches of mission. This controversy, to be treated later under the thread "Mission, Cultures, and Religions," had a very negative impact on Christianity in China. In 1700, there were about 200,000 Chinese Catholics and 150 Western missionaries in China (Irvin and Sunquist 2012, 397). However, in 1724 the Chinese emperor expelled most of the missionaries, churches were torn down, and the number of Christians in China dropped dramatically. An exception was the province of Sichuan, which received many migrants and was religiously more tolerant; "the number of Christians is estimated to have grown from under five thousand to more than forty thousand by the end of the century," and "similar growth was seen in Inner Mongolia, Guzhou, and Yunan" (ibid., 398).

The growth of Christianity throughout Asia during 1600–1800 was also influenced by competing political/economic powers from Europe and ecclesiastical differences. In the East Indies many Catholic communities were founded in Flores and Timor under the Portuguese, while several Reformed communities formed in the areas under the Dutch East India Company (VOC) with its center in Jakarta. In the Indian subcontinent the Portuguese and French governments supported Catholic mission efforts, while the British, Dutch, and Danish companies did not generally support Protestant mission efforts. But German Lutherans Bartholomäus Ziegenbalg and Heinrich Plütschau were sent by the king of Denmark to southeast India. By 1800, minority Catholic communities had continued to grow in the present-day Indian states of Karnataka, Kerala, Tamil Nadu, and Andhra Pradesh. The tremendous growth of Catholicism in the Philippines slowed in 1609 when the Spanish faced attacks from the Dutch and Muslims. While the church remained under Spanish control through the seventeenth and eighteenth centuries, a strong Filipino adaptation of Christianity developed. Korea stands out as an exception in Asia, since Christianity did not come through Western agents. Members of the Korean embassy in Beijing brought Chinese Christians writings, including those of Ricci, back to Korea, and a small Christian community developed there. Despite subsequent persecution by the Korean king, Christians met secretly, and there may have been as many as ten thousand Christians in Korea in 1800 (Irvin and Sunquist 2012, 401).

Africa

Christianity in Central Africa centered around the Kingdom of Kongo, which had been under indigenous Christian rule since the beginning of the sixteenth century. In 1607, the Jesuits opened one college in Luanda, capital of Angola, the Portuguese colony south of Kongo, and another in 1624 in São Salvador (present-day M'banza Congo in northwest Angola), then the capital of the Kongo Empire and the home of a resident bishop in 1619. A catechism was translated into the local Kikongo language from the Portuguese version in 1624. The Capuchin missionaries, who came to Kongo in 1645, over the next two centuries "were closer to West Africans and developed a more intimate knowledge of African Christianity than any other European order" (Irvin and Sunquist 2012, 212). By the end of the seventeenth century over 300,000 were baptized in Central Africa (ibid., 213). While the Kingdom of Kongo as a united entity had almost collapsed by the eighteenth century, the Portuguese colony of Angola was expanding.

Interestingly, the first Roman Catholic missionaries in East Africa were Augustinians, trained in Goa. They began in the capital of the Kingdom of Mombasa (in present-day Kenya) and later on islands off the coast. Some six hundred were baptized by the end of the first year (Irvin and

Sunquist 2012, 222). Christianity spread as far south as Mozambique and Zimbabwe, but mostly "through Portuguese traders, soldiers and sailors, and their slaves" (ibid.). The relationship between Christians and Muslims, who already had a strong presence along the east coast, was marked by both peaceful relations and violence. Tragically, the traffic in enslaved people from the Zambezi River region to Brazil began during this time period, and very sadly, members of religious orders were often involved in this practice.

During the period from 1600 to 1800 the decline in Portuguese trade and influence in Africa and the accompanying increase by Dutch and British economic interests affected Christianity on the continent. In the seventeenth century the Dutch militarily took over Portuguese strongholds and factories throughout Asia—such as in Indonesia, India, and Ceylon—and in Elmina, Ghana, and Cape Town, South Africa. In the eighteenth century the British included much of coastal Africa in its growing economic network between America and Asia. For example, "In the 1730s, the British surpassed the Portuguese in slave trade, transporting an estimated 170,000 Africans to America during that decade alone" (Irvin and Sunquist 2012, 325). The interests of the Netherlands, England, and Denmark were primarily economic. Generally, they restricted Catholic activity, and Protestant efforts initially were normally limited to chaplaincy in the colonial settlements.

We now turn to Southern Africa, where Holland had its biggest impact in Africa. It had established a colony in Cape Town in the 1650s. Toward the end of the seventeenth century a number of Christian groups, such as the French Huguenots, came in order to escape political intolerance at home. After some initial conflicts a rather tentative peace was reached between the colonists and the local Khoikhoi (Hottentots) people. The Dutch used enslaved labor from other parts of Africa and Malay people, who were Muslims, from the East Indies. The Moravians, members of the Brethren who had fled from Czechoslovakia to Germany and who had a strong sense of mission, sent Georg Schmidt as a missionary to the Dutch colony in 1737. He founded an agricultural community of Khoikhoi people in Baviaanskloof, over fifty miles from Cape Town, and had the first baptism in 1742. He was eventually forced to leave southern Africa because his ordination was not recognized by the Dutch authorities. The Moravians were not allowed to return until 1792. At that time, they reestablished a community in Baviaanskloof, renamed Genadendal (Valley of Grace), which had over a thousand inhabitants by 1800. "Europeans and Africans lived together with a significant degree of dignity and prosperity" (Irvin and Sunquist 2012, 333).

Along with the Moravians, other Christians contributed to the beginning of the abolitionist movement. Two influential voices in Europe were those of two African Christians who wrote about the real experience of slavery. Olaudah Equiano, known also as Gustavus Vassa, was captured from an Igbo village (in present-day Nigeria), taken as an enslaved person to Barbados, Virginia, and England, where he received baptism and education. He eventually was allowed to purchase his freedom from his owner, who was a member of the Society of Friends (Quakers). Equiano worked with Granville Sharp, a strong opponent to slavery in England, and in 1789 published a narrative of his own enslavement. His earlier request to the Anglican bishop of London for ordination and commissioning to Africa as a missionary had been denied. One of his collaborators in England was Ottobah Cugoano, who had been taken into slavery from the Fanti people in Ghana to Grenada in the Caribbean. He also became Christian and received his freedom. His memoir, a powerful commentary on slavery, was published in England in 1787 and translated into French the following year. "Without question, it was these African Christian voices in the heart of the empire that proved to be most significant in turning the tide of public opinion in England at the end of the eighteenth century" (Irvin and Sunquist 2012, 329). After an initial failed attempt, Sharp and others formed a settlement for former slaves and other Africans called Freetown in Sierra Leone in 1792.

Following up on the account of Ethiopia in the last chapter, both the Portuguese and the Roman Catholic Church in the seventeenth century continued to strive to bring Ethiopians under their authority. After several rebellions Ethiopia "turned decisively away from Rome and the West, and looked even more toward India and the Orthodox traditions of the East" (ibid., 219). Monasticism continued to provide spiritual and theological foundations. In the eighteenth century Ethiopia was suffering due to internal political fracturing and theological divisions. At the end of this century the *abuna* (patriarch of Ethiopia appointed by the Coptic pope in Alexandria) Yosab III was a strong advocate for urgent social reforms and a sign of hope over thirty years.

The Caribbean and Latin America

With a decline in profits from gold and silver, tobacco and sugar became the major exports from the Caribbean in the seventeenth century. Particularly due to the labor-intensive production of sugar, the numbers of enslaved peoples from Africa increased dramatically; the population of many Caribbean islands consisted of an African majority by 1700. Holland and Britain now entered as major colonial powers, and Spain and Portugal declined. In the eighteenth century Britain took the lead in the slave trade, "transporting approximately 2.5 million Africans to the Caribbean and South America between 1690 and 1807" (Irvin and Sunquist 2012, 418). British political and economic ambitions conflicted with religious ones. The Church of England (Anglican) policy that enslaved or indentured persons would eventually be freed upon baptism was denied in America. The Anglican Morgan Godwyn, an advocate for enslaved Africans, voiced his protest to this change in Westminster Abbey. Other single Christian voices against slavery included several Quakers, the Puritan pastor Richard Baxter, Jesuits Alonso de Sandoval and Peter Claver, and Capuchins Epiphane de Moirans and José de Jaca.

In general, Protestant churches in the Caribbean, like the Catholic Church, worked closely with the secular colonial authorities, whereby the "governors generally were expected to establish parishes, appoint priests, and ensure financial support for the church" (ibid., 228). The Anglicans began in St. Christopher (present-day St. Kitts) and Barbados. In the eighteenth century the Moravians established their first community in America on St. Thomas; George Liele, a Baptist of African descent, founded churches in Jamaica and the Bahamas; and Methodism was growing, especially among those of African heritage. The Roman Catholic Church did not expand as much, mostly due to the lack of priests, especially after the Jesuits were suppressed.

The focus of Portuguese colonial investments in Asia and Africa shifted to Brazil with the discovery of gold in 1693. While the profit from gold would not be so great, the arrival of tens of thousands seeking quick wealth bolstered the presence and expansion of the Portuguese in America. Paramilitary bands, *bandeirantes*, went into western areas of Brazil seeking indigenous people for enslaved labor sugar production and domestic labor. As introduced in Chapter 5, the Jesuits had established a system of reductions (*reducciones*) or Christian settlements to protect the indigenous people and combine the best of indigenous and Portuguese cultures. Antonio Ruiz de Montoya, a *mestizo* from Peru who initially worked as a Jesuit in Argentina and Paraguay, was assigned in 1613 to serve the Túpi-Guarani people in Brazil. He founded eleven missions, but eventually he led a massive migration of Guarani almost a thousand miles to Argentina to distance them from raiding parties. Due to his pleas to King Philip IV of Spain, the Guarani were allowed to bear arms in 1641 to protect themselves. António Vieira, a Portuguese-born Jesuit, spoke strongly against the injustice of the Inquisition in Portugal and on behalf of the human rights of the indigenous peoples in America. German-speaking Jesuit Johann Philipp Bettendorf, like Vieira, served as the superior of the Jesuit mission in Brazil and was a linguist and defender of the Túpi-Guarani. Lourenço da Silva de Mendonça, a former enslaved person and a Brazilian mulatto of Angolan and European descent, went to Portugal, where he was appointed as the procurator of the Confraternity of Our Lady Star of the Negroes. His description of the horrible reality of slavery along with the appeal of the Capuchins in Kongo led Pope Innocent XI to issue a condemnation of the Atlantic slave trade. Unfortunately, it had little impact.

The dominance that Spain had over Portugal in Europe carried over into Spanish America through much of the seventeenth century. Spanish colonial rule was conducted through two viceroyalties: Peru consisted of most of South America; and New Spain consisted of Central America, the Caribbean, Mexico, and a large area north of the Rio Grande River. The church was integrated into the political and social structure, strictly stratified with the Europeans at the top, the pure indigenous and African peoples at the bottom, and those of mixed heritage in between. In addition to two government and three church universities founded earlier, the Jesuits, Dominicans, and Franciscans founded schools in the seventeenth century that served primarily to train priests and government administrators. The acquisition of much land and wealth by religious congregations often led to problems and corruption. A secular priest, Juan de Palafox y Mendoza, who later became a bishop and visitator general of Mexico, was a figure of reform in this regard. A growing number of lay associations or confraternities provided a venue for more lay involvement in works of social service and charity.

The Catholic Church was well established in Latin America, and Protestants were officially not allowed to work there. In the eighteenth century a number of social protests and uprisings "arose from the experience of the indigenous, the enslaved, and the oppressed who were politically, socially, and often religiously on the underside of Spanish power" (Irvin and Sunquist 2012, 428). The most successful revolt occurred in Saint-Dominique (Haiti) under the leadership of the freed slave Toussaint L'Ouverture, who would die in a French prison in 1803. The following year a free nation renamed Haiti was "the first to abolish slavery in the Americas" (ibid., 429). The Catholic Church remained the official church in Haiti. In other parts of the Caribbean and Latin America, church authorities and religious orders, with the exception of the Jesuits, normally sided with the colonial powers in the face of social unrest.

North America

We begin with Spanish colonialism in North America. Ponce de León named a peninsula *la Florida* in 1513, but after several explorations and failed attempts, a permanent settlement was not established in Florida until 1565 in St. Augustine. By 1602, there were a number of Spanish forts and Franciscan missions from northern Florida to what is now South Carolina. In the west, after some Spanish explorations north of the Rio Grande, the capital for the new province of New Mexico was established in 1610 in

Santa Fe. A number of indigenous peoples, whom the Spanish collectively called *Pueblos*, lived in small towns or villages. Other Native Americans like the nomadic Navajo (Dine) and Apache had recently moved into this area. Franciscans without invading armies were allowed to establish their missions to peacefully create a new Pueblo society. "Unlike many regions of Spain's American empire, limited contact with the Europeans and the Franciscans' paternalistic protection prevented the Pueblos from succumbing to mass diseases or being decimated by enslavement" (Irvin and Sunquist 2012, 251). By the mid-seventeenth century many had accepted Christianity, and some had moved into the Franciscan missions. However, due to growing tensions a Pueblo rebellion in 1680 drove out the colonists and most of the Franciscans from Arizona and New Mexico. Spanish rule returned to this area by the end of the seventeenth century, and many settlers followed.

In response to the colonial advance of Russia in Alaska, the Spanish expanded their colonial presence over to the West Coast. Jesuit Francisco Kino, under whose leadership fifteen missions were established in the present-day Mexican states of Baja California and Sonora, defended the rights of the local Pimas and opposed slavery. When the Jesuits were expelled by the king of Spain in 1767, the Dominicans and Franciscans continued the mission work. Under the leadership of Junípero Serra the Franciscans founded twenty-one missions from San Diego to San Francisco in the present-day state of California. "Without question, harsh methods of coercion were at times employed by the Franciscans, but it was not the general practice" (ibid., 448). Serra successfully brought formal charges against the governor for strong military action. By 1800, the foundations for Christianity were well established in California.

While searching for a route to China, the French explorer Jacques Cartier landed in Newfoundland (present-day Canada) in 1534 and within a couple years established trading settlements for furs in Quebec and Montreal. While the trading relationship with the First Nations (Native American) peoples began under fairly amicable terms, the local people soon began to die from the European diseases. The Jesuits (Blackrobes), who arrived some seventy years later, attempted to use a more accommodational approach to mission among the semi-nomadic peoples. Jean de Brébeuf, Isaac Jogues, four other Jesuits, and two French laymen were killed during the period of 1642–1649 when they were caught in the war between the Iroquois and Huron nations. Collectively they are now known as the North American Martyrs. Two Native American Christian women, Kateri Tekakwitha and Catherine Ganneaktena, were important early figures of First Nations Christianity. Ursuline Sister Marie de l'Incarnation arrived in Quebec in 1639 and founded "the first school for girls in northern America" (Bevans and

Schroeder 2004, 182). In the late part of the eighteenth century, after defeat at the hands of England in 1763, France ceded its colonies in America to the British. With time, Canada was divided into French and English regions, with Montreal and York (present-day Toronto) as their respective capitals. The former supported the Roman Catholic Church and the latter the Church of England.

The first permanent settlements of the English in North America were in Jamestown, Virginia, in 1607, and Plymouth, Massachusetts, in 1620. While the Church of England was the official religion, many of the settlers were members of dissenting church groups looking for freedom. This included the Puritans, who strove to purify the Church of England of all vestiges of the Catholic Church. They first landed in Salem, Massachusetts, in 1630, in order to form a new Christian society. "More than twenty thousand people crossed the Atlantic over the next decade from England to New England" (Irvin and Sunquist 2012, 254). They expanded into the colonies of Massachusetts and Connecticut. The Puritan John Eliot established fourteen separate settlements (called praying Indian towns) for Native Americans who became Christian and culturally European. However, fighting eventually broke out, and as a result, the Native Americans lost their land and in some cases their freedom through enslavement, and they were forced to move west. In contrast to the situation south of the Rio Grande, there was very little intermarriage between the Europeans and the indigenous peoples. In addition, since dissension was not welcomed under the Puritans' strict ideology, some, like Roger Williams, were forced to leave. Williams started a new settlement that became the colony of Rhode Island, noted for its religious tolerance. Other early colonies were Virginia, New Amsterdam (New York), Maryland, and Pennsylvania.

Many Europeans came to the English colonies as indentured servants, but they were theoretically able to pay off their debt or crime after five to ten years and be set free. Even potential freedom was not the case for the enslaved persons from Africa, even if they became Christian. "By 1750, some fifty thousand enslaved persons a year were being imported by British ships to American colonies" (Irvin and Sunquist 2012, 261). The African diaspora shaped a new expression of Christian faith. "The form of Christianity they created in America was from its inception an Africanized religion, abolitionist at the core, and capable of sustaining people's struggles and hopes across many centuries" (ibid., 260).

At the beginning of the eighteenth century "the Puritan political experiment had fairly well run its course, and a greater degree of toleration accompanied by a new sense of rationalism was taking hold" (Irvin and Sunquist 2012, 435). Within this context a religious revival, called the Great Awakening, swept through the colonies with people such as preacher-theologian Jonathan Edwards and revival preacher George Whitefield leading the way. Sarah Osborn, who experienced an "awakening" through a sermon by Whitefield, started a Religious Female Society. At times as many as five hundred enslaved and freed women, men, and children gathered in her home in Rhode Island. "Revivalism triggered democratic impulses . . . rendering all equal before God in the experience of conversion, and calling all . . . to be engaged in a life of service and devotion" (ibid., 440). The Baptists, born a century earlier in England, had established churches in the southern colonies before the Great Awakening. Some Africans joined Baptist churches in Virginia, "where blacks and whites worshipped together for a time" (ibid., 442). New efforts to evangelize Native Americans were carried out by Moravians, who contributed much toward educating Cherokee leaders and negotiating their land rights in Georgia, and by David Brainerd in Massachusetts and New Jersey with the Lenape people. Algonquian-speaker Samson Occom, who was ordained by the Presbytery of Long Island, New York, in 1759, and was instrumental in the foundation of Dartmouth College ten years later, is "widely regarded as the first Native American to publish works in English" (ibid.).

After ten years of war between England and France tensions percolated into open hostility between England and its colonies in 1775 over the issue of taxes. The Declaration of Independence was signed in 1776, and after five years of war, the thirteen colonies were on their way to forming the new nation of the United States. The First Amendment of the US Constitution prohibited an official religion, making the United States "the first nation-state rooted in the European reality of Christendom to so disestablish Christianity" (Irvin and Sunquist 2012, 454). Those who benefitted immediately from this freedom of religion were Jews, most of whom were of Spanish and Portuguese origins; and Roman Catholics, under the leadership of John Carroll, who in 1789 was elected by the clergy and then confirmed by Rome as the bishop of Baltimore, the first bishop in the United States. Freemasonry, the quasi-religious organization to which George Washington and Benjamin Franklin belonged and which shared much with the Deism beliefs of many of the nation's leaders, in many ways "served as a civil religion" (ibid., 458) for the United States. At the same time, new churches emerged and others grew. An Episcopal Church independent of the Church of England was formed around 1790; a Lutheran school of theology (Hartwich Seminary) was established in 1797 in New York City (and would eventually be established as Hartwick College in Oneonta, New York); Methodists who had been in the colonies in the 1760s developed as an independent Methodist Episcopal Church under the leadership of Francis Asbury and Thomas Coke; Baptists had grown to more than 750 congregations by 1800. African Americans founded the African Baptist Church and the African Methodist Episcopal Church, under the leadership of Andrew Bryan and Richard Allen, respectively. David George planted a number of black Baptist churches in Nova Scotia and later another in the new colony of Freetown in Sierra Leone.

For a political map of the Americas at the end of the eighteenth century, see Map 8.

Europe

At the beginning of the seventeenth century, rationalism and science were growing in importance, while the role of religion was declining in relevance. Copernicus had already posed the theory that the earth revolved around the sun and not vice versa. Galileo supported the Copernican view with his invention of a telescope and soon found himself under house arrest and censorship by the Inquisition. Francis Bacon developed a new inductive scientific method. René Descartes established rationality as normative, thereby providing "the foundations for a revolutionary turn in European philosophy that was as far reaching as that of Copernicus" (Irvin and Sunquist 2012, 266). Major changes were occurring in the political-religious arena as well. The 1555 Peace of Augsburg was not a long-term solution. Tensions between Catholics and Protestants contributed to the Thirty Years' War—"one of the bigger blots on Christian history in Europe" (Norris 2002, 176). The Treaty of Westphalia in 1648 marked the beginning of the modern idea of the nation-state, that is, politics are to be shaped by national and not religious identity. This treaty provided "the roots of what would come to be called 'secularization' or the 'secular state' in Europe" (Irvin and Sunquist 2012, 268). And, competing interests of European nations affected the rest of the world, as noted earlier in this chapter.

This time of change and violence was also a time of renewal within the Roman Catholic Church. In 1622, Pope Gregory XV established the Congregation for the Propagation of the Faith to reclaim the responsibility of the Catholic Church, not of political powers like Spain and Portugal, for missionary efforts. Members of new religious congregations responded to moral and spiritual decline and the needs created by overcrowded cities and the bubonic plague. Jane Frances de Chantal founded the Congregation of the Visitation in 1610; Vincent de Paul founded the Vincentian congregation in 1625 to reach out to the peasants, and eight years later cofounded the Daughters of Charity with Louise de Marillac to minister to abandoned children and prisoners.

Various movements were at work within Protestantism in the seventeenth century. First of all, German Lutherans and Reformed churches in continental Europe developed a scholastic orthodoxy of Luther and Calvin,

Map 8: North and South America in the Late Eighteenth Century

whereby confessions were seen as "a means of protecting the church from grievous error" (Irvin and Sunquist 2012, 278). Second, from the Anabaptist groups who were persecuted in the sixteenth century, the Mennonites now established themselves in Holland and certain parts of Switzerland and Germany, while a Reform group known as the Amish moved to Germany and later to the North American colony of Pennsylvania. Third, the situation in England was more complex. Civil war broke out in 1642 between the supporters of the monarchy and those of the parliament. The Puritans, who first appeared in sixteenth-century England to bring Calvinistic reform, had their strongest influence at this time. After the civil war the parliament sponsored an assembly of church leaders who over nine years produced documents, including the Westminster Confession, which "represent the high-water mark of English-speaking Reformed scholasticism" (ibid., 288). After the restoration of a limited monarchy in 1661, congregations of the Church of England returned to following their Thirty-Nine Articles, while many nonconforming congregations continued to follow the Westminster Confession. A new spiritual movement under the leadership of George Fox developed into the Society of Friends, or Quakers, which, like the Puritans, represents the Protestant stream of the "religion of the heart" for which the ultimate concern was "a genuine inner experience of Christian life that did not rest on what they considered to be external formalities" (ibid., 278). Another significant development in England was the emergence of the Baptists and the Free Church ideal—"free from government control, made up of members who had been baptized after a public profession of faith" (ibid., 291). The Act of Toleration in 1689 opened the door for broader religious tolerations of the growing number of Christian denominations. Finally, another stream within Protestantism was forming through interaction with science and rationalism, particularly through philosophers Thomas Hobbes and John Locke, into what influenced Deism and Unitarianism. All of these developments in England had a major impact on Christianity in North America as noted above.

In the eighteenth century the gap between science and religion and the tension between reason and revelation continued to grow within the context of the Enlightenment. In France, "a concern for freedom and open inquiry in the seventeenth century had turned antireligious by the end of the eighteenth century" (Irvin and Sunquist 2012, 346). In the face of such challenges, the churches strove to renew themselves. For the Catholic Church this was manifested again in terms of new religious orders such as the Passionists and Redemptorists responding to spiritual and social needs.

Among Protestants there were "currents of moderation" (ibid., 353) with established church status for Lutherans, Reformed, and Anglicans. However, on the other side, there was "a cluster of movements that came to form an evangelical consensus around the need or desire for more experiential forms of Christianity" (ibid., 355). Pietism began in the seventeenth century under the leadership of Philipp Jakob Spener, who assisted in the founding of the University of Halle in 1694, which soon became the center for Pietist learning in Germany and beyond. One of its graduates, Nikolaus Ludwig von Zinzendorf, was the founder of the Moravians. Moravians in the British colony of Georgia met the itinerant preacher George Whitefield and brothers John and Charles Wesley—three persons who shared prayer and outreach ministry during their days in Oxford. John developed local Methodist societies with lay preachers to provide "a vision of realizable holiness for daily life" (ibid., 361). In 1774, he published a pamphlet condemning slavery. While John thought that this movement would provide spiritual renewal within the Church of England, the Methodists eventually became a separate church entity in North America in 1784 and in England in 1795. Charles Wesley contributed much to Methodism after his brother's death. Others who were a part of the broader evangelical revival in England from within the Anglican Church included John Newton and William Wilberforce, influential in the founding of the colony of Sierra Leone.

The eighteenth-century changes in politics and religion took place against the background of major technological, economic, social, and environmental changes—referred to as the Industrial Revolution. Cities were growing rapidly, the French government was nearly bankrupt due to a series of wars, famine was a reality, and social unrest was growing between those in authority and commoners, including the growing middle class. The ideas of "liberty, equality, and fraternity" drawn from the Enlightenment and the American Revolution contributed to the situation. The storming of the Bastille stronghold in Paris in 1789 marked the beginning of the French Revolution. In 1790, the church was incorporated into the state, monastic orders were banned, and all clergy were to declare allegiance to the government. As the revolution turned more violent, thousands of priests and nuns were imprisoned, deported, or executed. The monarchy was officially abolished in 1792. The revolution ended in 1799, when General Napoléon Bonaparte led a coup d'état. This marked "the beginning of a new era in European history . . . [in which] the relationship between state and church in European society would be dramatically changed" (Irvin and Sunquist 2012, 370).

Orthodox Churches

The situation of Orthodox Churches, as defined in Chapter 5, became more complex during the period of 1600–1800. Those living, on the one hand, under the Safavid Dynasty and Shia Islam in Persia, and, on the other, under

Ottoman Turks and Sunni Muslims in Egypt, Palestine, Anatolia, Serbia, Albania, Armenia, and Georgia, faced the continual challenge of living as a minority community within Muslim rule, with the addition of "the pressures of Catholic and Protestant missions from the West" (Irvin and Sunquist 2012, 296). By the eighteenth century large sections of Balkan lands, such as Armenia, that had been traditionally Christian had become predominantly Muslim. However, as the Muslim Ottoman Empire weakened, there was a "revitalization of Orthodoxy in the Balkans and elsewhere under Ottoman rule . . . primarily the result of the monastics whose teachings and writings inspired devotion mixed with nationalism" (ibid., 382).

Orthodoxy in Russia and Ukraine was intertwined with the politics and culture of tsarist rule in Russia. To the west, the number of Orthodox declined with the growth of Polish and Lithuanian Catholics, and Latvia was politically divided between Poland and Sweden, which were officially Roman Catholic and Lutheran, respectively. However, at the same time, the Orthodox Church expanded as Russia spread eastward into Siberia and Alaska. Peter the Great had a major and controversial impact on eighteenth-century Russia. While being credited with introducing economic and cultural reforms, he also is known for using violent means to achieve those ends. He began as joint tsar with his half-brother and ended with the title of emperor. In terms of Christianity, he replaced the patriarch with a Most Holy Synod and put severe restrictions on monastic life. This trend continued after Peter's death to the point that by the 1760s "the number of monasteries in Russia had been reduced by half" (Irvin and Sunquist 2012, 377). However, a renewal of monasticism was under way by the end of the century.

The seventeenth and eighteenth centuries included a variety of religious and secular encounters on a global scale. Christians engaged new peoples in America, Africa, Asia, and Siberia. It was a time of the horrible Thirty Years' War and inspiring spiritual renewals. The human tragedy of enslaved Africans continued to be a pressing issue. We shall now trace the development of the six threads of tradition over this period.

Threads of Christian Tradition

Scripture

After the age of reforms Protestant scholastics developed theories of biblical interpretation whereby they "insisted upon the 'full' and 'verbal' inspiration of Scripture" (González 1994, 103). Everything ("full") in the Bible is directly inspired by God, including the exact words ("verbal"). With time, the new movements of Moravians, Pietists, Methodists, and the Great

Awakening emphasized "the need for personal piety rather than strict, cold orthodoxy" (ibid.). One of the major academic contributions came through the work of German Pietists P. J. Spener and A. H. Francke at the University of Halle, introduced earlier, "to equip gifted students with the knowledge of Semitic and Slavonic languages," reflecting "the stress placed by Pietism upon the study of biblical languages and versions" (Rogerson et al., 105).

At the same time, a very different approach to interpreting scripture, under the influence of rationalism and the former Renaissance period, was developing into what would become the historical-critical method. Deist philosopher John Locke maintained that the amount of truth present in scripture was dependent upon reason. Scholars began to study the historical, literary, and cultural context of the text itself. Old Testament scholar Benedict Spinoza laid out the principle that "theories of consistency and authority must arise from the text, and must not be imposed upon the investigation of the text" (Rogerson et al., 102). For example, the New Testament should not determine the interpretation of the Old Testament. The writing of Roman Catholic Richard Simon "was the first significant attempt to write a critical history of the Old Testament using techniques of textual and redaction criticism" (Ormerod, 320). Anglican Brian Walton in 1657 compiled an extensive comparative study of scriptural texts, which included "the Ethiopic version of the New Testament and Persian for the Gospels, in addition to the Syriac and Arabic versions" (Rogerson et al., 323). Several scholars bridged the spiritual and critical approaches to scripture in the eighteenth century. Lutheran Pietist J. A. Bengel in 1742 published a work "in which he set out to elucidate the New Testament as a guide to life with commentary based on sound philology" (ibid., 325), a work much used by John Wesley. Halle professor S. J. Baumgarten published biblical commentaries "for the spiritual building-up of the readers" (ibid., 106), while including the works of other scholars, such as English Deists. Baumgarten's successor, J. S. Semler, who has been called "the father of modern biblical criticism" (ibid., 107), further developed the historical method by maintaining that every word of the Bible was not divinely inspired, but he also held that faith was a prerequisite for understanding religious matters.

Bible translation was a priority for Protestants. In the seventeenth century Lutheran doctor and theologian Peter Heyling translated the gospel of John into Amharic, the spoken language of Ethiopia. Under the Dutch Reformed influence in the East Indies, initially bibles and prayer books in Dutch were provided for the Dutch colonists, but during the eighteenth century, "portions of scripture and devotional books had been published in Malay, Taiwanese, Tamil, and Sinhalese, including an entire translation of the Bible into Malay" (Irvin and Sunquist 2012, 409). Pietist missionary Ziegenbalg translated the New Testament into the Indian language of Tamil.

In Europe, during a great literary period in England including the work of William Shakespeare, a new English translation, known as the King James Bible, was published in 1611.

Translating scriptures was also important for other Christian churches. The first translation of the entire Bible in Armenian was published in Amsterdam in 1666. Peter the Great of Russia ordered that the Bible be translated into some vernacular languages as the Orthodox faith spread. Maronite scholar Abraham Ecchellensis, while working at the Propagation of the Faith office in Rome, "helped to revise the Arabic version of the Bible for missionary use among Muslims," and later he "helped to produce the Syriac and Arabic portions of the Paris Polyglot Bible" (Irvin and Sunquist 2012, 301). Valignano promoted the translation of some scripture into Japanese, but for some reason the Jesuits didn't translate the Bible into Chinese, although they had permission from Rome to do so.

The Bible continued to serve a key role in most Protestant worship, preaching, and spirituality. For example, the Pietist Francke in 1710 started the Cansteinsche Bible Institute in Halle, where inexpensive bibles were printed first in German and then in other languages. By the time of Francke's death in 1727, "ten thousand copies of the Bible were being printed and sold annually" (Irvin and Sunquist 2012, 356). In North America, Puritan Anne Hutchinson used the practice of neighborhood home meetings to hold Bible studies in her home in Boston, "at which she taught her own interpretation of scripture" (ibid., 255). Partly due to her criticism of some Puritan preachers and the general lack of tolerance for dissension in Massachusetts, she was eventually exiled from the colony. As for Catholics, Bishop John Carroll was a "tireless promoter of the reading of scriptures" and promoted the publication of the "Rome-approved Douay-Rheims translation of the Bible for English readers in America" (ibid., 457). Finally, during the classical developments in church music in the eighteenth century, famous composers like Johann Sebastian Bach (1685–1750) and George Frideric Handel (1685–1759) based much of their music on biblical themes and passages.

Liturgy, Sacraments, and Art

After a period of momentous and quick liturgical change in the sixteenth century, described in Chapter 5, the situation leveled out over the next two hundred years. This was particularly true with the eucharistic liturgy of the Roman Catholic Church due to the stabilizing effect of the Council of Trent. Partly in reaction to the Protestant emphasis on vernacular liturgies, translations of the Latin missal were forbidden (with the exception of Chinese, noted below). The laity during mass would normally read devotional books to receive spiritual benefits or pray the Rosary. Reception of the Eucharist by the laity during the liturgy declined in some areas in the seventeenth century due to the emphasis by Jansenism on human sinfulness and therefore the need for confession before receiving communion. The canon law provision was that Catholics receive communion once a year during the Easter season, but now "the rule that was laid down as a minimum became a norm instead" (Martos, 291).

However, the Enlightenment spirit of freedom, the growing tension between France and Rome, and the desire to reestablish Gallican or French heritage provided the context for proposed changes toward the end of the eighteenth century. Holy Roman Emperor Joseph II attempted to curb the pope's authority, and he established directives to make the liturgy simpler and more understandable. In order to achieve this and address possible abuses associated with multiple masses for financial motivation, the Synod of Pistoria in 1786 "went even further directing that there should be only one altar in each church, one Mass on each Sunday, and outright condemning the use of Latin in the liturgy" (Foley, 245). It is estimated that in France by the time of the French Revolution, "80 out of 130 dioceses had abandoned the liturgy of Trent and were following a neo-Gallican form of liturgy" (ibid., 290).

China was an exception in the seventeenth century. In 1615, Pope Paul V gave permission for the scriptures to be translated into classical Chinese and for future Chinese priests to celebrate mass and administer the sacraments in Chinese, since they lacked sufficient knowledge of Latin. An official Chinese translation of the Roman Missal was published in 1670 and was possibly used until a suspension of this permission in 1688 from Rome. The Jesuit Ludovico Buglio as the chief translator generally followed a literal translation methodology but the choice and naming of major feasts reflect his cultural and political sensitivities. For example, Finding the Holy Cross was made into a major feast, probably to impress the Chinese emperor with the power of Christianity with the reference to the importance of the symbol of the cross for Constantine's victory (see Seah, 107).

With the Rites Controversy, Latin became the norm everywhere. Also, increased persecution of Christians in China toward the end of the eighteenth century affected the shape of worship. "Small communities of Christians met for prayer and worship on a regular basis. Some of them practiced baptism, but without priests they did not celebrate the Eucharist" (Irvin and Sunquist 2012, 398). In other Catholic situations the meaning of the Eucharist was expressed according to local cultures. "De Rhodes also adapted traditional Christian liturgy within the Vietnamese context" (Bevans and Schroeder 2004, 191). In Kongo, the people "would beat drums, play instruments, and even shoot guns in the air" as they sang the Gloria at mass, and often salt was put in the baptismal water because, according to that African worldview, salt was seen as "a means of warding off evil spirits" (Irvin and Sunquist 2012, 213, 215). In Peru, the feast of Corpus Christi became a public celebration including Incan cultural aspects, and throughout Latin America, Sunday mass "became both a religious and a social event" (ibid., 243).

Worship among the Orthodox churches continued to be closely linked to national identity. Following the call for church reform by several tsars in Russia, Patriarch Nikon in the seventeenth century introduced liturgical reforms "to bring the Russian Church into conformity with Greek liturgical practices" (Irvin and Sunquist 2012, 313). Those resisting such changes, known as Old Believers, "continued to hold on to the traditional Russian liturgical practices for centuries to come" (ibid., 314). With the rapid growth of the Catholic Church in Croatia, the Orthodox monastery of Marča entered an agreement to affiliate with Rome in 1611. They "were allowed to continue to worship in Croatian, following the eastern Orthodoxy liturgy, but were required to insert into their services of worship an acknowledgement of the pope in Rome" (ibid., 299). This of course raised serious objections from other Orthodox leaders. The Syriac liturgy was still celebrated by both the Catholic and Orthodox Syrian churches of the Saint Thomas tradition (treated later under "Ministry and Organization"). However, during the eighteenth century, as noted in Chapter 5, "the Syrian Roman Catholic priests gradually lost their understanding of Syriac, so that the Syriac Mass became meaningless, even to the priests" (ibid., 415).

In terms of Protestantism, the understanding and celebration of the Eucharist continued in much the same way in Lutheran, Reformed, and Anglican churches, as described in Chapter 5. New Christian movements and denominations brought new worship styles. Some followed a more open practice in terms of who could receive the Eucharist or communion, while a preacher like Jonathan Edwards wanted to restrict "admission to Communion to those whom he considered to be truly converted" (Irvin and Sunquist 2012, 438). Representing other "religions of the heart," the Puritans "had placed considerable emphasis on the experiential dimension of 'true' religion" (ibid., 435) and the importance of preaching. Methodists and Baptists were open to emotional expressiveness in worship, and this would lead to "the flowering of distinctive free church styles of worship" (Foley, 246). In Christian communities of enslaved people in North America, "liturgical forms of music and prayer were adapted to African cultural patterns" (Irvin and Sunquist 2012, 442). Quakers spent their time in silence until the Spirit spoke through someone in the gathering.

The "religion of the heart" stream of Protestantism emphasized the personal, internal aspects of the faith. However, the English Puritans and

German Pietists in general still affirmed the external practice of the sacraments, although some "went further along the lines of inward religion ... weakening considerably their emphasis on external sacraments, scripture, or church authorities" (Irvin and Sunquist 2012, 279). Having said that, the majority of Protestants embraced the sacraments of the Lord's Supper (Eucharist) and baptism, though the practice differed in form and regularity. In terms of baptism, the variance in the practice of infant and adult baptism was described in the previous chapter. The Baptists, representing the emerging free church model, introduced the practice of baptism after a public profession of faith. The Synod of Dort (1617–1618) of the Dutch Reformed Church, with other denominations in attendance, was divided on the question of whether Asian, African, or Native American children could be baptized (see Daniels 2017a).

In terms of the attitude of the Orthodox Church to other churches, the ecumenical patriarch with the support of the patriarchs of Alexandria and Jerusalem issued a decree in 1755 of not accepting the validity of baptisms outside the Orthodox Church. This was in response to proselytism by Catholics and Protestants in areas of Orthodox presence. As a whole, the Russian Orthodox Church did not accept this Orthodox ruling and continued to accept other baptisms as long as "the individual [would] undergo chrismation (or confirmation) upon entering a Russian Orthodox Church" (Irvin and Sunquist 2012, 385). On the other side, Catholic, Lutheran, and Calvinist churches continued to accept Orthodox baptisms.

The Council of Trent had affirmed seven sacraments in the Roman Catholic Church. The 1614 revision of the Roman sacramentary required priests for the sacrament of Penance to hear confessions from behind a screen, primarily to protect the anonymity of those confessing. Furthermore, some bishops at Trent "had expressed the hope that private confession could become a vehicle for giving spiritual counseling to the faithful, but outside of monasteries and convents this hardly ever happened" (Martos, 358). In reality, most considered penance simply a requirement before receiving communion. The Jansenists wanted to apply more rigorous standards, such as not allowing persons to receive communion until the required penance was completed, and they also questioned the consequences of imperfect contrition. This stricter understanding and practice was ultimately not accepted by the church.

In the seventeenth century the sacrament of anointing was simplified, and priests were to conditionally anoint those whose immediate death was not absolutely certain. As for matrimony, the Catholic Church continued to affirm that it had the right to maintain marriage laws for all Christians. However, from the beginning of the reforms, "other Christian churches developed their own wedding ceremonies and considered them valid, and as a matter of fact for over two centuries afterward almost all marriages in Europe were church marriages" (Martos, 441). The French Revolution will effect a change in this around Europe in the nineteenth century. It is interesting to note that for the Moravians, "Marriage was considered a sacrament, and the entire community was involved in celebrating the consummation of marriages among their members" (Irvin and Sunquist 2012, 357). While the sacrament of orders did not change at this time, the developing practice of priestly ministry is discussed below in "Ministry and Organization."

In terms of the arts, the lack of opportunity for the laity to participate much in Roman Catholic liturgies "led to a renewed emphasis on church music and architecture . . . to arouse in people a sense of the sacred" (Martos, 290). "The music that had begun as plain chant in medieval times developed into polyphony during the Renaissance and into elaborate choral and orchestral works during the Baroque period" (ibid.). However, congregational singing was generally not highly valued in Catholic worship. Catholics did develop vernacular hymnody, for example, in German-speaking areas in response to Protestant German hymns. In Spanish America such vernacular singing "was a practice that helped missionaries both attract converts and impart religious teaching" (Foley, 263). Hymns were composed in local languages such as Nahuatl, Mochica, and Quechua. Furthermore, music was a rare avenue for cultural exchange as indigenous and European styles combined in producing a unique contribution to baroque music in the Jesuit reductions, through, for example, the Moxos and Chiquitos of Bolivia. In the Asian context a Vietnamese woman convert from Buddhism who was baptized as Catherine in the seventeenth century "wrote a book of poems that was set to music as a type of catechism. [These] songs became popular and were sung by Christians and non-Christians alike" (Irvin and Sunquist 2012, 185).

Back in Europe major developments in church music occurred in the eighteenth century, primarily among Protestants through such persons as Charles Wesley, John Newton, and Isaac Watts. There was also a shift from baroque to classical music with large pipe organs and new instruments like the piano. The influence of these changes on religious music is clearly seen, for example, in the famous works of Bach and Handel (see Irvin and Sunquist 2012, 366), both German Lutherans. As for Orthodox Christians in the Ottoman Empire, "Byzantine chant was sung in monasteries like those of Mount Athos in Greece and St. Catherine's on Mount Sinai" (Bevans 2009, 278).

As for architecture, the elaborate baroque style was developed mostly by Catholics. Church interiors "grew more elaborate, with decorative painting and sculpture designed to capture the eye and stimulate the religious imagination even while mass was going on" (Martos, 290). Protestants in general preferred simpler architecture and an emphasis on the pulpit. With the emphasis more on the auditory—preaching and music—than the visual, the architecture of Protestant churches shifted "from processional to auditorium space—from a place that emphasized movement to one that focused on hearing—contribut[ing] to the increased popularity of seating" (Foley, 257). The introduction of pews started with Protestants and then moved to Catholics, especially in northern Europe and North America.

In general, Protestants were much more austere and hesitant regarding the use of art and images compared to Catholics. The English Puritans took a strong stance against what they considered the improper use of images by the Church of England. In contrast, in response to the Catholic Japanese desire for religious art, Valignano had started a school for training Japanese, and later Chinese, Christian artists. While they were taught European styles, "one finds some Japanese features in later works in some of the few surviving images" (Irvin and Sunquist 2012, 182). Icons continued to be very important for the spiritual life of Orthodox communities, especially in Russia. The influence of the baroque style from the West on Russian Orthodox paintings led to a heated conflict. One recalls the iconoclast controversy of the eighth and ninth centuries.

Ministry and Organization

Among the many developments of Protestant and evangelical churches during this period, a number of models of church organization (polity) and ministry developed. The episcopal hierarchical model assigns the central role of authority over a local church to bishops, but there is no universal authority such as a pope or patriarch. An ordained priest (or rector) leads a congregation. The churches of the Anglican communion—for example, the Church of England and the Episcopal Church in the United States—most clearly represent this model and refer to themselves as catholic, in distinction to the Roman Catholic Church. Today, the United Methodist Church and some Lutheran groups have variations of this model.

A second model, the presbyterial type of church governance, drawing upon Calvin in Geneva and Knox in Scotland, developed in this way: Each local church has a body of elected elders (session or consistory), a group of local churches is governed by a higher assembly of elders (presbytery), a group of presbyteries can become a synod, and a national grouping of synods can be gathered as a general assembly. Congregations have ordained pastors or ministers. Presbyterians, for example, trace their roots to the 1560 Scots Confession and the Church of Scotland. Presbyterial polity is associated with Reformed churches.

And finally a third model, the congregationalist, emphasizes the responsibility of each autonomous congregation for its own affairs, that is, free from the authority of bishops or presbyteries. Congregations are led by one or more elected elders as pastors and/or by ordained deacons. This was originally influenced by the Anabaptists' egalitarian idea of church. The Puritans brought congregationalism to North America, where in turn it influenced the Baptists and later many others. These three forms of church organization were clearly represented in developments in England and North America and later transported to other parts of the world.

However, some adaptations occurred in North America. While Congregationalists and Baptists could ordain those considered called and qualified from local congregations for leadership and ministerial roles, the Anglicans had to have candidates for priesthood ordained in England because there was no bishop in America. The increased number of priests coming from England in the eighteenth century could still not meet the pastoral needs in the colonies. "Anglican congregations in the American colonies turned to lay leadership, or 'readers,' who were chosen from among their own ranks and who led services, often even preaching, but who did not administer the sacraments" (Irvin and Sunquist 2012, 435). Lay preachers, including women, were very significant for Methodists. William Tennent is credited with founding in 1727 "the first training school for Presbyterian pastors in North America" (ibid., 436); Arumugam Pillai was the first Indian Lutheran pastor in 1733; Antigua-born and ex-enslaved Rebecca Protten was ordained in 1746 by the Moravians, "making her quite likely the first woman of African descent to undergo the rite in a Protestant or evangelical church tradition" (ibid., 420); and Episcopalian bishop Samuel Seabury began ordaining clergy in America in 1785. Women had more opportunities for leadership and ministry among the Moravians, Society of Friends, Methodists, and Baptists than in other churches.

"Among many of these Protestant or evangelical churches, internal fracturing accelerated throughout the course of the eighteenth century . . . due in some instances to an increased desire for spiritual renewal . . . [and in other cases] it had to do with resistance to the state" (Irvin and Sunquist 2012, 370–71). The birth of Methodism is an example of the former, while the division among Presbyterians in Scotland after 1732 over the issue of the appointment of clergy by wealthy nobles represents the latter. At the same time, Calvinist preacher George Whitefield "liked to tell his listeners that there were no Presbyterians, Quakers, Baptists, Methodists, or even Catholics in heaven . . . [because they] were all simply known as Christians there" (ibid., 438).

While church governance among some was moving toward more congregational and egalitarian forms, the Roman Catholic Church followed a strict episcopal style under the centralizing authority of the pope. The post-Tridentine establishment of seminaries and other reforms helped to produce better-educated priests, whose preaching improved in terms of both regularity and quality. While Protestants understood ordination more in terms of role or function, Catholic theologian Robert Bellarmine insisted on the indelible character or mark of ordination, but also, on a human and ministerial level, he held that the role of the priest is not "one of rigidly performing an external rite" (Bernier, 186). One of the main influences on the reform of the clergy that developed in the seventeenth century was the French school of spirituality, led by Cardinal Pierre de Bérulle and Jean-Jacques Olier, founders of the French Oratorians and Sulpicians, respectively. On the one hand, it fostered an effective spirituality of the clergy, but on the other hand, it also promoted an "exalted notion of ordained priesthood" (ibid., 198). Consequently, "priests also continued to dominate the other ministries in the church, and in this respect, there was little change in the pattern of ministry" (Martos, 512). The major exceptions came through the ministry of religious orders, to be treated in the following section.

Beyond these general ministerial patterns, which affected the entire Catholic Church, other developments occurred outside Europe. While there had already been an African bishop in 1520, only a handful of African or mixed-race priests were trained in the seventeenth and eighteenth centuries through the seminary opened in 1596 on the island of São Tomé to work with the small number of missionary priests. However, in Kongo, the lay catechists who did most of the catechetical teaching and provided pastoral ministry "were usually bilingual and did much of the work that a friar or secular priest did in other places" (Irvin and Sunquist 2012, 212). In the first half of the seventeenth century in Asia, the Jesuits promoted priesthood ordination and vibrant lay ministry among the Japanese and Vietnamese. Admittance to ordination was slower in China. Luo Wenzao (Gregorio López) was consecrated the first Chinese bishop in 1685, and he ordained three Chinese priests three years later. The situation was even slower in the Spanish territory of the Philippines. The first Filipino was ordained in 1698, and several more the following year, about 180 years after Magellan's arrival. Shifting to North America, François de Laval, the first Catholic bishop of Québec, had established a seminary in Canada in 1663, while Bishop Carroll opened the first Catholic seminary in the United States in Baltimore in 1791. In terms of laity and ministry, some confraternities in Spanish America "dedicated themselves to providing for the poor, preparing their members for the Eucharist, or ministering to the dying and the dead" (ibid., 244).

We now turn to church organization and ministry beyond Catholic and Protestant churches. In terms of the Orthodox churches, the Old Believers who resisted the reforms initiated by Patriarch Nikon, introduced above, separated from the state-supported Russian Orthodox Church in the middle of the seventeenth century and suffered much persecution as a result. In the eighteenth century the tsar Peter the Great replaced the patriarch with a Most Holy Synod, which remained the main church body for two centuries. The endorsement of this change by the ecumenical patriarch in Istanbul and a couple other patriarchs "helped to legitimate the synod as an alternative to a patriarch in the Russian Orthodox Church" (Irvin and Sunquist 2012, 376). With Russian eastward expansion, the first Orthodox bishop in Alaska was consecrated in 1799. As for Orthodox under Ottoman Muslim rule, the authority of the ecumenical patriarch over the churches embracing the Chalcedonian formulation shifted to more regional leadership in the provinces. Furthermore, the Ottomans often asked the Armenian patriarch, also now based in Istanbul, to attend to the affairs of "the various non-Chalcedonian millets, or religious 'nations,' including the Copts, West Syrians, East Assyrians, and Maronites" (ibid., 306).

In southwest India the Saint Thomas Christians in 1653 divided into the Syrian Orthodox (Mar Thoma Church) and Syrian Catholic churches (with both an Eastern and a Western rite), a division existing until today. The former welcomed a new ecclesiastical link with the West Syrian (Jacobite) patriarch of Antioch to replace the ancient link with the East Syrian Church. "Efforts were made to begin to restore aspects of the ancient Syrian tradition that had been lost after the Synod of Diamper, thereby joining the Indian Church again to its Asian roots" (Irvin and Sunquist 2012, 198). At the same time, the Syrian Catholic Church flourished under "local, indigenous leadership that had been properly ordained" (ibid.). The Orthodox are often called Mar Thoma, while those in union with Rome are known as the Syro-Malabar Church.

The Roman Catholic Church continued to form new church bodies of Christians from other ancient Christian churches. These included the Syro-Malabar Church (India), Roman Catholic Ukrainian Church (Ukraine), Coptic Catholic Church (Egypt), Greek Melkite Catholic Church (Lebanon), Armenian Catholic Church (Armenia), and Syrian Catholic Church (Persia). They continued with their own leadership under a patriarch or similar authority and with their traditional liturgical, linguistic, and ministerial customs, while also acknowledging the authority of the pope of Rome. Historically they were called "uniate" churches, but today they are described as Eastern churches, with their own rites and in communion with the Roman Catholic Church and its Western rite.

An interesting intersection of Latin West and East Syrian streams of Christianity occurred in China. As seen in Chapter 3, a stone stele or monument was erected outside of Chang'an in 781 that presented an account of Christianity during the T'ang Dynasty. The stele was hidden as that dynasty ended, but then unearthed hundreds of years later, in 1625, when the Jesuits were in China. This was "the evidence that proved that Christianity was not a new religion to China, and that it had been previously approved by emperors," and this "surprising discovery helped encourage the Jesuits, empower Chinese Christians, and open the ears of Chinese intellectuals" (Irvin and Sunquist 2012, 177).

Spiritual, Religious, and Social Movements

In the two centuries after the Age of Reforms, a new type of spirituality emerged "which emphasized finding God in everyday life—creating a spiritual climate favorable to lay Christians" (Sheldrake, 107). The Protestant beginnings were described in the last chapter, and they continued into the seventeenth century. Representative of Lutheran spiritual writing was Johann Arndt's *True Christianity,* in which his primary concern was "the development of the inner Christian life in daily practice" (Irvin and Sunquist 2012, 281). Furthermore, "for many people the most beautiful expression of Lutheran spirituality is its rich musical tradition, with such composers as Schütz, Buxtehude, and the genius of Bach" (Sheldrake, 112).

The next wave of this spiritual and religious movement was through the various forms of the "religion of the heart." One of the richest expressions of Reformed and Calvinist spirituality was through the English Puritans. One of the great classics—"known to Catholics and Protestants alike" (Sheldrake, 120)—was John Bunyan's *Pilgrim's Progress*, which he wrote during a twelve-year term of imprisonment in England for preaching without a license. Bunyan's book "tells the story of a traveler named Christian, who, directed by one named Evangelist, journeys from the City of Destruction . . . to eventually arrive at the Celestial City, which is the goal of the soul" (Irvin and Sunquist 2012, 292). German Pietism affirmed that "conversion to God, inner transformation, and holiness of life expressed in good works were more vital than a mere affirmation of doctrinal orthodoxy" (Sheldrake, 144). Moravians, Methodists, Baptists, and the Great Awakening movement all highlighted the experiential aspect of spirituality. At the same time, Congregationalist revivalist Jonathan Edwards strove to maintain the importance of religious experience and sound doctrine. Furthermore, John Wesley was suspicious of any spirituality that did not include action or service of the needy, and the Society of Friends had a spirituality in which "social justice actions are not separate from listening to the Spirit" (Holt, 86). David Bosch described the Moravians as "Protestantism's 'answer' to the very best there was in Catholic monasticism" (1991, 255). The major difference is that Moravian monastics included married couples and families.

The book *Martyrs Mirror*, which contained poetry, stories of martyrs, and confessional statements, helped immigrating Mennonites of the Anabaptist communion "maintain their distinct community values and spirituality" (Irvin and Sunquist 2012, 365). In the eighteenth century, as a result of the Great Awakening, many African Americans accepted Christianity and adapted it to their African heritage, thereby "converting Protestant Christianity from Europe into a distinct and often independent African form of Christianity" (ibid., 441).

Similar to Protestants, Roman Catholics continued their development of popular spirituality, as described in the last chapter. In Poland, the Byzantine icon, "The Black Madonna," had been housed in the famous pilgrimage center in Jasna Góra in the city of Częstochowa since 1382. John Kazimierz, the king of Poland, attributed the 1655 defeat of the invading Swedish army in Jasna Góra to the intervention of the Virgin Mary, and he declared Mary the Queen of Poland. The Black Madonna of Częstochowa continues until today to be a central symbol of Polish national identity (see Stanley 2018, 52–53). In addition to the many devotions to Mary and the Eucharist, a new spiritual practice based on the Sacred Heart of Jesus, a symbol of the humanity and compassion of Jesus, was associated with the visions of a French cloistered nun named Margaret-Mary Alacocque. It is interesting that "a strikingly similar devotion to the Sacred Heart of Christ was present among English Puritans in the same period, for example in the writings of Thomas Goodwin" (Sheldrake, 133). In another context many aspects of European popular piety were transferred to and transformed in Latin America into an enduring form of popular religiosity that includes devotion to saints, festivals, and pilgrimages.

New developments in Catholic spirituality shifted from Spain in the sixteenth century to France in the seventeenth. The French priest Francis de Sales wrote a devotional guide, *Introduction to the Devout Life*, "for lay people seeking to experience the presence of God in their everyday lives without denouncing the world" (Irvin and Sunquist 2012, 271). Cardinal Bérulle, a friend of de Sales, is considered the founder of the French school of spirituality, mentioned earlier for its importance in renewing clerical spirituality. He also developed spiritual resources for laypeople. Two movements represented contrasting points. First, Cornelius Jansen was the central figure in developing Jansenism, with its strict moral approach and strong emphasis on human sinfulness. Second, Quietism is a mystical form of spirituality that promotes an excessive passive surrender to God's will. Both Jansenism and Quietism were eventually condemned by the church, but "in some ways a moderate form of Jansenist moralism and penitential asceticism continued to influence much Roman Catholic spirituality into the twentieth century" (Sheldrake, 138). Interestingly, the general concerns of the Quietists and other Catholic spiritual reformers somehow overlapped with those of Protestants seeking the "religion of the heart," and "there was considerable reading of one another's work and even dialogue among some of the major figures" (Irvin and Sunquist 2012, 278).

Significant religious developments by women in Latin America took two forms. First, women in the *beaterio* "did not actually take vows but lived in semicloistered settings intended to protect them and to facilitate religious devotion and mentoring" (ibid., 240). Second, many more women sought to live in established convents that were expanding rapidly. Many convents then developed schools for girls, but most of these girls already had social and/or economic advantages. Juana Inés de la Cruz of seventeenth-century Mexico "was probably the most significant Christian woman known in this period" in Latin America (Norris 2002, 191). She went from life in the royal court to the convent, where she studied theology, music, science, and literature; amassed a library of over four thousand books, "reportedly the largest" in Latin America at the time (Irvin and Sunquist 2012, 241); and produced writings in Castilian Spanish, Latin, and Nahuatl. She attracted people seeking her counsel as well as a number of critics. She eventually sold all her books, gave the money to the poor, and withdrew further into a life of penance and prayer.

The Catholic Church was also renewed through the founding of new religious orders such as the Vincentians, Daughters of Charity, Passionists, Redemptorists, Congregation of the Visitation, and the Brothers of the Christian Schools (De La Salle Brothers). The situation of admitting non-Europeans to older religious proceeded much more quickly in Asia than in America. The Dominican Martin de Porres, who was "one of the first persons of African descent to be admitted to a religious order" (Irvin and Sunquist 2012, 244), dedicated his life to caring for the sick and needy in Lima, Peru. One of the first religious orders founded in America was the Bethlehemites, who were dedicated "to care for the imprisoned, the sick, the poor, and others who were without means" (ibid., 239). In this chapter we have noted, on the one hand, the dedicated witness and service of religious orders, and, on the other hand, such scandalous behavior as owning slaves and perpetuating racism. Religious orders went through a very difficult time near the end of the eighteenth century. Due to a variety of political, economic, and religious factors, the Jesuits were suppressed in 1773, and all monastic orders were banned in France in 1790 during the French Revolution.

Throughout this section and the entire chapter we have seen how Christianity was challenged during 1600–1800 by social and economic movements and developments like the slavery system, social classes in Latin America and India, the status of women around the world, the Industrial

Revolution and urbanization, and revolutions in France and North America. At the same time, Christianity contributed to protecting and enhancing the status and role of women in some areas of the Americas, Europe, and Asia. Also, the burgeoning publishing enterprise enhanced such movements as the Great Awakening.

The Russian Orthodox Church in the seventeenth century turned to the Greek Orthodox for spiritual renewal in response to external pressures from the Catholic West. In the eighteenth century it faced internal pressures of monastic restrictions under several tsars. However, the religious revival of Russian Orthodox Christianity was sparked by the birth of new women's religious communities and the contributions of three monastic figures. Paisii Velichkovskii used earlier spiritual writings from the monks of Mount Athos, which "proved to be a major influence in rejuvenating Orthodox spirituality in monasteries throughout Russia" (Irvin and Sunquist 2012, 378). Tikhon of Zadonsk responded to the pastoral and spiritual needs of the laity, and he was greatly influenced by Arndt's *True Christianity*. The monk Seraphim of Sarov drew people seeking healing, and he likewise strove to extend spiritual teachings beyond the monastery to laypeople.

Generally speaking, in terms of spiritual and religious movements, a "vast majority of Christians in all churches and communions continued to hold on to what they considered to be classical orthodox doctrines . . . [and at the same time there] was an increased amount of emphasis placed on experiential dimensions of Christian faith" (ibid., 371).

Theological Developments

While the treatment of theology in the last chapter began in America, we start here in Asia. Based on a positive assessment of culture, Valignano promoted an accommodational policy for Jesuit missionaries. In terms of theology, Ricci, through his engagement in the Confucian and scientific world of China, had the "opportunity to lay the foundation for the same sort of marriage between a philosophy, Confucianism, and the Christian faith as Thomas Aquinas had performed with Aristotelianism" (Ross, 128). De Nobili and de Rhodes made similar attempts with Hindu philosophy and Vietnamese culture. Regarding the latter, theologian Peter Phan maintains that the accomplishments of Rhodes "far surpassed what the official church of his times could have dreamed of, even in its most catholic moments" (1998, 202).

In Europe various types of Roman Catholic theology developed through the seventeenth century. First, a polemic theology refuting Protestants was represented by the Jesuit Robert Bellarmine. Second, some theologians began focusing on specialized areas of theology, such as dogmatic theology and moral theology. Third, spiritual theology mushroomed through the writings of the French school of spirituality and persons like Francis de Sales. Beyond these types of theology, Jansenism on the theological issue of grace and works stood for "a greater emphasis on human sinfulness, and consequently a greater emphasis on the work of grace in redemption" (Irvin and Sunquist 2012, 275). In the eighteenth century "the so-called theological manual began to replace Aquinas' *Summa Theologiae* as the basic text in seminaries . . . to pass on the correct teaching of the church as articulated at Trent and against Protestantism" (Bevans 2009, 278). During this same time, the outstanding moral theologian Alphonsus de Liguori, founder of the Redemptorist order, developed "his perspective of 'equi-probabilism,' which was a kind of middle course between positions that were too rigid or too lax" (ibid.).

Protestant theology in the seventeenth century developed the scholastic orthodoxy of Luther and Calvin. Lutheran theologian Johann Gerhardt "was one of the first to formally locate the doctrine of scripture at the beginning of a theological system" (Irvin and Sunquist 2012, 280), as he wrote a nine-volume "masterpiece of Lutheran orthodoxy that became the standard for generations" (Norris 2002, 198–99). Arndt, mentioned earlier for his influential spiritual writing, was concerned with "recovering something of the spirit of Martin Luther's own original mystical theology" (ibid., 281). Dutch Reformed theologian of the University of Leiden Jacobus Arminius challenged Calvinist teaching by maintaining the role of free will and the universal offer of atonement (salvation). In response the Synod of Dort of the state church in the Netherlands condemned his teachings in 1618–1619 after his death and issued a statement that "quickly became a touchstone of Calvinistic orthodoxy throughout northern Europe" (ibid., 283). The Swiss theologian Francis Turretin published a three-volume work that "stands as the most complete systematic exposition of Calvinist scholastic theology in the seventeenth century" (ibid., 285).

The major wave of Protestant theology of the eighteenth century, in reaction to Protestant orthodoxy, was that of the "religion of the heart." Coming out of the Pietist movement of Lutheranism, Zinzendorf held a prominent role for the Holy Spirit as "Mother" in his theology and work, and his writings "call for a warm, almost erotic, relationship with Christ" (Bevans 2009, 276). John Wesley adopted Arminian theology, developed from Arminius and propagated in Methodism and the Great Awakening. Jonathan Edwards, "perhaps the greatest Protestant theologian of the age" (ibid., 277), made a major contribution "to shift the emphasis in theology from one's beliefs in doctrines alone to the realm of affections in determining the case for an individual's salvation" (Irvin and Sunquist 2012, 437). The Quaker John Woolman maintained the inseparability of spirituality and justice, as "evidenced in his strong opposition to slavery and in his respect for the culture and religion of the Native Americans" (Bevans 2009, 278).

Among the Orthodox under Muslim rule not much theology was written. In Russia, Kiev was an important place of learning, "but what was studied there were the works of Reformed, Lutheran, and Roman Catholic theologians from the West" (ibid., 279). However, there were several significant theological and spiritual scholars, such as Tikhon of Zadonsk, mentioned above, in the eighteenth century.

Mission, Cultures, and Religions

The Roman Catholic Church attempted to free itself from the *patronatus* agreement with Spain and Portugal by reclaiming its primary responsibility for mission by establishing the Congregation for the Propagation of the Faith in 1622. A seminary for the Society of Foreign Missions was established in Paris in 1663 to prepare diocesan clergy for mission and to promote indigenous priests and bishops around the world. "Since the church was not able to name the bishops in Asia, Africa and the Americas—this was still a legal right of the civil authorities of Spain and Portugal—the papacy appointed vicars apostolic, who could exercise episcopal duties but did not have territorial authority" (Bevans and Schroeder 2004, 192). This latter action led to some longstanding conflicts.

The section "Christianity in Asia" described how Jesuits like Ricci, de Nobili, and de Rhodes carried out Valignano's *modo soave* by accommodating themselves and the Christian message to the contexts of China, India, and Vietnam. Rather than hoping for many baptisms, Ricci's primary goal of mission was that "when the Jesuits and the faith they proclaimed were no longer alien but in some sense Chinese, then a truly Chinese and Christian Church could be built which could then take up the task of the conversion of the nation" (Ross, 135). Ricci allowed Chinese Christians to participate in ancestor veneration rituals, and we noted earlier the significant contributions of Catholic Chinese like Xu Guangxi, Yang Tingyun, and Xu Candida. De Nobili also hoped to show that being a Christian and an Indian was not incompatible. "Although his dream was not realized, he proposed establishing a seminary in India and teaching Christian dogma based on certain principles of Hindu philosophy" (Bevans and Schroeder 2004, 190). In contrast to the situation in China and India, many people were baptized in Vietnam through the efforts of de Rhodes. Also, "Vietnamese Christians themselves carried out most of the work of evangelism, teaching, and apologetics" (Irvin and Sunquist 2012, 186). In Asia, Chinese, Vietnamese, and Japanese Catholic men and women played key roles in spreading and deepening the Christian faith. We also noted above that an African (Miguel de Apresentacão) did mission work in India and an Indian (Joseph Vaz) did the same in Ceylon.

In terms of issues related to other cultures and religions, many factors contributed to what became known as the Rites Controversy. The growing conflict in Asia between the accommodational and tabula-rasa approaches, followed by the Jesuit-minded missionaries and the others, respectively, was brought to Rome for resolution in the mid-seventeenth century. The primary issues were the term used for God in China, the participation by Christians in funerals and ancestor rituals in China, rituals related to the caste system in India, and the degree to which sacramental rites could be adapted to accommodate cultural sensibilities. The two offices of the Vatican curia that were consulted upheld both positions according to the reports each side presented. When most of the missionaries in China were together under "house arrest" in 1667–1668, they reached a workable agreement that lasted about twenty years. However, the conflict resurfaced in Europe within the broader situation of tension between the political and economic implications of the *patronatus* and Congregation for the Propagation of the Faith policies, the Jesuits and other religious orders, the Portuguese and the French, and the contrasting theological attitudes toward human nature and the culture of Jansenism (strong base in France) and of probabalism (primarily of the Jesuits).

When the controversy returned to Asia, the Chinese emperor, in response to a request from the Jesuits, declared in 1707 that only those missionaries who received an imperial permit (*piao*) by agreeing to follow the approach of Ricci could remain in China. Four bishops and a number of missionaries received the permit. In 1715, Pope Clement XI published a prohibition against the accommodational approach. Emperor Yongzheng then expelled all missionaries and closed churches, and in 1736 his successor and son "imposed the death penalty for anyone practicing and embracing Christianity" (Irvin and Sunquist 2012, 177). Rome issued a bull in 1742 condemning Chinese Christians who practiced rituals honoring their ancestors. Church rulings also affected Jesuit accommodational efforts in the Indian context, and there would never again be such Christian outreach to Brahmins. The prohibition of Christians participating in ancestor veneration will remain until 1939.

Before 1600, different understandings and practices of mission stood in stark contrast to one another within the Americas and between the Americas and Asia. During 1600–1800, the strict contrast was very apparent within Asia itself, as manifested in the Rites Controversy. One major issue underlying this conflict was the issue of collaboration or confrontation between colonialism and mission. Second, the basic theological difference was in terms of salvation and culture. Third, the particular mission context led to different responses. For example, the Jesuits in China assessed ancestor veneration from the intellectual understanding of Confucian scholars, while the other missionaries formed their opinion from the actual practice of the rites by ordinary Chinese. Also, de Rhodes "had a less appreciative attitude than Ricci and his fellow Jesuits in China . . . due to the fact that de Rhodes's perspective was drawn from that of the common people, not the scholars and philosophers" (Bevans and Schroeder 2004, 191). At the same time, de Rhodes "did recognize that filial piety is such a central value in Vietnamese culture, and so he substituted alternative Christian practices" (ibid.).

The consequences of the conflicts underlying the Rites Controversy were not as dramatic in Catholic mission outside of Asia, but they were still reflected in various approaches. Many bishops, clergy, and religious supported the colonial regime in the Caribbean and Latin America, while at the same time, others took prophetic stances against the atrocities. While an attitude of patronizing the indigenous peoples was predominant among missionaries and church officials, religious communities such as the Jesuits and Augustinians upheld the human dignity and values of the indigenous peoples in Latin America. In Africa, in contrast to the motivation of the Portuguese *patronatus* system, Congregation for the Propagation of the Faith assigned the Capuchin order in Kongo "to establish Christian communities and catechize local people" (Irvin and Sunquist 2012, 212–13). At the same time, missionaries in East Africa were involved in the slave trade. The extensive mission work of the Franciscans in the western regions of North America includes accounts of both defending the indigenous peoples and using coercion rather than invitation. The church-directed rather than state-directed mission in the French areas of America included a more accommodational approach by men and women, lay and cleric missionaries, and First Nations Christians. While Europe was not considered a mission territory at that time, new religious orders like the Redemptorists and Passionists were preaching and offering spiritual guidance to the poor and those on the fringes of the church in Europe. "Although these efforts were mostly directed toward people who had been baptized as children into the Christian religion, they were patterned after the efforts being conducted in other parts of the world by Catholic missionaries who were working to convert new believers to the Christian faith" (ibid., 351).

In terms of Protestant mission, motivation for mission generally disappeared within Lutheran orthodoxy. "However, as with the Anabaptists earlier, the Pietist movement would break through to provide an active missionary response" (Bevans and Schroeder 2004, 196). Pietist theologian and pastor A. H. Francke was instrumental in developing the new University of Halle "as one of the most important centers for missionary and ecumenical efforts taking place throughout the world" (Irvin and Sunquist 2012, 356). Two of its missionaries, Ziegenbalg and Plütschau, developed in India "a model of mission that became very significant for future Protestant missionary work" (Bevans and Schroeder 2004, 196). One of its graduates, Zinzendorf, founded the Moravians, who had a strong commitment to mission. They advocated on behalf of the dignity of enslaved persons, Native Americans, and women, and they strove to break the connection between the church and state, for example in South Africa. Since generally "the Protestants of the first two centuries still operated within the framework of a close liaison between church and state" (Bosch, 261), this practice by the Pietists, as well as the Anabaptists and Puritans, was an exception to the norm.

During the seventeenth and early eighteenth centuries in areas under the colonial rule of the Netherlands, England, Denmark, and Sweden, chaplains served those on the company ships and the small number of settlers, but "efforts to missionize outside the boundaries of the forts or settlements were for the most part not welcomed" (Irvin and Sunquist 2012, 326). However, changes were beginning to occur. Dutch Reformed Gisbertus Voetius was "one of the first Reformed theologians to work out a full-fledged theology of missions, arguing that Christians needed to seek to plant new churches in regions where there were currently no existing Christian communities" (ibid., 284). In New England, Puritan pastor John Eliot learned the Algonquian language and established "praying Indian towns" so that newly baptized Native Americans could retain their new faith and also become culturally European. The Anglican bishop of London in 1701 founded the Society for the Propagation of the Gospel in Foreign Parts. It began sending missionaries to North American colonies the following year to focus their energies on the colonists, but they also would reach out to enslaved Africans and Native Americans. Written by Jonathan Edwards, the biography of David Brainerd, who did mission work with Native Americans, "came to exercise a great deal of international influence on Protestant missions in subsequent years" (ibid., 446). Revival movements in many forms were stimuli for mission in Europe and North America. The 1792 settlement of Freetown will become a very important base for mission by Africans in West Africa in the nineteenth century. We noted above that the Baptist George Liele, born in Virginia and of African descent, had founded churches in the Caribbean in the eighteenth century, and he is considered the first missionary from the United States.

The foundation of the Russian Orthodox Church in Alaska followed the accommodational approach. Following the presence of Russian fur traders and settlers, eight monks and two novices arrived in Alaska in 1793. They learned the vernacular languages, translated the liturgy, and proposed establishing a seminary there for training indigenous priests. "By 1800 over ten thousand members of several indigenous ethnic groups along the coastal region had been baptized" (Irvin and Sunquist 2012, 474).

Understanding the relationship between mission, on one side, and culture and other religions, on the other, requires some background. Europeans thought of culture and religion as two separate categories. All held that Christians could not maintain allegiance to anything from another religion. However, they had a positive or negative theology of culture, represented by the accommodational and tabula-rasa approaches, respectively. In the Rites Controversy the Jesuit-minded missionaries considered the ancestor rituals as cultural and, according to their theological perspective, permissible for Christians; others considered ancestor rituals as part of another religion and therefore not compatible with Christian faith. The former considered it as ancestor veneration, which is acceptable in the Catholic Church, and the latter as ancestor worship, which is not. Today, ancestor rituals in an Asian context (and the religious-cultural worldview of indigenous peoples in America, Africa, and Oceania) are probably best understood not as either cultural or religious (a dichotomy), but as both cultural and religious.

In terms of culture, the Congregation for the Propagation of the Faith, in 1659, within forty years of its founding, issued a positive statement toward non-Western cultures: "Do not regard it as your task, and do not bring any pressure to bear on the peoples, to change their manners, customs, and uses, unless they are evidently contrary to religion and sound morals. What could be more absurd than to transport France, Spain, Italy, or some other European country to China?" (Bevans and Schroeder 2004, 192). Jesuits, shaped by Italian humanism and the philosophy of probabalism, received this as an affirmation of Valignano's *modo soave*. The translation of liturgical texts into Chinese by Buglio, mentioned above, "reveals the way the Jesuits negotiated and navigated Chinese culture and politics of the literati, Roman theology, and ecclesiology" (Seah, 119).

Furthermore, an examination of the translations of post-Tridentine catechisms reveals a high degree of accommodation. Brébeuf in North America invented new words—for example, for *Eucharist*—for the Huron (Steckley, 160–63), and fellow Jesuit de Nobili used Sanskrit and Tamil narrative content and style to translate Catholic doctrine for a Tamil audience (Nardini, 232–49). The Spanish Franciscan Juan de Plasencia adapted the "Our Father" in the Filipino catechism to include, for example, the phrase "give us today our daily rice" (see Bevans 2009, 263). In Africa some cultural elements were included in the liturgy and sacraments in Kongo, and the Portuguese Augustinian António da Conceição, as the ecclesiastical superior of the Zambezi River region, worked "to translate the catechism into the local language and argued strongly that all church leaders should become fluent in it, something that was almost unheard of in seventeenth century southeast Africa" (Irvin and Sunquist 2012, 225).

On a grassroots level many cultural-religious elements of indigenous peoples and Africans fused with Spanish Catholic practices and devotions in Latin America and the Caribbean and Philippines, sometimes in ambiguous ways. Normally, Protestants had a negative theology of culture, but at the same time, the importance of Bible translation and indigenous church leadership implicitly affirmed the value of local languages and cultures. The Orthodox in Alaska continued to hold a very positive theology of culture.

As for other religions, the Jesuits and other likeminded church personnel generally had a somewhat positive attitude toward what we would call today the cultural-religious worldview and practices of indigenous peoples in Asia, America, and Africa. But they had a very negative attitude toward established world religions other than Christianity. "The Jesuits seemed to be particularly intent on attacking Buddhism, which they considered to be nothing more than vulgar idolatry, and Taoism, which they considered superstition" (Irvin and Sunquist 2012, 174–75). In China, they positively engaged Confucianism, which they considered a philosophy and imperial ideology. In Vietnam, de Rhodes engaged Confucianism in a more critical manner, but also had conversations with Buddhist monks, one of whom was baptized and became a Jesuit. De Nobili learned Sanskrit and engaged the Brahmin caste, as a social group, and accepted certain practices into Christianity that he considered Hindu culture, not Hindu religion. In the Muslim Mughul Empire of northern India during a period of religious tolerance at the beginning of the seventeenth century, the Jesuits had a positive relationship with the Muslim rulers. Jerónimo Xavier, grandnephew of Francis Xavier, built "a literary foundation for Christianity in India during this period," including a life of Christ and a psalter in Persian (ibid., 201). Furthermore, "Xavier produced a Hindustani catechism in 1611, while a German Jesuit produced a Sanskrit grammar to begin ministry among Hindus" (ibid.). The period of religious tolerance ended in 1632, but missionaries like de Rhodes continued working there. The former Brahmin Vaz was accepted as "a legitimate religious person" by a Buddhist ruler in Ceylon (ibid., 208).

In Africa the Capuchins took a confrontational stance and "sought to exorcize the spirits they encountered in traditional African religionists and destroy what they considered as the Africans' idols" (Irvin and Sunquist 2012, 213). As we noted earlier, along the east coast of Africa the relationship between Christians and Muslims included both peaceful collaboration and violent hostility. "Matters of religion usually overlapped with political and economic issues among local populations" (ibid., 222). In terms of Judaism, Portugal had exiled to Brazil some Jews suspected of holding their Jewish faith after being baptized. When the religiously tolerant Dutch took control over part of Brazil, Jews there were able to found the first synagogue in America in Recife in 1636. After the Portuguese retook that area of Brazil, some of the Jews moved to a Dutch colony on Manhattan "to establish a synagogue in New Amsterdam, the first in North America" (ibid., 234). "There were approximately two thousand Jews living in the United States" in 1776 (ibid., 455).

Conclusion

In 1600–1800, Christianity as a global movement "maneuvered" between various sets of issues—relationship of church and state (mission and colonialism), religion of the head versus religion of the heart, positive and negative attitudes toward culture, and hierarchical and egalitarian models of church and society. The following description of a Sunday morning in a Guaraní reduction in Paraguay reflects such dynamics:

> When the Fathers come out from their prayers, the doors are opened; the women enter the church through the three doors of the portico, and the men through the side doors. The boys remain in the patio of the Fathers; and the girls go to the cemetery. In the middle of the church, between the men and the women, with their backs to the women, stand four Indians with the clearest voices, and everyone else is kneeling. The four begin the Lord's Prayer and other prayers [in the Guaraní language], which everyone repeats. Then the others sit, while the four continue to stand. The four then begin the Catechism. . . . The boys and their leaders in the patio, and the girls in the cemetery, do everything that the men and women do in the church. (Cardiel, 133; cf. Koschorke, 333)

7

Colonialism, Progress, and Mission

ca. 1800 to ca. 1900

The spread of Christianity around the globe that we have followed in the past two chapters continues into the nineteenth century, but with new developments. At the end of the eighteenth century the absolute authority of monarchies was being replaced by the birth of nation-states and the separation of church and state. Nationalism developed a sense of manifest destiny, that is, being chosen for a unique destiny in history. Europe and later the United States experienced significant economic, technological, and scientific growth, labeled as the Age of Progress. This contributed to false notions of cultural superiority and bringing a "higher civilization" into the imperialistic enterprise.

> Whereas in earlier centuries the essential factor that divided people was *religious*, people were now divided according to the levels of *civilization* (as interpreted by the West). This led to the next criterion of division—*ethnicity* or *race*—now interpreted as the matrix out of which civilization (or the lack of it) was born. The "civilized," however, not only felt superior to the "uncivilized," but also responsible for them. (Bosch, 312)

To the first two *C*'s of colonialism—commerce and civilization—would eventually be added the third *C* of Christianity. While the affairs of the mercantile companies began as strictly secular in nature, in the second half of the nineteenth century "colonial expansion would once again acquire religious overtones and also be intimately linked with mission!" (Bosch, 303). For the most part the motivations of missionaries blended with those of their nations, but Pietism and neo-Pietism strove to promote purified Christian values within Protestantism. Protestant mission work played the major role in the expansion of Christianity in this century, but Catholics would join in as well after recovering from the effects of the French Revolution and Napoleonic rule. Tensions between Protestants and Catholics were generally exported around the world.

This chapter has drawn much from Sheridan Gilley and Brian Stanley, eds., *The Cambridge History of Christianity: World Christianities c. 1815–c. 1914* (2006) and the unpublished manuscript of chapters 1–8 of Irvin and Sunquist, *History of the World Christian Movement*, volume 3 (unpublished). We begin our brief historical survey in the newly independent countries of Latin America and the Caribbean.

Historical Context

The Caribbean and Latin America

At the beginning of the nineteenth century most of Latin America and the Caribbean—except for the British and Danish colonies and the newly independent Haiti—were under the influence of the Roman Catholic Church. However, political independence, which received additional impetus from the Napoleonic wars against Spain and Portugal, would also bring some changes to the religious context.

In the Spanish territories most of the bishops and members of higher clerical orders tended to support the colonial governments, while the lower clergy were often more supportive of the independence movements. For example, in Mexico, the *criollo* (a person of Spanish descent, born in Latin America) priest Miguel Hidalgo led the revolution that eventually achieved Mexico's independence in 1821, ten years after Hidalgo's execution. The then-empire of Mexico was greatly reduced in size over the next thirty years with the formation of the United Provinces (later Republic) of Central America and the ceding of Texas and the entire "Southwest area" to the United States after the war between the two countries. In terms of the church, the Vatican refused to acknowledge the nationhood of Mexico and claimed the right to continue the colonial practice of Spain to nominate bishops. After an invasion of Mexico by Napoleon III of France, the Republic of Mexico was reestablished in 1867 under President Benito Pablo Juárez García, a member of the indigenous Zapotec people. Within the postcolonial environment, antichurch legislation followed. Church properties were taken, and the political authority of bishops was reduced. Mexico attempted to expel all *peninsulares* (Spanish-born persons living in Latin America), which included all the bishops at that time. Simón Bolívar, while not alone, played a major role in independence movements throughout Spanish America, which also included the emancipation of enslaved persons. While not compelled by law, most of the bishops and many priests and religious who were *peninsulares* left South America.

In contrast with Spanish America, Brazil declared its independence in 1822 without a revolution. At the same time, the economy of the country was still very dependent upon slave labor for producing coffee, cotton, tobacco, and sugar. With the opening of its ports in 1808 to ships of other nations, Brazil had already begun to receive Lutherans from Germany, Anglicans and Presbyterians from Britain, and later many Methodist and Baptist former plantation owners from the United States. In terms of the Catholic Church, Rome wished to exercise more authority by directly appointing the bishops and strengthening clerical leadership through stronger seminary education. Due to the latter, the number of local priests increased, while the *peninsular* priests decreased.

Political independence movements in the Caribbean were accompanied by a number of revolts by enslaved peoples and an economy shifting away from such a strong dependence on sugar and tobacco. Religiously, there was also a shift from established state churches to more pluralistic religious societies. The early years of Protestant presence was already noted in Chapter 6. By the first part of the nineteenth century Baptists were the largest Protestant group among persons of African descent in the Bahamas, and the first Baptist church was established in Trinidad in 1816.

Across Latin America and the Caribbean in the nineteenth century the Roman Catholic Church eventually adjusted to the new political climate and got some degree of official recognition. Protestant churches, which began to appear more regularly, were planted by missionaries from other countries as well as by some indigenous church leaders from within Latin America (see Irvin and Sunquist unpublished, ch. 1). Relations between Catholics and Protestants were often rather tense.

North America

The history of Christianity in North America in the nineteenth century centers on the rapidly expanding United States. The population increased from four million in the thirteen colonies in 1790 to over seventy-five million about one hundred years later. This was due to the large territorial expansion through the Louisiana Purchase from France, a treaty with England for the Oregon Territory, the annexation of Texas and the Southwest after the war with Mexico, the purchase of Alaska from Russia, and the annexation of Hawaii. The United States also assumed colonial rule over the Philippines, Puerto Rico, and Guam after the Spanish-American War. Rapid industrial and economic development and an increased sense of manifest destiny accompanied this growing national identity, which also influenced mission work both domestically and internationally. Unfortunately, people who were dominated in the process suffered greatly.

Native Americans experienced territorial displacement, cultural annihilation, and even genocide. This included the Cherokee "Trail of Tears" in 1838, the killing of the buffalo herds, and the massacre at Wounded Knee (in South Dakota) in 1890. While the majority of the church personnel were "children" of the manifest destiny mentality, there were some exceptions. Eleven pastors were jailed for helping the Cherokee resist (see Irvin and Sunquist unpublished, ch. 2). After the United States annexed land from Mexico, many Spanish-speaking peoples became second-class citizens in another nation.

In the first half of the nineteenth century African enslaved persons "forged an alternative, and largely clandestine, belief system sometimes called the 'invisible institution' that worked in the shadow of the master's religion" (Sensbach, 431). When they were freed after the Civil War (1861–1865), new waves of racial oppression and violence occurred through "Jim and Jane Crow" segregation and the Ku Klux Klan. Within this context the independent African Methodist Episcopal Church (AME) and the African Methodist Episcopal Zion Church (AMEZ) were formed. Soon these denominations and the Baptists were training black clergy.

Religious renewal, treated in Chapter 6, continued. Many new religious movements emerged that would reshape not only the religious landscape of the United States and eventually have an impact throughout the world. Presbyterians, Methodists, and Baptists attended large Camp Meetings, with as many as twenty thousand in attendance. A movement known as Restorationism—designed to restore the faith and practice of New Testament Christians—also contributed to a larger period of revivalism, the Second Great Awakening. Charles Finney was one of the major figures. As a revivalist preacher he linked explicit and total acceptance of Christ with social justice, particularly abolitionism and women's rights. Finney influenced the early formation of the Holiness movement in the United States, which would spread in many directions. A very important person for this movement in the later part of the century was Dwight Moody. He held evangelistic campaigns and summer conferences and established the Chicago Evangelization Society to prepare laity for mission; the society's school became known as the Moody Bible Institute. This revival spirit spilled out into the founding, for example, of the Boston Female Society for Missionary Purposes, the American Board of Commissioners for Foreign Missions (ABCFM), and later the Student Volunteer Movement for Foreign Missions (SVM). These are included under the thread "Mission" below.

Roman Catholics, still a minority in the United States, increased in number due to immigration, especially from Ireland and Germany, and the annexation of Texas and the Southwest. Two key figures in the nineteenth century were Elizabeth Ann Seton, who founded the Sisters of Charity of St. Joseph, and Isaac Thomas Hecker, who founded the Missionary Society of St. Paul (Paulists). Catholics established institutions of higher education, including Georgetown (the first of many Jesuit schools), Villanova, and Notre Dame. In Canada, Catholics remained very strong in Québec and later grew in Toronto through German and Irish immigration. Canada became an independent country in 1867. The Orthodox Church continued to grow along the west coast, especially in Alaska, among Russian immigrants and Native Americans. Innocent Veniaminov, a very important missionary in Alaska, was later ordained a bishop and became the metropolitan of Moscow. Other Orthodox churches that appeared across North America consisted of immigrants from Russia, Greece, and the Balkans.

Europe

After naming himself emperor in 1804, Napoléon brought Spain, the Netherlands, and parts of Germany and Italy under his authority through several military operations. His armies suffered devastating losses in their retreat from Moscow during the harsh Russian winter of 1812 and in the final defeat by an English army at Waterloo in Belgium in 1815. The Congress of Vienna was held in 1814–1815 to reestablish political boundaries in Europe in the aftermath. Pope Pius VII, who had been imprisoned by Napoléon for five years, restored the Jesuits upon his release and carried out other measures to reestablish the authority of the Roman Catholic Church. However, the situation of church-state relations had changed forever.

Dramatic changes in Europe from the Industrial Revolution were felt around the world. For example, the appearance of steam locomotive trains spread from England, the United States, and Russia to India and China. Efforts to market the products of the new European factories fueled economic/political expansion through colonialism that was blatantly seen, for example, in the Opium Wars in China in the 1840s and the "scramble for Africa" in the Berlin conferences of 1884–1885. A similar economic disparity between Europe and the rest of the world appeared within Europe itself with the creation of the urban poor accompanied by underemployment, crime, and poor housing.

The ongoing development of the ideas of freedom of thought and expression influenced both Catholic and Protestant churches. On one hand, some Protestants linked social progress in Europe with the reign of God—an understanding that could easily be used to support manifest destiny. On the other hand, as in North America, those in revival movements stressed the priority of personal religious experience over the new ideas of liberalism and rationalism. The emphasis on freedom and equality supported a much stronger level of participation by women in mission work.

To respond to the rapidly changing worldview, many Christians in Europe at the beginning of the century drew upon the emerging movement of Romanticism, which represented a cultural rejection of the growing rationalism and industrialization in Europe. At the same time, many new voices continued to challenge religion in general and Christianity in particular. Karl Marx described religion as the opiate of the people, while also criticizing the "fetishism" of capitalism. From another direction, Søren Kierkegaard criticized religion as being reduced to ethics and the idea of Christendom itself. Charles Darwin's theory of evolution challenged the long-held understanding of God's involvement in creation. By the end of the century, in order to protect religion from these new ideas, many looked for new notions of an infallible source of truth, whether it was the Bible, the church, or the pope.

The decline in the political influence of the Catholic Church spread around Europe. At the same time, strong papal leadership would eventually strengthen the church's importance in terms of teaching authority. Pope Gregory XVI reinvigorated Catholic missionary activity. Pius IX, who was pope for thirty-two years, published the *Syllabus of Errors* in 1864 condemning ideas linked with the Enlightenment. He also called the First Vatican Council in 1869–1870 to strengthen the Vatican's teaching authority through the doctrine of papal infallibility.

In 1800, the parliaments of Great Britain and Ireland created the United Kingdom. That brought an end to the serious restrictions by the Irish parliament against Catholics and their bishops (see Irvin and Sunquist unpublished, ch. 3). However, later the British allowed a potato famine to occur in Ireland, and consequently many Irish—the majority Catholic—migrated to the United States. In England, John Henry Newman was a prominent member of the Oxford Movement, which was concerned with the lack of attention to sacraments among Anglicans. Newman joined the Roman Catholic Church, was ordained a priest, and later became a cardinal. Others from the Oxford Movement also joined the Roman Catholic communion.

After the death of John Wesley in 1791, the Methodists separated from the Anglican Church to form their own church. After several decades they divided into the Wesleyan Methodist Conference and the Primitive Methodist Church. A Methodist couple, William and Catherine Booth, founded a society later named the Salvation Army to reach out to the urban poor. The Baptist Missionary Society founded by William Carey in 1792 provided a major boost for the vibrant nineteenth-century Protestant missionary movement. Also, various youth and student mission organizations contributed to this trans-Atlantic movement. The Young Men's Christian Association

(YMCA) and the Young Women's Christian Association (YWCA) were founded in London in 1844 and 1855, respectively.

On the European Continent a number of theologians in Germany, drawing on speculative philosophy and the Enlightenment, developed a theological stream that became known as liberalism. Pietistic evangelical revivalism stood on the other side theologically. At this time, Roman Catholics faced much opposition in Germany under the nationalistic program of Chancellor Otto von Bismarck. However, many Roman Catholic missionary societies of men and women were founded in France throughout the nineteenth century. Protestants in France, who gained citizenship through the French Revolution, formed the Paris Evangelical Mission Society in 1822. As a final note, the Dutch Reformed Church experienced a number of divisions on theological grounds during this century.

Africa

As many nations of the Caribbean and Latin America were finding political independence through the nineteenth century, European nations were extending their colonial, and later imperial, actions farther into Africa. While a small portion of the African continent was under direct European colonial control in 1870, practically the whole continent was colonized thirty years later, after the meetings held in Berlin in 1884–1885 convened by Bismarck divided up Africa among the colonial powers in the "scramble for Africa" (see Map 9). At the same time, internal African conflicts included the role of African kingdoms and other ethnic groups in capturing fellow Africans for enslavement.

The history of Egypt, the Coptic Church, and Sudan reflect this reshaping process. With the withdrawal of Napoléon's troops from Egypt by 1802 and the ongoing decline of the Ottoman Empire, a military officer named Muhammad Ali gained administrative control of the country and initiated a process whereby Egypt would become a political and economic power in the region through the development of commerce, military forces, and eventually the building of the Suez Canal. Egypt extended its influence over sections of Saudi Arabia, Syria, and Sudan, to the border of Uganda. The Sudanese suffered greatly under harsh Egyptian rule that included enslavement and heavy taxes. With time Egypt came more and more under British control. Roman Catholic and Protestant missionaries were allowed into Egypt primarily to establish schools, which even included seminaries at one point. The Coptic Church, which had generally supported Muhammad Ali, experienced more freedom. Pope Cyril V in the latter part of the century established a number of new schools in Cairo and Alexandria—including the first Coptic school for girls, a new seminary, and schools for monks.

Map 9: The Colonial Partition of Africa in the Early Twentieth Century

Unfortunately, the British had a more negative attitude toward the Copts, who in turn found themselves more marginalized.

The Ethiopian Orthodox Church faced many challenges in the first part of the century. Dependence on the Coptic pope to appoint the Ethiopian patriarch (*abuna*) led to problems with two prolonged vacancies totaling over twenty-five years between appointments and with discontent over two appointees. The Ethiopian Orthodox Church also suffered under the pressure of Islam on one side, and Catholic and Protestant missionaries on the other. Near the end of the century war broke out between Ethiopia and Italy regarding Ethiopian independence. After being defeated in 1896, Italy recognized Ethiopia as an independent nation. This is considered a key turning point in the history of European colonialism and imperialism in Africa, as the words *Ethiopia* and *Ethiopianism* became equated with a call for African independence. "Ethiopia became a symbol of African redemption, a political and religious ideology that continued to inspire for generations to come" (Kalu 2006a, 583).

In West Africa the colonies of Sierra Leone and Liberia were established for those who had been enslaved. While initial attempts to settle in Sierra Leone were not successful, Clapham Sect (a group of Church of England social reformers) philanthropists from Britain purchased land in Sierra Leone for formerly enslaved persons who had become Christian. The first eleven hundred Africans to arrive in 1792 in this settlement of Freetown had been enslaved plantation workers in the United States, soldiers in the British army, and farmers in Nova Scotia. They came "with their own preachers, and they would not see missionaries there for almost twenty years" (Bevans and Schroeder 2004, 213). Samuel Ajayi Crowther was the outstanding leader of the Freetown mission outreach, in particular, and African Christianity in general.

The following are representative of the many Roman Catholic missionaries in Africa. Anne-Marie Javouhey, founder of the Sisters of St. Joseph Cluny, established a colony of freed slaves. Cardinal Charles Lavigerie founded men's and women's missionary congregations for Africa. Daniel Comboni, who worked in Sudan, conceived of a "Plan for the Regeneration of Africa by Africa."

Christianity in southern Africa was caught in the web of colonialism. In South Africa the Dutch Reformed farmers (Boers) moved inland to an area called the Transvaal under pressure from the incoming Anglican British. The British policy of outlawing enslavement early in the nineteenth century was a point of contention with the Dutch, who depended more on enslaved labor. In 1902, after two Boer Wars, the Dutch were defeated and put under British rule. The Zulu leader, Shaka, through negotiations and military operations built a strong Zulu nation that initially won some battles but eventually was defeated by the British and incorporated into the colony of Natal. On the other hand, a remarkable leader of the Sotho, Moshoeshoe, was able to establish the independent nation of Basutoland (present-day Lesotho).

Two extreme forms of imperialism were the British South Africa Company of the businessman Cecil Rhodes, covering the present-day countries of Zimbabwe and Zambia; and the Congo Free State, a private company owned by King Leopold II of Belgium in the Congo River region. Approximately five to ten million Africans died under Leopold's rule (see Irvin and Sunquist unpublished, ch. 4). On the whole the Catholic priests supported the Belgium king, while the Protestants from the United States generally did not.

Many Western missionaries had quick deaths in Africa due to malaria, such as the first four sent by the Protestant Basel Mission to the Gold Coast (within present-day Ghana) and the first three sent by the Catholic Society of African Missions to Sierra Leone. Other missionaries and church workers were killed. For example, Anglican bishop James Hannington of the London Missionary Society (LMS), Roman Catholic lay catechist Charles Lwanga, and over twenty others were executed during 1885–1887 in Buganda (in present-day Uganda).

A new expression of Christianity that began in the nineteenth century would later be called African Independent Churches (AICs). During this century the main impetus for this was attributed to the refusal of mission boards and church bodies in Europe or the United States to grant Africans full leadership of their own churches. In the first part of the century a Christian evangelist named Ntsikana led an independent movement in South Africa, and in 1892 another South African, Mangena Mokone, established one of the first independent churches on the continent to be founded by an African. Several years earlier, in the wake of the subsequent European dismantling of the work of Crowther, Mojola Agbebi had played a major role in establishing the Native Baptist Church in Lagos (Nigeria) in 1888.

South Asia and East Asia

In India colonial rule was shifting from the Portuguese, French, and Dutch to the British, and the primary missionary activity from Roman Catholics to Protestants, even though the British East India Company was initially not supportive of missionaries. For this reason William Carey had to move with his Baptist Missionary Society colleagues William Ward and Joshua Marshman (the Serampore Trio) and their families to the Danish colony north of Kolkata (Calcutta) in 1800. Around the middle of the century the British government took over direct rule of India from the British East India

Company, which involved working with local leaders, employing Indians as soldiers and civil servants, and being supportive of chaplaincy among European and Eurasian communities, which then led to missionary outreach among other communities.

Charles Simeon was a very influential founding member of the Church Missionary Society (CMS). While Anglicanism does not normally fit neatly within Protestantism, Simeon's strong evangelical approach gave the Anglican Church a Protestant "face" in India at the beginning of the nineteenth century (see Irvin and Sunquist unpublished, ch. 5). Early Anglican leaders included missionaries David Brown, Daniel Corrie, and Henry Martyn, and former Muslim Abdul Masih, one of the first two Anglican Indian priests. Methodists came from England, Presbyterians from Scotland and the United States, and Calvinist Methodists from Wales. By 1860 there were over twenty-seven Protestant mission societies and churches working in India.

Of course, the history of Christianity in India is much older. The ancient Saint Thomas or Syrian churches had developed into Orthodox Syrian and Syrian Roman Catholic churches, as noted in the previous chapter. While initially supporting the Saint Thomas Christians, the Anglicans eventually contributed to further divisions with the indigenous church.

While Roman Catholics were sidelined under British rule, by the end of the century they had almost doubled in number, particularly through conversions of Dalits (the lowest of the scheduled castes or untouchables). Clément Bonnard of the Foreign Mission Society of Paris (MEP) convened the important Synod of Pondicherry that endorsed a national hierarchy in India. Another important person for the Roman Catholic Church in India was Anastasius Hartmann, who was a vicar apostolic in both Patna in northern India and Mumbai (Bombay).

In neighboring Myanmar (then called Burma) the earlier presence of Roman Catholics had dwindled drastically by the beginning of the nineteenth century. Renewed missionary efforts began in 1870 under the auspices of the MEP and the Pontifical Seminary for Foreign Missions. The number of Catholics increased from three thousand to sixty thousand over the century. The Baptist missionaries in Burma included Felix Carey, the son of William Carey, Adoniram and Ann Hasseltine Judson—the first missionaries supported by the American Baptist Union in the United States—and later George Dana and Sarah Hall Boardman. Burma was annexed as a province of India in 1886.

The British were the first to unite Sri Lanka (then called Ceylon), and they recognized Buddhism as the official religion. Roman Catholic Indian missionaries began to replace the Europeans in order to serve the fairly large number of Catholic communities in Ceylon at the beginning of the nineteenth century (Irvin and Sunquist unpublished). However, there was always a shortage of priests. The number of Protestants had seriously declined by the beginning of the century, but then new Anglican, Baptist, and Methodist missionaries began arriving. Some tensions did surface between Catholics and Protestants and among Christians, Buddhists, and Hindus.

In contrast to what we have seen in the past two chapters, the history of Christianity in China in the nineteenth century also falls under the cloak of colonialism that was covering all of Asia. In order to establish a trade relationship to their advantage, the British introduced the importation of the addictive opium drug from India into China. The Qing rulers tried unsuccessfully to prevent this through strict laws and punishment. An international conflict developed into two Opium Wars. The consequences of two unequal treaties in 1842 and 1858 included ceding Hong Kong to Britain, the legalization of the opium trade, and the opening of additional Chinese ports for trade and diplomatic presence in Beijing with Britain, France, the United States, and Russia. China was opened to Western mission after 1860. Around this same time, the Chinese government was dealing with the army of the peasant-led Taiping Rebellion, founded by Hong Xiuquan. The apocalyptic and political rebellion was defeated by Chinese and British forces in 1864. The significant influence of Christianity on the Taiping leaders (see Irvin and Sunquist unpublished, ch. 6) would contribute to strong anti-Christian attitudes in the future.

The number of missionaries increased dramatically after 1860. Western Roman Catholics and Protestants held primary responsibility in the churches in China. However, there were also Chinese Christians like Liang Fa and Keuh Agong, who originally worked with two LMS missionaries, and later distributed Christian literature and served as evangelists for years in southern China (see Irvin and Sunquist unpublished).

Growing anti-foreign and anti-Christian sentiment led to attacks on Christian churches and homes and the deaths of some two hundred Protestant and Catholic missionaries and tens of thousands of Chinese Christians in 1898–1899. The full-scale Boxer Rebellion took over Beijing in 1900, which was quickly suppressed by a foreign military force from Europe, the United States, and Japan. This contributed to the sentiment that Christianity was complicit with Western imperialism.

Although Christianity was illegal in Korea at the beginning of the nineteenth century, Korean Catholics continued in their faith. Some French priests secretly entered the country, and an underground seminary was even opened. The government responded with persecutions. The first Protestant church was started in Korea in 1883 by Korean merchants, who were drawn to the Christian faith through Scottish Presbyterian missionaries in Manchuria. The treaty of 1882 between Korea and the United States opened up opportunities for Protestant missionaries and doctors to enter. By the end of the century Japan was taking control of Korea.

As in Korea, Christianity was illegal in Japan in 1800. Politically, through the nineteenth century Japan became a colonial power itself through rapid industrial and military development. In the mid-nineteenth century Protestant, Roman Catholic, and Orthodox missionaries were allowed into Japan, but initially few were baptized through their efforts. A French Catholic MEP priest found thirty thousand "hidden Christians" around Nagasaki whose ancestors had survived the seventeenth-century persecutions. The last legal restrictions against Christianity were removed in 1873, and the number of missionaries, especially Protestants from the United States, and Japanese converts increased. Almost one-third of Japanese Protestants at this time came from *samurai* families and often became Christians through Christian college education. However, Christianity declined at the end of the century as Japanese nationalism grew.

The political situation of the nineteenth century in Indochina—including the present-day nations of Vietnam, Thailand, Cambodia, and Laos—was shaped by the interplay of two regional powers in Vietnam and Siam (present-day Thailand), and the colonial competition between the French and British. In Vietnam, as part of their resistance to Western colonialism, the emperors persecuted foreign and Vietnamese priests and as many as one hundred thousand other Catholics. Despite this heavy persecution, the number of Catholics in Vietnam increased from three hundred thousand to approximately nine hundred thousand during the nineteenth century. In contrast to Vietnam, Siam maintained its political independence despite British colonial interests. Very few Siamese became Christians—the total of Roman Catholics and Protestants was only thirty-five thousand out of six million in 1900. Cambodia, initially caught between interventions by Vietnam and Siam, became a French protectorate in 1864. The small group of Christians in Cambodia suffered persecution. And the small mission effort in Laos "was terminated with the killing of twelve priests in 1884 and five more in 1889" (Phan 2006, 526).

When the Dutch East India Company went bankrupt at the end of the eighteenth century, Indonesia (then called the Dutch East Indies) became a formal Dutch colony, and with that the anti-Roman Catholic policy of the Dutch East India Company was rescinded. Catholic missionaries reconnected with surviving Catholic communities, founded under earlier Portuguese rule, and extended into new areas. Dutch Jesuits Cornelius le Cocq d'Armandville and Franz van Lith had major impacts in Flores and Java, respectively. Chinese medical doctor Paul Tsen On-Njie, baptized in Malaysia, formed a Catholic community on the island of Bangko off the coast of Sumatra (Sumatera), which appears to be the first church in

Indonesia with no trace to direct European origins (see Irvin and Sunquist unpublished, ch. 6). The extensive Protestant mission activity on Sumatra included the martyrdom of two ABCFM missionaries and the extensive work among the Batak groups by the German Ludwig Nommensen of the Rheinische Missionsgesellschaft (Rhenish Mission Society, RMG). The total number of Christians in Indonesia was only 540,000 (1.4 percent of the population) in 1900, but a remarkable increase would occur in the twentieth century.

Malaya consisted of the island of Singapore and certain states on the Malay Peninsula, including Malacca, which had been a strategic port city in the narrow passageway between Malaya and Sumatra for Muslim merchants since the fifteenth century. It was taken over by the Portuguese, the Dutch, and then by the British in 1824. The settlement of Singapore grew from less than a thousand people to over 100,000 during the nineteenth century and surpassed Malacca in importance as a commercial center. Over one-third of this growing population was Chinese merchants and indentured laborers, many of whom became Christian through the efforts of British and United States Protestants or French Catholics, and later by Chinese Christians (see Irvin and Sunquist unpublished). The introduction by the British of sugar, coffee, and rubber was followed by laborers brought from India and Sri Lanka. While the first were of the low castes and Hindu, with time many of the Indian immigrants were Roman Catholics, Anglicans, and Saint Thomas Christians. Most of the missionary work was done by the Foreign Mission Society of Paris and the London Missionary Society.

In the Philippines rebellion against Spanish rule surfaced throughout the nineteenth century. These movements were anticlerical, since many friars supported the landowners, and most of the religious order and secular priests were from Spain and supportive of the oppressive Spanish rule. However, there were exceptions, especially during the latter part of the century. Dominican Juan Villaverde worked for thirty years to improve the economic and social situation of the indigenous people on Luzon, the largest island of the Philippines. The Jesuit Jacinto Juanmartí y Espot was instrumental in building good relations with the Muslims on Mindanao. Many of the Filipino clergy were on the side of the common people. For example, three Filipino priests—Jacinto Zamora, Mariano Gómez, and José Burgos—were executed for their role in a rebellion outside Manila in 1872. Several highly educated children of the landowners, known as *Ilustrados* (enlightened ones), provided the intellectual spark for independence. One of the most influential *Ilustrados* and national heroes was José P. Rizal. A major rebellion was under way when the United States warships came into Manila in 1898. The United States refused to recognize the newly declared independent republic and claimed jurisdiction over the Philippines in light of the treaty with Spain. The first Protestant baptism in the Philippines occurred in 1899, followed by Protestant missionaries from the United States. Entering into the next century also brought the birth of an independent Filipino Church, Iglesia Filipina Independiente, under the leadership of Gregorio Aglipay.

Oceania

The vast area of Oceania, which was the last major region of the world to be touched by Christianity and Western colonization, went through extensive and rapid change in the nineteenth century. The initial encounter with Western explorers and sailors brought smallpox, venereal disease, firearms, and rum. Anthropologists distinguish four major cultural groupings among the indigenous people of this wide area: Polynesia, Micronesia, Melanesia, and Australian aboriginals. Much of the early missionary contact occurred in Polynesia—a large area including Hawaii, Easter Island (off the coast of Chile), New Zealand, Tonga, Tahiti, and Samoa. Among Polynesian people with a hierarchical social structure, the acceptance and spread of the Christian faith was often dependent upon the influence of local leaders, as had been the case earlier among the Germanic tribes in Europe. King Pomare II of Tahiti and Queen Kaahumanu of Hawaii are two examples. Protestant Pacific Islanders not only played an early major role in local church leadership but also in the spread of Christianity to others. LMS missionary John Williams, who arrived in Tahiti in 1817, immediately trained indigenous teachers, some of whom accompanied him to Cook Island. Tahitian church workers began their mission work, alongside missionaries from the West, in Hawaii in 1822 and in Tonga in 1826. In turn, Hawaiian church workers helped in establishing Congregational churches in the eastern part of Micronesia.

Due to the strong anti-Catholic attitude of the British government and the ambivalence of post-revolution France toward Catholics, the mission work of the Roman Catholic Church was limited at the beginning of the century. The newly formed Catholic orders working in Oceania were the Marists (Society of Mary), the Congregation of the Sacred Hearts of Jesus and Mary (later called the Picpus Fathers), and the Pontifical Institute of Foreign Missions. While most Catholic missionaries and church leaders were French, by exception the Catholic communities on Wallis and Futuna—between Tonga and Samoa—provided indigenous church leadership quite quickly. By the end of the century Catholics joined Anglicans, Lutherans, and other Protestants in initial missionary work in the Melanesian islands of the Solomons and New Guinea, which had an egalitarian social structure, in contrast to Polynesia.

The fourth cultural group of indigenous peoples in Oceania was the semi-nomadic hunters and gatherers of Australia, who began arriving there over forty thousand years ago from Southeast Asia. The original number of aboriginals, approximately seven hundred thousand in 1800, was reduced by as much as 75 percent within a hundred years due to disease and armed violence (see Irvin and Sunquist unpublished, ch. 7). None on the island of Tasmania survived colonialism. The British started to establish penal colonies for convicts from Europe in 1788 in the present-day site of Sydney. The Church Missionary Society sent chaplains for the prisoners and their keepers, and later a few Roman Catholic priests were allowed to accompany the Catholic prisoners from Ireland. After 1850, the settler population and the number of Protestants, Catholics, and Orthodox (from the Russian Antarctic expedition) grew rapidly. Key individual missionaries included the Anglican Samuel Marsden, who worked for social reform, and the Catholic Mary MacKillop, who worked for the education of the poor.

The history of Christianity in New Zealand is quite different. The indigenous Polynesian Maori, who arrived between 800 and 1300 CE, initially established trade relations, including guns, with the small group of British settlers. They had relatively good relations with the missionaries of the London Missionary Society, Wesleyan-Methodist Missionary Society, and later French Marists. Perhaps as many as half of the Maori became Christian in the first several decades of Protestant mission work in New Zealand. But during 1840–1858, the number of European settlers increased from two thousand to almost sixty thousand and the Maori decreased in number due to new diseases. The 1840 Treaty of Waitanga granted the Maori land rights but also made New Zealand a British colony. In the following years of fighting and tension, many white church leaders were caught between loyalties to their fellow Europeans and to the oppressed Maori. "While Maori clergy were ordained from 1853, they were given little opportunity to exercise leadership within these [church] structures, despite calls for a Maori bishop and representation" (Piggin and Davidson, 557). By the end of the nineteenth century Christianity had grown to the point that, for example, the Presbyterian Church of New Zealand established missions to China, India, and New Hebrides, and started home missions to the Maori and to the immigrant Chinese community (see Irvin and Sunquist unpublished, ch. 7).

Western Asia and Eastern Europe

The complex history of Christianity in Western Asia and Eastern Europe was intertwined with political conflicts. The Crimean War (1853–1856) saw France and England joining the Ottomans to defeat Russia, who were claiming authority over all Orthodox in the Ottoman Empire. The decline of the Ottomans, already noted in Chapter 6, had opened the door for the political independence of Greece in 1832, later among the Balkan states of Serbia and Romania in the nineteenth century, and Bulgaria and Montenegro in the early twentieth. Orthodox Christians also experienced more religious freedom leading to declarations of becoming autocephalous churches, to the disapproval of the ecumenical patriarch in Istanbul. Catholic and Protestant missionaries in the Middle East generally tried to convert Orthodox Christians to their churches, while Anglicans preferred not to do so. Maronite Christians in Lebanon were growing in number but also being persecuted by the Muslim community of Druze.

Most Armenians at the beginning of the nineteenth century were living in either the Ottoman Empire or Persian Empire, but in 1826, after a second Russian-Persian War, the original territory of Armenia and its Armenian Orthodox Church was under the strict control of the Russian government and Orthodox Church. The Armenian Orthodox who continued to live under Ottoman rule had more freedom, especially during the time of the Armenian patriarch Mkrtich Khrimian in Istanbul. The Ottomans also formally recognized the Armenian Catholic Church as a separate ecclesial body in 1831.

As noted above, Russia exercised strong political force during this century. After the defeat of Napoléon and the Congress of Vienna in 1815, Tsar Alexander I held political power over Russia, Poland, Finland, and Lithuania. He was succeeded by his brother, Nicholas I, who officially enforced the political slogan of "Orthodoxy, Autocracy, and Nationality," which points to the fact that the only religion allowed in Russia was that of the Orthodox Church, which continued to be under the control of the government. Jews and other non-Christians and many non-Russian nationals suffered the most under this situation (see Irvin and Sunquist unpublished, ch. 8). In addition, many who had become members of the Ukrainian and Belorussian Roman Catholic "uniate" or Eastern rite churches returned to the Orthodox Church. The nineteenth century was also a great period in Russia for literature (with writers like Pushkin, Dostoyevsky, and Tolstoy), spiritual and patristic renewal, and an increased role for women in monastic and religious life. Russian Orthodoxy was spreading to Japan, northern China, Alaska, North America, and Australia. At the same time, Roman Catholics and Protestants were going to Russia as missionaries. In particular, there were several streams of mission movements by Baptists after 1860 in the Ukraine, present-day Georgia, and Saint Petersburg. Politically, anarchist and socialist ideas are beginning to coalesce as Russia moved into the twentieth century with the arrival of Lenin.

The nineteenth-century history of Christianity intertwined with the other two *C*'s of commerce and civilization in a very ambiguous and troubling manner. At the same time, many non-Western indigenous Christians were very significant agents in the growth of Christianity in their own contexts and the further spread of Christian faith and values. We now trace the development of the six threads of tradition over this period.

Threads of Christian Tradition

Scripture

In terms of biblical interpretation, the historical-critical method developed in various ways during the nineteenth century. The search for the most accurate biblical text led, for example, to the publication by Karl Lachman of "a critical edition of the Greek New Testament on the basis of the ancient manuscripts" (Rogerson et al., 332) and the study of a newly discovered Old Syriac version of the four Gospels that predates Tatian's *Diatessaron*. The critical study of the synoptic gospels led to a recognition of the primary dependence upon Mark and a possible sayings source (identified as "Q" in the following century). Beyond these areas of biblical study was a much deeper issue of tension—"the relation between the Bible and the threat to the claim of supernatural religion" (ibid., 330). A major concern regarding the Old Testament was the status of the biblical accounts of creation. Regarding the New Testament, the main concern was the person of Jesus. As to the latter, various versions of a rationalist interpretation of the life of Jesus included the works of Friedrich Schleiermacher, David Strauss, and Ferdinand Baur. Schleiermacher studied at the Pietist University of Halle, while the Catholics Strauss and Baur were key figures in shaping the Tübingen school of biblical criticism.

In response to the challenges of the historical-critical method, many Christians insisted that the Bible is not subject to the critique of human methods, and "the more conservative gathered around the banner of the 'fundamentals' of the Christian faith and brought the doctrine of biblical inerrancy to the fore" (González 1994, 104). Some scholars, such as J. B. Lightfoot, provided a middle ground between the two approaches. In general, the Roman Catholic Church was not open to a critical study of the Bible at this time, but Pope Leo XIII in *Providentius Deus* (1893), the first encyclical on the Bible, "called for a major effort in biblical studies—not only a return to the original languages, but more specialist training . . . dedicated to the demands of the biblical texts" (Ormerod, 338).

The American Bible Society was formed in 1816 to foster the translation and distribution of the scriptures in the United States. In the second half of the century, C. A. Briggs introduced the historical methods of studying scripture at Union Theological Seminary in New York. As a result, he was suspended from Presbyterian ministry, but the historical-critical approach continued to spread. On the other hand, the Niagara Bible Conference, Moody Bible Institute, and Gordon Bible Institute represent the conservative approach to scripture. From another perspective, activist Elizabeth Cady Stanton with a group of women wrote a commentary on biblical passages that dealt with women—published as *The Woman's Bible* in 1895 and 1898—"to unmask the patriarchy that was present in the Bible, or at least in male interpretations of it" (Bevans 2009, 291).

Protestants continued to give high priority to translating the Bible. In Latin America they distributed it in Spanish, and over fourteen translations of scripture into indigenous languages had begun by the end of the nineteenth century (see Irvin and Sunquist unpublished, ch. 1). The Bible had been translated into only three African languages—Ge'ez (Ethiopia), Arabic, and Coptic by 1815, but that number had grown to twenty-eight major African languages by 1860 (see Irvin and Sunquist unpublished, ch. 4). These latter translations were by European and North American missionaries. By exception, Crowther would later translate the scriptures into his own language of Yoruba in Nigeria. Of many translations in Asia, Carey and Marshman alone contributed six translations of the entire Bible and another twenty-three translations of the New Testament in India (see ibid., ch. 5). Chinese convert Liang and LMS missionaries R. Morrison and W. Milne published the Bible in Chinese in 1823. In the Pacific Islands the local islanders played a major role in most of the Bible translation in their part of the world (see ibid., ch. 7).

Orthodox missionary bishop Veniaminov and Aleut chieftain Ivan Pan'kov translated the gospel of Matthew and other sections of the New Testament into Aleut in Alaska by 1828. The Russian Orthodox monk Nikolai translated the New Testament into Japanese. Back in Russia, the Academy of Kazan alone was responsible for translating the Bible into twenty-two different languages (see Irvin and Sunquist unpublished, ch. 8). And Ethiopian monk Abu Rumi translated the entire scriptures into the Amharic language of Ethiopia.

As seen in the last chapter, scripture continued to play a central role in church life, liturgy, and mission, particularly among the Protestants and Orthodox. Outstanding examples from the nineteenth century include the following. Many Chinese Christian "Bible women," either with Western missionaries or on their own, visited homes and neighborhoods in their local ministry of teaching the Bible (see Irvin and Sunquist unpublished, ch. 6). Presbyterian missionary Samuel A. Moffett developed a month-long program of Bible classes to train Korean evangelists. In Russia, Ukrainian peasants held Bible hours for studying scripture in their homes, and this movement, which developed as one of the Baptist streams in Russia, spread through the network of migrating farmworkers (see ibid., ch. 8).

Liturgy, Sacraments, and Art

The post-Tridentine form of the eucharistic liturgy in the Roman Catholic Church remained. "Though minor revisions of these rites occurred in succeeding centuries, the liturgical books published in the fifty years after Trent remained in force until the second half of the twentieth century" (Foley, 274). However, new forms sometimes emerged when Catholics were cut off from the West and/or the ministry of priests. During a period of persecution in Korea, Catholic Koreans taught the faith, led worship services, and even conducted baptisms in some cases (see Irvin and Sunquist unpublished, ch. 6). When the Western missionaries returned later in the century, Korean Catholics, like all Catholics of the Western rite, again celebrated the Eucharist in Latin, but the scriptures were read in Chinese, not Latin. (Catholics had not yet translated the Bible into Korean.) Under similar circumstances of no contact with the West, Sri Lankan Catholics developed their own patterns of worship that included adaptations to their language and culture (see ibid., ch. 5). Conflicts arose when Western missionaries returned.

In the West distinctions were made between a simple "low mass" that could be celebrated in twenty minutes and a "high mass" that could last over an hour with the addition of much music and ceremony. Theologically and spiritually, "attending" mass and receiving communion were understood primarily in individualistic terms. But in the nineteenth century some scholars "began to suggest that those who attended should participate in it in other ways besides devout watching" (Martos, 293). Beyond mass, other Catholic forms of worship included litanies, adoration of the Blessed Sacrament, and the Way of the Cross—all of which could be done individually or communally.

A major development that influenced Protestant liturgy was "for conversion itself to become a main function of worship" (White, 178). The origins of this shift can be traced to the camp meetings and Restorationism described earlier within the broader religious renewal movement in North America. The order of worship that developed consisted of a song or praise service, the sermon, and a harvest of new converts (indicating a public explicit acceptance of Christ in their lives) or "altar call." Most North American Protestant traditions eventually assimilated some of these elements, except for Anabaptists and Anglicans, and this form of worship "continues to expand rapidly, not only in familiar territory such as North America but also in almost every other part of the world" (ibid., 172).

African American enslaved Christians continued to develop their own style of liturgy. "A standard part of Afro-Christian worship was the 'ring shout,' when worshippers gathered African-style in a circle to dance, clap and sing praises in call-and-response fashion, communing with the spirit in an ecstatic trance that often lasted hours" (Sensbach, 432).

Baptism and Eucharist continued to be the most commonly shared sacraments among many churches and denominations, although the practice varied. A new movement in the United States, which became known as the Christian Church or Disciples of Christ, practiced "open communion" for members of all confessional traditions, and they practiced full-immersion baptism after a confession of faith. In contrast to others the celebrant of the Eucharist for the Christian Church and the Plymouth Brethren of England was a layman (see White, 175). The revivalist Finney used either the Baptist form of immersion or the pouring of water over the head according to the preference and background of those to be baptized. The Salvation Army did not have baptism or Eucharist; rather, the ritual of walking under the Salvation Army flag served as initiation into the movement.

One significant change regarding sacraments was that, after the French Revolution, France and most other European countries allowed people to marry before a civil magistrate, not only before a priest or minister. "These developments forced the Catholic hierarchy to reexamine the official teaching on marriage and determine more precisely when and how the sacrament was conferred" (Martos, 442). Many new questions for Catholic marriage tribunals were raised around the world, and the regulation of marriage became much more complex.

As for artistic expressions, many forms of worship music developed outside of Europe. Anonymous enslaved African Americans composed spirituals from songs sung in the plantation fields. "The biblical lyricism of the spirituals sometimes disguised other intention; to sing of 'stealing away to Jesus' might have been a coded expression of running away, and the 'Canaan land' of Exodus bore easy symbolic resemblances to the slaves' promised land, Canada" (Sensbach, 432–33). In parts of Polynesia hymns introduced by Protestant missionaries were adapted to traditional South Pacific chant style in place of the Western form of four-part harmonies (see Irvin and Sunquist unpublished, ch. 7). In the second half of the century, the Coptic Church paid more attention to church music and liturgical practices, and Pope Cyril IV prioritized the training of cantors (see ibid., ch. 4). Often the composition of music and Christian literature were linked. Ghanaian David Asante translated Paul Bunyan's *Pilgrim Progress* and wrote hymns in his native language of Twi (see ibid.). Vedanayakam Sastri of Tamil Nadu, India, wrote over five hundred Christian poems, many of which were later composed as hymns and popularized through his many public performances (see ibid., ch. 5).

While most churches around the world were built according to a Western architecture, there were exceptions. The Phát Diem Cathedral, which was designed by the Catholic Vietnamese priest Tran Luc at the end of the nineteenth century, displayed the cultural-religious symbols of the phoenix, dragons, and lotus blossoms throughout the church (see Irvin and Sunquist unpublished, ch. 6). In another part of the world the beautiful Saint Vladimir Cathedral was built in Kiev as part of the spiritual renewal of Russian Orthodoxy.

Ministry and Organization

Within Protestantism the revival movements of Restorationism and the Second Great Awakening and social/political factors all somehow influenced most churches and denominations in the United States. The democratic spirit affected all of them to various degrees, and the distinctions among confessional traditions started to blur significantly (see Irvin and Sunquist unpublished, ch. 2). The Methodists in the United States had the structures of organization and ministry with their circuit system of stations, developed under the leadership of Bishop Francis Asbury, to build upon the camp meetings dynamic. Normally, their itinerant preachers would travel and preach for three to ten years, and then marry and settle down in one locale while serving as an unpaid exhorter or pastor. The circuits were grouped into districts, with a superintendent; districts then formed a conference; and a general conference of the whole Methodist Episcopal Church met every four years. In England the Methodists who wanted to incorporate the camp meeting experience separated to form the Primitive Methodist Church, while the original group became known as the Wesleyan Methodist Conference. As noted earlier in this chapter, a number of new Protestant evangelical denominations emerged in England during this century. The ecumenical and international Conference on World Missions held in Liverpool in 1860 affirmed the importance of planting indigenous churches around the world. However, a dispute arose over whether these latter churches should conform to the "'technicalities' of western ecclesiastical principles" (see Stanley 2006, 456).

Ministry among Protestants was being localized around the world. The Lutherans ordained the first Indian in 1819, the Anglicans the first two in 1825. The Presbyterian Church quickly initiated Indians in ministry in the area of Punjab, and by 1890 most of the church leadership was local (see Irvin and Sunquist unpublished, ch. 5). The first Japanese citizen was ordained a Protestant minister in 1874, and the Japanese Christian Uemura

Masahisa helped to establish a seminary to train Japanese pastors in Japan. Many Protestant missionaries promoted ministry by Africans as catechists, pastors, and evangelists. Due in great part to the influence of Henry Venn in the Church Missionary Society, Crowther was ordained as the first African bishop of the Church of England in 1864. The Tahitian chief Auna, the first Polynesian to be ordained a deacon in the Anglican Church, was one of several Polynesians in the early stages of the work of LMS missionaries in Hawaii. The Wesleyans began ordinations in Tonga in 1847, and the ABCFM in Hawaii in 1849. Of LMS Polynesian workers, 46 percent were ordained by 1875 (see ibid., ch. 7). The first Mexican Methodist minister was ordained in 1872, and the Presbyterians opened a seminary in Mexico City in 1882.

Many Protestant women were itinerant preachers from the beginning of the nineteenth century, and some would eventually be accepted for ordination in some denominations by the end of century. In North America, Jarena Lee of African descent was a well-known AME itinerant preacher but did not succeed in convincing her church to allow women ordination. Julia Foote, another traveling evangelist, was the first woman ordained a deacon by the AMEZ in 1894, and a full elder in 1900. In her 1879 autobiography, *A Brand Plucked from the Fire,* she challenges other women to take up leadership in the church. The ordination of Clara Celestia Hale-Babcock in 1888 (or 1889) in the Disciples of Christ Church marked "one of the earliest ordinations of female pastors in the modern era" (Sunquist, 123). Finney, a key figure in the early Holiness movement, supported the ordination of women as preachers. Phoebe Palmer contributed much to the development of this movement through prayer meetings in her home, several publications, and forming connections with the Holiness Movement in England. The German Lutheran pastor Theodor Fliedner, having met Mennonite women deaconesses in the Netherlands, is credited with initiating the ministry of female deacons among Protestants in Germany in 1836 to offer social assistance to those in need (see Irvin and Sunquist unpublished, ch. 3). So many women received training in the Bible and nursing to join this movement that in less than thirty years "there were thirty houses for some 1,600 Protestant deaconesses spread throughout the world" (see ibid.). Lutherans brought this ministry to the United States, "but the [North] American Methodists fully developed the movement" (Robert 1996, 157) domestically and beyond. The extensive contribution of women to mission efforts is described later.

The major change in church organization in the Roman Catholic Church revolved around the papacy and the changes in church-state relationships. In response to its loss of temporal power after the French Revolution, Napoleonic rule, and the growth of nationalism in Europe, the Vatican reasserted its religious and moral authority. The ultramontane (over the mountains [Alps]) movement promoted a very high view of the pope's authority. Pius IX called the First Vatican Council (1869–1870), which would be remembered for the controversial doctrine of papal infallibility. It is important to note that such infallibility refers to the authority given to the church by Christ, not to the person of the pope but only when he is speaking officially (ex cathedra) on matters of doctrine and morals. Some sixty bishops left before the final vote, and many thought that the teaching was unnecessary, premature, and/or ill-timed. The council accepted the decree, but in fact the only generally accepted use of this infallibility to date has been the declaration in 1950 of the assumption of Mary.

The next pope, Leo XIII, held a much more open stance to the world, as shown, for example, in his endorsement of Catholic social teaching. However, the general stance of the Catholic Church in the nineteenth century was an affirmation of its religious authority in opposition to the "modern world." "And its monarchical organization was reflected in the paternalistic style of its ministry" (Martos, 514). The First Vatican Council was forced to close prematurely due to the political movement of republicanism and unification in Italy, called the *Risorgimento* (resurgence). As a result, the Catholic Church lost its political authority and claim to most of the Papal States in 1870. The following year Chancellor Bismarck initiated anti-Catholic legislation in Germany.

In postcolonial Latin America the Catholic Church still had political and economic power. However, many bishops and priests born in Spain (*peninsulares*) left either voluntarily or under pressure. In Mexico this provided an opportunity for a renewal of parish life through the ministry of local priests who were close to the people and who received good seminary training. Through a number of agreements between the Holy See and the new governments of Latin America, Roman Catholicism was named the official state religion and could own land, and the Vatican would now directly appoint the bishops. The first Latin American Plenary Council of 1899 in Rome, called by Leo XIII, focused on defending the faith and the church from a Vatican perspective; nonetheless, this meeting was important in that "it represented the reawakening of the collegial consciousness of the Latin American episcopacy and became the foundation for all the initiatives that would be taken in the future" (Dussel 1981, 106). In concluding this brief treatment of organization and ministry in Latin America, it is necessary to also mention that the lay confraternities continued to serve social and religious purposes, and unlike Mexico, most of Latin America suffered because of the lack of priests.

Steps were taken to foster indigenous ordained ministry in Africa, Asia, and Oceania. Cardinal Lavigerie founded one of the first seminaries in

Africa for training Catholic priests. The 1844 Synod of Pondicherry promoted the development of an indigenous hierarchy in India, which was supported by Rome. The first Sri Lankan priests were ordained in 1876. During the time of persecution in Korea, Korean seminarians were sent to a seminary in Macau for eventual ordination. Two seminaries were established in Japan in 1873, but the ordination of Japanese proceeded slowly. A seminary was started in Thailand in the seventeenth century, relocated to Vietnam and India, and finally moved in 1810 to Penang (in present-day Malaysia), making it a new center for Roman Catholicism in the region (see Irvin and Sunquist unpublished, ch. 6). Despite these initial attempts there was still a relative shortage of priests in most of East Asia and most of the existing priests were Western, even in the Philippines with its very high percentage of Catholics. One exception was Vietnam. In 1802, although all six Catholic bishops were French, the vast majority of priests were Vietnamese. In China, by 1900 there were more than eight hundred foreign priests and about five hundred Chinese ones, but no Chinese bishops until 1926 (see Bays and Grayson, 498). In the newer missionary area of Oceania, the Marist priest Louis Elloy strove to prepare Samoans for priesthood. By exception, four indigenous men of Wallis Island were ordained priests in 1886, and fairly soon the majority of priests on Wallis were indigenous. By 1890, two seminaries had been started in New Zealand. The further contribution of Catholic women and men in missionary activities is described below under the thread "Mission."

The following developments occurred in the nineteenth century in church organization and ministry beyond Protestant and Catholic churches. Following political independence the Orthodox in Greece declared themselves autocephalous under a synod that eventually had the archbishop of Athens as its head. However, more than two-thirds of the Orthodox who were ethnically Greek lived under Ottoman rule and remained under the jurisdiction of the ecumenical patriarch in Istanbul. At the same time, the Serbian, Bulgarian, and Armenian Orthodox Churches in the Ottoman Empire moved in the direction of becoming autocephalous churches in various forms, so the administrative role of the ecumenical patriarch in Istanbul decreased drastically. Until 1902, the small Orthodox community in Australia turned to the patriarch in Jerusalem as its ecclesiastical authority, and later to Athens.

For the Russian Orthodox Church, the Holy Synod that had assumed the role of the patriarch in the eighteenth century was under the control of the tsar in the nineteenth, including the appointment of bishops after 1855. Furthermore, the beginning of some state support of rural priests in Russia included the expectation of their endorsement of government policies (see Irvin and Sunquist unpublished, ch. 8). The Russian Orthodox in the United States looked to Russia as their ecclesial authority, while the

Orthodox from places such as Romania, Albania, and Syria maintained more independence and developed lay parish boards. The first Japanese Orthodox priest was ordained in 1874, and by 1890 there were twenty thousand Orthodox Japanese.

In the Coptic Church a group of lay leaders in 1874 established a Community Council of twenty-four elected members to oversee the economic, social, and legal business of the church. Conflicts among the members and between the council and the pope led eventually in 1904 to a reconstitution of the council with greatly reduced responsibility. The Mar Thoma Church of India, due to its interaction with the Anglican Church, experienced much internal tension among various groups with varying degrees of allegiance to traditional Syrian Orthodoxy and/or Anglicanism. A formal split occurred between the older Mar Thoma Church and a newly formed Syrian Orthodox Church with moderate reforms, such as using the vernacular language of Malayalam rather than Syriac in their liturgies. With time, the older church grew stronger while the newer one suffered further divisions and setbacks. Another type of church organization and ministry also began to emerge within new movements formed by African Christians, who normally separated from historic churches established in Africa by Western missionaries. This growing phenomenon is referred to as African Initiated Churches (AICs).

Spiritual, Religious, and Social Movements

One major spiritual movement of this century grew out of what we described in the last chapter as the "religion of the heart." Building upon the earlier spiritualities of the Puritans, Pietists, and Wesleyans, the evangelical revival in England developed a primarily Calvinist spirituality, which was characterized by the centrality of the Bible, conversion, the cross, prayer, moral responsibility, and a life of action (see Sheldrake, 160). Significant written works on spirituality include *A Treatise on Prayer* by Edward Bickersteth, one of the founders of the Evangelical Alliance, and *Evangelical Meditations* by Charles Simeon, an important leader in the evangelical movement. Across the Atlantic, the revival movements of Restorationism and the Second Great Awakening placed great emphasis on conversion and an experiential, rather individualistic spirituality. The Holiness movement, originally a renewal movement within American Methodism, strove to recover the Wesleyan focus on the perfection of love in the lives of all believers. A particular heritage of African American spirituality was reflected in the spirituals, which "resonate with deep emotions—especially suffering, the desire for liberation, and yet also profound hope" (ibid., 169).

Another development in spirituality is linked with the Oxford Movement in England. Like those of the evangelical revival, who were responding to religious apathy in society, those of the Oxford Movement were concerned with what they considered exaggerated emotionalism in religion. "There was an emphasis on an integrated spirituality of body, heart, and mind . . . and on the potential for union with God in Christ rather than the Calvinist stress on God's distance and a spirituality based largely on obedience to divine law" (Sheldrake, 163–64).

During the nineteenth century "Roman Catholic spirituality (with exceptions) tended to be restorationist and defensive rather than innovative" (ibid., 157). By exception, in order to combat religious indifference, some bishops in Europe initiated town or village missions that were similar to Protestant revivals. The Catholic missions included preaching, dramatizing scriptures, and celebrating the Eucharist. Popular spiritual piety also increased. Along with earlier forms—including the Rosary and eucharistic devotion—there was renewed interest in miracles, visions, saints, and the Virgin Mary. Apparitions of Mary to Bernadette Soubirous in Lourdes resulted in Lourdes becoming a major pilgrimage center. The declaration of Pope Pius XI in 1854 on the Immaculate Conception of Mary—being preserved from original sin—contributed to the growth of Marian devotion. During a period of persecution in Vietnam, some Catholics who fled into the forests experienced a vision of Mary, who assured them of protection and healing from certain sicknesses. This site continues to be a place of pilgrimage, and Our Lady of La Vang has become a central element of Vietnamese Catholicism, representing both the suffering of Christians and the relief they received from Mary.

The Carmelite nun Thérèse of Lisieux, whose spiritual writing was posthumously published in the *Story of a Soul*, proposed a spirituality of "the little way," which "offered a spirituality of small actions that influenced large numbers of people who sought a credible spiritual framework for every day, ordinary existence" (Sheldrake, 159). In the United States, Isaac Hecker, the former Methodist who founded the Catholic order of the Paulist Fathers, "rejected the world-denying tendencies of Catholic devotionalism and placed his emphasis on a 'democratic' spirituality of finding God in everyday realities and of Christian holiness shaped *in* the world" (ibid., 170).

The Russian Orthodox Church experienced a spiritual revival during the nineteenth century. Very popular spirituality works included the autobiography (*My Life in Christ*) of the priest John of Kronstadt and an anonymous book (*The Way of a Pilgrim*). While these spiritual writers were in a similar vein as the revivalists in the West, they did not focus on individual conversion but rather on the end of the spiritual journey (see Irvin and Sunquist unpublished, ch. 8).

Coming out of the spiritual movements described above, new churches, denominations, and other institutional religious expressions of Christianity developed. New Protestant evangelical denominations that arose in the United Kingdom in the nineteenth century included the Catholic Apostolic Church (Irvingites), the Plymouth Brethren, and the Free Church of Scotland. The Christian Church or Disciples of Christ developed during the early years of Restorationism. The Holiness movement led to the founding of the Wesleyan Methodist Connection, the Free Methodist Church, the Salvation Army, and the Church of God (Anderson, Indiana, USA). Large international Holiness gatherings were convened, especially in Germany, Switzerland, and England by 1874–1875. The millennial utopian Seventh-day Adventist Church and the restorationist Church of the Latter-Day Saints (Mormons) are two other forms of religious innovation in the United States. Developments toward the end of the nineteenth century included the Christian Science Church, with its primary concern with healing, and the millennial Watch Tower Bible and Tract Society, with its largest wing taking the name of Jehovah's Witnesses in the next century. Independent church movements in Africa and the Philippines represent new religious expressions emerging outside of Europe and North America.

Religious movements and developments in the Catholic Church were represented by religious congregations, especially for women—"the greatest expansion of religious life since the Reformation" (Sheldrake, 157). For example, the women's communities of the Religious of the Sacred Heart, Daughters of the Cross, and Little Sisters of the Poor were founded in France and Belgium. In 1900 in Europe there were more women in Catholic religious orders than there were men serving as priests, monks, and religious (see Irvin and Sunquist unpublished, ch. 3). In Latin America the number of religious men and women and their communities declined rapidly during the shifting relationship between the church and the newly independent states, but there was new growth after 1880 in religious orders across the continent. It is interesting to note that of the twenty-nine new congregations founded in Brazil alone during the period of 1880–1920, fourteen were new indigenous orders. While some religious orders in the United States owned slaves, others, such as the Oblate Sisters of Providence and the Sisters of the Holy Family, included women of African descent and served the African American community. The Carmelites of Mary Immaculate, the first Roman Catholic congregation in India, was founded by several Syro-Malabar priests in 1831. Mary MacKillop founded the Sisters of St. Joseph of the Sacred Heart in Australia in 1866. "The contribution of Middle Eastern Christians to Roman Catholic work can be illustrated very clearly by the increasing number of religious, who entered the orders in the Middle East" (Murre-Van den Berg, 469).

The Anglo-Catholic movement in the Church of England led to the foundation of a number of men's and women's communities. "Many of these groups spread from England to other parts of the Anglican Communion where other indigenous religious orders also emerged" (Sheldrake, 165). The large number of Protestant volunteer societies founded in this century was in some ways parallel to the Catholic orders.

Within the Orthodox world the spiritual revival in Russia contributed to the growth in the importance and number of monasteries. In addition, many Russian women formed unofficial religious communities that were in some ways similar to female Protestant missionary societies and some new Catholic women's congregations of that time (see Irvin and Sunquist unpublished, ch. 8). In Egypt, churches and Coptic women's monasteries were renovated.

A major social movement that affected Christianity was combatting slavery, which has been a thread throughout this chapter. All European nations had banned their ships from engaging in the trans-Atlantic slave trade by 1850. Slavery would come to an end in Latin America and the Caribbean mostly after political independence, but required a civil war in the United States. As noted in Chapter 6, Christian individuals and some churches were part of the earlier abolitionist movements in the eighteenth century, and this grew much stronger in the nineteenth. The significant persons in the United States for this cause include Richard Allen, Harriet Tubman, Isabella Baumfree (Sojourner Truth), and Frederick Douglass. The major impact of slavery on the church in Africa was already noted in the first part of this chapter.

Another significant social movement that influenced Christianity revolved around the fuller participation of women in the church. This movement included Protestant women deaconesses in Europe, Chinese and Indian Bible women, ordination of women in the Holiness movement, renewed monastic movements among Russian Orthodox and Egyptian Coptic women, and many new Roman Catholic women religious congregations, including the first for Australians, New Zealanders, African Americans, and the indigenous of Brazil. A number of Christian women played major roles in struggling for women's rights in society—from Josephine Butler fighting for women's right to vote in Europe to Hindu convert Pandita Ramabai pushing for women's rights in India and criticizing racism and colonialism.

Other social dynamics in Europe and North America were industrialization and urbanization. The church began to respond to this situation toward the end of the century through social reform movements, ministry among the poor, the Protestant Social Gospel movement, the publication of Catholic social teachings by Pope Leo XIII, and the work of such groups as the Salvation Army, YMCA, and YWCA. The church needed to respond to different social contexts and challenges in other parts of the world, such as the caste system in India, and the impact of colonialism around the world.

Theological Developments

Rather than beginning in the Americas or Asia, as in the past two chapters for this thread, we now begin with and focus on Europe. Bevans offers the following concise overview:

> Quite in contrast to the eighteenth, the nineteenth century was one of brilliant and creative theological thinking. It also produced major challenges to theology as scholars proposed ways of thinking that went beyond the bounds of traditional methods of interpreting the Bible and orthodoxy of doctrine. It was a time, however, that was very Eurocentric, with European Christianity at the height of its development. What is clear is that there was very little formal theologizing by people who were not Europeans or North Americans during this period, or if there was it was basically under the influence of Western theology and theologians. (2009, 294)

In terms of Protestant theology on the European continent, the German theologian Friedrich Schleiermacher is often called the "father of modern theology" (see Bevans 2009, 285). He kept his Pietist roots while also embracing the move toward Romanticism in Germany that emphasized intuition over reason. In contrast to the idea of the possibility of a rational, philosophical knowledge of God, he proposed that theology should be based on experience, the human consciousness/feeling of absolute dependence on God. Doctrine should not be taken literally. This was developed in his classic work *The Christian Faith* (1821). Lutheran theologian Albrecht Ritschl developed the work of Schleiermacher, but he took historical revelation rather than experience as his starting point. Ritschl was one of the proponents of what came to be called liberal theology, with its emphasis on the love rather than the judgment of God. German theologians Ferdinand Baur and David Strauss from the University of Tübingen, mentioned earlier in terms of their important contributions to biblical criticism, were influenced by Schleiermacher and the philosophy of G. W. F. Hegel. In contrast with this liberal theology in Germany, there was also a smaller group of theologians coming from evangelical revivalism, including Friedrich Krummacher, who drew from German Pietism and mysticism as well as the Catholic spirituality tradition (see Irvin and Sunquist unpublished, ch. 3).

The theological landscape in the Protestant and Anglican English-speaking contexts reveals some similar and yet different developments.

John McCloud Campbell of Scotland and Frederick Maurice of England are important representatives of those who opposed rigid Calvinism in favor of focusing on the "radically personal nature of God" (Campbell) and "reconciliation and the reign of God" (Maurice) (Bevans 2009, 289). Philip Schaff of Switzerland was one who brought the new ideas developing in Germany to the United States. He "proposed a move away from the individualist and rationalist understanding of Protestantism . . . and called for a move toward a more ecclesial and sacramental understanding of the church . . . [representing] the grand synthesis of Protestantism and Roman Catholicism, both leaving behind their imperfections" (ibid., 290). At the same time, on the one hand, strong trans-Atlantic theological developments from an English-speaking evangelical perspective included apocalyptic, dispensational, and/or Arminianist characteristics. On the other hand, the theologians at Princeton Seminary upheld the dogmatic standards of Calvinism against the innovations of the Second Great Awakening (see Irvin and Sunquist unpublished, ch. 2). Lutheran theologians in the United States included Princeton Seminary graduate Samuel Schmucker at one end of the continuum, and Carl Walther, the first president of the Lutheran Church–Missouri Synod, at the other.

Roman Catholic theology also included some diverse theological developments. Contrary to the general Catholic suspicion of the Enlightenment, a movement in the first half of the century attempting to engage the contemporary age was sparked by the philosophy of Friedrich Schelling and centered in the Catholic faculty at Tübingen University, which was established alongside the Protestant one in 1822. A couple of the key Catholic theologians were Johann Sebastian Drey and his student Johannes Kuhn. The latter developed an ecclesiology and theology of Christian tradition that would not be "very far from that laid out in Vatican II" (Bevans 2009, 281). However, Rome considered this and similar movements in France and Italy as a danger—"a kind of subjectivism that would lose sight of the objective truths of the faith, upheld and taught by the Roman magisterium" (ibid., 282). This led to the rise of the Roman school of theology of neo-Scholasticism. The Roman College, which was restored to the Jesuits in 1824 and renamed the Pontifical Gregorian University in 1873, became an important center of neo-Thomist, neo-Scholastic theology. Theologians Giovanni Perrone and Joseph Kleutgen of the Roman College were very influential in the declaration of the dogma of the Immaculate Conception and the opposition to the Catholic German school of theology, respectively. The subsequent *Syllabus of Errors* and the First Vatican Council reinforced the church's stance against anything related to the Enlightenment, modernism, and the French Revolution. While neo-Scholasticism was the dominant theology of the second half of the century, one outstanding exception was

John Henry Newman. After switching from the Anglican to the Roman Catholic Church, as noted earlier, he was often controversial. For example, "Newman marshaled his expertise in patristic thought to argue that there needs to be a wider dialogue between hierarchy and laity in the church" (ibid., 284). In closing, it is interesting to note that Russian Orthodox theology within its patristic renewal shifted toward mysticism and what is often called spiritual theology (see Irvin and Sunquist unpublished, ch. 8).

Mission, Cultures, and Religions

The nineteenth century was called the "Great Century" of mission by Kenneth Scott Latourette due to the tremendous amount of missionary efforts, particularly by Protestants and Anglicans, but also by Roman Catholics and Orthodox. Contributing external factors from the societal contexts included the Enlightenment, nationalism, scientific and technical progress, and the political and economic force of colonialism and imperialism. The latter two dynamics—progress and colonialism—caused long-lasting consequences for the recipients and are included with *mission* in the title of this chapter. This points to both the strong and complex interplay among these aspects and the very important role mission played in Christian history and tradition during this period, as noted throughout this chapter. At the same time, a wide variety of spiritual and religious renewal movements provided the internal motivation of many women and men from around the world for mission.

The initial Protestant mission work, described in the last chapter, burst open in this century. While many individuals contributed to this, the name of the British Baptist missionary William Carey (1761–1834) is most commonly associated with this new chapter in mission (see Irvin and Sunquist unpublished, ch. 5). In response to strict Calvinism, which negated the need for human activity to bring people to God, the 1792 publication of his booklet, *An Inquiry into the Obligation of Christians to Use Means for the Conversion of the Heathens,* led to the eventual foundation of the Baptist Missionary Society. "In order to 'use means' to effectively accomplish the missionary goal, Carey looked outside the ecclesiastical structures available at that time and drew upon an analogy from commerce: organizing a volunteer 'instrumentalist' society is like floating a company" (Bevans and Schroeder 2004, 211). Many organizations based on this society model—such as the LMS, CMS, ABCFM, and the Basel Mission—emerged quickly, and accompanying mission theologies eventually developed as well.

The ideology of social and political egalitarianism of the Enlightenment and the French Revolution influenced the volunteer nature and inclusion of both lay and ordained members in these mission societies. "Rather than depending on the authority of the institutional church and its official ministers, individual Christians could band together for a common cause . . . [and] the Enlightenment's optimistic view of humanity further supported the motivation to make a difference in the world either from one's home or by leaving it" (ibid., 212). Of course, the long history of revivalist movements likewise fueled this mission commitment.

In the beginning these societies were normally not denominationally or confessionally exclusive. The formation of the Evangelical Alliance in London in 1846 was very significant within this movement toward international and interdenominational mission collaboration. However, the central purpose of mission began "shifting from the earlier emphasis on individual conversion to the planting of distinctly confessional churches" (Bevans and Schroeder 2004, 213). Henry Venn and Rufus Anderson, longtime secretaries of CMS and ABCFM, respectively, separately developed the important "three-self" formula that became widely practiced among Protestants and Anglicans, whereby the goal of mission was to establish churches that were self-supporting, self-governing, and self-propagating.

In addition to the Western theological developments described above, there were also many non-Western Protestant and Anglican Christians who contributed to the thread of mission. One outstanding representative was Samuel Ajayi Crowther, considered "the foremost church leader in nineteenth-century Africa" (Bevans and Schroeder 2004, 213). Captured and enslaved as a boy from western Nigeria, Crowther was freed from a Portuguese slave ship by a British squadron, taken to Freetown, and baptized in 1825. After completing studies in Freetown and England, Crowther accompanied an expedition to the Niger Delta as a translator. He then completed his theological education in England, was ordained a priest with the Church of England, and returned to Freetown as a missionary for the Church Missionary Society. Crowther led successful all-African mission efforts in the area of the Niger River and was ordained a bishop in 1864. "In 1841, there were 107 European and 9 African and Asian missionaries in CMS, while thirty-two years later, under Venn's leadership, the CMS had 230 European and 148 African and Asian missionaries. In addition, African catechists, evangelists, traders, and clerks played important roles in spreading the Christian faith across Africa" (ibid., 214). The first part of this chapter also included the important contributions by Chinese Christians like Liang Fa and Keuh Agong, unnamed Korean merchants, and many Pacific Islanders. Many others can be added to this list, such as "Naga preachers and teachers who carried the gospel to new tribes" (Frykenberg, 487) in the Assam (Asom) area of northeast India; this pattern was replicated by other indigenous (tribal) people in northern India. However, when colonialism turned to the stronger form of imperialism in the 1870s and 1880s, such non-Western active participation would suffer under increased racism and paternalism. For example, Crowther's legacy and leadership would be challenged in this changing environment.

Another very strong aspect of this period was the dramatic increase in the official participation of Protestant women in mission. At the beginning of the century Mary Webb founded the Boston Female Society for Missionary Purposes to support British and North American mission activity financially and spiritually; this was at a time when a woman could only take part directly in foreign mission as the wife of a missionary. In the 1820s the ABCFM began sending single women to teach girls and young women among Native Americans and in Hawaii and India. Mary Lyon, considered "the female counterpart of Rufus Anderson" (Robert 1996, 93), founded Mount Holyoke Female Seminary in 1837 to prepare women teachers; it sent its first teacher for foreign mission six years later. The British Society for Promoting Female Education in the East was one of a number of such interdenominational organizations founded in Europe. Soon many other denominational women's missionary organizations, such as the Woman's Foreign Missionary Society of the Methodist Episcopal Church, were formed, so that by 1900 "over forty denominational women's societies existed, with three million active women, some despite sustained hostility from the men of the church" (ibid., 129).

The holistic mission activities of women included education, health, and evangelism. Generally speaking, schools were seen as a way of attracting students and parents to Christianity and of developing the literacy necessary for reading the Bible, but not all mission schools required their students to become Christian (see Irvin and Sunquist unpublished, ch. 5). Furthermore, the education of women prepared them for active participation in society and the church. For example, several Chinese Christian women's periodicals started in the 1880s and 1890s, and the first Chinese YWCA opened in 1890 (ibid., ch. 6). As an example of health and mission, Clara Swain, the first Western woman missionary doctor in India, received land from a Muslim ruler to build a clinic and training center, which became the first women's hospital in Asia (see ibid.). Moving beyond initial resistance to women engaged in direct evangelism, the long list of women doing evangelism (see Robert 1996, 50–56, 167–69, 200–205) included Western missionaries like Baptist Ann Judson in Burma, Southern Baptist Charlotte (Lottie) Moon in China, and many zenana workers visiting women's quarters in India. They, in turn, trained many more non-Western women for mission engagement, most notably the Bible women in China and India. "By 1909, the woman's missionary movement had employed 441 missionaries as 'evangelists and zenana workers,' but it had hired 6,154 'Bible women and native workers'" (ibid., 169). In addition, Yu Cido (Dora Yu), who is considered one of the most important Chinese women Christian leaders at this time, was among the first Protestant missionaries in Korea (see Irvin and Sunquist unpublished, ch. 6).

This mission theology of the Canadian Presbyterian Mission's Woman's Work for Woman movement was concerned with both salvation and civilization. In this way it was part of Western cultural imposition, but it also promoted the human dignity of women in the face of patriarchal ideas and practices. Women played a major role in mission in this century. In 1890, 60 percent of US Protestant missionaries were women. Women leaders from North America and England founded the international and ecumenical World's Missionary Committee of Christian Women in 1888, which "organized meetings and programs in conjunction with the Chicago World's Fair of 1893 and the Ecumenical Missionary Conference of New York in 1900" (Bevans and Schroeder 2004, 220).

The relationship between colonialism and full-scale imperialism in the last three decades of the century, on the one hand, and mission, on the other, was complex. For example, the well-known missionary and explorer David Livingstone opposed slavery and supported the role of Africans in mission work, but at the same time, he thought that colonialism and Christianity would provide Africans a prosperous life. "On the whole, the missionaries were children of their time; that is, they normally did not question colonialism in itself or the attitudes associated with manifest destiny. At the same time, most missionaries were very concerned about the welfare of the non-Western peoples, although today we would label their approach paternalistic and ethnocentric" (Bevans and Schroeder 2004, 216).

Several new forms of Protestant mission surfaced in the later years of the century. Many new missionary societies, called faith missions, demanded radical volunteerism, whereby missionaries worked with no financial guarantees. J. Hudson Taylor with others founded one of the first and most widely known ones—the China Inland Mission (today known as the Overseas Missionary Fellowship). "In reaction to the imperialistic situation, Taylor insisted that his missionaries not seek protection or favor from a foreign colonial government. They wore Chinese clothing and a braid or pigtail, which symbolized submission to the Chinese government" (Bevans and Schroeder 2004, 216). New student movements drew many young people for service and eventual leadership for world mission. The Student Volunteer Movement for Foreign Missions was founded under the inspiration of Dwight Moody and A. T. Pierson in 1888, and the World's Student Christian Federation by John R. Mott in 1895. While faith missions and some more evangelical missionary groups considered social outreach as secondary, other Christians were concerned primarily with social issues and these activities developed particularly in the United States into the

Social Gospel movement. Inspired by theologian Albrecht Ritschl and the writings of the Baptist minister Walter Rauschenbusch, this "development would eventually influence SVM and missionary-founded churches" (ibid., 217). As a final note on Protestantism and mission, Gustav Adolf Warneck, often considered the founder of the discipline of missiology, was appointed in 1896 as professor of mission studies at Halle. Furthermore, his writings are among the first by European Protestants to recognize that Christianity is a world religion, not a European religion (see Irvin and Sunquist unpublished, ch. 3).

The extensive Roman Catholic mission activity of the seventeenth and eighteenth centuries reached a low point in 1800, with possibly only three hundred missionaries left around the world, due to factors described in the last chapter, including the French Revolution. Despite this, Anne-Marie Javouhey of France founded the Sisters of St. Joseph Cluny in 1807 during Napoléon's rule, and she is "credited with initiating nineteenth-century Catholic mission efforts in Africa" (Bevans and Schroeder 2004, 223). The Jesuits were restored in 1814 and already numbered five thousand by 1848, of whom approximately 20 percent were serving in Asia, Africa, and the Americas (see Irvin and Sunquist unpublished, ch. 3). Pope Gregory XVI, who had been the prefect of the Sacred Congregation for the Propagation of the Faith, promoted missionary renewal during his papacy (1831–1848).

François Libermann of Orthodox Jewish background founded a missionary congregation that later merged with another to become the Holy Ghost Fathers (Spiritans), who would send more Catholic missionaries to Africa than any other congregation in the hundred-year period of 1860–1960. Charles Lavigerie, archbishop of Algiers and Carthage and later a cardinal, founded the Missionaries of Our Lady of Africa (the White Fathers) and a parallel women's community. On the one hand, Lavigerie focused on African agency in mission and was influential in fighting slavery on the international level, but he also "reminded his missionaries that they were working for France as well as for the reign of God" (Bevans and Schroeder 2004, 225). The Italian Daniel Comboni, who also founded two missionary congregations initially for Africa, "laid the foundation for recognizing the human dignity of indigenous peoples and their role in evangelization" (ibid.). The many newly founded men's and women's missionary congregations in Europe also included Oblates of Mary Immaculate, Society of Mary (Marists), Daughters of Mary Immaculate (Marianists), Mill Hill Missionaries, Society of the Divine Word, Missionary Sisters Servants of the Holy Spirit, Franciscan Missionaries of Mary, and Missionaries of the Precious Blood,

"While the primary role of Catholic women in mission at this time [the first part of the nineteenth century], similar to their Protestant counterparts, was teaching, they also were involved in a variety of charitable works and in the area of health, through nursing and establishing hospitals" (Bevans and Schroeder 2004, 224). Franciscan Sister Marianne Cope further developed the work of Damien De Veuster with lepers on the Hawaiian island of Moloka'i. Rose Philippine Duchesne of the Society of the Sacred Heart of Jesus initiated an approach to ministry among Native Americans in the United States whereby the sisters lived with the people rather than the children coming to the schools in town. Katherine Drexel committed herself and her significant family financial resources to the education of Native Americans and African Americans and founded the Sisters of the Blessed Sacrament for this purpose. She supported the eventual founding of Xavier University in New Orleans, the first African American Catholic institution of higher education, and she "became a strong voice for interracial justice and for women and mission in the United States" (ibid., 225). Suzann Aubert founded the first women's order in New Zealand, the Daughters of Our Lady of Compassion, to serve the Maori. The older Chinese women's congregation of Christian Virgins grew during the nineteenth century and developed ministries for orphans and the sick and dying. Generally speaking, there were ten times more Chinese women religious than priests and men religious in China through these years (see Irvin and Sunquist unpublished, ch. 6).

The nineteenth century is also considered a golden age of mission for the Orthodox Church. One of those who responded to the call for missionaries in 1828 by the Holy Synod in Russia was Macarius Gloukharev (Glukharev). With two companions he worked with nomadic peoples in the Atlai Mountains area of Siberia in the areas of Bible translation, medicine, and hygiene. "Contrary to contemporary Orthodox practice, he insisted on a long pre-baptismal preparation and later encouraged them to live in newly established Christian villages" (Bevans and Schroeder 2004, 227). Gloukharev was also influential in developing an Orthodox mission theology. Another key figure was the aforementioned Veniaminov, missionary to Alaska and bishop of an area from Siberia and the Aleutians to California. Later, as the metropolitan of Moscow, he was very influential in the foundation in 1870 of the Russian Orthodox Missionary Society. Orthodox mission activity also extended to Japan, China, and Korea. Within the new forms of religious communities of women developing in Russia, some also had specialized ministry to grief-stricken women and the poor—combining contemplation and service to the world (see Irvin and Sunquist unpublished, ch. 8).

The earlier Rites Controversy, described in Chapter 6, and the overarching context of colonialism and imperialism, had promoted a negative Christian attitude toward non-Western cultures. Few Western missionaries, as children of their time, acknowledged that local cultures maintained high ethical and religious values (see Irvin and Sunquist unpublished, ch. 4). However, there were exceptions. Among Catholic missionaries in Polynesia the traditional social structure was preserved on Wallis; Marist priest Louis Elloy demonstrated ways of creatively engaging the local culture in Samoa (see ibid., ch. 7); and Bishop Jean Baptiste Pompallier supported the acceptance of many elements of the Maori culture. In Asia some noteworthy examples of Protestant adaptations to local cultures included the approaches of the China Inland Mission in China; RMG missionary Nommensen in Indonesia; and Norwegian missionary Lars Olsen Skrefsrud and colleagues in northern India, who tried to distinguish between the heart of Christianity and its European expressions and to assist the Santal people in expressing the faith in their own way (see ibid., ch. 5). Meanwhile, Orthodox mission efforts continued to favor adaptation to local cultures.

Non-Western Christians were of course the primary agents of expressing their faith in their own culture. Using his "insider's" view, Crowther contributed to the Africanization of Christianity through "his acknowledgement of the richness of African culture" (Bevans and Schroeder 2004, 213). Tamil poet H. A. Krishna Pillai described Jesus Christ with Indian idioms (see Irvin and Sunquist unpublished, ch. 5). Polynesians often brought their music, drums, and dancing to Protestant worship, and Vietnamese Catholics expressed their culture through devotional practices around Our Lady of La Vang.

In general, there was tension and suspicion between Christianity and other religions in the nineteenth century. Crowther again provides an exception in this area. He "avoided the common language of denunciation and allegation in his encounters with Muslims" (Bevans and Schroeder 2004, 213–14). He used Arabic translations of the Bible and knew the Qur'an well enough to identify some points of common agreement with Christianity. Such engagement with Muslims in West Africa in the nineteenth century was not possible in other places, especially in the Ottoman and Persian empires (see Irvin and Sunquist unpublished, intro.). In the Ottoman Empire, Muslim conversions to Christian faith were illegal, but proselytizing activities with Jews were permissible. The London Society for Promoting Christianity amongst Jews, founded in 1809, was active in England, the United States, South America, and eventually in Palestine, where some believed that the conversion of the Jews was associated with the second coming of Jesus Christ. In the latter context medical mission became the primary vehicle for the society's purposes. While this was initially intended to promote individual conversions of Jews, medical mission became an opportunity for Christian witness with people of other religions and for better interfaith relationships (see ibid., ch. 8).

As for the relationship with Hinduism in India, Protestant and Anglican missionaries had conversion as their primary goal and education as the main activity. The handful of upper-caste Indians who became Christians through the educational work of the Scottish Presbyterian Alexander Duff became influential Protestant leaders as India moved toward independence. One of these students and converts, Krishna Mohan Banerjee, wrote articles in defense of female education and in critique of the caste system (see Irvin and Sunquist unpublished, ch. 5). We noted above the significant role of Pandita Ramabai, a Christian from Brahmin background, in advocating for social reform in India. At the same time, Christian mission influenced a variety of Hindu reform movements and figures that included Debendranath Tagore, Brahmo Samaj, Ramakrishna, and Swami Vivekananda, who spoke at the World's Parliament of Religions in Chicago in 1893. Irvin and Sunquist maintain that Zoroastrianism, Buddhism, Islam, and Hinduism in India all experienced some renewal in the nineteenth century, partly due to the influence of interfaith interactions with Christianity (see ibid.).

We conclude this section with two exceptional nineteenth-century examples of Western missionaries attempting to bridge the traditional cultural-religious worldview of non-Western indigenous peoples with the new message of Christianity through their choice of a local name for God. First, the Anglican bishop John William Colenso in Natal, South Africa, advocated for the use of *uNkulunkulu* as the Zulu God-name. "He believed that there was 'common ground' between African and Christian religion" (Colenso, 99). The use of this name not only raised a religious question, but it also had political implications in the colonial period (see ibid.). Second, German Lutheran missionaries proposed using the God-name *Altjira* for some aboriginal peoples in central Australia (see Moore). In both cases some missionaries opposed using these names for God, while some communities continue to use them today.

Conclusion

Colonialism and mission influenced Christian tradition around the globe in many ways. The nineteenth century also included new developments in biblical studies, many spiritual and religious renewal movements, an increased role of women in the church and mission, and growth of indigenous Christian communities. The following is an excerpt from the diary of Mary Kaaialii Nawaa, a Hawaiian (Polynesian) missionary affiliated with ABCFM who was sent to Mille in the Marshall Islands (Micronesia):

I had no thought in my widowhood to abandon the work of God. I determined to direct the work, to leave the meetings of the men with the deacons and conduct the women's meetings myself.... I had no wish or intention to return to Hawaii but only to wear out and lay my bones in this foreign land engaged in turning souls to the Lord. The people of Mille refused to part with me and promised to take good care of me. (Munro and Thornley, 219–20)

8

Post-Christendom West and Non-Western Christians

ca. 1900 to ca. 2000

Two major shifts or reversals occurred in Christianity in the twentieth century—the collapse of Christendom in the West and the rise of the Christian faith outside the West. The idea and reality of Christendom had developed in the West since the tenth century; another form of it existed in the Byzantine Empire even earlier, but ended in the fifteenth century. The high optimism of the 1910 Edinburgh Conference reflected the confidence of the church-state collaboration in the West and the sentiment and watchword of A. T. Pierson and John R. Mott—"The evangelization of the world in this generation" (see Bosch, 336–37). This was based on the false notion of the ongoing advance and perceived superiority of Christianity from the West. However, by the end of the century the situation in the West had shifted drastically, to the extent that "Christianity would not be recognized even as a cultural factor in Europe by the nations that today compose the European Union" (Sunquist, xvi). Furthermore, the center of the Orthodox Church in Russia would suffer under the rise of communism in 1917.

However, over the same period Christianity spread rapidly in other parts of the world, so that by the end of the twentieth century the majority of Christians were living in the Southern Hemisphere and Asia. "In 1893, 80 percent of those who professed the Christian faith lived in Europe and North America, while at the end of the twentieth century almost 60 percent live in Africa, Asia, Latin America, and the Pacific" (Bevans and Schroeder 2004, 242). Scott Sunquist notes that "a larger percentage of people attend church in China, Malaysia, Singapore, Indonesia, and South Korea than in almost any country in Europe today" (Sunquist, xvii–xviii). Massive migrations from the Global South (and East) to Europe, North America, and

Australia along with the rise of Pentecostalism and independent churches also contributed greatly to the shape of a world church.

The title for this chapter, "Post-Christendom West and Non-Western Christians," is taken from the eighth chapter of the work of Frederick Norris (2002, 238–76). Much material for this final chapter is drawn from Scott Sunquist, *The Unexpected Christian Century: The Reversal and Transformation of Global Christianity: 1900–2000* (2015), and from Hugh McLeod, ed., *World Christianities c. 1914–c. 2000*, The Cambridge History of Christianity (2006). We begin our brief survey of the historical context in Africa.

Historical Context

Africa

Most of the leaders at the Edinburgh Conference "had pretty much given up on Christianity in Africa" and/or thought that "Africa would become a Muslim continent" (Sunquist, xvi). No African spoke at Edinburgh. However, the number of Christians in Africa grew from 10 million in 1900 to 360 million by 2000, and there were more Christians than Muslims by the end of the century.

The First World War (1914–1918) affected the social-political and ecclesial context of Africa. For example, "The Anglo-French attacks on German colonies in Africa would implicate over half a million Africans as soldiers and many millions more as hapless porters" (Kalu 2006b, 197–98). The war also "severely disrupted the structure and moral economy of the missionary enterprise in Africa" (ibid., 201), particularly as Germany, England, and France deported or incarcerated missionaries of their enemies' nationalities. However, in the following decades the missionary efforts rebounded strongly due to the ecumenical spirit of the International Missionary Council (IMC), founded in 1921, the formation of a national council of churches, and massive efforts in education by both Protestants and Catholics. While most Western missionaries colluded with the ongoing colonial system, several did object. An example is J. H. Oldham's protest against the forced labor and heavy taxation of Africans. Also, Africans "returning from the war or from mines and plantations urged the presence of schools as a sign of development, the acquisition of white power . . . and a coping mechanism of the new times" (ibid., 205). Due to this and other factors, a massive movement to Christianity took place during this period.

Alongside the fast growth of Protestant and Roman Catholic communities, other African Christian movements that had begun in the late nineteenth century (described in Chapter 7) mushroomed in many forms throughout the twentieth century in sub-Saharan Africa. Zionist and

Apostolic churches emerged in South Africa; other independent movements in West Africa; and global Pentecostalism throughout Africa, with many grouped under the broader category of African Independent Churches (AICs). Simon Kimbangu of the Congo Free State (present-day Democratic Republic of the Congo) began a charismatic ministry of healing and preaching, including a prediction of the end of colonialism. The latter point led to his eventual death in prison, but the newly formed Kimbanguist Church would become the largest AIC, with over five million members by the end of the second millennium. "All over the continent, the nature, direction and pace of Christianity changed from the burst of the prophetic and spiritual revivals" (Kalu 2006b, 209). These developments are discussed in further detail below under the threads "Ministry and Organization" and "Spiritual, Religious, and Social Movements."

The Second World War opened the door for political independence and decolonization in Africa, affecting both political and religious areas. "Undoubtedly, missionary responses to nationalism varied during the decade 1945–54 according to individual whims, official or denominational/institutional policies, and regional contexts" (Kalu 2006b, 213). However, after independence the historic churches in general drew more upon African personnel and resources. Internationally, the Second Vatican Council (1962–1965) and the World Council of Churches (WCC) assemblies in Uppsala (1968) and Nairobi (1975) promoted and expanded these efforts by opening up to the modern world, embracing a more holistic understanding of mission and church, and opening the door for what would become known as indigenization, inculturation, and contextualization.

The relationship among the churches founded by Western missionaries and those founded by African Christians was rather complex. On the one hand, there was a call in the first half of the 1970s by some Africans for Western missionaries and church personnel to leave Africa. This debate pointed to the desire to break not from Christianity, but from its colonial form. At the same time, many of the first generation of African leaders were influenced by a Christian understanding of integral development and were sympathetic to the historic churches, such as Julius Nyerere with Catholicism in Tanzania, Kenneth Kaunda with Presbyterianism in Zambia, and Canaan Banana with Methodism in Zimbabwe. By the late 1980s the historic churches had to a significant degree shifted from their colonial past to predominantly African leadership, and new church-state relationships emerged as almost half of the African sub-Saharan countries moved toward multiparty democracies. Regarding the latter, Catholic bishops in Zaire and Benin, for example, chaired national conferences or councils during these political transitions, while others provided voices of prophetic criticism again oppressive systems, like the Anglican bishops in Kenya (see

Maxwell, 407). In the early 1990s the Vatican brokered a peace agreement in Mozambique, and Anglican Archbishop Desmond Tutu chaired the Truth and Reconciliation Commission in post-apartheid South Africa.

However, the horrifying 1994 genocide in Rwanda pointed to the ambiguous position of Christianity as a source of both life and death. Two million people were killed and another two million fled from Rwanda. While some priests and many Christians died in efforts to prevent the genocide, a number of church clergy and personnel were agents of this violence. "The vast majority of the perpetrators of the crimes of the genocide had been baptized and had some sort of Christian formation" (Maxwell, 418).

In spite of situations like Rwanda, Christianity was growing exponentially during the twentieth century in Africa. This movement, both in the historic and indigenous churches and both domestically and internationally, was primarily initiated and led by Africans. Some were formal, organized efforts, but "most of the expansion was the low-level face-to-face kind. . . . Enhanced communication and social mobility swelled the ranks of the proselytisers from labour migrants, catechists and evangelists to include nurses, teachers and civil servants on placement, returning students . . . and urban churches on 'crusade' determined to establish rural branches" (Maxwell, 408–9). The millions of refugees and migrants contributed to these mission activities.

In terms of northern Africa, Coptic Christians and Muslims united in gaining independence for Egypt in 1922. However, in the 1930s and 1940s the Copts were again marginalized under Islamic nationalism. This intensified when Islam became the national religion in 1971. In the interim, the Coptic pope Cyril VI from 1959 to 1971 "developed a reputation for church renewal through rebuilding and repairing churches" (Sunquist, 99). Similar to the situation in Egypt, the Christians in Sudan also faced restrictions and persecutions during this century. Sudan received its independence from the United Kingdom and Egypt in 1956. Ethiopia found itself under the grasp of Mussolini's Italy from 1935 to 1941. Later, in 1963, the reinstated Emperor Haile Selassie I helped found the Organization of African Unity, with headquarters in Addis Ababa.

Europe

The 1910 Edinburgh Conference, under the leadership of John R. Mott, was a very important event both religiously and politically, with the European states fully supporting extensive missionary efforts. Although the Roman Catholics and Orthodox were not included, the conference succeeded in bringing together Protestants and Anglicans of different ecclesiological and theological perspectives and marking "the beginning of one of the major themes of Christianity in the twentieth century: the ecumenical movement for global Christian unity" (Sunquist, 27). While there were very few non-Western participants, one of them, the future Anglican bishop in India, Vedanayagam Samuel Azariah, challenged the paternalistic attitudes of colonialism and appealed for Western missionaries to come as friends.

The conference, which reflected the high confidence of Western Christianity, quickly suffered a series of challenges. World War I (1914–1918) signaled a decline in the power and prestige of Europe, and on a global basis Western Christianity suffered "a crisis of credibility after such a bloody war, in which Christians were killing other Christians" (Sunquist, 17). "One of the most significant aspects of the First World War for Western Christians was the evident failure of the Vatican and of certain supranational Protestant bodies to mobilize the churches against the war" (Snape, 147). The war was followed by a global influenza pandemic (1918–1919) that claimed over fifty million lives in Europe, North America, and Asia, and then an economic collapse in the 1930s. While most German Catholics and Protestants initially supported the political rise of Adolf Hitler, a group of Lutheran and Reformed Christians—the Confessing Christians of Germany—wrote the Barmen Declaration, under the leadership of Karl Barth, to express resistance to Nazi rule. Hitler's government became more anti-Christian and very anti-Jewish and started World War II (1939–1945), which was even more destructive than World War I. Included in the war-related horrors were "the deaths of ten million victims of Stalin's social reconstruction and six million Jews during the Holocaust" (Bevans and Schroeder 2004, 240–41). And atomic bombs dropped by the United States resulted in "the destruction of two-thirds of the city area of Hiroshima and half of Nagasaki" (ibid.). Nationalism took precedence over religion for most. Christianity would not rebound to its former status in Europe.

A continuation committee that was formed from the Edinburgh Conference and drew upon the leadership of the Student Volunteer Movement became the IMC after World War I, in 1922. It provided the structure and inspiration for vibrant missionary efforts for the next four decades of the twentieth century. The WCC was founded in 1948 as a fellowship of Christian churches and denominations, and the IMC was integrated with the WCC in 1961.

In terms of the Roman Catholic Church, missionary efforts were revived after World War I. A key church event that occurred in Europe but had worldwide impact was the Second Vatican Council. Theologically and pastorally the Catholic Church opened itself to engaging with the world—shifting from the opposite stance it had taken since the French Revolution. This significant change opened the door for more respectful relationships with other Christians, non-Western peoples, and followers of other religions or no religion. Western European Christianity became particularly concerned with the issue of secularization and religion. In contrast to the First Vatican Council, 30 percent of the attending bishops had been born in the Global South. Particular contributions came from Africa's first cardinal, Laurean Rugambwa, and Brazilian Bishop Hélder Câmara. Câmara led a group of bishops, particularly from Latin America, during the council in unofficial discussions that produced a document called the "Pact of the Catacombs," proposing a radical vision of a church of and for the poor. This document was "forgotten and neglected until recently" (Bevans 2018, 708; see Pikaza and Antunes da Silva).

At the end of the Second World War, the communist state of the Soviet Union remained entrenched in Eastern Europe and expected those peoples, including the eastern half of Germany, to give their allegiance to the Kremlin. This marked the beginning of the Cold War between the political, military, and economic powers of the Soviet Union and the United States. Christians in Eastern Europe experienced various types of discrimination in education and employment and other restrictions under this atheist state. At one end of the spectrum, Eastern rite Catholics were declared illegal throughout Eastern Europe, and any manifestation of religious faith was illegal in Albania. At the other end, the Catholic University of Lublin in Poland functioned throughout the communist period. Generally speaking, a "combination of 'discretion' and 'valour' frequently characterized church life under communism" (Walters, 349).

In Poland the Catholic Church was recognized as the only moral authority and as the institution in opposition to the communist rule. The election of Cardinal Karol Wojtyła in 1978 as Pope John Paul II and his first visit to Poland the following year signaled a shift of power as it "was becoming clear that in Poland the Catholic church had greater legitimacy than the state" (Walters, 354). The Solidarity free trade union began in 1980, and after a period of protests and martial law, Poland inaugurated its post-communist government in early 1989 without violence. The fall of the Berlin Wall, which occurred later that same year, marked the end of the Cold War and, some would say, the end of the twentieth century. Independence movements spread quickly through Eastern Europe, and with them came religious freedom. However, the challenges that Christians faced in the post-communist period included lack of property, resources, and experience; lack of exposure to developments in the world and wider church circles, like Vatican II; and distrust between "those who had 'compromised' or 'collaborated' with secular authorities and those who had 'resisted' and had been persecuted or discriminated against as a result" (ibid., 360). Also, a high percentage of the people of Hungary, Estonia, and former East Germany claimed no religion as the millennium ended.

We return to western Europe to describe the shift toward a post-Christian West. The symptoms of Christian decline include "the weakening of orthodox beliefs and diminishing rates of observance among Christians; the growing numbers of those belonging to non-Christian religions or to no religion; and the declining influence of Christianity and the churches on morality, politics and the law" (McLeod 2006b, 324). While this shift can be traced from the Enlightenment through to World War II, the socially and politically turbulent 1960s are considered the turning point and the beginning of the steep decline in attendance at weekly church services. By 1999 in western Europe "the number of those with no religion was highest in the Netherlands (54 per cent), France (43 per cent) and Belgium (37 per cent)" (ibid., 325). However, at the same time, a vast majority of people in western Europe still identified as Christians, the churches still played a considerable role in public institutions, and new grassroots Christian movements had begun to emerge around Europe.

Asia

Similar to Africa, most of the countries in Asia became independent during the twentieth century, and Christianity grew significantly in terms of numbers and diversity. In India at the beginning of the century, most of the Roman Catholic bishops were from France or Italy, and until 1920 "all priests in Bengal, Tamil Nadu and Andhra were recruits from outside India" (Mallampalli, 423). The movement of Catholic Action, initiated by Pope Pius XI in 1931, provided guidelines for the involvement of Catholic laity in the church apostolate and in the political-social arena in India. The Catholic Bishops' Conference of India was established in 1944. Three years later India achieved its political independence, and there was a partitioning of the subcontinent into Pakistan and India, which was traumatic and bloody despite the nonviolent efforts of Mohandas Gandhi. In the post-colonial period, the Indian government prohibited the arrival of new missionaries into India and strictly monitored the use of international church financial resources. Within this context the Catholic Church fairly quickly shifted to training Indian clergy and church ministers. This increased in the 1960s with the vision of the Second Vatican Council. Interreligious dialogue in various forms would become very important as well. The vast majority of new Christians, both Catholic and Protestant, came from Dalit (formerly called untouchables), tribal (indigenous before the arrival of the caste system), and other marginalized communities. Albanian-born Mother Teresa (canonized a saint in 2016) is "among the most popular of all Christian figures in the twentieth century" (Sunquist, 48) for combining traditional piety with her care for the neediest in

Calcutta and eventually around the world through her congregation of the Missionaries of Charity.

The extensive Protestant missionary efforts were characterized by large-scale conversion movements and work in education and translation. Furthermore, even before the Edinburgh Conference, "the South Indian Missionary Conference in Madras drew nearly 150 missionaries representing forty-five missionary organizations" (Mallampalli, 425–26), and in 1938 the IMC met in Madras. This prepared the way for the birth of the Church of South India in 1947, which united Anglicans from India, Myanmar (Burma), and Sri Lanka (Ceylon) with Methodist, Presbyterian, Reformed, and Congregational churches in India. A similar Church of North India was established in 1972. After independence, Protestants also followed a path of the "Indianization" of church administration and ministry. M. M. Thomas from southern India, an outstanding ecumenical lay leader, was the only non-Western participant in the preparatory meetings of the WCC in 1948. "Furthermore, separate from its better-known origins in the United States, Pentecostalism emerged independently in 1906 in India, partly under the leadership of the former Methodist missionary Minnie Abrams, and in a girls' school headed by Pandita Ramabai" (Bevans and Schroeder 2004, 273). It should also be noted that the Mar Thoma Church was reaching out beyond its traditional social boundaries in the twentieth century. As a final point, starting in the late 1990s militant Hindu groups led violent attacks against Christians who were considered "foreigners" and a threat to a "Hindu India."

During the twentieth century the percentage of Christians in Southeast Asia doubled, from 10 percent to 20 percent, and Christians experienced "relative freedom in most of the region except Brunei, Laos, Vietnam and Myanmar" (Roxborogh, 437). After the Edinburgh Conference, Mott was influential in the formation of Christian councils in Thailand, the Philippines, and Burma in the 1920s. Under the Japanese invasion during the Second World War the churches suffered loss of life, property, and the presence of missionaries. At the same time, "Christians in the Japanese administration sometimes encouraged local believers and Japanese clergy were sent to assist" (ibid., 443). After the war local churches realized that they were able to survive without Western leadership, as nations likewise moved toward political independence, starting with Indonesia in 1945. However, this region of the world was caught in the Cold War after the communist victories in China, northern Korea, and Vietnam. After the 1954 Geneva Conference partition of Vietnam and the opportunity to migrate south or north, "about 1,400,000 Catholics in the north, including 60 per cent of the bishops, 70 per cent of the clergy and 40 per cent of the laity, went south" (ibid., 445). South Vietnam would fall to the communists in 1975 and many refugees fled as a result. By the end of the twentieth century, Christianity in Southeast Asia "took control of its own affairs and destiny, and grew to fiercely maintain an orthodox identity with an Asian face" (ibid., 448–49). At the same time, Iglesia ni Christo, founded by Felix Manalo in the Philippines, became the "largest independent church in Asia" and "is basically Unitarian in theology" (Bevans and Schroeder 2004, 269).

Dramatic shifts likewise occurred through the twentieth century in East Asia. Numerically speaking, the approximate percentage of Christians increased from 0.4 percent to 7.1 percent in the People's Republic of China, from 1.0 percent to 2.9 percent in Japan, from 0.4 percent to 2.1 percent in North Korea, from 0.5 percent to 39.9 percent in South Korea, and from 0.3 percent to 6.3 percent in the Republic of China (Taiwan) (see Young, 452). Beyond statistics, the gospel was "not only adopted but adapted" to form an Asian Christianity that was and is "remarkably resilient" (ibid., 451–52). Before 1945, the practices of the state religion of Shinto were imposed on Christians in Japan and its occupied areas of Taiwan and Korea. Japan's defeat in World War II was followed by other political and ecclesial changes. With the defeat of Chiang Kai-shek's Guomindang, or Chinese Nationalist Party, in 1948 by Mao Zedong's Communist forces, a mass exodus of mainlanders, including Protestants and Catholics, sought refuge in Taiwan and established the Republic of China there. The longstanding Taiwan Presbyterian Church would tend to favor the indigenous Taiwanese, while the Catholic Church was more pro-Guomindang.

Korea was divided after World War II between two spheres of influence: the Soviet Union and the United States. The outbreak of the Korean War in 1950 sparked a mass exodus of both Catholics and Protestants "from Pyongyang in the North, Korea's 'old' Jerusalem, to Seoul in the South, the 'new' Jerusalem" (Young, 464). While there was a "house church" movement in the North, the growth of Christianity in the South to almost 40 percent of the population by 2000 stands out as a remarkable phenomenon of the twentieth century. The Presbyterian Church with its many branches is by far the largest Protestant denomination in South Korea, and Catholicism also experienced revitalizing growth. In the political sphere Seoul's Catholic cathedral "became the symbol of resistance and the scene of student-led demonstrations . . . until Kim Young Sam, a former dissident, was elected in 1992, ending nearly fifty years of totalitarian rule" (ibid., 465). Beyond the historic mission churches, Korean Christianity consists of many independent Pentecostal churches, including the large Yoido Full Gospel megachurch that was founded by Paul Yonggi Cho in 1958.

We now turn to China. Following the anti-foreign and anti-Christian Boxer Rebellion in 1900, the newly arrived Catholic missionary Vincent Lebbe from Belgium insisted that "Chinese Christians should not have to become like foreigners in their own society, and that missionaries should distance themselves from European nationalistic interests to the point of missionaries becoming naturalized Chinese citizens in order to identify as closely as possible with the Chinese" (Bevans and Schroeder 2004, 244). We can compare Lebbe with the evangelical J. Hudson Taylor and the China Inland Mission from the last chapter. Despite such prophetic Western figures, paternalism among many missionaries and occasional waves of anti-foreign and anti-missionary sentiments continued. Others were charting the path for Chinese-initiated Christian movements. John Sung became "one of the greatest evangelists of the twentieth century, but since he ministered entirely in Chinese, and completely in China and Southeast Asia, few outside the region have heard of him" (Sunquist, 50). On the other hand, Watchman Nee was a very widely known Chinese Christian in the West through his extensive writing. He founded the Local Church (also called the Little Flock) in Shanghai in 1927, one of many such independent church foundations at this time in China.

The situation of Christianity shifted after Mao Zedong established the People's Republic of China. Under communism, the Three-Self Patriotic Movement was established in 1951 as the government agency to regulate the affairs of Protestants in China, and a parallel structure was soon put into place for Roman Catholics under the Chinese Patriotic Association. Rome vehemently opposed the Chinese Patriotic Association, particularly its appointments of bishops. The China Christian Council, which is now a member of the WCC, was established in 1980 to attend to the internal and ecclesiastical affairs of Protestant churches while the Three-Self Patriotic Movement continues to serve a more political function. The Protestant churches are supposed to register with both the Three-Self Patriotic Movement and China Christian Council. "Outside the TSPM/CCC umbrella one finds the unofficial Chinese-initiated, 'house church' population, which first began to increase phenomenally in the 1980s in rural areas" (Young, 461). Most of the hundreds of earlier churches of Watchman Nee became part of this underground church movement. There are also two parts of the Catholic Church in China—the one officially registered with the Chinese Patriotic Association, and the one that is unregistered or underground. The relationship between them ranges from antagonistic to rather friendly depending upon local contexts and changing times in China.

Latin America and the Caribbean

At the beginning of the twentieth century in Latin America "the situation of Christianity approximated the situation in Western Europe and North

America more than in Africa and Asia" (Sunquist, 34). The Catholic Church, to which the vast majority belonged, was trying "to reverse the legacy of 'Luso-Hispanisation' of the church during the colonial period, to accelerate processes of 'Romanization'" (Abel, 180), that is, to instill the uniformity of a Western universal church. "The programme of 'Romanization' was applied only slowly, and its overall achievement was uneven. It had a deep impact upon Argentina and southern Brazil, but little in Cuba and northern Brazil" (ibid., 181). The general situation of the separation of church and state during the post-independence period strengthened the Catholic Church in some countries and weakened it in others. For example, the Mexican revolution in 1910 created a strong antichurch, anticlerical environment, while Archbishop (later cardinal) Sebastião Leme of Rio de Janeiro was a key figure in revitalizing the church in Brazil. In general, the Catholic Church was not very engaged in social issues or indigenous rights at this time.

However, major changes occurred in the second half of the century. The Vatican encouraged the sending of missionaries from North America and Europe, established new dioceses with young bishops, and supported the establishment of a Latin American Bishops' Conference (CELAM) in 1955. Dom Hélder Câmara of Brazil was one of those young bishops who would play a significant role in the revitalization of the Catholic Church as "he began to develop his commitment to Catholic action on behalf of the poor and his organization of the laity in local communities" (Sunquist, 57). These grassroots groups would later be called *Communidades Ecclesiais de Base* (CEBs, basic ecclesial communities). Câmara brought this vision to Vatican II and to the CELAM 1968 conference in Medellín, Colombia. Liberation theology would grow out of this context.

Another key figure was Óscar Romero, archbishop of San Salvador in El Salvador. While he had been a friend of the ruling elite, he was transformed into supporting the local people after witnessing a brutal killing of innocent people by the national guard. His life commitment to justice for the poor led to his assassination while presiding at the Eucharist in 1980. More recent challenges for the Catholic Church included reaching out more to the large communities of indigenous peoples and those of African descent.

Another important shift in Latin America was the growth of Protestantism and Pentecostalism. By 1950, "Protestant churches had gained a small but well-established presence in Latin America" (Cleary, 379). A number of them contributed on the worldwide level, like Orlando Costas as head of the WCC and José Miguez Bonino as an important liberation theologian. The historic Protestant churches and the WCC also began working with the Catholic Church in Latin America on peace-and-justice issues.

The fastest Christian growth was in Latin American Pentecostalism, which traces its roots to Pentecost-like events in Chile, Brazil, and Central America. Although European or North American missionaries were present, "Latin Americans were far greater in number at the inception of the Pentecostal movement . . . [and] Pentecostalism assumed from the beginning a Latin American character" (Cleary, 380). Neo-Pentecostalism appeared in the 1970s and 1980s. By the year 2000, there were about fifty million Protestants and Pentecostals/neo-Pentecostals in Latin America, with the latter grouping making up about 75–90 percent of the total (ibid., 381). At the same time, believers in Umbanda, Candomblé, "and many other Afro-Brazilian religions make up nearly 4 percent of the population of Brazil . . . [and the] influence of these religions is not contained by the border of Brazil" (Sunquist, 157). It is also interesting to note that the formerly very small percentage of those who claimed "no religion" has grown in countries like Guatemala (12 percent), Chile (8 percent), and Brazil (7 percent) (see Cleary, 382).

During the twentieth century the Caribbean witnessed a shift in outside political influence from Britain to the United States, great economic hardships between the two world wars, and a greater diversification of its ecclesial and religious panorama. Until the 1960s, "European Christian denominations undoubtedly contributed to continued social and racial stratification" (Gerloff, 231). On the other hand, we had described in the previous two chapters the long and strong presence of the Baptists, coming originally from those of African lineage in the United States, among the communities of African descent in the Caribbean. Beginning in 1900, a religious revival came to the Caribbean with the arrival of the Salvation Army, Seventh-Day Adventists, and churches of the Holiness movement. Marcus Garvey of Jamaica, an early founder of the Pan-African movement, had great influence on the cultural, political, and religious scene in the Caribbean. The Rastafari movement, begun in the 1930s in Jamaica, considered Garvey one of its prophets. Pentecostalism likewise spread throughout the Caribbean, particularly in Puerto Rico and Cuba, and the charismatic movement within the Catholic Church was very strong. In terms of ecumenism, the Caribbean Conference of Churches, consisting of twelve major Christian bodies, including the Catholic Church, was established in 1973.

During the independence movements and other political changes, the churches were on both sides. In the Dominican Republic, the Catholic Church opposed US intervention in 1916, but approved it in 1965 when there was fear of the possibility of another communist Cuba. "In the English Caribbean, the Christian churches have given an uncertain and, in some cases, even a negative response to the movement for political independence of the 1970s. . . . [At the end of the century] large sectors of the churches are involved in defending human rights in the social, political and economic fields" (Lampe, 209).

North America

Christianity in the United States began the twentieth century with the optimism of the Edinburgh Conference, the energizing emergence of Pentecostalism, and the dangerous spirit of manifest destiny. During the immediate period of post–World War I abundance, "moderate and liberal Protestant congregations expanded their physical plants, broadened their services and increased their staff" (McDannell, 237). Most city-dwelling Christians were Roman Catholic Irish, Italian, Slavic, and Polish immigrants organized into national parishes, and the "number of Catholic schools doubled between 1916 and 1926" (ibid., 239). However, the stock market crash in 1929 and the subsequent economic depression devastated many moderate Protestant churches. "Disputes over the nature of the scriptures and the place of Christians in the modern world fragmented the Protestant community into 'fundamentalists' and 'modernists'" (ibid., 236). In relation to the former, the beginning of Pentecostalism in the United States was through the Holiness preachers Charles F. Parham in 1900 in Kansas and African American William Seymour, who led the Azusa Street revival in Los Angeles from 1906 to 1909. Pentecostal churches would enroll millions and quickly send hundreds of missionaries overseas. Canadian-born Aimee Semple McPherson, who founded the Pentecostal Foursquare Church in 1923, "pioneered radio preaching, large megachurches, and modern religious drama" (Sunquist, 126). Other radio ministers included the Catholic bishop Fulton Sheen and Lutheran Missouri Synod preacher Walter Maier.

While US Protestants continued their vibrant missionary outreach, the Catholic Church also considered the immediate postwar years as "America's Hour" for mission. The Catholic Foreign Mission Society of America (Maryknoll Fathers and Brothers) and the Mission Sisters of St. Dominic (Maryknoll Sisters) had already been founded in 1911 and 1912, respectively, as the official missionary societies of the US Catholic Church. They joined many who were members of international missionary congregations. The Catholic Students' Mission Crusade was founded in 1918. Parallel to ongoing Protestant social-gospel ministry, Catholic laywoman Dorothy Day, who is sometimes considered "the most influential and significant person in the history of Catholicism in the United States" (Bevans and Schroeder 2004, 246), and Peter Maurin founded in 1933 the *Catholic Worker* newspaper and movement, which soon included many Catholic Worker houses of hospitality for the most marginalized.

Following World War II and the beginning of the Cold War, the 1960s was a decade of transition in so many ways in the social, political, and moral arenas around the world, including the United States with the civil rights movement, Vietnam War protests, "sexual revolution," "drug culture," Cuban missile crisis, and assassinations of Dr. Martin Luther King Jr. and John and Robert Kennedy. This was also a time of transition for Christianity. Parallel to the ferment for transformation sparked by the Second Vatican Council for the Catholic Church, the winds of change were also blowing among Protestants, who were experiencing the growing tension between "fundamentalists" and "modernists." Many churches identified closely with the vision of the WCC and the newly created Division of World Mission and Evangelism (later the Commission on World Mission and Evangelism, CWME) with its focus on holistic mission and dialogue. However, the conservative and more evangelical churches, which were more focused on proclamation and the uniqueness of Christ, organized the Berlin Congress of Evangelism and the Wheaton Congress on the Christian World Mission, the latter in Illinois (United States), both in 1966. The 1968 WCC Assembly in Uppsala, Sweden, with its emphasis on humanization rather than salvation, was the final event to prompt the formation or birth of two distinct Protestant bodies.

Billy Graham, one of the foremost Protestant evangelists of the twentieth century, "had preached to more than 210 million people in 185 countries by the mid-1990s" (Sunquist, 63) and to many more through television, radio, and recordings. On a global level his association had sponsored the two 1966 conferences mentioned above and the 1974 International Congress on World Evangelization in Lausanne, Switzerland, which developed the Lausanne Covenant. "Graham, more than any other single figure, brought together evangelical streams within global Christianity" (ibid., 64). The churches that accept the Lausanne Covenant form the international body known as evangelicals. Donald McGavran's church growth movement and the modifications by Ralph Winter's approach in terms of "unreached people" were very important among evangelicals in the United States. Meanwhile, the WCC and CWME developed as the other main Protestant stream that became known as the conciliar (ecumenical) movement.

The transition years of the 1960s in the United States were also the beginning of the trend for people to be drawn more to a personal spirituality than to a formal religion. This was reflected in the decline in regular church attendance. However, in comparison with the rest of the Western world, "the decline in churchgoing and church membership slowed down considerably in that country [United States] in the later 1970s and early 1980s, while continuing with little interruption elsewhere" (McLeod 2006b, 341). Furthermore, "while Christians in North America were more likely than those in Europe to be actively involved in their churches, the number of declared secularists were by 2001 similar to the numbers in many European countries" (ibid., 344).

At the beginning of the twentieth century in Canada, Christendom still existed in the largely Catholic, French-speaking region of Quebec. Since the failed uprising against British rule in 1837–1838, the Catholic Church for the next 125 years was "the central institution in Quebec society, enjoying at least the nominal loyalty of the great majority of the French-speaking population" (McLeod 2006a, 16). "Overwhelmingly high levels of Catholic observance were maintained until the 1960s—a poll in 1965 found that 83 percent of Catholics in Quebec claimed to have attended church during the previous week" (ibid.). La Société des Missions Étrangères de la Province de Quebec was founded in 1921 to send diocesan priests for mission overseas. The Protestant English-speaking part of Canada witnessed the first ecumenical union across confessional lines when the United Church of Canada was formed from the Methodists, Congregationalists, and most of the Presbyterians in 1925. Church attendance among Protestants, which was not as strong as with the Catholics, began its decline in the late 1950s. Church attendance for all of Canada had dropped to 23 percent by 1990, but this figure "was still higher than in many European countries" (McLeod 2006b, 323). While the churches in the United States have been challenged to respond responsibly to the sexual-abuse accusations, the churches in Canada have also been dealing with abuse accusations related to the former residential schools for indigenous peoples. Most recently the Canadian Council of Churches was collaborating with the 2015 recommendations of the Truth and Reconciliation Commission for reconciliation and healing with the First Nations peoples.

Oceania

Social change continued in an accelerated rate across the many Pacific Island countries. In the first part of the twentieth century Western missionaries built upon the earlier Christian foundations in Polynesia and Micronesia and began new initiatives in the inland areas of Melanesia, particularly in present-day Papua New Guinea. World War II had a major impact on the Pacific area. "Foreign missionaries were evacuated, executed or interned, and tens of thousands of local men conscripted to assist the one million troops in the region. . . . With missionary leaders gone, and no church structures beyond the disrupted villages, Pacific Christianity emerged as self-reliant under local leadership" (Massam, 256). We already noted in Chapter 7 the key role played by Pacific Islander missionaries. The wave of political independence began with Western Samoa in 1962 and Fiji in

1964 (see Map 10). The Pacific Council of Churches, founded in 1966, was joined by the Catholic Church in 1976 in the post–Vatican II spirit of ecumenism. Independent church movements included the Melanesian Brotherhood and the Christian Fellowship Church in the Solomon Islands and a variety of millenarian-type movements, particularly among Melanesian peoples from the 1940s to the 1970s.

Australia and New Zealand became independent in the British Commonwealth in 1901 and 1907, and completely independent in 1986 and 1947, respectively. The Church of England was the largest denomination in both. The Uniting Church in Australia, established in 1977, included the Methodist, Presbyterian, and Congregational traditions. Social gospel and Catholic Action activities had been strong in the 1920s and 1930s, but decline in church attendance increased in the second half of the century. "For instance, in the Australian state of Victoria, the Anglican, Presbyterian and Methodist churches each lost about a third of their members between 1961 and 1976" (McLeod 2006b, 332). Aboriginal Australians and the Maori New Zealanders both continued to experience racism. Starting in the 1960s some churches supported these indigenous peoples in their appeals and actions for justice and recognition of their human dignity. The Anglican, Catholic, and Uniting churches in Australia apologized in the 1990s for wrongs they had committed toward the Aboriginal Australians.

Russia and Western Asia

Several important factors influenced Christianity in Russia and Western Asia in the twentieth century. First, the rise of communism in Russia in 1917 and the fall of the Berlin Wall in 1989 were bookends for a very difficult period of persecution and martyrdom for the Orthodox Church. As many as 600 bishops, 40,000 priests, and 120,000 monks and nuns were killed in Russia alone (see Sunquist, 78). Second, persecutions of Orthodox and other Christians in Western Asia, such as in Turkey, contributed further to the Christian decline in the area. For example, the authority of the ecumenical patriarch would become limited to the fewer than 100,000 Greek Orthodox who were living in Constantinople itself. Third, while in earlier centuries we could normally situate the bulk of a particular ethnic Orthodox church—like the Russian, Serbian, and Coptic Orthodox—in a certain geographic area, this would no longer be the case in the twentieth century due to persecution, migration, and globalization. Furthermore, the creation of the nation of Israel in 1947, the Six-Day War of 1967, and the ongoing Israeli-Palestine tensions, on the one hand, and the rise of the OPEC (Organization of the Petroleum Exporting Countries) nations in the 1970s and the political-religious renewal and resurgence of Muslim Arab

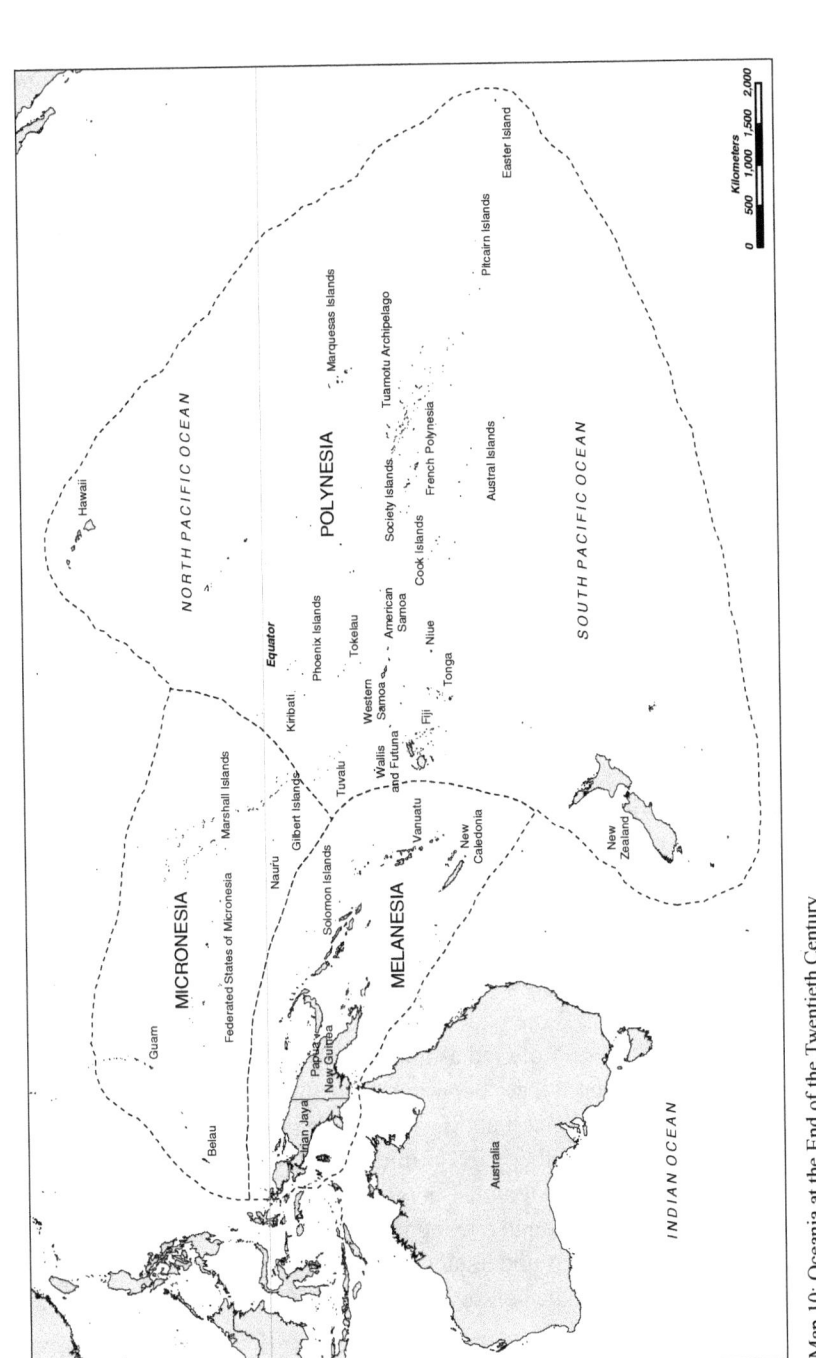

Map 10: Oceania at the End of the Twentieth Century

nations and groups on the other, have caused major disruptions not only in the West Asia region but on the global scene as well. For example, at the beginning of the century Lebanon had a Christian majority, most of whom were members of the Maronite Church. Then Lebanon was devastated by a flood of Palestinian refugees, a fifteen-year civil war, invasions by Syria, and interreligious conflicts. This led to violence, death, and migration. "During the twentieth century, 2.7 million Lebanese, mostly Christians, came to the Americas" (ibid., 146). Other Christian minorities in Iran, Iraq, and Syria have suffered greatly as well.

We have seen how the twentieth century was a period of several major reversals—with the end of Christendom in the West and the outstanding growth of Christian faith in much of the Global South. Church attendance declined in some areas, while new places of worship were springing up quickly in other places. Let us now follow the extensive developments of the six threads of tradition over this period.

Threads of Christian Tradition

Scripture

The historical-critical method of biblical interpretation of the nineteenth century (see Chapter 7) continued to be nuanced and appreciated by many while also being critiqued by others. Among Protestants, Albert Schweitzer's famous work *The Quest of the Historical Jesus* in 1906 "clearly showed that much of what supposedly objective scholars found in Jesus was a reflection of their own values and times" (González 1994, 104). At the same time, Barth insisted that "the results of historical and literary criticism of the Bible can and should be incorporated into theology" (in ibid.). One of the recurring and underlying challenges was bridging the gap between the culture and times of the Bible with contemporary times and contexts. Barth considered the "otherness" of God as the link, while New Testament scholar Rudolf Bultmann thought that "the bridge that allows us to appropriate the message of the NT is self-authenticity and self-understanding—a position that tended to dehistorize the NT" (in ibid., 105). Some Christians of very conservative and/or fundamentalist perspectives interpreted the scriptures literally and therefore discounted using the historical-critical method or any other scientific method for understanding the Bible.

In the second half of the century two other concerns gave birth to new hermeneutical approaches to scripture. First, the literary concern led, for example, to the use of rhetorical criticism, narrative criticism, reader-response criticism, and deconstructionism. Second, the sociopolitical concern attempts to identify more clearly how the cultural and social location of a particular individual or community affects biblical interpretation. These latter developments provide avenues for reading and interpreting the scriptures from new perspectives—such as by women, non-Western persons, and formerly marginalized groups. Theologian Justo González states that this new reading of the Bible "will take into account the contributions of many whose voices have scarcely been heard in the past, but whose insights are already proving to be both valuable and disturbing" (ibid., 106).

Initial shifts in the nineteenth century from the negative attitude of the Roman Catholic Church regarding the critical study of the scriptures greatly accelerated through the twentieth century. Marie-Joseph LaGrange established École Biblique in Jerusalem in 1890 and *Revue biblique* two years later. As a reaction to errors presumed to have come from the modernists, Pope Pius X founded the Pontifical Biblical Institute in Rome in 1909 to promote Bible studies and to train professors of Sacred Scripture. The Catholic biblical renewal continued after Pope Pius XII's 1943 encyclical *Divino Afflante Spiritu* (*Inspired by the Holy Spirit*), and especially following the Second Vatican Council and its 1965 monumental document *Dei Verbum* (*Dogmatic Constitution on Divine Revelation*, DV). The publication of the in-depth 1993 document "The Interpretation of the Bible in the Church" by the Pontifical Biblical Commission includes an excellent description and assessment of the various biblical methods of interpretation in the twentieth century.

The Second Vatican Council's reaffirmation of the importance of scripture for Christian faith and life mandated the church to make sure that "suitable and correct translations are made into various languages, especially from the original texts of the sacred books" (DV, no. 22). Also, these translation efforts could be done ecumenically, another fruit of Vatican II. Of course, Bible translation had been essential for Protestants and Orthodox for a long time, and this continued throughout the twentieth century. Wycliffe Bible Translators, founded in 1942, completed five hundred translations by 2000. The dramatic renewal of the post–Vatican II Catholic Church embraced the centrality of scripture within the liturgy, preaching, sacraments, and spirituality, and supported the growing practices of Bible study and sharing, like the *lectio divina* (divine reading) method introduced in 1950 under Pope Pius XII. It is interesting that this method is adapted to different contexts, for example, with more discussion in Latin America and more silent reflection time in Asia. The Bible continued to be central for the worship, preaching, and spiritual life of Christians of all other churches and denominations.

The translation and reading of scriptures ignited the global spread of Christianity particularly outside the West. Africans "mined the biblical resonances with indigenous worldviews" (Kalu 2006b, 198) and used the scriptures to express and deepen their Christian faith and practice as Africans. For the AICs "the word of God—whether it is through the written biblical text or a charismatic person—is of ultimate importance, to such a degree that Andrew Walls call them 'radical biblicists' and compares them with the Anabaptists of Western church history" (Bevans and Schroeder 2004, 266; cf. Walls 1996, 116). Independent churches and Pentecostals often brought their own charismatic and indigenous interpretations to the scriptures. In Latin America, Catholics began studying and reading the Bible more following the Second Vatican Council and the Medellín Conference. The CEBs "became an important element in applying biblical teaching to the laity, and in helping local communities organize to solve local community problems" (Sunquist, 57). For the Korean-initiated churches and most independent Christian movements in East Asia, "the Bible is read through a Pentecostal lens and without Euro-American blinkers" (Young, 465). Non-Western Christianity has a very strong biblical orientation.

In returning to the issue of biblical interpretation, some non-Western biblical scholars were wrestling with the newer forms of literary and sociopolitical methods, mentioned above, and developing other ones, such as those coming out of postcolonial, liberationist, and feminist contexts and perspectives. Biblical hermeneuticist R. S. Sugirtharajah described some of the presuppositions underlying some non-Western biblical interpretation in the following way: "that the meaning of the text is produced by mutual interaction between the reader and the text; that the reader engages the text and the text in turn engages the reader, and the meaning is the invention of the reader; that a specific meaning is perceived in the text by certain readers because of their particular social, cultural and religious location" (Sugirtharajah, 3).

Liturgy, Sacraments, and Art

Liturgy went through significant changes in the Catholic Church. Pope Pius X and the Benedictine Lambert Beauduin played significant roles in the early stages of this movement, which encouraged a call for the active participation of the people—"one of the grand themes of twentieth-century liturgical reforms—resonant with the global concerns of inclusion and liberation that widely marked the twentieth century" (Foley, 302). The practice of a dialogue mass, in which people recited the prayers of the mass (still in Latin) and responded to the presider, began in Europe in the 1920s. Permission for limited use of the vernacular languages of Paleoslav (Yugoslavia), Czech, Croatian, and Slovenian was granted in the first three decades of the century. The 1947 document of Pope Pius XII, *Mediator Dei*, affirmed the use of the vernacular and the liturgical movement, which culminated in the 1963 *Sacrosanctum Concilium* (*Constitution on the Sacred Liturgy*) of the Second Vatican Council. The twenty-year period after the council was generally one of openness and change that endorsed fully vernacular liturgies, active lay participation, the importance of scripture, and liturgical inculturation. However, since the mid-1980s, there has been a move toward "increasing caution, restriction, and retrenchment" (Foley, 303).

Liturgical renewal was also vibrant among Anglicans. The new liturgy of the Church of South India emphasized congregational participation and followed a structure nearer to that of the fourth and fifth centuries. "This new liturgy would be an encouragement to the rest of the Anglican world" (Spinks, 477) for a renewal that led to the publication of a new Church of England prayer book in 1980. However, worship services within Anglicanism "vary from a sung eucharist with choir and fully vested clergy in a cathedral, to an informal praise service without any traditional Anglican liturgical trappings" (ibid., 479). Revisions also occurred in the Reformed tradition. The 1983 liturgical book of German Reformed churches "represents a blending of the traditionally Reformed orders . . . together with newer orders reflecting the ecumenical consensus, and drawing on the patterns of the fourth and fifth centuries" (ibid.). The *Book of Common Worship* of 1993 gave North American Presbyterians "rites based on the classic rites of the fourth and fifth century, but thoroughly modern, with restored rites and ceremonies, such as the Holy Week services and the use of oil for anointing in baptism" (ibid., 480). New liturgies were created for amalgamating churches like the Australian Uniting Church. Examples of inculturated liturgies around the world are the incorporation of suitable Shinto customs in Korea, ceremonial dancing and traditional African elements in the Roman Catholic Zaire mass in Congo, and Pacific Islanders developing their own "Pacific way" in worship. While, on the one hand, liturgical experimentation in Africa "caused disquiet in many places as 'traditionalism' impeded progress," on the other hand, there was "the energy released by Vatican II and Uppsala which removed the restrictions of yesteryear, enabling the Africanization of the liturgy" (Kalu 2006b, 217).

Worship services within evangelical churches around the world were also conducted along a wide spectrum of styles during this century. The Bible-centered services normally included extensive preaching, as well as testimonies, prayer, singing, the offering, announcements, and special music. Preaching in African American evangelical churches had its own style of rhetoric and congregational participation. The revival services of television evangelists, of various Christian traditions, normally follow a threefold pattern of "preliminaries (heavy on the music), fervent sermon, and harvest (via mail for those not physically present)" (White, 191). Worship in megachurches, particularly in North America, "tend to be a blend of modern pop music, contemporary Christian music and choruses, with 'down to earth' talks (rather than 'sermons') on practical things of life, and minimum use of traditional Christian worship formulae" (Spinks, 481).

Worship for Holiness and Pentecostal communities normally is centered on "singing hymns and spiritual songs, testimony, preaching, an 'altar call' to respond to the conviction of sin, and being freed by the gospel message" (ibid., 482). Prayer services by Pentecostals and charismatics often includes speaking in tongues, the laying on of hands for healing, and other elements found in 1 Corinthians 12:4–12, while preaching and music styles vary greatly. Their spontaneity in prayer influenced other churches. Worship in independent churches and movements around the world is very diverse, although generally speaking they do not have elaborate formal liturgies or sacramental practices. Development within the great variety of AICs "was achieved by bringing traditional worship style into the church through song, dance, choruses and indigenous instruments . . . [and there] was an intentional quest of resonance in biblical symbols and themes" (Kalu 2006b, 208). Prophets and healing also play central roles in worship.

Following the Second Vatican Council, sacraments in the Catholic Church were revised into more contemporary language. In terms of cultural adaptation, the Vatican allows "for some variations in the rituals but they also put limits on the amount of variation that is permissible" (Martos, 143). The sacraments of baptism, confirmation, and Eucharist were grouped together as the sacraments of initiation, reclaiming the practice of the early church, and celebrated together at the Easter vigil for those who had gone through the restored catechumenate process of the Rite of Christian Initiation. The Faith and Order Commission of the conciliar WCC published a theological statement in 1982, after fifty years of discussion, entitled "Baptism, Eucharist, and Ministry." This document was affirmed by churches of the Reformed, Lutheran, Methodist, Anglican, and Orthodox families. It succeeded in bringing "various communions closer together by using language closer to the Bible and the early church writings" (Sunquist, 120). Many African Conciliar Protestants and Catholics strove to inculturate the sacraments. "While Roman Catholic priests challenged celibacy, their Protestant counterparts wanted to celebrate the eucharist with palm wine and kola-nut" (Kalu 2006b, 218). In terms of Pentecostals and sacraments, many "do not sense a need for frequent eucharistic celebrations," and for some, "it is linked to foot washing out of a sense of obedience to Jesus' example in John 13" (White, 201). And baptism of the Spirit is more important than baptism by water for most.

In terms of artistic expression Christian music proliferated during the second half of the twentieth century with the use of different musical instruments and particularly the addition of music from around the world.

"Many of the newer churches, both in the West and in the former 'mission lands,' were producing Christian music following tunes and styles that were more culturally familiar to them" (Sunquist, 123). Within the United States, Thomas Dorsey "developed the new musical form of gospel music" (McDannell, 245) within the African American context, and Southern Baptist churches, which sponsor a number of schools of sacred music, "have done much to raise the quality of music in terms of performance and professional standards" (White, 189). Several expressions in Christian art were directly linked with non-Western communities of faith. The "Jesus Mafa" paintings by the artist Bénédite de la Roncière, which depict the life of Jesus as an African, are based on the dramatic interpretation of Bible readings by a Christian community in Cameroon. A collection of commentaries by the peasants of Solentiname in Nicaragua, which were read at mass before the town was destroyed by military forces in 1977, became the inspiration for paintings done by the people when they returned to reconstruct their town after the overthrow of Somoza in 1979. Also, He Qi provided "a powerful Chinese interpretation to biblical scenes" (Bevans 2009, 313).

Ministry and Organization

The "North America" section above outlined the major development in Protestant ecclesial organization, whereby most churches by the end of the twentieth century would be members of the (conciliar) WCC and others the (evangelical) Lausanne Covenant. After the establishment of the IMC in 1922, the main interrelated themes within Protestantism were ecumenical unity and mission. "A number of subthemes—church independence, ordination of women, liturgical renewal, contextualization—flow out of the impact of the missionary experience and the struggle for Christian unity" (Sunquist, 113). The issue of liturgy was covered in the preceding section, and mission and contextualization are treated in the sixth thread. The other themes are touched upon here.

The 1910 Edinburgh Conference laid the foundation for the Faith and Order movement, which focused on doctrines, organization, and ministry, and the Life and Work movement, which focused on practical questions of action and social reform. They both later became WCC commissions. Around the midpoint of the century the divide between those focused on evangelism and those focused on social engagement led to a "division in Western Christianity and the shift of balance of Protestant Christianity to North America" (Sunquist, 115). Graham was a key person in this movement leading to the Lausanne Conference, that "in some ways was a parallel ecumenical movement, based not on faith-and-order discussions but on cooperation for worldwide evangelism" (ibid.). The formal births of the evangelical and ecumenical streams of Protestantism represented vitality in the West. At the same time, "the divisions that existed in African Christianity, Latin American Christianity, and Asia-Pacific Christianity were mostly exports from Europe. . . . Non-Western Christians found their own voice in the twentieth century, and in many instances they refused many of the Western divisions and Western theological assumptions" (ibid., 121).

In terms of ministry the issue of women's ordination was one of the obstacles for broader church unity. A few Protestant women had been ordained as pastors, deacons, and preachers in the nineteenth century, and the ordination of women increased in the next century, but not among larger Protestant churches until after World War II. Minnie Jackson Goins was ordained in 1904 as the first African American woman cleric by the United Brethren in Christ, which was later part of the United Methodist Church (see Sunquist, 123). The Assemblies of God began to ordain women in 1914, and Congregational churches in England in 1917. It is interesting to note that in 1933 "the first ordination of a woman in a Reformation-era church probably took place in Japan, not in the West . . . when Takahashi Hisano was ordained by the Nihon Kirisuto Kyokai, or the Presbyterian and Reformed Church of Japan" (ibid., 124). Generally speaking, the localization of ministry and church leadership among historic mission churches increased fairly quickly in postcolonial contexts. However, in the first two decades after independence in African countries, "poorly educated Protestant clergy felt themselves to be at distant disadvantage when dealing with a sophisticated post-colonial leadership" (Maxwell, 406).

Of all the transformations or themes of Christianity in the twentieth century, "the single most important is the rise of the 'fourth-stream' churches: those that are independent and rise up, or suddenly spring up, in local contexts" (Sunquist, 124). These spiritual churches, including Pentecostals and independent movements, generally emerge not from a tradition but directly through an inspiration of the Spirit. We have seen throughout this chapter the various ways that Pentecostalism began and spread quickly around the world. The portion of the population in Brazil who were Pentecostal jumped from 7 percent in 1970 to almost 45 percent some thirty years later. However, the significant overlap between Pentecostals and evangelicals also needs to be noted. "More than two-thirds of Latin American evangelical Christians identified themselves as Pentecostals in 2000" (ibid., 82–83). Pentecostalism had also begun to spread in the 1950s and 1960s in mainline Protestant, Catholic, and Orthodox churches, and most of these neo-Pentecostal or charismatic movements were eventually accepted within their denominations. The Catholic charismatic movement "now claims to include more than 100 million Roman Catholics" (ibid., 105).

The AICs often started due to "resistance to foreign (colonial) control of the churches and inspirited African leaders" (Sunquist, 129). These churches developed indigenous leadership and ministry that was particularly strong among women. The Kimbanguist Church, with over five million members, was the first AIC to start its own seminary and join the WCC in 1969. In Asia some of the indigenous spiritual movements were sparked through Western missionaries, but in China, for example, many were initiated by Chinese Christians—from those in the 1920s, described above, to the unregistered churches and house church movement in the second half of the century. Regarding the latter, some propose using the term *autonomous Christian communities* to reflect the size and complexity of their networks. "While it is extremely difficult to count the total number of persons in this Christian movement, estimates range from thirty to eighty million" (Bevans and Schroeder 2004, 269). "Since the 1980s, the official Protestant church has promoted the idea of a post-denominational church in China" (Anderson and Tang, 125). The spiritual churches of Latin America were closely linked with Pentecostalism, which grew rapidly, as stated earlier. "By the end of the twentieth century it was estimated that 95 percent of the Protestants in Chile were actually from Spiritual or Pentecostal heritage" (Sunquist, 131–32). Women also had opportunities for leadership, preaching, and teaching in these movements.

The spiritual churches around the world "seem to germinate below the surface of the Christian story and then suddenly grow and even blossom with little planning and no real strategy" (ibid., 133). At the same time, "independency was working the opposite direction of the ecumenical movement with which it was contemporaneous, and yet the independent and Spiritual churches have found ways to work together, often, but not always, in opposition to the Western churches" (ibid., 128).

Important changes also occurred in the Roman Catholic Church in organization. The Second Vatican Council, called by Pope John XXIII, was a watershed moment. It marked a change "from an essentially hierarchical understanding of the church to a consciousness that is rooted in the understanding of the church as a *community*" (Bevans 2009, 77). Organizationally, the church was now seen as a communion of local churches, or dioceses, each as the body of Christ in its own right. Dioceses were gathered into regional conferences of bishops, such as CELAM, AMECEA, and FABC, in Latin America, East Africa, and Asia, respectively. Further implications of collegiality included universal, regional, and diocesan synods, and presbyterial, diocesan, and parish councils. The development of BECs in Latin America and elsewhere was another expression of the church as community on a grassroots level. The Catholic Church also began official ecumenical dialogues with Orthodox, Anglicans, Conciliar Protestants, evangelicals, and Pentecostals. However, the spirit of ecumenism was not always strong on a regional level. For example, "the vast majority of Latin American Pentecostals shunned ecumenical dialogue and Catholic bishops did not have dialogue with Pentecostals as a high priority" (Cleary, 383).

In terms of ministry Lebbe was one of the first to point to the necessity of promoting indigenous leadership in China. He influenced the move toward the ordination of the first six Chinese bishops (in modern times) in 1926, the first Japanese bishop in 1927, and the first Vietnamese bishop in 1933. The major growth in the number of non-Western bishops, priests, and religious occurred after Vatican II. By 2000, more than 95 percent of the bishops in Asia and Latin America were indigenous, and "Africa had more than 80 percent who were local in origin" (Bernier, 208). The number of Catholic priests around the world remained about the same since 1970, but due to the large numerical growth of Catholics, the ratio of priests to Catholics continued to widen. However, while the number of priests grew in the Global South, there was a serious priest shortage in the West. This led to the closure and merging of parishes, and many are without a resident priest-pastor. Many priests to this day are coming to North America from other countries to fill this lacuna. The celibacy requirement has also been questioned by some.

The ministry of local catechists had already been important for a long time. "In the Belgian Congo, for example, 6,400 catechists were largely responsible for the considerable growth of Christian communities" (Norris 2002, 241). In many areas they increased in number and responsibilities. "They were vernacular intellectuals, interpreters of Christianity within Latin America.... In 2000 more than one million lay Catholics served as catechists, in effect acting as non-ordained ministers" (Cleary, 375). The Second Vatican Council reinstated the office of the permanent deacon, and a wide variety of different ministries were opened up for Catholic laity. The Catholic Church did not allow the ordination of women, but they assumed other new ministerial roles in great numbers, including that of catechist, family life coordinator, and pastoral associate.

The Orthodox situation shifted greatly during the twentieth century. We saw above in the "Russia and Western Asia" section that due to communism, persecution, and migration, many Orthodox moved from their homelands to Europe and North America—creating a strong diaspora presence. New York became the headquarters of the Russian Orthodox Church Outside of Russia in 1950, and the Moscow patriarchate granted autonomy and autocephalous status to the Orthodox Church in America in 1970. The great Orthodox leader Athenagoras, as archbishop of North and South America for seventeen years, strove "to unite the various streams of ethnic-Orthodoxy and at the same time work within Roman Catholic and Protestant contexts" (Sunquist, 99). He continued in this vein as the ecumenical patriarch in Constantinople from 1948 until 1972 in two significant ways. First, with Pope Paul VI in 1965 he lifted the 1054 anathema between their two churches; and second, he worked closely with the WCC, for which the Eastern Orthodox was a founding member. Ethiopian emperor Selassie I called an Oriental Orthodox Conference in 1965 that drew together Armenian, Syrian, Egyptian, and Ethiopian representatives. "The 1988 CWME Orthodox consultation in Neapolis, Greece, marked a closer collaboration and reconciliation between the Eastern Orthodox and representatives of the Oriental (non-Chalcedonian) Eastern Churches, including Armenian, Syrian, Jacobite, Coptic and Ethiopian communities" (Bevans and Schroeder 2004, 265).

The Orthodox endured hardships in their homelands. For example, the Copts and other Christians in Egypt after 1971 "returned to the narrow and limited *dhimmi* status of 'protected' non-Muslim natives living in a Islamic state" (Sunquist, 98). Generally speaking, women had a larger role in the Orthodox Church in comparison with earlier times. While the Orthodox grew numerically, their Christian proportion declined. "In 1900, 22 percent of the world's Christian population was Orthodox (116 million), but by 2007 it was only 10 percent (221 million)" (ibid., 81).

Spiritual, Religious, and Social Movements

Our survey of Christian spiritual movements begins with the spiritual churches. The roots of Pentecostalism and charismatics movements can be traced to Wesley, the Holiness movement, and/or indigenous revival movements around the world. "What was new in Pentecostalism was the identification of Wesley's 'second blessing' with the biblical 'baptism in/ with the Holy Spirit' (Luke 3:16; Acts 1:5)" (Holt, 101). The outward signs of this baptism are speaking in tongues and other spiritual gifts listed in 1 Corinthians 12, including healing and prophecy. Speaking in tongues was a required verification in the early years of Pentecostalism in North America, but that was not always the case in later developments and other contexts. As a "religion of the heart," Pentecostalism offers emotional and experiential faith with a strong sense of community and the call to change one's behavior. One of the most notable reasons for the growth of Pentecostalism is "how it has attracted the least, the lost, and the lonely with nothing but a message and a promise of spiritual power" (Sunquist, 127). Catholic charismatics combined Pentecostal features with traditional Catholic spirituality like sacraments and Marian devotions. In Brazil, both the CEBs and charismatic groups "drew Catholics together in worship and fellowship in the pattern of past Catholic lay associations" (ibid., 105).

The spirituality of the independent churches was expressed and experienced in a wide variety of ways. Often Pentecostal and charismatic elements were combined with indigenous ones. Common features of the AICs include "revelation through prophecy, trances and dreams; the importance of healing within a holistic context; and some identification with Levitical law" (Bevans and Schroeder 2004, 266). Independent churches in China "often have Confucian concerns for a moral and ethical life mixed with Daoist openness to the mysterious and mystical" (Sunquist, 131). In terms of the spirituality of the large Chinese house-church movement, "some are clearly Pentecostal, others are on the margin, while many are simply the conservative evangelical type" (Anderson and Tang, 125). Most independent churches in Latin America are very Pentecostal.

Spirituality in the twentieth century in the historic churches included bringing together mysticism and social-political concerns, sometimes in creative tension. Evelyn Underhill of the Anglican Church developed a strong link between mysticism and social awareness, was very involved in spiritual direction and the new retreat movement, and it is said "that she helped to keep spirituality alive in the Church of England between the world wars" (Sheldrake, 175). Well-known for his provocative book *The Cost of Discipleship*, the German Lutheran Dietrich Bonhoeffer called for a "religionless Christianity" to restore the costly commitment to God. He was arrested by the Gestapo in 1943 for his anti-Hitler stance and executed in a concentration camp two years later. The Catholic Trappist (Reformed Cistercian) monk Thomas Merton, the author of the autobiographical *Seven Storey Mountain*, is often considered the greatest Catholic spiritual writer of the twentieth century. He is known "for his attempts to rearticulate the contemplative-monastic life for a contemporary audience . . . [for] his special contribution to Christian-Buddhist dialogue, and for his later commitment to issues of social justice and world peace" (ibid., 185). At the grassroots level today the New Monasticism movement among Protestants attempts to blend monastic values with social action in daily life.

Along with the representatives of spiritual giants mentioned in the preceding paragraph, another "striking feature of Christian spirituality during the twentieth century is the many ways in which it became more democratic—that is, how it passed increasingly out of the controlling hands of religious authorities and spiritual elites such as clergy or, in the Catholic tradition, members of religious orders" (Sheldrake, 200). In terms of the laity in the Catholic Church, the Second Vatican Council called all the baptized to holiness and full participation in church life. The *cursillo* (short course) movement, which began in the 1940s in Spain out of the pilgrimage experience of some Catholic men, spread around the world and became one of the first important spiritual resources for Catholic laity after Vatican II.

Soon retreats, spiritual direction, *lectio divina* (praying with scripture), centering prayer, and the charismatic movement would represent a wide range of spiritual resources available to all Catholics and other Christians. During the first part of the century popular spirituality from the previous century included the Rosary, Forty Hours services, novenas, and Marian devotions, which were often associated with prayers to overcome communism. While there was some decline in these devotions after the council, these spiritual practices returned strongly in the 1980s. Spiritual growth and Christian action were also nurtured by confraternities and associations, primarily of the laity, like the Legion of Mary, Knights of Columbus, Daughters of Isabella, Altar and Rosary Society, and Holy Name Society. In Latin America, the "cursillo lay leaders and their priest-chaplains emphasized an evangelical change of heart" (Cleary, 369), and the CEBs provided the venue for both prayer meetings and social involvement on the parish and neighborhood levels.

There were many other new developments in spirituality. First, ecumenical spirituality was embodied in the Taizé community and Focolare movement. Second, following the line of Merton in terms of interreligious dialogue in the area of spirituality, the Benedictine monk Bede Griffiths, for example, lived as a Christian *sannyasi* in the state of Tamil Nadu, India, for about twenty-five years in an ashram, which welcomed spiritual seekers and visitors, both Christian and Hindu. Third, there were new dialogues with traditional indigenous spiritualities of the Americas, Australia, and the Pacific Islands. Fourth, feminist spiritualities, which first emerged primarily among white women in the United States, also "have appeared applicable to African American experience (Womanist spirituality) and Latina or Hispanic experience (Mujerista spirituality)" (Sheldrake, 193). For a fuller picture of the explosion of spirituality from a global perspective, see the work of Abraham and Mbuy-Beya (1994) and the last three chapters of Wiseman (2006). Finally, while, on the one hand, church attendance in the West was in decline, on the other hand, there was a growing interest in spirituality that was not associated with Christianity as a religion.

Many of the spiritual movements described above became formal religious movements and institutions, particularly with the spiritual churches. Early Pentecostal churches in the United States included the Church of God in Christ, Assemblies of God, the Church of God (of Cleveland, Tennessee), and the Pentecostal Holiness Church. Today the Assembleia de Deus in Brazil "is the largest Pentecostal denomination in the world" (Sunquist, 132). Likewise, there was also a vibrant burst, both in terms of quantity and diversity, of formal independent churches—including the Kimbanguist Church, Iglesia ni Christo, Little Flock, and Yoido Full Gospel megachurch. "The continent-wide Organization of African Independent

Churches, formed in 1978 and later renamed Organization of African Instituted Churches, became an associate council of the WCC in 1998" (Bevans and Schroeder 2004, 266). Within Protestantism, the establishment of the WCC and Lausanne Movement were major worldwide religious moments. The twentieth century also witnessed the amalgamation of denominations, such as the Church of South India, and the birth of new ones, such as American Baptist Churches USA. Religious movements in Catholicism can be described in terms of renewed and new religious congregations and (primarily) lay movements, such as Focolare, Communion and Liberation, Sant'Egidio, L'Arche, and the Neocatechumenal Way. Regarding religious societies, while the number of Western-born members declined in the twentieth century, there was an increase from those born outside the West, especially for women. For example, in Africa in 1989 "members of female religious orders outnumbered their male counterparts by at least five times" (Maxwell, 410).

Generally speaking regarding the West in 2000, "Christianity was still by far the largest religion in western Europe, North America and Australia, but in all these regions of the world there had been a considerable increase during the last four decades of the millennium in the numbers of those belonging to other religions or to none at all" (McLeod 2006b, 324). New religious movements in the West included the Church of Scientology, Universal Life Church, Transcendental Meditation, New Age, and Wicca.

A central social movement that affected Christianity was migration. "Between 1800 and 1925, one in five Europeans moved out of Europe" (Sunquist, 137), and many Indians and Chinese were recruited to provide cheap labor in Africa, the United States, and areas of the British Empire. Following World War II the migration trend changed, with the vast majority of migrants moving from the Global South (and East) to Europe, North America, and Australia. Furthermore, almost 75 percent of immigrants coming to the United States today are Christians (see ibid., 147). Thus, the church in the United States is becoming more reflective of world Christianity. Conversely, the large influx of Muslim migrants from North Africa and Western Asia to western Europe has contributed to the shift from the Christendom idea there. For example, "in France about 10 percent of the population is now Muslim" (ibid., 137). Furthermore, the complex phenomenon of migration accelerated between and within countries around the world. The main causes of migration are urbanization, economics, politics, globalization, wars, religion, the environment, and disease. We also noted above extensive Orthodox migration.

The situation of women continued to have a great influence in the twentieth century. The role of women in ministry was strong from the beginning in the Pentecostal and independent churches, and expanded within

Protestantism in the second half of the century, although initially the issue of women's ordination was a point of contention. Protestant and Catholic women missionaries did much to improve the situation of women around the world. For example, Ewha Womans University, originally established by Mary Scranton, an American Methodist missionary, grew into one of the major women's universities in the world, and it has produced many women leaders in South Korea. This is indicative of the increase in ministerial and leadership roles of non-Western women in Christianity. The Ghanaian Methodist theologian Mercy Amba Oduyoye contributed on a worldwide level as the WCC deputy general secretary, and in "recruiting and empowering women in the global church" (Sunquist, 44). This leads us into the next thread.

Theological Developments

Following the lead of Stephen Bevans, our treatment of theology is separated into the periods before and after the Second Vatican Council, which was "almost certainly the most significant religious 'event' of the twentieth century" (Bevans 2009, 297). The time preceding the council was marked by energetic theological initiatives for Conciliars, evangelicals, Catholics, and Orthodox, and the period afterward was even more engaging and complex as Pentecostals and more women and men from every corner of the world began to contribute to theological developments.

As for Protestant theology in this first period, we start with Karl Barth, whom some have called "the most significant theologian of the twentieth century" (Bevans 2009, 297). "Barth's radical Christocentric theology, with his devastating critique of nineteenth century liberalism, initiated a theological reformation" (Sunquist, 69). Barth's theology, often identified with neo-orthodoxy, stressed the transcendence of God. Due to his involvement with the Barmen Declaration and his ongoing stance against Hitler, Barth was dismissed from his teaching position in Germany and then accepted a teaching position in Switzerland. His major publication, though never completed, was his thirteen-volume *Church Dogmatics*, which "ranks as one of the greatest works of systematic theology in Christian theological history" (Bevans 2009, 299). Barth taught that the church was for mission. "Barth's theology of the church (along with others) had a direct impact on the Second Vatican Council" (Sunquist, 70).

German-born Paul Tillich left his homeland for the United States when Hitler took over and became an internationally respected theologian. With his "method of correlation," he strove to explain the Christian faith in response to the existential questions of his time and context. Reinhold Niebuhr, Tillich's colleague at Union Theological Seminary in New York

City, developed his thought around what he called "Christian Realism." Niebuhr believed that humanity could transcend its "finitude not by trying to be like God but by trusting God and imitating Christ, whose combination of perfect freedom and human finitude shows the way of true humanity" (Bevans 2009, 301).

Most Orthodox theologians fled to the West. Georges Vasilievich Florovsky, who taught in both France and the United States, wrote extensively about patristic theology, and he was "one of the most active of Orthodox theologians in the Faith and Order Commission of the WCC" (Sunquist, 74). Two other exiled Orthodox theologians were Sergei Nikolaevich Bulgakov and Vladimir Nikolaevich Lossky.

Renewal among Roman Catholic theologians in the first part of the century came from two schools of thought—the historical approach to Thomism and Transcendental Thomism. Marie-Dominique Chenu was one of the leaders of the former school and Yves Congar the most famous. Congar wrote "perhaps the first systematic reflection on the theology of the laity" (Bevans 2009, 304), and then, despite being exiled from teaching for a time due to his call for church reform, he was very influential as one of the *periti* (official theological advisers) for Vatican II. Henri de Lubac, who fought against Nazi anti-Semitism in France, made his greatest theological contributions on the Eucharist and the relationship between grace and nature. The "theology of perhaps the two most important Catholic theologians of the century" (ibid., 303) came from the second school of Transcendental Thomism—Karl Rahner and Bernard Lonergan. Most of Rahner's publications came in the form of essays, as found in his twenty-three-volume *Theological Investigations*. He was very influential both as a *peritus* at the council and afterward. As Bevans notes, "Some theologians would contend" that in comparison with Rahner, the work of Lonergan would "hold more promise for the future" (ibid., 306). Lonergan's most well-known works are *Insight: A Study of Human Understanding* and *Method in Theology*. Other major Catholic theologians who were influential before and after Vatican II include Hans Urs von Balthasar, Edward Schillebeeckx, Pierre Teilhard de Chardin, Joseph Ratzinger (who became Pope Benedict XVI), and John Courtney Murray.

As for the theological initiatives after the Second Vatican Council, we now shift our approach from a denominational to a geographical one. "In many ways, after Vatican II what mattered more in theology was not so much one's church affiliation as one's 'social location': one's gender, one's culture, one's generational identity—in short, one's *context*" (Bevans 2009, 297). The Medellín CELAM conference opened the door for doing theology in Latin America in a new way—from the perspective and experience of the poor. The publication of *A Theology of Liberation* by Gustavo Gutiérrez laid the foundations for the development of Latin American liberation theology by Catholic men and women like Clodovis and Leonardo Boff, Ivone Gebara, Jon Sobrino, Maria Clara Lucchetti Bingemer, Juan Luis Segundo, Ignacio Ellacuría, and the United Methodist José Míguez Bonino. Initially, liberation theology also drew from the political theology of German theologians Jürgen Moltmann and Johann Baptist Metz, and also from Marxist thought, which prompted some sharp caution from the Vatican. However, in the last years of the century liberation theology continued to evolve with additional influences from "Latin American popular religion, indigenous cultures, the Catholic Charismatic movement, the challenge of Pentecostalism, Latin American feminists, and minority groups such as indigenous peoples and those of the African diaspora" (ibid., 311). The first of many international meetings of *teología india* (indigenous theology) was held in Mexico in 1990. Early key theologians included two Catholic priests—Eleazar López Hernández, a Zapotecan Indian from Mexico, and Nicanor Sarmiento Tupayupanqui, of the Quechuan community of Peru.

In South Asia, D. T. Niles of Sri Lanka offered leadership for the WCC, and as a theologian "used local religious concepts (in his case Buddhism was more important) to develop a Christian vocabulary and theology for Asia" (Sunquist, 45). At the same time, M. M. Thomas of India was more interested in Christianity's role in postcolonial nation building, while also being "one of the most influential theologians in the WCC during the 1960s and 1970s" (ibid., 50). Catholic theologians included the Indians Raimon Panikkar, George Soares-Prabhu, D. S. Amalorpavadas, and Michael Amaladoss, and the Sri Lankan Aloysius Pieris. Turning to Southeast Asia, Catalino G. Arévalo was "perhaps the most eminent Filipino theologian" immediately after Vatican II (Bevans 2009, 312), and Filipina theologian Virginia Fabella was key in founding the Ecumenical Association of Third World Theologians (EATWOT). They represent many Catholic theologians from this part of Asia (see ibid., 312–13). Several Methodist bishops made major theological contributions as well. Filipino Emerito Nacpil promoted "the independence of Asian theological thinking" (ibid., 312), and the Malaysian Hwa Yung wrote the widely known book *Mangoes or Bananas?* and also served on the Lausanne Movement board of directors. In East Asia the life of the political theologian K. H. Ting was controversial. As the head of the Chinese government's China Christian Council, he "helped to reintroduce the Chinese church to the world at the WCC's 1991 Canberra meeting ... [and] argued for greater religious freedom" (Sunquist, 54). Two outstanding Japanese Protestant theologians were Kazoh Kitamori, who wrote *Theology of the Pain of God*, which became "a classic in twentieth-century theology" (Bevans 2009, 313), and Kosuke Koyama, who authored *Water Buffalo Theology* and other examples of Asian contextual theology.

We now turn to the vast area of African theology. Similar to Latin America, "African theology focuses on the poverty and marginalization of African peoples, and call for liberation . . . [and] closer to the Asian emphasis [it] focuses on African cultural values and the resources to be found in African Traditional Religions" (Bevans 2009, 314–15). The liberation focus was particularly strong with Protestant South Africans, but also among others, like the Catholic Congolese Bénézet Bujo. Two representatives, among many, of the cultural theological trend are the Protestant John Mbiti and the Catholic Charles Nyamiti, both of East Africa. Prominent African women theologians include Mercy Oduyoye, Musimbi Kanyoro, and Afua Kuma. Borrowing a phrase from Bevans, this short paragraph can "just scratch the surface of a lively theological world that includes Pentecostals, Evangelicals, Catholics, and members of the huge number of African Independent/Initiated Churches" (ibid., 315).

Significant theological developments occurred in Oceania as well. Australian Gideon Goosen published *Australian Theologies: Themes and Methodologies into the Third Millennium*, which provides an excellent survey of the work being done in the areas of "aboriginal theology, ecological theology, feminist theologies, and theology and economics" (Bevans 2009, 313–14). Neil Darragh, one of the leading Catholic theologians in New Zealand, has contributed much in the area of theology and ecology, and compatriots Susan Smith and Cathy Ross, Catholic and Anglican, respectively, have written important works on women and mission. Much contextual theology of Melanesia was published in several issues of the *Point* journal of the ecumenical Melanesian Institute in Papua New Guinea.

While theology certainly mushroomed dramatically since 1965 outside of the West, much theology continued to be produced in Europe and North America (see Bevans 2009, 315–21). The following is simply a thumbnail sketch. Theologians who contributed to the lively ecumenical discussions about the relationship of Christianity to other religions include Paul Knitter, John Hick, Gavin D'Costa, Harold Netland, and S. Mark Heim. Evangelical theologians include Carl F. Henry, Donald Carson, Miroslav Volf, and Alister McGrath. The large cohort of systematic theologians includes Peter Hünermann, David Tracy, Thomas O'Meara, Elizabeth Johnson, Richard Gaillardetz, Bradford Hinze, Robert Schreiter, Douglas John Hall, and Rowan Williams. The Greek Orthodox bishop and theologian John Zizioulas is representative of several Orthodox theologians in the West. The growing field of feminist theology was established by women such as Letty Russell, Rosemary Radford Ruether, Elizabeth Johnson, Elisabeth Moltmann-Wendel, and Anne Clifford. Much has also been written in the areas of ecology, reconciliation, globalization, and the relationship of religion and science. In looking back at this rich variety of theological developments, "the vast majority recognize the importance of context in any theological effort" (ibid., 317).

By century's end much theology was being done by members of "subaltern" groups in Europe and North America. In terms of black theology, the Protestants James Cone, Cecil Cone, Major Jones, J. Deotis Roberts, and Gayraud Wilmore laid the groundwork. Black Catholic theologians include M. Shawn Copeland, Bryan Massingale, and Jamie Phelps. Womanist black theology also developed, represented by theologians such as Emilie Townes and Katie Cannon. The large number of those who broke new ground in Latinx theology is represented by people like Virgilio P. Elizondo, Orlando O. Espín, Arturo Bañuelas, Roberto Goizueta, Allan Figueroa Deck, Gary Riebe-Estrella, and Jean-Pierre Ruiz. Women like Ada María Isasi-Díaz contributed to a feminist Mujerista theology. While most of the above-mentioned Latinx theologians are Catholics, the prolific theologian and historian Justo L. González is just one of the growing number of Protestants. More recently, Asian American theology has been produced by persons like Catholics Peter Phan and Jonathan Tan, Methodists Roy Isao Sano and Jung Young Lee, Presbyterian David Ng, feminist Chung Hyun Kyung, and Pentecostal Amos Yong. Indigenous theologians in North America include Vine Deloria and George Tinker. NAIITS (formerly the North American Institute for Indigenous Theological Studies) was established at the turn of the millennium.

Mission, Cultures, and Religions

While the nineteenth century has been called the Great Century of Mission, Andrew Walls asserts that "the most remarkable century in the history of the expansion of Christianity has been the twentieth" (2002, 64). While Christianity was declining in the West, it was expanding throughout the rest of the world. Mission in the Roman Catholic Church has been described by Schreiter (1994) as passing through four stages during the twentieth century—certainty, ferment, crisis, and rebirth. The period of certainty before Vatican II was a continuation from the previous century, although there were indications of forthcoming changes. For example, Vincent Lebbe spoke against the link between colonialism and mission, and he encouraged the localization of church leadership in China; Charles de Foucauld was influential in introducing the model of mission as presence in Morocco; Henri Godin and Yvan Daniel challenged the geographical notion of mission with the publication of their pamphlet *France, pays de mission?* (France, a mission country?) in 1943. The catalyst was the Second Vatican Council. It opened a new understanding of mission, in terms of the primary trinitarian missionary (*missio Dei*) nature of the church, a stance of dialogue between the church and the world, and a new understanding of the nature of other religions (see Bevans and Schroeder 2004, 249–51). The Vatican II document *Ad Gentes* (*Decree on the Mission Activity of the Church*) and other conciliar documents laid the groundwork for these major shifts. The ten years after the council, as a period of crisis, were marked by many questions regarding the motivation for mission and much uncertainty due to other rapid post-conciliar changes. There were, however, also many signs of new life, like the Medellín conference, *cursillo* movement, and dissolution of the *ius commissionis*, whereby mission was now in the hands of every bishop and diocese rather than the Vatican assigning missionary congregations to them.

Schreiter designates the 1975 promulgation of the apostolic exhortation *Evangelii Nuntiandi* by Pope Paul VI as the beginning of the rebirth of mission. It was based on the reign-of-God theology and the experience and reflection of church leaders of the world church at a 1974 synod in Rome. Other regional gatherings that later nuanced this new understanding and practice of mission included the 1979 CELAM conference in Puebla (Mexico), the 1986 FABC assembly in Tokyo, two US bishops' documents in 1986 on economic justice and on mission, and an AMECEA meeting in Moshi (Tanzania) the same year. In 1990, Pope John Paul II issued the encyclical *Redemptoris Missio* (RM). While affirming the *missio Dei* and reign-of-God theologies of *Ad Gentes* and *Evangelii Nuntiandi*, respectively, this christocentric encyclical reaffirmed "the central place of Christ and the church in salvation history and the importance of mission *ad gentes*" (Bevans and Schroeder 2004, 254). The practice of mission "as a single, but complex reality" (RM, no. 41) includes multiple components such as proclamation and witness, interreligious dialogue, justice/peace and the integrity of creation, and liturgy and prayer (see ibid., 348–95). By the end of the century the majority of Catholic missionaries came from the Global South, and the many newly founded, non-Western missionary societies were represented by the Missionaries of Guadalupe (Mexico), the Daughters of Divine Love (Nigeria), and the Foreign Mission Society of Korea.

We introduced many of the events and developments regarding mission within Protestantism in the preceding section, "Historical Context." We shall now frame this development according to the same four stages used above to describe the Catholic understanding of mission, namely, certainty, ferment, crisis, and rebirth. The period before and after the Edinburgh Conference was a time of great optimism and certainty, but new movements were also stirring. Karl Graul laid the foundations for the so-called *Volkskirche* (people's church) mission model, which promoted grounding the church on the cultural characteristics of a people; Roland Allen proposed accelerating the church-planting endeavor to avoid perpetuating a dependency relationship with the West; Daniel Fleming "criticized missionaries for their attitudes of cultural and racial superiority, and he insisted on separating Western culture from indigenous expressions of Christianity" (in Bevans and Schroeder 2004, 257). A major indication of the intra-Protestant tension regarding mission was twofold. W. E. Hoking was the chairman of the committee that studied and wrote a summary (called *Rethinking Missions*) in 1932 of the Laymen's Foreign Missions Inquiry (LFMI), which offered a serious appraisal and critique of the situation of mission through a very extensive interview process. Second, at the request of the IMC, the Dutch lay missionary Hendrik Kraemer published a response in 1938 against the liberalism of the LFMI report. The long list of key missionaries during this period included, from the Indian subcontinent alone, people like C. F. Andrews, E. Stanley Jones, V. S. Azariah, Ida Scudder, and D. T. Niles.

The moment of ferment included several events. The first meeting of the new CWME in 1963 in Mexico City "pointed to the fact that God's mission was not geographically bounded; rather, one should talk of 'mission on six continents'" (Bevans and Schroeder 2004, 260). Anglican scholar and missionary Stephen Neill in 1964 wrote that "the age of missions is at an end; the age of mission has begun" (572). These shifts are similar to those of Vatican II. On the one hand, the split over issues of mission and theology became sharper within Protestantism, but on the other hand, this was also a moment of ferment with the pending "births" of two distinct and vibrant evangelical and conciliar movements that would each carry out this new understanding of mission. The moment of crisis from the mid-1960s to the mid-1970s was characterized by the divisive 1968 WCC Uppsala Assembly, postcolonial independence, a proposal by some for a missionary moratorium, and growing tensions between conservatives and liberals.

Several events marked the stage of initial rebirth in the mid-1970s. The 1974 Congress on World Evangelization developed the Lausanne Covenant. The Lausanne Committee for World Evangelization (LCWE) was established to carry out the mandate of the covenant and was the heart of what became known as the Lausanne movement. "Another organization, the World Evangelical Fellowship (WEF) . . . also has offered a number of important mission-related consultations, sometimes in conjunction with the LCWE" (Bevans and Schroeder 2004, 261). The evangelical stream of Protestantism articulated its particular vision of mission around explicit proclamation. At the same time, the inclusion of social justice in the covenant was due to the perspectives and input of those known as radical evangelicals and many from the Global South like René Padilla and Samuel Escobar. The 1989 LCWE missionary conference held in Manila, popularly called Lausanne II, produced the important Manila Manifesto, which reaffirmed "the primacy of proclamation but also includes dialogue, a strong concern for the poor and a more holistic approach" (ibid., 262). In 1987, the World Evangelical Fellowship moved its international headquarters to Singapore, and it chose its first non-Western international director in 1992.

After the Uppsala Assembly the conciliar stream of Protestantism began to discover and clarify its new understanding and practice of mission during the 1975 WCC Assembly in Nairobi and the 1980 CWME Conference in Melbourne. "Nairobi marks the beginning of a new phase in the development of ecumenical mission theology, as seen as an attempt to reconcile 'churchly' and 'worldly' approaches to mission" (Scherer, 126). The 1982 WCC document *Ecumenical Affirmation: Mission and Evangelism* was one of the most important ecumenical mission statements. WCC and CWME assemblies and consultations continued to articulate their multifaceted understanding of mission, including "wholistic" evangelism (Stuttgart, 1987); stewardship of creation (San Antonio, 1989); justice, peace, and the integrity of creation (Seoul, 1990); and reconciliation (Canberra, 1991). Lesslie Newbigen, one of the most important mission practitioners and academics in the conciliar movement, "established in 1982 the Gospel and Our Culture program as a forum for a missionary encounter with post-Enlightenment culture in the West" (Bevans and Schroeder 2004, 264). Again, one notes parallels with what was occurring in the Catholic Church. In terms of mission specifically by Christians of the Global South, "Protestant Christians in the non-Western world not only resisted older colonial models of missionary involvement but also quietly developed their own theology, liturgy, and music even as Western theologians and Christian institutions struggled to find their new place as partners in missionary obedience" (Sunquist, 121–22). Furthermore, for "the Protestant Asian, African, and Latin American missionaries, Reformation-era distinctions (denominations) held little sway" (ibid., 82).

While Orthodox churches couldn't send out missionaries during the first part of the century, they carried out a mission of presence in their new diaspora situations. However, the transitional 1960s was also a time of renewal in mission for them. Bishop Anastasios Yannoulatos established a journal in mission studies and a new Orthodox Missionary Society called *Porefthendes* ("Go ye"). "The Greek Orthodox supported missionary efforts initially in Uganda, Kenya, Korea and Alaska, and later in other African and Asian countries" (Bevans and Schroeder 2004, 264–65). An Orthodox Advisory Commission to the CWME, established in 1973, articulated its understanding of mission, while Catholics, conciliars, and evangelicals were doing the same. The primary focus of Orthodox mission was on common witness, liturgy, proclamation, and mission as "liturgy after the liturgy." In looking ahead, the Council of the Orthodox Church produced a major mission document in 2016 entitled "The Mission of the Orthodox Church in Today's World."

The Edinburgh Conference was concerned with order, statistics, and unity, but this "businesslike efficiency in 1910 is ironically developing at the same time as modern Pentecostal movements and revival movements in East Asia and Africa" (Sunquist, 24). Spiritual churches represented spontaneity, flexibility, and rapid diversification in terms of Christian life and mission. These churches "have always been strongly missionary in their identity, both in preaching a message of 'fullness of the Holy Spirit' to Christians in the world (as a type of renewal) and in evangelizing the non-Christians" (ibid., 82). They approach the missionary task with certainty and confidence. Moreover, they connect very directly with the spiritual concerns and worldview of the people. For AICs, if mission does not take ancestors, magic, and impurity into full account, "it is missing something very serious, and can scarcely maintain that the Good News has been proclaimed effectively" (Oduro et al., 22). Furthermore, "salvation is important for the here and now: for *here*, in ordinary life (not only in heaven); and *now*, at the time when a person might be in danger (not only for the time after death)" (ibid., 27). In Latin America the spiritual/Pentecostal churches reached out to the poor. While some preach a prosperity gospel of health and wealth, many others address the underlying social needs and "are engaged in educational work, orphanages, and even politics" (Sunquist, 132). For the Chinese spiritual churches, "missionary concerns for China have always been part of these movements, but by the end of the twentieth century concern for missionary work to western China and non-Chinese cultures began to appear" (ibid., 131).

The tremendous amount of missionary work by women in the nineteenth century continued into the first decades of the twentieth. Among North American Protestant missionaries around 1916 "missionary women outnumbered missionary men by nearly two to one in the major mission fields" (Robert 2002, 5). Helen Barrett Montgomery was the first woman to lead a major denomination when in 1920 she was elected president of the Northern Baptist Convention. However, that year also marked the beginning of a quick shift of integrating the separate women's missionary societies into male-dominated ones and a rise of fundamentalists who "began emphasizing the subordination of women to men . . . [and] claimed that the Bible restricted the ministry of women" (ibid., 9). But thanks to the efforts of Western missionary women, in Madras "the 1938 meeting of the IMC had the largest representation of non-Western Christian women in the history of ecumenical Protestantism" (ibid., 12) at that point in history. Many women were able to have prominent roles in mission in the Holiness and Pentecostal churches. "Women in Latin America, excluded from most church leadership in the Roman Catholic Church, became preachers and teachers in Pentecostal culture" (Sunquist, 133). After World War II, "the mainline denominational issue of women's rights in the church, including ordination, became separated from support for women missionaries except in the smaller denominations with traditions of women's ordination" (Robert 2002, 18). At the same time, the participation of non-Western women in the multifaceted dimensions of mission grew throughout the century.

The extensive mission involvement of Catholic women, many of whose stories appeared in *Woman's Work for Woman*, continued into the twentieth century, primarily through women's religious congregations. Anna Dengel founded in 1925 "the first Catholic congregation of women to work as physicians, surgeons and obstetricians" (Bevans and Schroeder 2004, 245). After Vatican II, religious women participated greatly in the expanded practice of mission that included liberation and social justice in Latin America, and addressing poverty, apartheid, and violence in Africa. Subsequent changes included the dramatic growth in the contributions of Western and non-Western Catholic laywomen (single and married) and non-Western religious women in mission around the world. However, as a general comment regarding all Christian women, one can say that often "the freedom of the gospel bearer collides with gender barriers—in the culture of both the missionary and of the new Christians" (Robert 2002, 27).

At the end of this lengthy description of mission one notices again the major shift from the West to the rest of the world in terms of Christianity and mission. Second, Christians involved in mission, in multiple senses, are not only "professional" missionaries or those officially sent by a mission organization or Christian community, but also ordinary Christians "gossiping the gospel" as in the early church.

In terms of culture, Catholics after the Second Vatican Council changed from a very negative attitude to a positive one toward non-Western cultures, from tabula rasa to accommodation and beyond. Pope Paul VI in 1969 in Uganda proclaimed, "You must have an African Christianity" (cf. Kalu 2006b, 197). This represents immediate efforts in inculturation around the world. However, some restrictions and cautions were raised starting in the 1980s. The Catholic Church also became more accepting of much popular religiosity, which expressed the link between culture and faith. Conciliar, ecumenical Protestants also shifted from a rather negative to a more positive approach to culture. Generally speaking, evangelical Protestants maintained a more negative assessment of culture throughout the century, while the Orthodox maintained a positive one—both following their underlying historical theological position. Of course, there were exceptions, nuances, and variations for these four Christian confessional families, according to different contexts. And all of them included some form of critique of aspects of every culture that are contrary to the gospel. In terms of the spiritual churches, the Pentecostals had a negative attitude toward culture, while some of the independent churches could be more positive. One of the main reasons for the rapid spread of the latter is that "many of the indigenous churches in Africa, Asia, and Latin America communicate the message in patterns that are more culturally appropriate for their neighbors" (Sunquist, 82). The work of *teología india* (indigenous theology) in Latin America is also a concrete attempt to engage indigenous culture with the gospel.

Parallel to its shift in understanding cultures, the post–Vatican II Catholic Church also assumed a positive attitude toward other religions. The 1991 *Dialogue and Proclamation* outlined the four avenues for interreligious dialogue in daily life, shared action, theological exchange, and religious experience. Regarding the last area, Pope John Paul II and leaders or representatives of other religions came together and prayed in their own ways in Assisi in 1986 and 2002. A similar openness occurred in the WCC beginning in the 1950s, with people like the British Anglicans M. A. C. (Max) Warren and Kenneth Cragg proposing approaches of presence, witness, and dialogue with those of other religions. The conciliar (ecumenical) Christians clarified the distinctive character of dialogue and proclamation in the 1979 WCC publication *Guidelines on Dialogue with People of Living Faiths and Ideologies*. Evangelicals continued to affirm the primacy of proclamation and the invitation to baptism. Between conciliars and evangelicals, the "theological, or, more exactly, missiological tension developed between the call to be peacemakers through dialogue and the call to be witnesses to all nations" (Sunquist, 164). While Pentecostals shared the evangelicals' stance toward other religions, the Pentecostal theologian Amos Yong (2008) affirmed that Christians should not look down on followers of other religions and should be open to offering and receiving friendship. Another interreligious phenomenon is that some followers of other religions worship Jesus Christ without joining an institutional church, as is the case with Hindu devotees of Christ.

Challenges for any type of interreligious interactions grew during the twentieth century due to events and situations such as the Jewish holocaust, Middle Eastern conflicts around the state of Israel, birth of radical Muslim groups like the Taliban, Christian fundamentalism, extreme Hinduism in India, and terrorist attacks and wars. It is important to note that "religious violence has been complex, seldom purely about religion" (Sunquist, 169). While the West has also contributed to the cycle of violence, many Christians around the world also participated in peacemaking efforts.

Conclusion

With major reversals in the twentieth century within Christianity, the expressions of the various threads of Christian tradition naturally underwent significant changes while still being faithful to the Christian core. One of the major developments was the emergence of Pentecostalism and independent churches. We close with an excerpt from the testimony of Amos Swelindawo, bishop of an AIC Zionist church in South Africa:

> My local congregation never talks or thinks about mission. It is not necessary, because they just know that here in the township and in the factories and in other work places they are witnesses for Christ. . . . Here in the city, our public preaching of the Word is often not fruitful. However, our witness within and outside the church, the way in which we live as Christians, is most important for the mission of our church. (Oduro et al., 107–8)

Conclusion

In the Introduction I introduced two images. First of all, as rain and snow fall on the earth, create waterways, bring forth fruit, and return to the heavens (see Isa 55:10–11), so God's mission of love, salvation, and justice continues to be lavished on humanity and all creation, and all are being drawn back to God. Condensation forms waterways in the form of creeks, streams, rivers, and lakes as water finds its way back to the oceans—twisting and turning through the terrain of different contexts and over a period of thousands of centuries. This image captures the power of God's word in itself to bear fruit and return to God. Humanity, created in God's image, has tried to participate in this mystery of the *missio Dei* over time and place. The new and growing field of world Christianity provides a framework for this global and inclusive perspective. At the same time, we remember that the waterways created by the flowing of God's Spirit are bigger than our historical records and the Christian movement itself.

Second, I used Steven Bevan's image of the passing of the baton in a relay race to represent both the "stuff" of Christian tradition and the act of traditioning—the noun and the verb of the Christian response. We have traced six threads of this multi-streamed tradition through eight time periods. Each chapter has acknowledged and portrayed a glimpse of the depth, breadth, and magnitude of the diverse ways through which Christians have understood and expressed their tradition and how Christians have passed on this tradition from one generation to the next, from one culture to another, and from one context to another. And we have seen how these human efforts have been (and continue to be) marked by both grace and sin.

I hope that the huge amount of detail in these pages has not been experienced as an overwhelming challenge for one's memory, but rather as an invitation to appreciate the broad sweep of the Christian tradition from a global perspective—many of the specific examples perhaps being new to us. Ideally, this book has provided a taste of the feast of plenty, which is not a display of the vast variety of "their" Christian traditions, but rather it is the vast richness of "our" Christian tradition.

We ended Chapter 8 with the words of Amos Swelindawo of an African Independent Church pointing to the underlying principle of Christian discipleship: "Our witness within and outside the church, the way in which we live as Christians, is most important for the mission of our church" (Oduro et al., 107–8). In Chapter 1 we heard about how "gossiping the gospel" by ordinary Christians, with and without words, was probably the main way that Christians contributed to God's mysterious and wonderful plan of drawing all back to God. We need to continue to be bold and faithful disciples in shaping and handing on the baton of Christian tradition for the ultimate goal of participating in God's mission.

Works Cited

Abel, Christopher. "Latin America, c. 1914–1950." In *World Christianities c. 1914–c. 2000*, ed. Hugh McLeod, 179–96. New York: Cambridge University Press, 2006.
Abraham, K. C., and Bernadette Mbuy-Beya, eds. *Spirituality of the Third World*. Maryknoll, NY: Orbis Books, 1994.
Anathil, George M. *The Theological Formation of the Clergy in India*. Pune, India: Pontifical Athenaeum, 1966.
Anderson, Allan, and Edmond Tang. "Independency in Africa and Asia." In *World Christianities c. 1914–c. 2000*, ed. Hugh McLeod, 107–27. New York: Cambridge University Press, 2006.
Aristides. "The Apology of Aristides the Philosopher." In *The Ante-Nicene Fathers*, trans. D. M. Kay, vol. 9. New York: Charles Scribner's Sons, 1925.
Bays, Daniel H., and James H. Grayson. "Christianity in East Asia: China, Korea and Japan." In *World Christianities c. 1815–c. 1914*, ed. Sheridan Gilley and Brian Stanley, 493–512. New York: Cambridge University Press, 2006.
Bellitto, Christopher M. *Ten Ways the Church Has Changed*. Boston: Pauline Books and Media, 2006.
Bernier, Paul. *Ministry in the Church: A Historical and Pastoral Approach*. Second ed. Maryknoll, NY: Orbis Books, 2015.
Bevans, Stephen B. *An Introduction to Theology in Global Perspective*. Maryknoll, NY: Orbis Books, 2009.
———. "Second Vatican Council." In *Encyclopedia of Christianity in the Global South*, vol. 2, 708–10. Lanham, MD: Rowman and Littlefield, 2018.
Bevans, Stephen B., and Roger P. Schroeder. "Keeping Current: The 'New' Church History." *New Theology Review* 16/4 (2003): 79–81.
———. *Constants in Context: A Theology of Mission for Today*. Maryknoll, NY: Orbis Books, 2004.
Bosch, David J. *Transforming Mission: Paradigm Shifts in Theology and Mission*. Maryknoll, NY: Orbis Books, 1991.
Cabrita, Joel, David Maxwell, and Emma Wild-Wood, eds. *Relocating World Christianity: Interdisciplinary Studies in Universal and Local Expressions of the Christian Faith*. Leiden: Brill, 2017.
Cardiel, Jose. *Las Misiones de Paraguay*. Madrid: CAMBIO 16, 1989.
Celano, Thomas of. *The Lives of Saint Francis of Assisi by Brother Thomas of Celano*, trans. A. G. Ferrers Howell. London: Methuen and Co., 1908.

Chidester, David. *Christianity: A Global History*. New York: HarperCollins Publishers, 2000.

Cleary, Edward. "The Transformation of Latin American Christianity, c. 1950–2000." In *World Christianities c. 1914–c. 2000*, ed. Hugh McLeod, 366–84. New York: Cambridge University Press, 2006.

Coakley, John W., and Andrea Sterk, eds. *Readings in World Christian History*. Volume 1: *Earliest Christianity to 1453*. Maryknoll, NY: Orbis Books, 2004.

Cochrane, Steve. "East Syrian Monasteries in the Ninth Century in Asia: A Force for Mission and Renewal." *International Bulletin of Missionary Research* 38/2 (April 2014): 80–83.

Colenso, Gwilym. "uNkulunkulu: Bishop John William Colenso and the Contested Zulu God-name in Nineteenth-Century Natal." In *Translating Wor(l)ds: Christianity across Cultural Boundaries*, ed. Sabine Dedenbach-Salazar Sáenz, 97–125. Baden-Baden, Germany: Academia Verlag, 2019.

Cowe, S. Peter. "Armenian Christianity." In *The New Westminster Dictionary of Church History*. Volume 1: *The Early, Medieval, and Reformation Eras*, ed. Robert Benedetto, 47–50. Louisville, KY: Westminster John Knox Press, 2008.

Daniels, David. "The Global South: The Synod of Dort on Baptizing 'Ethnics.'" In *The Protestant Reformation and World Christianity: Global Perspectives*, ed. Dale T. Irvin, 96–119. Grand Rapids, MI: Eerdmans, 2017a.

———. "Honor the Reformation's African Roots." *The Commercial Appeal* (Memphis), October 21, 2017b.

Diognetus, Epistle of. Anonymus. Second century.

Dussel, Enrique. *A History of the Church in Latin America: Colonialism to Liberation*. Grand Rapids, MI: Eerdmans, 1981.

Eusebius. *Church History*. In *Nicene and Post-Nicene Fathers*, ed. Philip Schaff and Henry Wace, vol. 1, second series. Peabody, MA: Hendrickson Publishers, 1994.

Foley, Edward. *From Age to Age: How Christians Have Celebrated the Eucharist*. Revised and expanded edition. Collegeville, MN: Liturgical Press, 2008.

Frykenberg, Robert Eric. "Christians and Religious Traditions in the Indian Empire." In *World Christianities c. 1815–c. 1914*, ed. Sheridan Gilley and Brian Stanley, 473–92. New York: Cambridge University Press, 2006.

Gerloff, Roswith. "The African Diaspora in the Caribbean and Europe from Pre-emancipation to the Present Day." In *World Christianities c. 1914–c. 2000*, ed. Hugh McLeod, 219–35. New York: Cambridge University Press, 2006.

Gilley, Sheridan, and Brian Stanley, eds. *World Christianities c. 1815–c. 1914*. The Cambridge History of Christianity, vol. 8. New York: Cambridge University Press, 2006.

González, Justo. "How the Bible Has Been Interpreted in Christian Tradition." In *The New Interpreter's Bible*. vol. 1, 83–106. Nashville, TN: Abingdon, 1994.

———. *Christian Thought Revisited: Three Types of Theology*. Revised edition. Maryknoll, NY: Orbis Books, 1999.
———. *The Changing Shape of Church History*. St. Louis, MO: Chalice Press, 2002.
Goosen, Gideon. *Australian Theologies: Themes and Methodologies into the Third Millennium*. Strathfield, Sydney: St. Paul's, 2000.
Green, Michael. *Evangelism in the Early Church*. Grand Rapids, MI: Eerdmans, 1970.
Gutiérrez, Gustavo. *Las Casas: In Search of the Poor of Jesus Christ*. Maryknoll, NY: Orbis Books, 1993.
Hastings, Adrian. *A World History of Christianity*. Grand Rapids, MI: Eerdmans, 1999.
Holt, Bradley P. *Thirsty for God: A Brief History of Christian Spirituality*. Minneapolis, MN: Augsburg Fortress, 1993.
Ignatius of Antioch. "Ignatius of Antioch: 'Letter to the Magnesians.'" In *The Apostolic Fathers*, trans. Kirsopp Lake, vol. 1, 197–211. New York: G. P. Putnam's Sons, 1919.
Irvin, Dale T. *Christian Histories, Christian Traditioning: Rendering Accounts*. Maryknoll, NY: Orbis Books, 1998.
Irvin, Dale T., and Scott W. Sunquist. *History of the World Christian Movement*. Volume 1: *Earliest Christianity to 1453*. Maryknoll, NY: Orbis Books, 2001.
———. *History of the World Christian Movement*. Volume 2: *Modern Christianity from 1454–1800*. Maryknoll, NY: Orbis Books, 2012.
———. *History of the World Christian Movement*. Volume 3: 1800–2000. Maryknoll, NY: Orbis Books, unpublished.
Jenkins, Philip. *The Next Christendom: The Coming of Global Christianity*. New York: Oxford University Press, 2002.
———. *The Lost History of Christianity: The Thousand-Year Golden Age of the Church in the Middle East, Africa, and Asia—and How It Died*. New York: HarperCollins Publishers, 2008.
Kalu, Ogbu U. "Ethiopianism and the Roots of Modern African Christianity." In *World Christianities c. 1815–c. 1914*, ed. Sheridan Gilley and Brian Stanley, 576–92. New York: Cambridge University Press, 2006a.
———. "The African Christianity: From the World Wars to Decolonization." In *World Christianities c. 1914–c. 2000*, ed. Hugh McLeod, 197–218. New York: Cambridge University Press, 2006b.
Kazoh, Kitamori. *Theology of the Pain of God*. Reprint edition. Eugene, OR: Wipf and Stock, 2005 (1946).
Koschorke, Klaus, et al., eds. *A History of Christianity in Asia, Africa, and Latin America, 1450–1990*. Grand Rapids, MI: Eerdmans, 2007.
Koyama, Kosuke. *Water Buffalo Theology*. Maryknoll, NY: Orbis Books, 1974.
Lampe, Armando. "Christianity in the Caribbean." In *The Church in Latin America 1492–1992*, ed. Enrique Dussel, 201–15. Maryknoll, NY: Orbis Books, 1992.

Latourette, Kenneth Scott. *Three Centuries of Advance: A.D. 1500–A.D. 1800*, vol. 3 in *A History of the Expansion of Christianity*. New York: Harper & Row, 1939.

Macy, Gary. *The Banquet's Wisdom: A Short History of the Theologies of the Lord's Supper*. Second edition. Maryville, TN: OSL Publications, 2005.

Mallampalli, Chandra. "South Asia, 1911–2003." In *World Christianities c. 1914–c. 2000*, ed. Hugh McLeod, 422–35. New York: Cambridge University Press, 2006.

Martos, Joseph. *Doors to the Sacred: A Historical Introduction to Sacraments in the Catholic Church*. Revised and updated. Liguori, MO: Liguori Press, 2001.

Marty, Martin. *The Christian World: A Global History*. New York: Random House, 2007.

Massam, Katherine. "Christian Churches in Australia, New Zealand and the Pacific, 1914–1970." In *World Christianities c. 1914–c. 2000*, ed. Hugh McLeod, 252–61. New York: Cambridge University Press, 2006.

Maxwell, David. "Post-colonial Christianity in Africa." In *World Christianities c. 1914–c. 2000*, ed. Hugh McLeod, 401–21. New York: Cambridge University Press, 2006.

McDannell, Colleen. "Christianity in the United States during the Inter-war Years." In *World Christianities c. 1914–c. 2000*, ed. Hugh McLeod, 236–51. New York: Cambridge University Press, 2006.

McGowan, Anne, and Paul F. Bradshaw. *The Pilgrimage of Egeria*. Collegeville, MN: Liturgical Press, 2018.

McLeod, Hugh. "Being a Christian in the Early Twentieth Century." In *World Christianities c. 1914–c. 2000*, ed. Hugh McLeod, 15–26. New York: Cambridge University Press, 2006a.

———. "The Crisis of Christianity in the West: Entering a Post-Christian Era?" In *World Christianities c. 1914–c. 2000*, ed. Hugh McLeod, 323–47. New York: Cambridge University Press, 2006b.

———, ed. *World Christianities c. 1914–c. 2000*. The Cambridge History of Christianity, vol. 9. New York: Cambridge University Press, 2006c.

Moffett, Samuel Hugh. "East Asian Christian Approaches to Non-Christian Cultures." *Missiology: An International Review* 15/4 (October 1987): 473–86.

———. *A History of Christianity in Asia*. Volume 1: *Beginnings to 1500*. Maryknoll, NY: Orbis Books, 1998.

Moore, David. "The Wanderings of Altjira, Christianity, and the Translation of Sacred Words in Central Australia." In *Translating Wor(l)ds: Christianity Across Cultural Boundaries*, ed. Sabine Dedenbach-Salazar Sáenz, 127–56. Baden-Baden, Germany: Academia Verlag, 2019.

Morris, James H. "Rereading the Evidence of the Earliest Christian Communities in East Asia during and prior to the T'ang Period." *Missiology* 45/3 (2017): 252–64.

Mullin, Robert Bruce. *A Short World History of Christianity*. Louisville, KY: Westminster John Knox Press, 2008.

Munro, Doug, and Andrew Thornley, eds. *The Covenant Makers: Islander Missionaries in the Pacific*. Suva, Fiji: Pacific Theological College and the Institute of Pacific Studies at the University of the South Pacific, 1996.

Murre-Van den Berg, Heleen. "The Middle East: Western Missions and the Eastern Churches, Islam and Judaism." In *World Christianities c. 1815–c. 1914*, ed. Sheridan Gilley and Brian Stanley, 458–72. New York: Cambridge University Press, 2006.

Nardini, Giulia. "Robert Nobili's *Vivâha dharma*: A Case of Cultural Translation." In *Translating Catechisms, Translating Cultures*, ed. Antje Flüchter and Rouven Wirbser, 223–51. Leiden: Brill, 2017.

Neill, Stephen. *A History of Christian Missions*. Revised edition. London: Penguin Books, 1964, 1986.

Norris, Frederick. *Christianity: A Short Global History*. Oxford: Oneworld Publications, 2002.

———. "Timothy I of Baghdad, Catholicos of the East Syrian Church (780–823): Still a Valuable Model." *International Bulletin of Missionary Research* 30/3 (July 2006): 133–36.

Oduro, Thomas, Hennie Pretorius, Stan Nussbaum, and Bryon Born. *Mission in an African Way: A Practical Introduction to African Instituted Churches and Their Sense of Mission*. South Africa: Bible Media and Christian Literature Fund, 2018.

Ormerod, Neil. *Re-visioning the Church: An Experiment in Systematic-Historical Ecclesiology*. Minneapolis: Fortress Press, 2014.

Pachuau, Lalsangkima. *World Christianity: A Historical and Theological Introduction*. Nashville, TN: Abingdon Press, 2018.

Palmer, Martin. *The Jesus Sutras: Rediscovering the Lost Scrolls of Taoist Christianity*. New York: Ballantine Wellspring, 2001.

Phan, Peter. *Mission and Catechesis: Alexandre de Rhodes and Inculturation in Seventeenth-Century Vietnam*. Maryknoll, NY: Orbis Books, 1998.

———. "Christianity in Indochina." In *World Christianities c. 1815–c. 1914*, ed. Sheridan Gilley and Brian Stanley, 513–27. New York: Cambridge University Press, 2006.

Piggin, Stuart, and Allan Davidson. "Christianity in Australasia and the Pacific." In *World Christianities c. 1815–c. 1914*, ed. Sheridan Gilley and Brian Stanley, 542–59. New York: Cambridge University Press, 2006.

Pikaza, Xabier, and José Antunes da Silva, eds. *The Pact of the Catacombs: The Mission of the Poor in the Church*. Estella, Spain: Editorial Verbo Divino, 2015.

Pope John Paul II. *Redemptoris Missio* (*On the Permanent Validity of the Church's Missionary Mandate*). December 7, 1990.

Pope Paul VI. *Evangelii Nuntiandi* (*On Evangelization in the Modern World*). December 8, 1975.

Robert, Dana. *American Women in Mission: A Social History of Their Thought and Practice*. Macon, GA: Mercer University Press, 1996.

———, ed. *Gospel Bearers, Gender Barriers: Missionary Women in the Twentieth Century.* Maryknoll, NY: Orbis Books, 2002.

———. *Christian Mission: How Christianity Became a World Religion.* Chichester, UK: Wiley-Blackwell, 2009.

Rogerson, John, et al. *The Study and Use of the Bible.* Volume 2 of *The History of Christian Theology,* series ed. Paul Avis. Grand Rapids, MI: Eerdmans, 1988.

Ross, Andrew C. *A Vision Betrayed: The Jesuits in Japan and China, 1542–1742.* Maryknoll, NY: Orbis Books, 1994.

Roxborogh, John. "Christianity in South-East Asia." In *World Christianities c. 1914–c. 2000,* ed. Hugh McLeod, 436–49. New York: Cambridge University Press, 2006.

Sanneh, Lamin. "World Christianity and the New Historiography." In *Enlarging the Story: Perspectives on Writing World Christian History,* ed. Wilbert Shenk, 94–114. Maryknoll, NY: Orbis Books, 2002.

Scherer, James. *Gospel, Church, and Kingdom: Comparative Studies in World Mission Theology.* Minneapolis: Augsburg Press, 1987.

Schmemann, Alexander. *The Historical Road of Eastern Orthodoxy.* New York: Holt, Rinehart, and Winston, 1963.

Schreiter, Robert J. "Changes in Roman Catholic Attitudes toward Proselytism and Mission." In *New Directions in Mission and Evangelization 2: Theological Foundations,* ed. James Scherer and Stephen Bevans, 113–25. Maryknoll, NY: Orbis Books, 1994.

Seah, Audrey. "The 1670 Chinese Missal: A Struggle for Indigenization amidst the Chinese Rites Controversy." In *China's Christianity: From Missionary to Indigenous Church,* ed. Anthony Clark, 86–120. Leiden: Brill, 2017.

Sensbach, Jon. "African-American Christianity." In *World Christianities c. 1815–c. 1914,* ed. Sheridan Gilley and Brian Stanley, 429–42. New York: Cambridge University Press, 2006.

Sheldrake, Philip. *A Brief History of Spirituality.* Malden, MA: Blackwell Publishing, 2007.

Shenk, Wilbert, ed. *Enlarging the Story: Perspectives on Writing World Christian History.* Maryknoll, NY: Orbis Books, 2002.

Sloane, O. O'C. "Catenae, Biblical." In *New Catholic Encyclopedia,* 2nd ed., vol. 3, 258–59. Detroit: Thompson/Gale Group, 2003.

Smith, Susan E. *Women in Mission: From the New Testament to Today.* Maryknoll, NY: Orbis Books, 2007.

Snape, Michael. "The Great War." In *World Christianities c. 1914–c. 2000,* ed. Hugh McLeod, 131–50. New York: Cambridge University Press, 2006.

Spinks, Bryan. "Liturgy." In *World Christianities c. 1914–c. 2000,* ed. Hugh McLeod, 471–82. New York: Cambridge University Press, 2006.

Stanley, Brian. "Christian Missions, Antislavery, and the Claims of Humanity." In *World Christianities c. 1815–c. 1914,* ed. Sheridan Gilley and Brian Stanley, 443–57. New York: Cambridge University Press, 2006.

———. *Christianity in the Twentieth Century: A World History*. Princeton, NJ: Princeton University Press, 2018.
Stark, Rodney. *The Rise of Christianity*. San Francisco: HarperCollins Publishers, 1996.
Steckley, John. "Inventing New Words: Father Jean de Brébeuf's Wendat Catechism of 1632." In *Translating Catechisms, Translating Cultures*, ed. Antje Flüchter and Rouven Wirbser, 129–69. Leiden: Brill, 2017.
Stewart, John. *Nestorian Missionary Enterprise: The Story of a Church on Fire*. Edinburgh: T & T Clark, 1928.
Sugirtharajah, R. S., ed. *Voices from the Margin: Interpreting the Bible in the Third World*. New edition. London: Society for Promoting Christian Knowledge, 1991; Maryknoll, NY: Orbis Books, 1995.
Sunquist, Scott W. *The Unexpected Christian Century: The Reversal and Transformation of Global Christianity, 1900–2000*. Grand Rapids, MI: Baker Academic, 2015.
Tan, Jonathan Y., and Anh Q. Tran, eds. *World Christianity: Perspectives and Insights*. Maryknoll, NY: Orbis Books, 2016.
Tang, Li, and Dietmar W. Winkler, eds. *From the Oxus River to the Chinese Shores: Studies on East Syriac Christianity in China and Central Asia*. Orientalia—Patristica—Oecumenica, vol. 5. Zürich and Münster: LIT Verlag, 2013.
Tertullian. *Apology*. In *The Fathers of the Church, Tertullian: Apologetical Works and Minucius Felix: Octavius*, trans. Rudolph Arbesmann, Emily Daly, and Edwin Quain. New York: Fathers of the Church, 1950.
———. *On Prescription against Heretics*. In *Ante-Nicene Fathers*, ed. Alexander Roberts and James Donaldson, vol. 3. Peabody, MA: Hendrickson Publishers, 1994.
Walls, Andrew. *The Missionary Movement in Christian History: Studies in the Transmission of the Faith*. Maryknoll, NY: Orbis Books, 1996.
———. "Eusebius Tries Again: The Task of Reconceiving and Re-visioning the Study of Christian History." In *Enlarging the Story: Perspectives on Writing World Christian History*, ed. Wilbert Shenk, 1–21. Maryknoll, NY: Orbis Books, 2002.
Walters, Philip. "The Revolutions in Eastern Europe and the Beginnings of the Post-Communist Era." In *World Christianities c. 1914–c. 2000*, ed. Hugh McLeod, 348–65. New York: Cambridge University Press, 2006.
White, James. *Protestant Worship: Traditions in Transition*. Louisville, KY: Westminster/John Knox Press, 1989.
Wilken, Robert Louis. *The First Thousand Years: A Global History of Christianity*. New Haven, CT: Yale University Press, 2012.
Wiseman, James A. *Spirituality and Mysticism: A Global View*. Maryknoll, NY: Orbis Books, 2006.
Yong, Amos. *Hospitality and the Other: Pentecost, Christian Practices, and the Neighbor*. Maryknoll, NY: Orbis Books, 2008.

Young, Richard Fox. "East Asia." In *World Christianities c. 1914–c. 2000*, ed. Hugh McLeod, 450–67. New York: Cambridge University Press, 2006.

Yung, Hwa. *Mangoes or Bananas? The Quest for an Authentic Christian Theology*. Oxford: Regnum, 1997.

Index

Abelard, Peter, 129–30
Abraham, K. C., 279
Abraham Ecchellensis, 190
Abraham of Tiberius, 94
Abrams, Minnie, 258
Abū Qurrah, Theodore, 94
Act of Toleration, 186
Ad Gentes decree, 8, 27, 286
Addai of Edessa, 9, 27
Afonso I, King of Kongo, 140
African Independent Churches (AICs), 272, 284, 293
  African leaders, as inspiring, 275
  common features of, 278
  growth in, 236, 253
  missionary endeavors, 289
  as radical Biblicists, 270
  in South Africa, 220, 292
African Methodist Episcopal Church (AME), 184, 214, 233
African Methodist Episcopal Zion Church (AMEZ), 214, 233
African-American spirituality
  conversions to Christianity, 200, 207
  "invisible institution," working within, 214
  liturgical music and prayer, 192, 231, 236, 273
  Protestant church membership, 183, 263, 271
  role of women in, 196, 238, 239, 247, 274, 279
Agbar VIII, King of Oshroene, 9
Agbebi, Mojola, 220
Aglipay, Gregorio, 225
Agong, Keuh, 222, 243
Alacocque, Margaret-Mary, 200
Albert the Great, 116
Alcuin of York, 82, 84, 85, 93, 96

Alexander III, Pope, 105
Alexander of Hales, 118, 129
Alexandria, 11, 27, 41, 64, 78
  Arianism of, 37–39
  Coptic presence, 52, 87, 178, 217
  Ethiopian Christianity in, 40
  mysticism of the Alexandrian school, 84
  patriarchs of, 80, 90, 111, 125, 159, 193
  as a theological center, 13–15, 18, 22, 25
Alexius Comnenus, Emperor, 102
Alighieri, Dante, 119, 130, 143
Allen, Richard, 184, 239
Allen, Roland, 286
Alopen of Syria, 74, 93
Álvares Cabral, Pedro, 138, 141
Ambrose of Milan, 16, 47, 59
American Board of Commissioners for Foreign Missions (ABCFM), 214, 224, 233, 242, 243, 244, 249
Amish faith, 186
Anabaptist tradition, 135, 150, 160, 230, 270
  baptism practices, 154
  egalitarian idea of church, 144–45, 158, 196
  images, strong stance against, 155
  Martyrs Mirror, centrality of text for, 200
  missionary work, 206–7
  nonviolence stance, 168
  persecution of, 147, 186
  Radical Reformation and, 156
Anchieta, José de, 166
Anderson, Rufus, 243, 244
Andrews, C. F., 287

Anglican tradition, 154, 213, 230, 232, 258
  in the American colonies, 196
  Book of Common Prayer as central to, 146, 160
  Catholic-Anglican relations, 147, 275–76
  Edinburgh Conference, Anglican participation in, 254–55
  establishment approval for, 156, 186
  liturgical renewal efforts, 271
  Methodist separation from Anglican Church, 216
  missionary endeavors, 179, 222, 225, 227, 242, 243
  Reform movement, arising from, 135
  Saint Thomas Christians and, 221, 224
  Underhill, influence on, 278
  WCC, Anglican presence in, 291
Anicetus, Pope, 21
Anselm of Canterbury, 128, 129, 130
Anselm of Laon, 115
Anthony, Saint, 39, 55
António da Conceição, 208–9
Aphrahat (Aphraates) of Persia, 59, 61
Aquinas, Thomas, 59, 116, 202
  Summa Contra Gentiles, 129, 132
  Summa Theologiae, 129, 130, 203
  on transubstantiation, 118
Arévalo, Catalino G., 283
Arianism, 33, 47, 49, 58, 59
  Arian mosaics of Ravenna, 51
  divinity of Jesus, denying, 57
  exile of believers, 38, 64
  of the Germanic peoples, 37, 43, 62, 85
  Third Council of Toledo as combating, 81
Aristotle, 115–16, 118, 129
Arius of Alexandria, 37–38, 57
Armandville, Cornelius le Cocq d', 223
Arminianism, 203, 241
Arminius, Jacobus, 203
Arndt, Johann, 199, 202, 203
Asante, David, 231
Asbury, Francis, 183, 232
Assemblies of God, 274, 279
Assumption of Mary, 234
Athanasius of Alexandria, 38, 39, 40, 45–46, 55, 57, 58, 62

Athenagoras of Athens, 276–77
Aubert, Suzann, 247
Augsburg Confession, 144
Augustine of Hippo, 46, 62, 92, 97, 106, 164
  Alexandrine school, as influenced by, 16
  allegorical methodology, developing, 47
  as Augustine of Canterbury, 63, 82
  monasticism, promotion of, 53
  Monica as mother of, 59
  Pelagianism, responding to, 60
Augustinians, 126, 143, 144, 151, 174, 176, 206, 208
Auna of Tahiti, 233
Averroes (Ibn Rushd), 132
Avicenna (Ibn Sina), 129
Ayala, Felipe Guamán Poma de, 163
Azariah, Vedanayagam Samuel, 255, 287
Azusa Street Revival, 263

Balthasar, Hans Urs von, 282
Banana, Canaan, 253
Banerjee, Krishna Mohan, 249
Báñez, Domingo, 149
Bañuelas, Arturo, 285
Baptist tradition, 156, 199, 213, 230, 231, 246
  American Baptist Churches USA, 280
  black Baptist churches, 183–84, 220, 262
  camp meeting attendance, 214
  free church style of worship, 186, 192, 193
  missionary endeavors, 207, 220, 221, 222, 227, 242, 244
  Northern Baptist Convention, 289
  Southern Baptist churches, 273
  women, preaching available to, 196
Bar Hebraeus, Gregory, 124–25, 131
Bardaisan of Edessa, 10, 26–27, 28, 29
Barmen Declaration, 255, 281
Barnabas, Saint, 7, 8
Barth, Karl, 255, 268, 281
Basel Mission, 220, 242
Basil of Caesarea, 39, 54, 55, 58
Basilides of Alexandria, 14
Baumfree, Isabella, 239
Baumgarten, S. J., 189

Baur, Ferdinand, 228, 240
Baxter, Richard, 179
Beauduin, Lambert, 270
Bede the Venerable, 63, 84, 85, 93
Beguines, 106–7, 118, 123, 126, 128, 131, 160
Bell, Johann Adam von, 174
Bellarmine, Robert, 197, 202
Bellitto, Christopher, xvi
Belorussian Roman Catholic Church, 227
Benedict of Nursia, 39, 43, 55
Benedict XVI, Pope (Joseph Ratzinger), 282
Benedictines, 106, 270
  accommodation approach, as practicing, 82, 97
  catenae and florilegia as favored theological themes, 60
  Cluny reform of Benedictine life, 125
  missionary efforts, 44, 62–63
  monastic tradition, 53, 55, 90–91, 96, 126, 127, 279
Bengel, J. A., 189
Berika, Ebedjesu bar, 130
Bernard of Clairvaux, 103, 114, 125, 129
Bernier, Paul, 21
Bérulle, Pierre de, 197, 200
Bettendorf, Johann Philipp, 179
Bevans, Stephen, 61, 130, 163, 240, 281, 282, 284, 293
Bible women, 229, 239, 244
Bickersteth, Edward, 236
Bismarck, Otto von, 217, 234
Blandina of Vienne, 23–24, 28
Boardman, Sarah Hall, 221
Boff, Leonardo, 283
Bolívar, Simón, 212
Bonaventure of Bagnoregio, 116, 118, 129, 130
Bonhoeffer, Dietrich, 278
Boniface (Wynfrith of Crediton), 82, 89, 96–97
Bonino, José Miguez, 261, 283
Bonnard, Clément, 221
Booth, William and Catherine, 216
Boris I, King of Bulgaria, 79
Bosch, David J., 98, 199
Boston Female Society for Missionary Purposes, 214, 244
Brainerd, David, 183, 207

Brébeuf, Jean de, 181, 208
Briggs, C. A., 229
Brigid of Kildare, 43, 53
Brothers and Sisters of the Common life, 117, 126, 159–60
Brown, David, 221
Bryan, Andrew, 184
Buglio, Ludovico, 191, 208
Bujo, Bénézet, 284
Bulgakov, Sergei Nikolaevich, 282
Bulls of Donation, 138
Bultmann, Rudolf, 268
Bunyan, John, 199, 231
Burgos, José, 224
Butler, Josephine, 239

Caecilian of Carthage, 36–37
Cajetan, Thomas, 157, 164
Calvinist tradition, 135, 146, 193, 195, 196, 242
  Calvinist scholastic theology, 184, 203
  the Elect, concept of, 154
  of English Puritans, 186, 199
  in evangelical revival of England, 236
  Institutes of the Christian Religion, 145, 164
  Knox, collaboration with Calvin, 150
  missionary presence in India, 221
  ordained ministry, stance on, 158
  rigid Calvinism, opposition to, 241
  on transubstantiation, 153
  worldly asceticism, in favor of, 160
Câmara, Hélder, 256, 261
camp meetings, 214, 230, 232
Campbell, John McCloud, 241
Cannon, Katie, 285
Capuchins, 140, 147, 160, 176, 179, 180, 206, 209
Carey, Felix, 221
Carey, William, 216, 220, 229, 242
Caribbean Conference of Churches, 262
Carmelite order, 126, 161, 237, 238
Carroll, John, 183, 190, 197
Cartier, Jacques, 181
Cassian, John, 39, 55
Cathars (Albigenses), 106, 115, 117, 121, 126, 131, 132
Catherine of Aragon, 145–46
Catherine of Siena, 123, 127, 130, 131–32
Catherine of Vietnam, 194

Catholic Apostolic Church (Irvingites), 238
Catholic Foreign Mission Society of America, 263
Catholic Students' Mission Crusade, 263
Catholic Worker (newspaper), 263
Chantal, Jane Frances de, 184
charismatic movement, 25, 28, 272
    AICs, charismatic elements in, 270, 278
    Catholic charismatic movement, 262, 274, 277, 279, 283
    early charismatics as church leaders, 20, 159
    Montanism, charismatic characteristic of, 13, 24
    Pentecostal tradition and, 157, 253
Charlemagne, Emperor, 67, 85, 97
    cannon law, promoting, 54, 89
    force and coercion as methods of, 93, 96
    Latin, making the official language of theology, 82, 86
    marriage laws during reign of, 87–88
Charles V, Emperor, 139, 144, 147
Chenu, Marie-Dominique, 282
Chicago Evangelization Society, 214
Chi-Lieh, Bishop, 75
China Christian Council, 260, 283
Ching-ching (Adam), 75, 93, 95
Cho, Paul Yonggi, 259
Christian Science Church, 238
Church Missionary Society (CMS), 221, 242, 243
Church of God, 238, 279
Church of Jesus Christ of Latter Day Saints (Mormons), 238
Clare of Assisi, 106, 123, 126, 131
Claver, Peter, 179
Clement of Alexandria, 14, 16, 26, 27, 29, 31
Clement XI, Pope, 205
Clovis, King of the Franks, 43, 61–62
Cluny reform, 91, 105, 121, 125
Coke, Thomas, 183
Colenso, John William, 249
Comboni, Daniel, 219, 246
Commission on World Mission and Evangelism (CWME), 264, 287, 288
Concordat of Worms, 102

Confessing Christians of Germany, 255
Congar, Yves, 282
congregationalist model of church, 195–96
Congregationalists, 196, 199, 225, 258, 265, 266, 274
Congress of Vienna, 215, 227
Constantine, Emperor, 33–38, 40, 42, 44, 47–48, 54, 57, 63, 191
Contarini, Gasparo, 157
Cope, Marianne, 247
Copeland, M. Shawn, 285
Coptic Catholic Church, 198
Coptic tradition, 125, 131, 219, 236
    Coptic as a liturgical language, 39, 49, 87, 96
    Coptic popes, 52, 148, 163, 178, 217, 219, 231, 254
    in Egypt, 33, 39, 65, 111, 112, 148, 217, 239, 254, 277
    monastic tradition, 80, 239
    Monophysite formulation, as holding, 58, 64
    as non-Chalcedonian, 39, 64, 147, 198, 277
    scripture translations into Coptic, 39, 46, 229
Cornelius, Pope, 13, 21
Cornelius the Centurion, 7
Corrie, Daniel, 221
Cosmos the Indian Navigator, 42
Costas, Orlando, 261
Council of Basel-Ferrara-Florence-Rome, 123, 125
Council of Chalcedon, 41, 51, 57
Council of Constance, 123
Council of Constantinople (I), 38, 58
Council of Constantinople III (Sixth Ecumenical Council), 93
Council of Elvira, 53
Council of Ephesus, 55
Council of Jerusalem, 7, 8, 20, 29
Council of Lima (I), 151, 152
Council of Lima III, 151, 166
Council of Mexico (I), 152, 158
Council of Nicaea (I), 41, 51, 57, 58, 59
Council of Nicaea II (Seventh Ecumenical Council), 57, 79
Council of Peru (I, III), 158
Council of Pisa, 123

Council of Toledo III, 81
Council of Trent, 122, 151, 158
   clerical reforms produced by, 153
   as a Counter-Reformation event, 157
   institutional reforms and, 146, 164
   sacramentality revisions, 154, 193
   stabilizing effect of, 190
   Vulgate canon, officially recognizing, 46, 149
Cragg, Kenneth, 291
Cranmer, Thomas, 150
Crowther, Samuel Ajayi, 219, 220, 229, 233, 243, 244, 248
Crusades, 101, 102–4, 122, 127, 132
Cugoano, Ottobah, 178
cursillo (short course) movement, 278
Cyril of Alexandria, 38
Cyril of Byzantium, 79, 86, 97

Dana, George, 221
Daniel, Yvan, 285
Darragh, Neil, 284
Daughters of Charity, 147, 184, 201
Daughters of Divine Love, 286
Daughters of Our Lady of Compassion, 247
Daughters of the Cross, 238
Day, Dorothy, 263
De La Salle Brothers, 201
De Nobili, Robert, 174, 202, 204, 208, 209
De Veuster, Damien, 247
Decius, Emperor, 11, 14
Deck, Allan Figueroa, 285
"Decree of Union," 125
Deism, 183, 186, 189
Deloria, Vine, 285
Demetrius of Alexandria, 14
Dengel, Anna, 290
Dhouda of Gascony, 92
Diocletian, Emperor, 11, 35, 36
Dionysius Exiguus, 54
Dionysius of Alexandria, 16
Dionysius the Areopagite, 58
Disciples of Christ, 231, 233, 238
Dominic of Caleruega, 106, 132
Dominicans, 116, 138, 157, 162, 180, 201, 224
   as a mendicant order, 126, 131
   missionary endeavors, 132, 133, 142, 165, 175, 181
   preaching as specialty of, 106, 115
   prominent Dominicans, 128, 129
   reducciones, role in establishment of, 139
   scholastic method, promoting, 149
   Third Order members, 127, 130
Donatism, 13, 33, 36–37, 38, 44, 55, 59, 64
Dorsey, Thomas, 273
Douglass, Frederick, 239
Drexel, Katherine, 247
Drey, Johann Sebastian, 241
Duchesne, Rose Philippine, 247
Duff, Alexander, 249
Dutch Reformed Church, 189, 193, 203, 207, 217, 219

East Assyrian Church, 198
East Syrian Church, 40, 87, 94, 98
   in Asia, 67, 73, 75, 110
   Council of Nicaea, representation at, 38
   Dyophysite Christology of, 38
   images, not allowing in churches, 88
   monastic tradition, 40, 55–56, 61
   Patriarch Denha of, 124–25
   Persian identity, 41, 46, 64, 71
   Saint Thomas Christians, ecclesiastical link with, 10, 141
   Syriac liturgy, use of, 69, 120, 155
Eastern rite churches, 124, 148, 227, 256
Eck, Johann, 164
Ecumenical Association of Third World Theologians (EATWOT), 283
Edessa, 11, 30, 64, 69, 103
   Bardaisan of Edessa, 26–27, 29
   first public churches in, 9, 17
   as a theological center, 10, 25, 27, 41
Edict of Constantinople, 35, 44
Edict of Milan, 35, 36
Edinburgh Conference, 251, 252, 254–55, 258, 263, 273, 286, 289
Edwards, Jonathan, 183, 192, 199, 203, 207
Egeria of Spain, 64–65
Elias of Nisibis, 130, 133
Eliot, John, 182, 207
Elizabeth of Hungary, 123, 132
Elizondo, Virgilio P., 285
Elloy, Louis, 235, 248

Ephrem the Syrian, 40, 51, 56, 59, 61, 62
Equiano, Olaudah (Gustavus Vassa), 178
Erasmus of Rotterdam (Desiderius Erasmus), 143–44, 150, 159–60, 161
Escobar, Samuel, 287
Espín, Orlando O., 285
Eugenius III, Pope, 103
Eusebius of Caesarea, 11
Eustochium of Rome, 46
Evangelii Nuntiandi apostolic exhortation, 286

Fa, Liang, 222, 229, 243
Fabella, Virginia, 283
Felicitas of Rome, 13, 24, 25–26, 28
Finney, Charles, 214, 231, 233
First Vatican Council. See Vatican I
Fleming, Daniel, 287
Fliedner, Theodor, 233
Florovsky, Georges Vasilievich, 282
Focolare movement, 279, 280
Foley, Edward, 18, 48, 118, 167
foot washing, 272
Foote, Julia, 233
Foucault, Charles de, 285
Fourth Lateran Council, 106, 117, 118, 120, 124, 132
Fox, George, 186
Francis, Pope, 105
Francis of Assisi, 106, 115, 116, 122–23, 129, 132, 134, 291
Francis Xavier, 142, 151, 152, 158, 162, 164, 166, 167, 172, 209
Franciscans, 107, 115, 146, 174
  Aquinas, Franciscan critics of, 130
  Asia presence in, 109, 110, 148
  India, presence in, 141, 152
  local culture, respect shown to, 120, 151, 165, 208
  missionary efforts, 117, 140, 142, 180–81, 206, 246–47
  preaching style, 119, 132
  reducciones, establishing, 139
  Second Order of, 106, 112, 131
  spiritual renewal of the common folk as goal of, 116
  Third Order of, 126, 133, 160
  transubstantiation, understanding of, 118

Francke, A. H., 189, 190, 206
Freemasons, 183
Frumentius of Axum, 40, 62

Gakko, Ashikaga, 167
Ganneaktena, Catherine, 181
Garvey, Marcus, 262
Gelasius I, Pope, 52
Genghis Khan, 101, 107, 109, 110
George, David, 184
Gerhardt, Johann, 203
Gertrude of Helfta, 128, 130
Gilley, Sheridan, 212
Gloukharev, Macarius, 247
Gnosticism, 14, 15, 23, 27, 30, 37, 53, 105
Godin, Henri, 285
Godwyn, Morgan, 179
Goins, Minnie Jackson, 274
Goizueta, Roberto, 285
Gómez, Mariano, 224
González, Justo L., 27, 269, 285
Goodwin, Thomas, 200
Goosen, Gideon, 284
Gordon Bible Institute, 229
Graham, Billy, 264, 273
Graul, Karl, 286
Great Awakening, 199, 200, 202
  in the American colonies, 182–83
  Arminian theology, as propagating, 203
  personal piety, emphasis on, 188–89
  Second Great Awakening, 214, 232, 236, 241
Greek Melkite Church, 198
Gregory I (Gregory the Great), 47, 52, 54, 63, 82, 84, 92, 97
Gregory IX, Pope, 107
Gregory Nanzianzen, 58
Gregory of Datev, 131
Gregory of Nyssa, 57, 58
Gregory Palamas, 128, 130
Gregory the Illuminator, 11, 27
Gregory the Wonderworker, 25
Gregory VII, Pope, 102, 121
Gregory XI, Pope, 123
Gregory XV, Pope, 184
Gregory XVI, Pope, 216, 246
Griffiths, Bede, 279
Groote, Gerard, 126, 159

Guadalupe, Our Lady of, 139, 162, 164, 166
Gutiérrez, Gustavo, 282–83

Hadrian II, Pope, 86, 97
Hale-Babcock, Clara Celestia, 233
Hall, Douglas John, 284
Handel, George Frideric, 190, 194
Hannington, James, 220
Hartmann, Anastasius, 221
He Qi, 273
Hecker, Isaac Thomas, 215, 237
Henrique of Kongo, 140
Heyling, Peter, 189
Hidalgo, Miguel, 212
Hilary of Poitiers, 59
Hilda of Whitby, 88–89
Hildegard of Bingen, 127, 130
Hinze, Bradford, 284
Hisano, Takahashi, 274
historical-critical method, 47, 189, 228, 229, 247, 268
Hoking, W. E., 287
Holiness movement, 214, 233, 236, 238, 239, 262, 277
Holy Name Society, 279
Holy Roman Empire, 67, 89, 97, 103, 191
homoousios (same substance) formulation, 57
Hong Xiuquan, 222
Hooker, Richard, 164
hospital ministry, 53–54, 123, 161, 168, 247
hospitality service, 56, 106, 263
Hugh of St. Victor, 115, 129
Hulagu of the Mongols, 107, 109
Hünermann, Peter, 284
Hus, John, 104, 119, 124, 145
Hutchinson, Anne, 190
Hutter, Jakob, 145

Ignatius of Antioch, 9, 20, 25
    Catholic Church, first use of term, 21–22
    heresies, responding to, 26, 30
    as a martyr, 10, 24, 28
Ignatius of Loyola, 139, 149, 160–61, 168
Immaculate Conception, 237, 241
Innocent III, Pope, 106

Innocent XI, Pope, 180
Inquisition, 104, 106, 122, 141, 157, 179, 184
Irenaeus Of Lyons, 12, 14, 29, 30
    as a bishop, 21, 28
    humanity, focus on theme of, 11, 26
    Type C theology of, 27
Irene, Empress, 79
Irvin, Dale, 53, 143, 212, 249
Isaac of Nineveh, 91–92
Isasi-Díaz, Ada María, 285
I-ssu of Persia, 75

Jaca, José de, 179
Jacob Baradaeus of Edessa, 45
Jacob of Serugh, 59
Jacobite Orthodox Church, 78, 87, 91
    "Decree of Union," invited to consider, 125
    as non-Chalcedonian, 64, 147, 277
    as West Syrian, 45, 46, 64, 124, 131, 147, 198
James, son of Zebedee, 8, 20
James (Jacob) of Nisibis, 38, 59
Jansen, Cornelius, 200
Jansenism, 191, 193, 200, 203, 205
Javoujey, Anne-Marie, 219
Jehovah's Witnesses, 238
Jeremiah II, Patriarch, 159
Jerome, Saint, 46, 47, 149
Jesuits, 179, 181, 209, 241
    accommodational policy of, 202, 204
    Asia, suppression of Jesuits in, 171
    Catholic Reformation, founded as part of, 139, 147
    in China, 174, 176, 190, 191, 198–99, 205–6, 208
    Christian villages, as developing, 140, 165
    Dutch Jesuits, 223, 224
    Ignatius of Loyola as founder, 139, 160–61
    in Japan, 142, 151, 152, 162, 164, 166–68, 172, 190, 197
    restoration of, 215, 246
    Russia, missionary work in, 148
    in Spanish America, 180, 194, 201
Jesus Prayer, 91

Joachim of Fiore, 116
Jogues, Isaac, 181
John Chrysostom, 47
John of Damascus, 79, 93
John of Kronstadt, 237
John of Monte Corvino, 110, 117, 120
John of Plano Carpini, 109
John of the Cross, 161, 165
John Paul II, Pope, 58, 256, 286, 291
John Scholasticus, 54
John XXIII, Pope, 275
Johnson, Elizabeth, 284
Jones, E. Stanley, 287
Jones, Major, 285
Joseph II, Emperor, 191
Juan de Plasencia, 208
Juana Inés de la Cruz, 201
Juanmartí y Espot, Jacinto, 224
Juárez García, Benito Pablo, 212
Judson, Ann Hasseltine, 221, 244
Julian of Constantinople, 40, 45, 62
Julian of Norwich, 130
Juliana of Cornillon, 118
Justin Martyr, 9, 15, 26, 27, 29
Justinian, Emperor, 44–45, 49, 54, 62, 78, 79, 90

Kaahumanu, Queen, 225
Kaunda, Kenneth, 253
Kazimierz, John, 200
Kempis, Thomas à, 126
Kierkegaard, Søren, 216
Kimbangu, Simon, 253
Kimbanguist Church, 253, 275, 279
King, Martin Luther, Jr., 264
King James Bible, 190
Kingdom of Axum, 39–40, 80
Kino, Francisco, 181
Kitamori, Kazoh, 283
Kleutgen, Joseph, 241
Knights of Columbus, 279
Knox, John, 146, 150, 153, 154, 195
Kollman, Paul, xiv
Koyama, Kosuke, 283
Kraemer, Hendrik, 287
Krummacher, Friedrich, 240
Kublai Khan, 107, 109, 110
Kuhn, Johannes, 241
Kyung, Chung Hyun, 285

Lachman, Karl, 228
LaGrange, Marie-Joseph, 269
Las Casas, Bartolomé de, 138–39, 152, 163, 165, 167
Latin American Plenary Council, 234
Latourette, Kenneth Scott, 242
Lausanne Committee for World Evangelization (LCWE), 287–88
Lausanne Covenant, 264, 273, 287
Lausanne Movement, 280, 283, 287
Laval, François de, 197
Lavigerie, Charles, 219, 234–35, 246
Laymen's Foreign Missions Inquiry (LFMI), 287
Lebbe, Vincent, 259–60, 276, 285
Lee, Jarena, 233
Lee, Jung Young, 285
Legazpi, Miguel Lopez de, 143
Legion of Mary, 279
Leme, Sebastião, 261
Leo, Emperor, 78
Leo II, Pope, 82
Leo IX, Pope, 102, 122
Leo XIII, Pope, 228, 234, 239
León, Ponce de, 180
Liang Fa, 222, 229, 243
Liele, George, 179, 207
Lightfoot, J. B., 228
Liguori, Alphonsus de, 203
Lioba (Leoba) of the Franks, 82, 89, 97
Lith, Franz van, 223
Little Sisters of the Poor, 238
Liturgy of Saint James, 87
Livingstone, David, 245
Llull, Ramón, 133
Locke, John, 186, 189
Lombard, Peter, 115, 120, 129
London Missionary Society (LMS), 220, 222, 224, 225, 226, 229, 233, 242
London Society for Promoting Christianity amongst Jews, 248
Lonergan, Bernard, 282
López Hernández, Eleazar, 283
Lossky, Vladimir Nokolaevich, 282
Lourenço of Japan, 166
L'Ouverture, Toussaint, 180
Lubac, Henri de, 282
Luo Wenzao (Gregorio López), 197

Lutheran Church-Missouri Synod, 241, 263
Lutheran tradition, 135, 154, 195, 241, 255, 278
  baptism, stance on, 154, 193, 272
  Brazil, Lutheran presence in, 213
  celebration of the Eucharist, 192
  established church status for, 186
  as evangelical, 144, 145, 147, 156, 159
  Hartwich Seminary, establishing, 183
  indigenous Lutheran clergy, 196, 232
  missionary efforts, 176, 206, 225, 249
  musical tradition, 194, 199
  Pietism, as linked with, 189, 240
  Russia, Lutheran works studied in, 204
  scholastic orthodoxy of, 185, 203
  Sweden as a Lutheran country, 188
  women, role in the church, 158, 233
Lwanga, Charles, 220
Lyon, Mary, 244

MacKillop, Mary, 226, 238
Macrina of Caesarea, 58
Magellan, Ferdinand, 143
Al Mahdi, Caliph, 72, 83, 93, 94
Mahmud of Ghazni, 110
Maier, Walter, 263
Maimonides, Moses, 129, 132
Malpanate system, 124
Manalo, Felix, 259
Manichaeism, 31, 74
Manifest Destiny, 211, 213–14, 215, 245, 263
Mao Zedong, 259, 260
Mar Dinkha IV, 58
Mar Sergis (Sergius), 74
Mar Thoma Church, 198, 236, 258
Marcella of Rome, 46
Marcionites, 15, 26–27, 30
Marie de l'Incarnation, 181
Marillac, Louise de, 184
Marists (Society of Mary), 225, 226, 235, 246, 248
Maronite tradition, 87, 150, 190
  as Eastern rite Catholics, 124
  in Lebanon, 78, 227, 268
  as non-Chalcedonian, 78, 93, 198

Marsden, Samuel, 226
Marshman, Joshua, 220, 229
Martel, Charles, 81
Martin de Porres, 162, 201
Martin I, Pope, 93
Martin of Tours, 39, 53, 55, 62
Martin V, Pope, 123
Martyn, Henry, 221
martyrdom, 1, 25–26, 39, 49
  in Asia, 10–11, 13, 172, 175, 224
  of Boniface and companions, 96
  Franciscan emphasis on, 131
  martyria in honor of, 48
  Martyrs Mirror, 200
  North Africa, martyrs of, 112, 133
  North American Martyrs, 181
  Orthodox Church and, 266
  in the Persian Empire, 36, 55, 79
  Rome, Peter and Paul martyred in, 22
  veneration of, 12, 23–24, 28
Maryknoll religious communities, 263
Masahisa, Uemura, 232–33
Masih, Abdul, 221
Massingale, Bryan, 285
Maurice, Frederick, 241
Maurin, Peter, 263
Maxwell, David, xiii
Mbiti, John, 284
Mbuy-Beya, 279
McGavran, Donald, 264
McGrath, Alister, 284
McLeod, Hugh, 252
McPherson, Aimee Semple, 263
Mechthild of Hackeborn, 128, 130
Mechthild of Magdeburg, 128, 130
Medellín Conference, 270
Mediator Dei encyclical, 270
Meister Eckhart, 128, 130
Melanchthon, Philip, 144
Melania the Younger, 39, 46, 55
Mellitus, Abbot, 63
Mendouça, Lourenço da Silva de, 179
Menelik of Ethiopia, 111
Menezes, Aleixo de, 141
Mennonites, 145, 156, 186, 200, 233
Merici, Angela, 161
Meroë, Kingdom of, 3, 80
Merton, Thomas, 278
Meruzanes of Armenia, 11

Methodist Episcopal Church, 183, 232, 244
Methodist tradition, 213, 265, 266, 272, 283, 285
  camp meeting dynamic, as part of, 214, 232
  Church of England, split from, 187, 216
  missionary endeavors, 221, 233, 258, 281
  personal piety, emphasis on, 188–89
  Primitive Methodist Church, 216, 232
  Wesleyan Methodists, 216, 226, 233, 236, 238
  women, role in, 196, 233, 244
Methodius (Byzantine missionary), 79, 86, 97
Metz, Johann Baptist, 283
Michael Palaeologus, Emperor, 112
Michelangelo, 155, 165
Miguel de Apresentação, 175, 204–5
Milne, W., 229
Mission Sisters of St. Dominic, 263
Mkrtich Khrimian, Patriarch, 227
il modo soave (sweet, gentle way), 166, 172, 204, 208
Moffet, Samuel Hugh, 61
Moffett, Samuel A., 229
Moirans, Epiphane de, 179
Mokone, Mangena, 220
Moltmann, Jürgen, 283
Monophysite Christology, 38, 39, 41, 42, 45, 58, 72, 78, 80, 147
Montanism, 13, 22, 24, 53
Montano, Benito Arias, 149
Montesinos, Antón de, 138
Montgomery, Helen Barrett, 289
Montoya, Antonio Ruiz de, 179
Moody, Dwight, 214, 245
Moody Bible Institute, 214, 229
Moon, Charlotte (Lottie), 244
Moravian tradition, 187, 194, 196
  missionary endeavors, 177, 179, 183
  personal piety, emphasis on, 188–89, 199
  Zinzendorf as founding, 187, 207
More, Thomas, 143
Morrison, R., 229
Mott, John R., 245, 251, 254, 258
Mount Athos, 91, 128, 194, 202

Mount Holyoke Female Seminary, 244
Muhammad Ali of Egypt, 217
Mullin, Robert Bruce, xiii
Murray, John Courtney, 282
mystery religions, 2, 3, 14
mystical theology, 58, 84, 240, 242, 278
  Bonaventure on, 116, 130
  of Calvin and Luther, 160, 203
  Eucharist, mystical devotion to, 127
  of the Greek East and Latin West, 91, 134
  Pseudo-Dionysius, contributions to, 56
  Quietism as a mystical form of spirituality, 200
  women mystics, 107, 123, 127–28, 130, 161

Nacpil, Emerito, 283
Nawaa, Mary Kaaialii, 249–50
Nee, Watchman, 260
Neill, Stephen, 30, 287
New Monasticism movement, 278
Newbigen, Lesslie, 288
Newman, John Henry, 216, 242
Newton, John, 187, 194
Ng, David, 285
Niagara Bible Conference, 229
Nicene Creed, 50, 57
Nicholas Black Elk, ix
Nicholas II, Pope, 122
Nicholas IV, Pope, 124
Nicholas of Lyra, 116
Niebuhr, Reinhold, 281–82
Nikolai (monk), 229
Nikon, Patriarch, 192, 197
Niles, D. T., 283, 287
Nilus of Sorka, 163
Nkuwu of Soyo, King, 140
Nommensen (missionary), 248
Norbert of Xanten, 125
Norbertines, 125, 131
Norris, Frederick, 137, 252
North American Institute for Indigenous Theological Studies (NAIITS), 285
Ntsikana of South Africa, 220
Nubian tradition, 45, 87
  Christian presence in, 40, 67, 80, 99, 112

Muslim influence on, 111, 139
one-nature formula, as embracing, 38, 64
Nyamiti, Charles, 284
Nyerere, Julius, 253

Oblate Sisters of Providence, 238
Occom, Samson, 183
Oduyoye, Mercy Amba, 281, 284
Old Believers, 192, 197
Oldham, J. H., 252
Olier, Jean-Jacques, 197
On-Njie, Paul Tsen, 223
Order of Brothers and Sisters of Penance, 106
Organization of African Independent Churches, 279–80
Origen of Alexandria, 14, 16–17, 26, 27, 31, 83
Osborn, Sarah, 183
Osroene. See Edessa
Otto I, Emperor, 83
Oxford Movement, 216

Pachomius of Egypt, 39, 40, 55
Pachuau, Lalsangkima, xiii, xvii
Pact of the Catacombs, 256
Padilla, René, 287
Palafox y Mendoza, Juan de, 180
Palmer, Phoebe, 233
Pan'kov, Ivan, 229
Pantaenus the Philosopher, 10, 14, 26, 27
papal infallibility doctrine, 216, 234
Papias of Phrygia, 21
Parham, Charles F., 263
Paris Evangelical Mission Society, 217
Patrick of Ireland, 39, 43, 53, 55, 62
Paul III, Pope, 138–39
Paul of Antioch, 133
Paul V, Pope, 191
Paul VI, Pope, 277, 286, 290
Paula of Rome, 46
Paulists (Missionary Society of St. Paul), 215, 237
Peace of Augsburg, 147, 184
Pelagius of the British Isles, 60
Pentecostal tradition, 157, 253, 272, 277, 281
  in Asia, 258, 259
  Catholic Church, dialogue with, 276
  charismatic interpretation of scripture, 270
  culture, negative stance towards, 291
  indigenous elements, adapting, 278
  in Latin America, 261–62, 274, 275, 283, 289
  in North America, 263, 279
  rise of, 252, 292
  women, roles in ministry, 280–81, 290
Pepin, King (Pippin the Short), 54, 81, 85, 89
Perpetua of Carthage, 13, 24, 25, 28
Perrone, Giovanni, 241
Petrarch, Francesco, 143
Phan, Peter, 202, 285
Phelps, Jamie, 285
Philip (Deacon), 6–7, 11, 22
Philip II of Spain, 143
Philip IV of Spain, 179
Philip of Moscow, 148
Philo of Alexandria, 14
Phoebe, Deaconess, 22
Picpus Fathers, 225
Pieris, Aloysius, 283
Pierson, A. T., 245, 251
Pietist tradition, 188, 203, 211
  evangelical piety, 126, 217, 236
  German Pietism, 189, 193, 199, 240
  University of Halle as a Pietist center, 190, 206–7, 228
Pillai, Arumugam, 196
Pillai, H. A. Krishna, 248
Pius IX, Pope, 216, 234
Pius V, 162
Pius VII, Pope, 215
Pius X, Pope, 269, 270
Pius XI, Pope, 237, 257
Pius XII, Pope, 269, 270
Plütschau, Heinrich, 176, 207
Plymouth Brethren, 231, 238
Polycarp of Smyrna, 11, 21, 23, 25, 28
Pomare II, King, 225
Pompallier, Jean Baptiste, 248
Poor Clares, 106, 112, 131
predestination, 164
Presbyterian tradition, 196, 229, 233, 285
  Book of Common Worship, use of, 271
  camp meetings, attending, 214
  missionary endeavors, 213, 221, 222, 226, 232, 245, 249, 253

Presbyterian and Reformed Church of Japan, 274
Scots Confession, tracing roots back to, 195
Taiwan Presbyterian Church, 259
in United Church settings, 258, 265, 266
Primitive Methodist Church, 216
Protten, Rebecca, 196
Providentius Deus encyclical, 228
Pseudo-Dionysius, 56, 58
Puritan tradition, 179, 236
Church of England, stance against, 182, 195
missionary endeavors, 182, 207
in North America, 190, 196
Pilgrim's Progress, as a favored text of, 199
religion of the heart and, 186, 192–93, 200

Quakers (Society of Friends), 178, 179, 186, 192, 196, 199, 203–4
Quietism, 200–201

Rabanus Maurus of the Franks, 84
Radegunde of Gaul, 39, 43, 53, 55
Rahner, Karl, 282
Ramabai, Pandita, 239, 249, 258
Rastafari movement, 262
Rastislav of Moravia, King, 79
Remigius of Reims, 61, 62
Restorationism, 214, 230, 232, 236, 238
revivalism, 183, 214, 215, 217, 240
Rhodes, Alexandre de, 174–75, 191, 202, 204, 206, 209
Rhodes, Cecil, 220
Ricci, Matteo, 172, 174, 176, 202, 204, 205, 206
Richard of St. Victor, 129
Riebe-Estrella, Gary, 285
Rites Controversy, 175, 191, 205–6, 208, 247
Ritschl, Albrecht, 240, 246
Rizal, José P., 224
Roberts, J. Deotis, 285
Roman Catholic Ukrainian Church, 148, 159, 198, 227
Romanticism, 216

Romero, Óscar, 261
Roncière, Bénédite de la, 273
the Rosary, 127, 162, 191, 237, 279
Ross, Cathy, 284
Ruggieri, Michele, 172
Ruiz, Jean-Pierre, 285
Abu Rumi of Ethiopia, 229
Russian Orthodox Church, 137, 155
baptism, stance on, 193
communism, suffering under, 251, 266
government control over, 227, 235
Greek Orthodox Church, separating from, 159
leadership mantle of, 101, 114
Moscow patriarchate, 113, 148, 276
Russian Orthodox Missionary Society, 247

Sahagún, Bernardino de, 151
Saint Thomas Christians, 110, 114, 134, 147, 224
Anglican support for, 221
church buildings, lack of images in, 156
denominational split, 141, 198
East Syrian Church, link to, 10, 159
Malpanate system, adopting, 124
Syrian liturgy, celebrating with, 151, 155, 192
Salazar, Domingo de, 143
Sales, Francis de, 200, 203
Salmerón, Alfonso, 149
Salvation Army, 216, 231, 238, 239, 262
Sam, Kim Young, 259
Sandoval, Alonso de, 179
Sano, Roy Isao, 285
Sastri, Vendanayakam, 231
Sauma, Rabban Bar, 110, 124
Schaff, Philip, 241
Schelling, Friedrich, 241
Schleiermacher, Friedrich, 228, 240
Schleitheim Articles, 145
Schmidt, Georg, 177
Schmucker, Samuel, 241
Scholastica of the Benedictines, 53
Schreiter, Robert, 284, 285, 286
Schweitzer, Albert, 268
Scotus, John Duns, 130
Scranton, Mary, 281

Scudder, Ida, 287
Seabury, Samuel, 196
Second Ecumenical Council, 112
Second Vatican Council. See Vatican II
Selassie I, Emperor, 254, 277
Semler, J. S., 189
Seraphim of Sarov, 202
Sergius of Constantinople, Patriarch, 92–93
Serra, Junípero, 181
Seton, Elizabeth Ann, 215
Seventh Day Adventists, 238, 262
Seymour, William, 263
Sharp, Granville, 178
Sheen, Fulton, 263
Simeon, Charles, 221, 236
Simeon the New Theologian, 91
Simon, Richard, 189
Simons, Menno, 145
Sisters of Charity of St. Joseph, 215
Sisters of St. Joseph Cluny, 219, 246
Sisters of St. Joseph of the Sacred Heart, 238
Sisters of the Blessed Sacrament, 247
Sisters of the Holy Family, 238
Sixtus V, Pope, 157
Skrefsrud, Lars Olsen, 248
Smith, Susan E., 284
Social Gospel movement, 239, 246, 263, 266
Société des Missions-Étrangères du Québec, 265
Solomonic Revival, 111–12, 128
Soto, Domingo de, 165, 167
Soubirous, Bernadette, 237
Sozzini, Fausto, 146
Sozzini, Lelio, 146
Spener, Philipp Jakob, 187, 189
Stanley, Brian, 212
Stanton, Elizabeth Cady, 229
Stark, Rodney, 22–23
Stephen, Saint, 6
Strauss, David, 228, 240
Student Volunteer Movement for Foreign Missions (SVM), 214
Sublimis Deus papal bull, 138–39
Sugirtharajah, R. S., 270
Sung, John, 260
Swain, Clara, 244

Swelindawo, Amos, 292, 293
Syllabus of Errors document, 216
Synod of Diamper, 141, 158, 193, 198
Synod of Dort, 193, 203
Synod of Dvin, 42
Synod of Pistoria, 191
Syriac tradition, 68, 83, 85
  Book of Steps regarding, 56
  Diatessaron text, role in, 84, 228
  Ephrem the Syrian, 59, 61
  Indian Christianity, influence on, 42, 87, 141, 151, 155, 192, 198, 221
  scripture translations into Syriac, 9, 16, 46, 149–50, 151, 189, 190, 228
  Syriac as a liturgical language, 18, 32, 49, 51, 87, 95, 236
  Syrian theology, 10, 27, 58, 59
  West Syrian Church, 45, 46, 64, 78, 124–25, 131, 147, 198
  See also East Syrian Church
Syro-Malabar Church, 198, 238

T'ai-tsung, Emperor, 74, 75
Taizé community, 279
Tamerlane (Timor Lenk), 101, 110, 113, 141
Tan, Jonathan, xiii, 285
Tatian the Assyrian, 9, 16, 24, 27–28, 84, 228
Taylor, J. Hudson, 245, 260
Teilhard de Chardin, Pierre, 282
Tekakwitha, Kateri, 181
Tennent, William, 196
Teresa of Avila, 130, 149, 161, 165
Teresa of Calcutta, 257–58
Tertullian of Carthage, 13, 22, 24, 26, 27, 28, 29, 36
Theodora of Constantinople, 40, 44, 45, 62, 80, 90
Theodore of Mopsuestia, 47
Thérèse of Lisieux, 130, 237
Thomas, Apostle, 10, 27
Thomas, Gospel of, 9, 15
Thomas, M. M., 258, 283
Thomas of Cana, 41
Thomas of Celano, 134
Tikhon of Zadonsk, 202, 204

Tillich, Paul, 281
Timothy I, Patriarch, 72, 73, 83, 90, 93, 94, 95
Ting, K. H., 283
Tinker, George, 285
Tiridates III, King, 11
Townes, Emilie, 285
Tran Luc, xiii, 232
transubstantiation, 117–18, 119, 121, 152
Treaty of Westphalia, 184
Turretin, Francis, 203
Tutu, Desmond, 254
Typayupanqui, Nicanor Sarmiento, 283

Ulfilas of the Goths (Wulfila), 43, 62
Underhill, Evelyn, 278
Unitarian tradition, 135, 146, 147, 157, 186, 259
United Brethren, 145, 274
United Methodist Church, 195, 283
Urban II, Pope, 103
Ursulines, 147, 161, 181

Valentinus of Alexandria, 14
Valignano, Alessandro
   accommodational approach, 142, 152, 166, 167–68, 174, 202, 204
   Japanese Catholicism, influence on, 151, 158, 162, 164, 190, 195
   modo soave model, promoting, 166, 204, 208
Valla, Lorenzo, 149
Vatican I, 216, 234, 241, 256
Vatican II, 241, 257, 261, 271, 282
   Ad Gentes decree, 8, 27, 286
   Catholic laity as affected by, 276, 278
   ecumenism, encouraging spirit of, 266
   modern world, opening up to, 253
   non-Western cultures, changing attitude towards, 290
   period of certainty prior to, 285
   sacraments, revising into contemporary language, 272
   scripture, reaffirming importance of, 269–70
   significance of, 275, 281
   theological shifts, 255–56, 287
   transformation of, 264
Vaz, Joseph, 175, 205, 209
Velichkovskii, Paisii, 202

Veniaminov, Innocent, 215, 229, 247
Venn, Henry, 233, 243
Victor I, Pope, 21
Vieira, António, 179
Villaverde, Juan, 224
Vincent de Paul, 184
Vincentians, 147, 184, 201
Vitoria, Francisco de, 149
Vladimir, King, 79
Vladimir of Kiev, Prince, 88
Voetius, Gisbertus, 207
Volotsky, Joseph, 163
Vulgate Bible, 46, 84, 149

Waldensians, 105–6, 115, 117, 121, 123, 126, 131
Waldo of Lyons, 105, 117
Walls, Andrew, 270, 285
Walther, Carl, 241
Walton, Brian, 189
Ward, William, 220
Warren, M. A. C. (Max), 291
Watch Tower Bible and Tract Society, 238
Way of the Cross, 230
Webb, Mary, 244
Wesley, Charles, 187, 194
Wesley, John, 187, 189, 199, 203, 216, 277
Wesleyan Methodist Conference, 216, 232
Whitefield, George, 183, 187, 196
Wilberforce, William, 187
William of Ockham, 130
William of Rubruck, 109, 133
Williams, John, 225
Williams, Roger, 182
Winter, Ralph, 264
Wiseman, James A., 279
Woolman, John, 203–4
World Council of Churches (WCC), 261, 273, 281
   African Churches in, 275, 280
   China Christian Council as members, 260
   Eastern Orthodox membership, 277, 282
   ecumenical openness, encouraging, 291
   Faith and Order Commission statement, 272

Index   317

IMC, integration with, 255
South Asian representation, 258, 283
Uppsala Assembly, 253, 264, 271, 287, 288
World Evangelical Fellowship (WEF), 287
World Parliament of Religions, 249
Wycliffe, John, 104, 117, 119, 121, 124

Xavier, Jerónimo, 209
Ximénez de Cisneros, Francisco, 146, 150, 157
Xu Candida, 174, 204
Xu Guangxi, 174, 204

Yaballaha, Patriarch, 110
Yajiro of Japan, 142, 151, 152, 166
Yang Tingyum, 174, 204
Yannoulatos, Anastasios, 288

Yeshuyab II, Patriarch, 69, 72, 73, 74, 90, 94
Yong, Amos, 285, 291
Yongzheng, Emperor, 205
Young Men's Christian Association (YMCA), 216–17, 239
Yu Cido (Dora Yu), 244–45
Yung, Hwa, 283

Zamora, Jacinto, 224
Zar'a Ya'iqob, Emperor, 140
Ziegenbalg, Bartholomäus, 176, 189, 207
Zinzendorf, Nikolaus Ludwig von, 187, 203, 207
Zionist churches, 214, 252–53, 292
Zizioulas, John, 284
Zumárraga, Juan de, 164–65
Zwingli, Ulrich, 135, 144–45, 152–53, 154, 155

www.ingramcontent.com/pod-product-compliance
Lightning Source LLC
Chambersburg PA
CBHW071400300426
44114CB00016B/2131